FIGHTER WING

A Guided Tour of an Air Force Combat Wing

THE TOM CLANCY MILITARY LIBRARY

TOM CLANCY

FIGHTER WING

A Guided Tour of an Air Force Combat Wing

HarperCollins*Publishers*

The views and opinions expressed in this book
are entirely those of the author,
and do not necessarily correspond to those
of any corporation, air-force, or government organization
of any country.

HarperCollins*Publishers*
77-85 Fulham Palace Road,
Hammersmith, London W6 8JB

Published by HarperCollins*Publishers* 1996
5 7 9 8 6 4

First published in the USA by
Berkley Books 1995

A catalogue entry for this book
is available from the British Library

ISBN 0 00 255527 1

Set in Times Roman and Palatino

Printed and bound in Great Britain by
Caledonian International Book Manufacturing Ltd, Glasgow

DEDICATION

This book is dedicated to four members of the 366th Wing,
who died while serving with the Wing in 1994.

Major Morton R. Graves III, USAF (34th Bombardment Squadron)
Captain Jon A. Rupp, USAF (34th Bombardment Squadron)
Captain Kathleen J. Hale, USAF (366th Medical Group)
Staff Sergeant Don Antikainen (389th Fighter Squadron)

They died while serving, without acclaim or fanfare. Gunfighters, Warriors, and
Americans. We just thought that you should know, because their friends, families,
and fellow airmen loved them, and miss them. Please love them too, because the
noblest of our ideals have always been protected for us by warriors.

Contents

Acknowledgments

Thanks to all the people who made this book special. Once again, we start with my partner and researcher, John D. Gresham. His work on this book took him across the country many times, where he had some very interesting experiences. Whether he is talking over the finer points of precision-guided weapons with contractors or having the ride of his life in the back of a fighter, he always brings a special touch to the books of this series. We also have again benefited from the wisdom and efforts of series editor Professor Martin H. Greenberg. Once again, Laura Alpher is to be complimented for her marvelous drawings, which have been such a pleasure to see, and have added so much to these books. Thanks are also due to Craig Kaston, whose photographs appear here for the first time. Tony Koltz, Mike Markowitz, and Chris Carlson again need to be recognized for their outstanding research and editorial support — so critical and timely. Thanks again goes to Cindi Woodrum, Diana Patin, and Roselind Greenberg for their support in backing the rest of us up as we moved toward completion.

A book like this would be impossible to produce without the support of senior service personnel in leadership positions, and this one is no exception. Our first thanks go to Dr. Richard Hallion, the Chief Historian of the Air Force and a long-time friend. He was there at the start with solid advice on the structure of the book, and advice on how to make it all happen. We also have our greatest thanks for two senior USAF officers, General John M. Loh and General Charles A. Horner. Both of these officers, in the sunset of their careers, gave us valuable time and support, and we cannot repay their trust and friendship. Thanks also to Colonel John Warden at the Air Command and Staff College for sharing his special insights with us. Out at Nellis AFB, NV, there was Lieutenant General Tom Griffith, who runs the world's finest air warfare training center. Also at Nellis were Brigadier General Jack Welde, commander of the 57th Wing; Colonel John Frisby of the Adversary Tactics Division; Colonel Bud Bennett, who commands the 554th Range Control Squadron; and Colonel Bentley Rayburn of the USAF Weapons School, who gave us run of their facilities and personnel during our visit. Other notable help at Nellis AFB came from Lieutenant Colonel Steve Anderson, who commands the USAF Thunderbirds; Lieutenant Colonel Steve Ladd, who runs the 549th Joint Training Squadron known as AIR WARRIOR; Major Steve Cutshell in the Nellis Adversary Tactics Shop; and Lieutenant Colonel Ed LaFontaine, who has built the USAF Combat Search and Rescue School. The legendary Blake Morrison and Marty Isham, the team behind *USAF Weapons Review,* were instrumental in getting the details right. Finally, there were two wonderful young USAF officers: Major Gregory Masters and Captain Rob Evans, who were kind enough to share their personal Gulf War experiences with us.

Another group that was vital to our efforts, less well known but equally important, were the members of the various USAF public affairs offices (PAOs) and protocol organizations that handled our numerous requests for visits and information. Tops on our list were Major Dave Thurston, June Forté, and Carol Rose of the Pentagon PAO. Down at Air Combat Command, Colonel John Miller, Colonel Mike Gallager, and Captains John Tillis, Katie Germain, and Michele DeWerth worked hard to get their story across. Out at Nellis AFB, NV, Major George Sillia made our visit both memorable and livable in the incredible heat of April 1994. Out at the USAF Space Command, Colonel Dave Garner helped get the space story across to us. At the intelligence agencies, there was Jeff Harris and Major Pat Wilkerson at NRO, Linda Miller and Judith Emmel at NSA, and Dwight Williams at DARO. Other helpful PA officers included Lieutenant Colonels Bruce McFadden and Charles Nelson, Major Jim Tynan, Captains Tracy O'Grady and Brett Morris, and Lieutenant Chris Yates. Thanks to you all.

Out at Mountain Home AFB, ID, we had the high honor of living with as fine a group of people as you will ever meet: the personnel of the 366th Wing, The Gunfighters. Our biggest thanks go to the wing commander, Major General (Selectee) David McCloud. This career fighter pilot is a man on the move, and his willingness to share the limited time of his unit in a frantic year was above and beyond the call of duty. In addition, the wing staff deserves some mention. Colonel Robin Scott was always helpful, whether briefing us on wing deployments or the finer points of playing "Crud." Lieutenant Colonels Gregg Miller and Rich Tedesco were there to show us the art of ATO building. And the wing PAOs, Captain Christi Dragen and Lieutenant Don Borchelt, were fantastic in their tolerance and patience. We also want to recognize the assistance of the Wings' various squadron commanders: Lieutenant Colonels John Gauhn, Stephen Wood, Larry New, Frank Clawson, Lee Hart, William K. Bass, and Jay Leist. And then there was Lieutenant Colonel Tim Hopper, the commander of the Wings' 34th Bombardment Squadron. Tim is one of the awesome young combat leaders in the Air Force today, and he tolerated having us there to see the best and the worst of his career, and still kept on going. God bless Tim, because the nation needs officers like him. Another special leader is Brigadier General Silas Johnson, the commander of the 552nd Airborne Control Wing, and we are proud to know him. Also, thanks to Brigadier General J. C. Wilson, the commander of the 28th Bombardment Wing at Ellsworth AFB, SD, for showing us the "heavy iron" of the Air Force.

Again, thanks are due to our various industrial partners, without whom all the information on the various aircraft, weapons, and systems would never have come to light. At the aircraft manufacturers there was Lee Whitney, Barbara Anderson, Robert Linder, Tim Courson, Lon Nordeen, Gary Hakinson, Martin Fisher, and Jerry Ennis of McDonnell Douglas; Joe Stout, Donn Williams, Karen Hagar, Jim Ragsdale, Jeff Rhodes, Eric DeRitis, Susan Walker, James Higginbotham, Terry Schultz, Doug McCurrah, and Robert Hartman of Lockheed Martin; Mike Mathews, James Walker, Eric Simonson, Tony Pinella, and Tom Conard of Rockwell International; John Visilla, Tony Contafio and Patty Alessi at Northrop Grumman; Milt Furness, Cynthia Pulham, and Susan Bradley of Boeing; and finally, Jim Kagdis and Foster Morgan of Boeing Sikorsky. We also made and renewed many friendships at the various missile, armament, and system manufacturers including: Tony Geishanuser and Vicki Fendalson at Texas Instruments; Larry Ernst at General Atomics; Glenn Hillen, Bill West, Kearny Bothwell, and Cheryl Wiencek at Hughes; Tommy Wilson, Adrien Poirier, Edward Ludford, Dave McClain, and Dennis Hughes at Loral; Jody Wilson-Eudy at Motorola; Nurit Bar of Rafael USA, and last, but certainly not least, Ed Rodemsky, LeAnn McNabb, and Barbara Thomas of Trimble, who again spent so much time and effort to educate us on the latest developments of the GPS system. Also, for all the folks who helped us at Pratt & Whitney and Westinghouse, thanks to you all.

Again, we give thanks for all of our help in New York, especially Robert Gottlieb, Debra Goldstein, and Matt Bialer at William Morris. At Berkley Books, our appreciation again goes out to our editor, John Talbot, as well as David Shanks, Patty Benford, Jacky Sach, and Jill Dinneen. To friends like Tony Tolin, Dave Deptula, Matt Caffrey, Jeff Ethell, Jim Stevenson, Norman Polmar, Bob Dorr, Roger Turcott, and Wilber Creech, thanks again for your contributions and wisdom. And for all the folks who took us for rides, thanks for teaching the ignorant how things work for real. For our friends, loved ones, we once again thank you. For being there when we can't, God bless you all.

Foreword

As a lifelong practitioner of airpower in the field, I have often had opportunity to watch the coming and going of my profession's technical, political, tactical, and organizational changes. And after more than three decades of service in the Air Force, I have to admit that radical and volatile change seems to be the lot of those who wear the blue suit. While reading this superb book, I was continually reminded that few aspects of modern warfare remain constant. Nowhere is this more evident than in the dramatic technological changes driving the employment of airpower. In this work, Tom Clancy defines better than anyone this new role of air power and what it means to the nation.

Four significant events have transformed my understanding of airpower during this period of dramatic change—all four of them occurring in a brief eighteen-month span.

The first happened on the day the air war began in the Persian Gulf, January 17th, 1991. I was then the Air Force Vice Chief of Staff, and we were sitting in the Air Force Operations Center in the Pentagon . . . our war room. It seemed ironic that we, along with the rest of the world, were watching the attack live on CNN, just as if it were *Monday Night Football*. As our F-117A stealth fighters struck targets in the heart of Baghdad, B-52s were launching standoff missiles safely from the Persian Gulf against targets in Northern Iraq; and these were followed by attacks throughout Iraq by an array of other aircraft. This was the first genuine test of our modern air force, and particularly of radar-evading stealth planes equipped with the precision munitions in which we had invested so heavily following the Vietnam War. Although at the time I was confident and optimistic, I still had grave anticipation and many unanswered questions as our planes flew into the formidable anti-aircraft defenses of Iraq. How many planes and pilots would be lost? Would we achieve air supremacy, and destroy the enemy's war-making capability quickly and decisively? Had our intense aircrew training in exercises such as Red Flag prepared our crews for the rigors of modern air warfare? We wondered if our planning decisions were right. As history was to prove, they were.

The second date is February 28th, 1991, the day President Bush ordered a cease-fire. The war had been won, quickly and decisively, and our forces had sustained minimal casualties. Our people had performed magnificently, demonstrating superb professional competence, discipline, and leadership. The results surpassed even my own expectations. While the entire world marveled at the total domination by our air forces, and the demonstrated effectiveness of "smart" bombs and stealth technology, the essential role of modern land-based airpower had been established. Airpower performance had now caught up with airpower theory, and its decisiveness was now a fact of modern warfare strategy. Viewing the confusion in Baghdad on CNN, when our first planes evaded Iraqi radar and caught the Iraqi armed forces by surprise, convinced a skeptical public of the immense value of stealth weapons in future air wars. In addition, the precision munitions, so clearly described in this book, assured destruction of military targets without unnecessary civilian casualties. Our total air dominance allowed unrestricted surveillance of all enemy ground movements, while denying that same capability to Saddam Hussein. With impunity, we were able to destroy his war-making capability and demoralize his soldiers to the point of ineffectiveness. And finally, this victory of airpower validated the realism of our training programs as well as the superb performance and competence of our pilots and aircrews.

When I first discussed this book with Tom, I mentioned another date with particular personal meaning. On March 26th, 1991, I assumed command of Tactical Air Command (TAC). It was the dream command assignment for any fighter pilot. And yet, who would have guessed then that I'd be the last head of that proud organization, with its rich tradition and honored history . . . a history that included our proud performance in the Gulf War, when our people basked in the glory of their victory with the boisterous phrase "It can't get any better than this!" In fact, when I became the TAC commander, I knew that high point could not last, and that we were very quickly traveling a new and uncharted course; for I was already aware that we had to undertake the painful processes of downsizing and restructuring, while simultaneously maintaining our combat capability. With our "too easy" victory in the Gulf, and the end of the perception of foreign threat, the American public and national leadership felt confident enough in our national defense to conclude that a drastic reduction would not sacrifice security.

The time had come to downsize the Air Force and formulate a complete plan for its reorganization. With increased competition for scarce budget dollars, the military would get a far smaller share. In a short period we eliminated nearly one third of our personnel and retired 35% of our aircraft. Most of our overseas bases were closed; our people and equipment would now be primarily located in the continental United States. The decision was made to value technology and intense training over numbers. We'd now have a highly trained, but smaller force. In addition, the primary Air Force mission had changed. Where before the focus was on nuclear deterrence and a single major adversary, now we saw a multifaceted requirement to project power and strike anywhere in the world. Thus was born the new mission statement: Global Reach/Global Power. This book chronicles the restructuring of the U.S. Air Force to meet the new mission.

The fourth date of great importance to me is June 1st, 1992. On that day, we witnessed the merger of Strategic Air Command (SAC), TAC, and elements of the Military Airlift Command (MAC), and the birth of Air Combat Command (ACC). This new organization provides combat-ready air forces for any regional theater commander in chief. By far the largest U.S. Air Force command, ACC has about a quarter million active-duty, reserve, and civilian members; and it has nearly three thousand aircraft, including virtually every bomber, fighter, and reconnaissance, command-and-control, electronic warfare, and theater transport plane in the U.S. Air Force inventory. To say there was trepidation by SAC, MAC, and TAC members at the thought of such a merger is an understatement. Thus, as the first commander of ACC, I found it important to assure our people that neither SAC, MAC, nor TAC was losing in a "corporate takeover." This was a friendly merger, not a hostile takeover. And in reality, all the different components from the various commands *were* winners: SAC had prevailed by preventing nuclear war for over forty years. TAC and SAC had combined to win the Gulf War decisively. And MAC had kept both of the other commands equipped and supplied so that they might accomplish their combat missions.

This book details several of the lessons learned in the Gulf War, lessons that have led to many of the decisions that have reshaped today's Air Force. Of major importance is the integration of airpower needed to assure rapid deployment. Consequently, the Air Force can support the decisions of the national leadership within hours and days, not weeks. Composite wings at Pope Air Force Base, Moody AFB, and Mountain Home AFB are made up of squadrons with all the parts (bombers, fighters, tankers, and other support units) needed to deploy instantly and take the battle anywhere in the world.

Tom Clancy will introduce you to one of these composite wings: the 366th based at Mountain Home AFB, Idaho. Readers will visit each squadron and learn its part in supporting what he accurately calls "this miniature air force." Our 366th Wing is indeed a microcosm of the command as a whole. Of particular interest will be watching some of the realistic training exercises used by ACC people to sharpen their skills. You will participate in war games at Nellis AFB, Nevada, as aircrews simulate real battle situations against enemy aircraft and threats on the ground. And then Clancy, the expert storyteller, will take you into the future. You will join the 366th as it is deployed to action in Vietnam. While this scenario is fiction, the descriptions are real. The time or place might change, but the story could easily be a picture of the future.

As a result of our "easy" success in the Gulf War, the American public has a level of expectation that will be difficult to maintain in the future. What is now expected is a quick, painless, 99–0 victory with few casualties against *any* adversary. But clearly, we can't look back at success and assume we can do it again as easily. And so the author wisely questions the wisdom of making massive cuts in military spending, and wonders about the impact on national defense. He discusses reductions in force and airlift capability, and challenges the notion that we could now conduct a Persian Gulf–type war with the same efficiency and success as the first time around. Of particular significance to ACC is the future of the bomber force and of the B-2 Spirit. Bombers provide the air commander with assets that have an intercontinental range, a large payload of precision-guided weapons, and a sense of immediacy. They can have a big impact within hours of being called into action. Preserving our capability to build bombers is important for the nation. Yet it is not the only vital national capability that we must try to preserve. In addition, the ability to produce and deploy stealthy tactical aircraft like the F-22 must be protected, for it must be procured in adequate numbers to replace the fleet of F-15 Eagle fighters that now rule the skies. This issue of aircraft quality is of vital importance: The F-15s that are the foundation of our fighter force today will soon be challenged by new generations of fighters and missiles developed by both our adversaries and our allies. In earlier wars we used simpler weapons. When we needed more of them, we had the industrial capacity to produce them quickly and in large numbers. But today we cannot rapidly "turn on the spigot" for the high-tech weaponry required to respond to changes in the world situation. These capacities have to be protected, so that we will have the "just in case" advantage that may be needed in the future.

In this book you will learn about the sophisticated aircraft ACC would provide to the commander in chief of a unified command in a war zone. From the versatile F-16, to our reliable workhorse C-130, to the high-flying U-2 spy plane, and the state-of-the-art flying wing B-2, you will see the capabilities and limitations of each plane, and clearly understand the unique role of each in battle. A strike aircraft is only as effective as the skill of the crew and the lethality of weapons it carries. In this book you will find excellent descriptions of air-to-air missiles, air-to-ground munitions, unguided bombs, and base defense weapons. This is critical for an understanding of modern airpower. With fewer planes, each must have far more capacity to destroy targets and greater ability to survive an attack.

As this book demonstrates, the future capability of our military lies not only in new weapons, but in a style of leadership that gets the most return from our limited resources . . . the most output for a given input. The leadership at Air Combat Command has tried to create a working climate that inspires trust, teamwork, quality, and pride. The goal is to delegate authority and responsibility to the lowest level and to give every member of the team, regardless of rank, a sense of ownership in the product or mission. For no one person or community in ACC is more or less important than anyone else. The outstanding, highly trained young men and women in this command are the reason I am confident in their ability to respond to any national crisis.

Airpower has come of age. This book chronicles the creation of a command with a unique culture—the U.S. Air Force Air Combat Command. It possesses the leadership, the combat power, and the highly trained, competent people to provide the world's best combat air forces anywhere in the world, at any time, to win quickly, decisively, with overwhelming advantage and few casualties. Tom Clancy does a masterful job of telling us all about it. I am proud to have served as the first commander of Air Combat Command, and proud to commend this book to your reading pleasure.

John M. "Mike" Loh
General, USAF (Retired)
July 1995

Introduction

In August 1914, a British aviator patrolling the skies above Mons, in Belgium, spotted the advance of von Kluck's German army toward the British Expeditionary Force. Interviewed for TV five decades later, the pilot recalled the reaction of senior officers when he reported the news . . . they didn't believe him. Pilots soon took cameras with them to give proof of their sightings to skeptical general officers whose vision was limited to the view from the ground.

Before long, both sides were flying reconnaissance missions, and hostile aviators were firing pistols at one another. Then machine guns. And soon after that, aircraft were designed as aerial killers—the first fighters. They were delicate, unstable constructs of wood and wire, usually underpowered by inefficient engines. But they could fly. And the learning curve was steep back then. One day, someone asked, "If you can hang one engine on an airframe, why not two, or even more? If you can see to shoot, you can see to drop a weapon, can't you?" Thus began the age of the bomber.

It was the Germans at Verdun, in the bitter weather of February 1916, who first made actual the concept we now call airpower—the systematic application of tactical aircraft to control a battlefield (the definition will change and develop). The objective was to seal off the battlefield from French aviation, denying the enemy the ranging eyes needed to see behind the German trench lines; and as it turned out, the plan didn't work terribly well. Still, others saw what the Germans tried, and recognized that it could be made to work. By the end of the war, aircraft were attacking infantry on the ground. And for the first time soldiers knew what field mice had long understood: The target of an aerial predator feels as much psychological burden as physical danger.

Between the wars, a handful of visionary officers in Britain, Italy, Germany, Japan, Russia, and the United States grappled with the theory of airpower . . . and with its practical applications in the next, inevitable war. The most famous of these, the Italian Guilo Douhet, proposed the first great "philosophy" of airpower: Bomber and attack aircraft can reach far into the enemy's rear to attack the factories that make the weapons and the railroads and roads and bridges that transport them to the fighting front. It was Douhet's view that airpower alone—without armies or navies—could bring victory in war. In other words, if you smash enough factories, railroads, roads, and bridges, you'll bring your enemy to the point where he will lie down and wave the white flag.

Douhet was too optimistic. An air force is remarkable not only for what it can do, but for what it cannot. The unchanging truth of warfare is that only infantry can conquer an enemy—infantry is people, and only people can occupy and hold ground. Tanks can roll across ground. Artillery can punish and neutralize ground. And airpower—which is at heart longer-range artillery—can punish and neutralize over long distances. But only people can take up residency there.

Yet airpower can have a powerful effect, and this fact was not lost on the German General Staff. In May 1940, when another German attack violated French soil at a place called Sedan, French soldiers excused their rapid departure from the battlefield by saying, "But *mon lieutenant,* bombs were falling."

The second global conflict announced the importance of airpower in terms that no one could ignore. Now, huge fleets of aircraft attacked everything they could reach—and that reach was ever growing, for aviation science advanced rapidly. Engineering talent tends to follow the excitement of discovery and possibility. Engineers who had once devoted their skills to developing steam engines for ships or railroad locomotives found more exciting work. The great breakthroughs in engine power came first, and those drove improvements in airframe design.

By the beginning of the Second World War, Daimler-Benz and Rolls-Royce had both developed water-cooled in-line engines exceeding a thousand horsepower. In America, Allison did the same, and Pratt & Whitney began production of their monster, two-thousand-horsepower R-2800 radial engine in East Hartford, Connecticut. More efficiently cooled, simpler, and capable of absorbing catastrophic battle damage, the Double-Wasp and its close relatives would power a variety of successful tactical aircraft (F-6F Hellcat, F-4U Corsair, TBF/TBM Avenger, P-47 Thunderbolt, etc.), plus numerous types of bombers and transport aircraft.

The Republic P-47 Thunderbolt, called "the Jug" by its pilots for its brutal and decidedly ungraceful lines, was originally designed by Alexander Cartvelli as a high-altitude interceptor, and it would distinguish itself as an escort fighter for the bomber fleets of the 8th Air Force over Germany. But the Thunderbolt carried a total of eight heavy .50-caliber machine guns, and could also carry bombs and rockets. Its rugged construction and immense armament rapidly led pilots to experiment with other forms of hunting. Soon Jug drivers were flying low on missions they sometimes called Rodeos, for their wild and woolly character: If it moved, it was fair game. Such missions inspired the German Army to coin a new word, *Jabo*—short for *Jagdbomber,* literally "hunting bomber," spoken with alarm and respect. But the P-47 was more than that. Other countries had aircraft with similar missions. The Russian Il-2 was a dedicated low-level attack bird with an evil reputation among those whom it hunted, but it required a fighter escort. The Thunderbolt was something else. It could hold its own in a swarm of enemy and friendly fighters—now called a "furball"—*and* go low to make life miserable for the people on the ground. And that—though hardly recognized at the time—was a revolution of sorts. Using a single aircraft for more than one mission was so logical that the Jug's ability to do more than one mission *well* seems to have been overlooked. Alexander Cartvelli accidentally invented the multi-role aircraft. Today, the name of the game is multi-role aircraft.

So just what can airpower do? It can make life thoroughly miserable for an enemy—especially if you can hit exactly what you want to hit. Toward this goal, America continues to lead the world. "If you can see it, you can hit it," goes the saying. Following this usually comes, "If you can hit it, you can kill it." That way of thinking shaped American air doctrine. Dive bombing and close air support were first systematized by the United States Marine Corps in Nicaragua during their early interventions there. In the late 1930s, the Army Air Corps (later the Army Air Force) adopted the ultra-secret Norden bombsight to bring systematic accuracy to high-altitude bombing. In World War Two, the AAF experimented successfully with the "Razon" and "Mazon" TV-guided bombs. And the Germans conducted similar experiments, sinking an Italian battleship with their radio command guided Fritz-X bombs.

Such weapons have been improved over the years. Most of us can remember watching "the luckiest guy in Iraq" on CNN. During the Gulf War, his car was perhaps two hundred yards from the impact point of a two-thousand-pound guided bomb on an Iraqi bridge. Bridges are always worth destroying. So are factories, aircraft on the ground, radio and TV towers, and microwave relays. So too, especially, are the places which generate signals and commands . . . because commanders are there, and killing commanders is ever the quickest way of disrupting an army. Or a whole nation. Using precision-guided munitions can be likened to sniping with bombs. All warfare is cruel and ugly, but such munitions are less cruel and ugly than the alternatives.

With the recent advent of precision-guided munitions to attack the command centers of the enemy nation with great selectivity and deadly accuracy, the promise of airpower is finally being realized. But this fulfillment is not always what people wish it to be. You want a "surgical strike," find yourself a good surgeon. Surgical strikes do not happen in war. Yet the phrase continues to be approvingly employed in speeches by those (usually by elected or appointed politicians) who don't know what the hell they are talking about. To state things simply, surgeons use small and very sharp knives, held with delicacy by highly trained hands, to invade and repair a diseased body. Tactical and strategic aircraft drop metal objects filled with high explosives to destroy targets. The technology is much improved over what it once was, but it will never be surgically precise. Yes, the qualitative improvement over the past fifty years is astounding, but no, it isn't magical. All the same, you would be wise not to make yourself the object of the deadly attention of American warplanes.

The newest revolution—also American in origin—is stealth. When researching *Red Storm Rising*, I traveled to what was then the headquarters of the Tactical Air Command at Langley Air Force Base in the Virginia Tidewater.

There, a serious and laconic lieutenant colonel from Texas looked me straight in the eye and announced, "Son, you may safely assume that an invisible aircraft is tactically useful."

"Well, gee, sir," I replied, "I kinda figured that out for myself."

Seemingly a violation of the laws of physics, stealth is really a mere perversion of them. The technology began with a theoretical paper written around 1962 by a Russian radar engineer on the diffraction properties of microwave radiation. About ten years later an engineer at Lockheed read the paper and thought, "We can make an invisible airplane." Less than ten years after that, such an airplane was flying over a highly instrumented test range and driving radar technicians to despair. Meanwhile men in blue suits slowly discarded their disbelief, saw the future, and pronounced it good. Very good. Several years later over Baghdad on the night of January 17th, 1991, F-117A Black Jets of the 37th Tactical Fighter Wing proved beyond question that stealth really works.

The stealth revolution is simple to express: An aircraft can now go literally anywhere (depending only on its fuel capacity) and deliver bombs with a very high probability of killing the target (about 85 to 90% for a single weapon, about 98% for two), *and in the process it will give no more warning than the flash and noise of the detonation.* Meaning: The national command authorities (an American euphemism for the president, premier, or dictator) of any country are now vulnerable to direct attack. And for those who believe that the USAF was not trying to kill Saddam Hussein, be advised that maybe his death was not the objective. Maybe we were just trying to turn off the radio (i.e., command-and-control system) he was holding. A narrow legal point, but even the Pentagon has lawyers. However one might wish to put it, we *were* trying, and Hussein was a lucky man indeed to avoid the skillful attempts to flip off that particular switch. Whoever next offends the United States of America might wish to consider that. Because we'll try harder next time, and all you have to know is where that offending radio transmitter is.

As in *Submarine* and *Armored Cav,* I'll be taking you on a guided tour of one of America's premier fighting units and its equipment. In this case, the unit is the 366th Wing based out of Mountain Home AFB, Idaho. As organized today, the 366th is the Air Force's equivalent of the Army's 82nd Airborne or 101st Air Assault Division—a rapid-deployment force that can be sent to any trouble spot in the world on a moment's notice. The 366th's job is to delay an aggressor until the main force of USAF assets arrive in-theater, ready to go on the offensive. But before we visit these daring men and women in their amazing flying machines, let's take a look at the technologies that enable an aircraft to move, see, and fight.

Airpower 101

Weʼve all seen TV cartoons that show some clever character fashioning a set of wings and then trying to fly like a bird (with thanks to Warner Bros., Chuck Jones, and Wile E. Coyote). Usually, the sequence ends with the character in a bruised and battered jumble at the bottom of some horrendous precipice, pleading for help. Fitting wings to your arms and flapping them like a bird and leaping off cliffs looks silly, and so we laugh; yet thatʼs just how humans tried for several hundred years to achieve flight. Needless to say, it didnʼt work. It canʼt. The approach has to fail because it does not take into account the basic forces that affect flight.

Essentially, two forces help you get into the air and stay there. These forces are called thrust and lift. Working against them are another pair of forces that try to keep you grounded. These forces are called weight (mass and gravity) and drag; and their practical application to fly an aircraft safely from point A to point B constitutes the engineering discipline of aerodynamics.

For an engineer designing a combat aircraft, ignoring those forces seems as absurd as traveling backwards in time. At the same time, he or she must press the limits imposed by those forces as far as possible. You want a combat aircraft to fly as close to the "edge" as you can make it. By definition. Putting this another way: To really understand the edge, you have to understand the basic forces. And so, before we look at how well various combat aircraft succeed in approaching the edge, letʼs spend a little time going over the four forces—thrust, lift, weight, and drag.

THRUST

This is the force that causes an aircraft to move through the air. It is provided by an aircraftʼs engines, and has the same effect on the aircraft whether it is pulled through the air with a propeller or pushed with a jet engine. Thrust is conventionally measured in pounds or newtons. The more thrust an aircraftʼs engines can generate, the faster the aircraft will travel, and the more lift the wings will provide. Similarly, when you step on your carʼs accelerator, the engine produces more power, the wheels spin faster, and the car moves along the road at a higher speed. This action also causes the air to move past the car at a higher speed.

In the world of combat aircraft design, the engineʼs raw propulsion power is expressed as its thrust-to-weight ratio. This ratio compares the amount

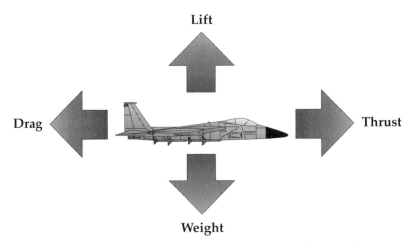

Lift

Drag

Thrust

Weight

An illustration of the four primary forces on a powered aircraft: thrust, drag, lift, and weight.

JACK RYAN ENTERPRISES, LTD., BY LAURA ALPHER

of thrust that the engines can produce to the weight of the aircraft. The higher the ratio, the more powerful the aircraft. For most combat aircraft, this ratio is around 0.7 to 0.9. However, really high-performance models, like the F-15 and -16, have thrust-to-weight ratios greater than 1.0 and can accelerate while going straight up!

LIFT

Lift is the force that pushes an object up due to the unbalanced movement of air past it. In an aircraft, the unbalance comes from the different curvature of the upper and lower surfaces of the wings (the upper surface has more curve than the lower), and the movement of air is provided as a consequence of the engine's thrust. When the moving air comes in contact with the leading edge of the wing, the air separates. Part of the flow passes over the top of the wing, and the remainder below. Given the shape of an aircraft's wing, the air stream on top has to travel a greater distance than the stream below. If both air streams are to arrive at the trailing edge at the same time, then the air stream above the wing must have a higher speed.

In aerodynamics, there is a simple, but neat, relationship between the speed of a gas and its pressure: The faster a gas travels, the lower its pressure and vice versa. This principle is called Bernoulli's Law, in honor of the 18th-century Italian scientist who first investigated it experimentally. So if the air stream above the wing is moving faster than the air stream below the wing, air pressure above the wing will be lower than below the wing. This difference causes the air below to push upward and "lift" the wing up. As the speed of an aircraft increases, the pressure difference grows and produces more lift. This wing's angle, called the angle of attack (AOA) of the aircraft, can have a significant effect on lift.

Initially, lift increases as AOA increases, but only up to a certain point. Beyond this point, the AOA is too large and the air flow over the wing stops. Without the air flow, there is no pressure difference and the wing no longer produces lift. When this situation occurs, the wing (and the aircraft) is said to have stalled. Now, a high AOA isn't the only thing that will cause an aircraft to stall. If an aircraft's speed gets too low, the air no longer moves fast enough over the wings to generate adequate lift, and again the aircraft will stall—and any pilot will tell you that stalls can be really bad for your health.

DRAG

Drag is the force that wants to slow the aircraft down. In essence, drag is friction; it resists the movement of the aircraft. This is a tough concept to grasp, because we can't see air. But while air may be invisible, it still has weight and inertia. We've all taken a walk on a windy day and felt the air pushing against us. That is drag. As an aircraft moves through the air, it pushes the air out its way, and the air pushes back. At supersonic speeds, this air resistance can be very significant, as a huge amount of air is rapidly pushed out of the way and the friction generated can rapidly heat the aircraft's body to temperatures over 500° F/260° C.

There are two types of drag, parasitic and induced. Parasitic drag is wind resistance associated with the various bumps, lumps, and other structures on an aircraft. Anything that makes the aircraft's surface rough or uneven, like bombs, rivet heads, drop tanks, radio antennae, paint, and control surfaces (rudder, canards), increases the aircraft's wind resistance. Induced drag is more difficult to understand because it is directly linked to lift. In other words, if lift is being generated by the wings, so too is induced drag. Since drag is unavoidable, the best that can be done is to minimize it and understand the limits it places on the aircraft's performance. And the limits are significant. Drag degrades the aircraft's ability to accelerate and maneuver and increases fuel consumption, which affects combat range/radius. Therefore, a good understanding of drag is needed not only by aircraft designers, but by aviators as well.

WEIGHT

Weight is the result of gravitational attraction of the Earth, which pulls the mass of the aircraft toward the Earth's center. As such it is in direct opposition to lift. Of all the forces involved with flying, gravity is the most persistent. To some extent, we can control the other three. But gravity is beyond our control. In the end, it *always* wins (unless you're riding a spacecraft fast enough to escape the Earth's gravity entirely—about 25,000 mph [40,000 kph]!). Thrust, lift, and drag are all accounted for in the design process of the aircraft. But when thrust or lift become insufficient to maintain the aircraft aloft, gravity will bring the plane down.

Engines

Once you understand the physics of flight, and you can build a sufficiently lightweight power plant, getting an aircraft into the air is a relatively simple matter. But operating high-performance aircraft in the hostile environment faced by today's military aircraft is quite another thing. These machines are anything *but* simple.

With complexity comes problems. The heart of a good aircraft is a good engine—the thing that makes it *go!* More fighter programs have been plagued by engine troubles than by any other source of grief. So, what's the big deal in making a good jet engine, you might ask? Well, try and imagine building a 3,000-to-4,000 lb./1,363.6-to-1,818 kg. machine that produces over seven times its own weight in thrust and is made with tolerances tighter than the finest Swiss watch. It has to operate reliably for years, even when pilots under the stress of combat or the spur of competition push it beyond its design limits.

To give you a better picture of how exact these engines are made, look at a human hair. While it may look pretty thin to you, it would barely fit between many of the moving parts in a jet engine. That's what I mean by tight tolerances! Now, let's spin some of those parts at thousands of revolutions per minute and expose a few of them to temperatures so high that most metal alloys would melt instantly. One can now begin to appreciate the mechanical and thermal stresses that a jet engine must be designed to handle every time it runs. Should even one of the rapidly rotating compressor or turbine wheels fail under these stresses and come into contact with the stationary casing, the resulting fragments would shred the aircraft just as effectively as missile or cannon fire.

Since a combat aircraft's performance is so closely tied to its propulsion plant, the limits of engine technology are constantly being pushed by designers and manufacturers. Their goal is to design an engine that is lighter than its predecessors and competitors, but produces more thrust. To accomplish this, an engine designer almost always has to bet that a new emerging technology or two will work out as anticipated. Occasionally, this means taking some pretty big risks. Risks that usually turn into problems that get widely reported in the media. For example, engine-development problems in the mid-1950s almost wrecked major aircraft companies, when airframes like the McDonnell F-3H Demon and Vought F-5U Cutlass had to wait months—or even years—for their engines to be developed. So, just how far has jet engine performance come along in the past forty years? Let's take a quick look.

In the mid-1950s, the U.S. Air Force began operating the North American F-100 Super Sabre, nicknamed the "Hun." Powered by a single Pratt & Whitney J57-P-7 engine, an axial-flow turbojet generating up to 16,000 lb./7,272.7 kg. of thrust, and aided by the newly developed afterburner, it was the first supersonic fighter, achieving a top speed of Mach 1.25. With confidence growing in the axial-flow turbojet engine, new fighter designs quickly showed up, and in 1958 the first McDonnell F-4 Phantom II flew. In the world of combat aircraft, the F-4 is legendary. During the Vietnam War it proved to be a formidable fighter bomber, and it still serves in some air forces. Powered by two giant General Electric J79-GE-15 turbojet engines, each generating up to 17,900 lb./8,136 kg. of thrust, the Phantom, or the "Rhino" as it was affectionately called, could reach speeds up to Mach 2.2 at high altitudes.

To illustrate the axial-flow turbojet, consider the J79 engine and its five major sections:

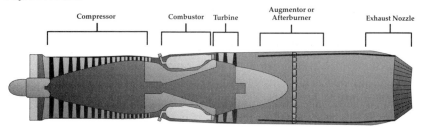

A schematic cutaway of a typical turbojet engine, such as the Pratt & Whitney J79.

JACK RYAN ENTERPRISES, LTD., BY LAURA ALPHER

At the front of the J79 is the compressor section. Here, air is sucked into the engine and compacted in a series of seventeen axial compressor stages. Each stage is like a pinwheel with dozens of small turbine blades (they look like small curved fins) that push air through the engine, compressing it. The compressed air then passes into the combustor section, where it mixes with fuel and ignites. Combustion produces a mass of hot high-pressure gas that is packed with energy. The hot gas escapes through a nozzle onto the three turbine stages of the engine's hot section (so-called because this is where you find the highest temperatures). The stubby fan-like turbine blades are pushed by the hot gas as it strikes them. This causes the turbine wheel to spin at very high speed and with great power. The turbine wheel is connected by a shaft which spins the compressor stages which compact the air flow even further. The hot gas then escapes out the back of the turbojet and this flow pushes the aircraft through the air. When the afterburner (or augmentor) is used, additional fuel is sprayed directly into the exhaust gases in a final combustion chamber, or "burner can" as it is known. This provides a 50% increase in the final thrust of the engine. An afterburner is required for a turbojet to reach supersonic speeds. Unfortunately, using an afterburner gobbles fuel at roughly three to four times the rate of non-afterburning "dry"-thrust settings. For example, using full afterburner in the F-4 Phantom II would drain its tanks dry in just under eight minutes. This thirst for fuel was the next problem the engine designers had to overcome.

The axial flow turbojet became the dominant aircraft propulsion plant in the late 1950s because it could sustain supersonic flight for as long as the aircraft's fuel supply held up. The term "axial" means along a straight line, which is how the air flows in these engines. Up until that time, centrifugal (circular) flow engines were the military engines of choice—they were actually more powerful than early axial flow turbojets. But centrifugal flow engines could not support supersonic speeds.

Instead of a multiple stage compressor, centrifugal flow engines used a single stage, pump-like impeller to compress the incoming air flow. This drastically limited the pressure (or compression) ratio of the early jet engines, and therefore the maximum amount of thrust they could produce. The comparison between the air pressure leaving the last compressor stage of a jet engine and the air pressure at the inlet of the compressor section is how the pressure ratio is defined. Because the pressure ratio is *the* key performance characteristic of any jet engine, the axial flow designs had more growth potential than other designs of the period. Therefore, the major reasons why axial flow engines replaced centrifugal flow designs was that they could achieve higher pressure ratios and could also accommodate an afterburner. Centrifugal flow simply could not move enough air through the engine to keep an afterburner lit. By the mid-1960s, it became apparent that turbojet engines had reached their practical limitations, especially at subsonic speeds. If combat aircraft were going to carry heavier payloads with greater range, then a new engine with greater takeoff thrust and better fuel economy would have to be designed. The engine that finally emerged from the design labs in the 1960s was called a high-bypass turbofan.

At first glance, a turbofan doesn't look all that much different from a turbojet. There are, in fact, many differences, the most obvious being the presence of the fan section and the bypass duct. The fan section is a large, low-pressure compressor which pushes part of the air flow into the main compressor. The rest of the air goes down a separate channel called the bypass duct. The ratio between the amount of air pushed down the bypass duct and the amount that goes into the compressor is called the bypass ratio. For high bypass turbofans, about 40% to 60% of the air is diverted down the bypass duct. But in some designs, the bypass ratio can go as high as 97%.

I know this doesn't appear to make a whole lot of sense. Don't you need more air, not less, to make a jet engine more powerful? In the case of turbofans, not so. More air is definitely not better. To repeat, pressure ratio is the key performance characteristic of a jet engine. Therefore the designers of the first turbofans put a lot of effort into increasing this pressure ratio. The result was the bypass concept.

If an engine has to compress a lot of air, then the pressure increase is distributed, or spread out, over a large volume. By reducing the amount of air

A schematic cutaway of a typical turbofan engine, such as the Pratt Whitney F-100.

JACK RYAN ENTERPRISES, LTD., BY LAURA ALPHER

Fan   Compressor   Combustor   Two–Stage Turbine   Augmentor or Afterburner   Exhaust Nozzle

Bypass Duct

flowing into the compressor, more work can be done on a smaller volume, which means a greater pressure increase. This is good. Then the designers increased the rotational speed of the compressor. With the compressor stages spinning around faster, more work is done on the air, and this again means a greater pressure increase. This is better. The bypass duct was relatively easy to incorporate into an engine design, but unfortunately, a faster spinning compressor proved to be far more difficult.

There were three major problems:

1. Getting more work out of the turbine so that it could drive the compressor at higher speeds.
2. Preventing the compressor blades from stalling when rotated at the higher speeds.
3. Reducing the weight of the compressor so that the centrifugal stresses would not exceed the mechanical strength of the alloys used in the compressor blades.

Each problem is a formidable technological challenge, but mastering all three took some serious engineering ingenuity.

Getting more work out of a turbine is basically a metallurgy problem: To produce the hotter gases needed to spin the turbine wheels faster, the engine must run hotter. Next, if the turbine's weight can be reduced, more useful work can be extracted from the hot gases. Both require a stronger, more heat-resistant metal alloy. But developing such an alloy is a difficult quest. In working with metals, you don't find high strength and high heat resistance in the same material. The solution was found not only in the particular alloy chosen for the turbine blades, but also in the manufacturing technique.

Traditionally, turbine blades have been constructed from nickel-based alloys. These are very resistant to high temperatures and have great mechanical strength. Unfortunately, even the best nickel-based alloys melt around 2,100° to 2,200°F/1,148° to 1,204°C. For turbojets like the J79, in which the combustion section exit temperature is only about 1800°F/982°C, this is good enough; the temperature of the first stage turbine blades can be kept well below their melting point. But high bypass turbofans have combustion exit temperatures in the neighborhood of 2,500°F/1,371°C. Such heat turns the best nickel-based turbine blade into slag in a few seconds. Even before the blades reached their melting point, they would become pliable, like Silly Putty. Stretched by centrifugal forces, they would quickly come into contact with the stationary turbine case. Bad news.

Nickel-based alloys still remain the best material for turbine blades. So improvements in strength and heat resistance depend on the blade manufacturing process. The manufacturing technology that had the greatest effect on turbine blade performance was single-crystal casting.

Single-crystal casting is a process in which a molten turbine blade is carefully cooled so that the metallic structure of the blade forms a single crystal.

Most metallic objects have a crystalline structure. For example, you can sometimes see the crystal boundaries on the zinc coating of new galvanized steel cans, or on old brass doorknobs etched by years of wear. When metal objects are cast, the crystals in the metal form randomly due to uneven cooling. Metal objects usually break or fracture along the boundaries of crystal structures. To melt a crystalline object, the heat energy must break down the bonds that hold the crystals together. The bigger the crystals the more energy it takes. If these crystalline boundaries can be eliminated entirely, a cast metal object can have very high strength and heat resistance, qualities highly desirable in a turbine blade.

The first step in forming a single crystal structure is to precisely control the cooling process. In turbine blade manufacturing, this is done by very slowly withdrawing the mold from an induction furnace. This works like your microwave oven at home, only a lot hotter. Controlled cooling by itself, however, will not produce a single crystalline structure. For that you also need a "structural filter."

So the molten nickel alloy is poured into the turbine blade mold, which is mounted on a cold plate in an induction furnace. When the mold is filled, the mold/cold plate package is slowly retracted from the furnace. Immediately, multiple crystal structures begin to form in a crystal "starter block" at the bottom of the mold. But because the cold plate is withdrawn vertically, the crystals can only grow toward the top of the starter block. At the top of the block is a very narrow passage that is shaped like a pig's curly tail. This pigtail coil is the structural filter, and it is only wide enough for one crystal structure to travel through. When the single crystal structure reaches the root of the turbine blade, it spreads out and solidifies as the

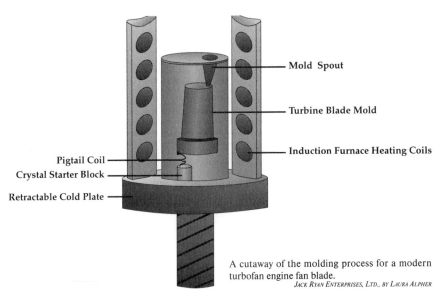

Mold Spout

Turbine Blade Mold

Induction Furnace Heating Coils

Pigtail Coil

Crystal Starter Block

Retractable Cold Plate

A cutaway of the molding process for a modern turbofan engine fan blade.
Jack Ryan Enterprises, Ltd., by Laura Alpher

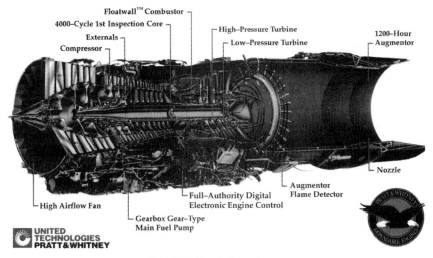

Floatwall™ Combustor
4000–Cycle 1st Inspection Core
Externals
Compressor
High–Pressure Turbine
Low–Pressure Turbine
1200–Hour Augmentor
Nozzle
Augmentor Flame Detector
High Airflow Fan
Full–Authority Digital Electronic Engine Control
Gearbox Gear–Type Main Fuel Pump

UNITED TECHNOLOGIES
PRATT&WHITNEY

A cutaway of the Pratt & Whitney F100-PW-229 turbofan engine.

JACK RYAN ENTERPRISES, LTD., BY LAURA ALPHER

blade mold is slowly withdrawn from the furnace. Once it is completely cooled, the turbine blade will be a single crystal of metal with no structural boundaries to weaken it. It now only requires final machining and polishing to make it ready for use.

While single-crystal turbine blades are very strong and heat resistant, they would still melt if directly exposed to the hot gases from the combustion of a turbofan engine. To keep molten turbine wheels from dribbling out the back end of the engine, a blanket of cool air from the compressor is spread over the turbine blades. This is possible because complex air passages and air bleed holes can be cast directly into the turbine blades. These bleed holes form a protective film of air, which keeps the turbine blades from coming into direct contact with the exhaust gases, while simultaneously allowing the turbine blades to extract work from those gases. Earlier non-single-crystal turbine blade designs had very simple cooling passages and bleed holes that were machined out by lasers or electron beams, and didn't provide as much thermal protection.

Thanks to single-crystal casting technologies, the turbine sections of turbofans not only operate at higher pressures and temperatures than turbojets, but are smaller, lighter, and more reliable. For example, a quick comparison between the J79 and the F100 shows that the turbine section that drives the compressor has shrunk from three large stages to two smaller ones.

The remaining problems resulting from a turbofan's higher pressure ratio include preventing the compressor blades from stalling at higher rotational speeds, and reducing the compressor section's weight. Weight is particularly critical, since every extra pound/kilogram has to be compensated for by the aircraft's designers. Fortunately, the solution to compressor stalling also reduces the compressor's overall weight.

Consider the problem: As the rotational speed of the compressor increases, so too does the speed of the airflow. At some point the airspeed becomes so high that a shock wave forms and the compressor "stalls." This is very similar to what happened to many early straight wing jet and rocket-powered aircraft when they went supersonic. As the aircraft exceeded the speed of sound, a shock wave (a virtual "wall" of air) formed which caused the wing to undergo "shock stall" and lose all lift. In an engine, excessive shock-induced drag stalls the airflow and the compressor is unable to push the air any further. In aircraft design, the remedy for shock stall was to sweep the wings back. The same solution works for turbofan engine compressor blades. Sweeping back the compressor blades not only avoids shock stalling, but allows the blades to do more work on the air because they are moving faster. This raises the pressure ratio. Since these higher-speed, swept-back compressor blades are much more efficient in compacting air, a smaller number of compressor stages are required to achieve a desired pressure ratio. A smaller number of stages means a reduction in the overall weight of the compressor and the engine itself. Again, comparing the J79 and the F100, we can see an overall reduction in the number of compressor stages from seventeen in the J79 to thirteen for the F100 (or really only ten if we exclude the fan section). Compressor weight has also been reduced through the use of titanium alloys in about half of the stages towards the front of the engine. Although titanium is lighter than nickel alloys, it cannot be used further aft than the midsection of the compressor (due to heat-resistance limits of titanium alloys), so heavier steel alloys are used in the remaining stages. Still, there is a significant weight saving from the use of titanium where it is applicable, and the current generation of fighting turbofan engines has greatly benefited as a result.

Once the problems with higher rotation speed compressors was solved, turbofan engines generally replaced the turbojet as the propulsion plant of choice for high-performance military aircraft. Their superior thrust made them a natural choice for the new generation of high-performance aircraft like the F-15 and F-16 that came on-line in the mid-1970s.

The latest version of the Pratt & Whitney F100 family, the F100-PW-229, is generally considered to be the best fighter engine in the world today. It is capable of delivering over 29,000 lb./13,181.8 kg. of thrust in afterburner, as well as providing improved fuel economy in dry-thrust ranges. Although it's not the first turbofan engine used in a fighter design (the F-111A was fitted with the Pratt & Whitney TF30), the F100 engine was the first true "fighting" turbofan, and is the propulsion plant for all of the F-15-series aircraft and the majority of the F-16 fleet as well. The F100 engine first flew in July 1972 in the first prototype F-15; and by February 1975, the Eagle had established eight world records for rapid climbing, streaking past the records held by the turbojet powered F-4 Phantom and the Soviet MiG-25 Foxbat.

The improvement in fuel economy at subsonic speeds came about because the smaller quantity of higher-pressure air entering the combustion chamber mixed better with the fuel and burned more completely. Since the fuel burns more efficiently, turbofans have about 20% lower specific fuel consumption at subsonic speeds; and as an added bonus they do not produce as much smoke as a turbojet. This was a major tactical improvement. In Vietnam, the F-4 Phantom II usually announced its presence by the plumes of smoke belching from its twin J79 turbojets.

Another significant improvement in fuel economy and overall engine performance came with the development of an advanced electronic-control system called Full-Authority Digital Engine Control or FADEC. FADEC replaced the old hydromechanical control system found on turbojets, responding faster and more precisely to changes that the engine experiences in flight. Factors that FADEC monitors include aircraft angle of attack, air pressure, air temperature, and airspeed. Since FADEC can monitor considerably more parameters than a hydromechanical system, it is constantly fine-tuning the engine to maximize its performance.

Not everything about a fighting turbofan engine is an improvement over a turbojet. For instance, the afterburner of a turbofan actually consumes far more fuel (about 25% more) than its counterpart on a turbojet. Because so much of the air entering a turbofan goes through the bypass duct, the afterburner is supplied with a larger supply of oxygen-rich air. With the greater amount of oxygen available for combustion, more fuel can be sprayed into the afterburner to produce even more thrust. For turbofan engines, the afterburner provides about a 65% increase in thrust (compared with 50% for a turbojet). The good news is that aircraft equipped with fighting turbofans don't need to use afterburners as often. The latest version of the F100 produces as much thrust without afterburner as the J79 does with it. Now, an F-15C still needs the afterburner to sustain supersonic flight, but it can cruise at high subsonic speeds, loaded with external fuel tanks and missiles, without using this fuel-guzzling feature.

Presently, all high-performance fighters are subsonic aircraft, with the ability to make short supersonic dashes through the use of afterburners. But the USAF's next-generation Advanced Tactical Fighter (ATF) will be required to sustain cruise speeds above Mach 1.5 (at altitude) *without* the use of its afterburners. The only way this can be done is to have the core (the compressor, combust, and turbine section) of a turbofan produce more thrust than even the current-generation fighting turbofans. With the help of advanced computer-modeling techniques, called computational fluid dynamics, the compressor and turbine blades of the new engine are shorter, thicker, and more twisted than those in the F100. Thus, the F119-PW-100, the engine chosen for the new F-22 fighter (winner of the ATF competition), has fewer stages in the compressor and the turbine (three stages in the fan, six in the compressor, and two stages in the turbine). Even with these changes, supersonic cruise could not be achieved. To get the needed thrust, the bypass ratio had to be further reduced, and more air sent through the core of the engine.

The F119 engine on the F-22 is technically a low-bypass turbofan, with only about 15% to 20% of the air going down the bypass duct. Now, this low-bypass ratio seems to conflict with all I've said about the advantages of high-bypass turbofans. However, a high-bypass-ratio turbofan is designed to give good performance at *subsonic speeds!* For supersonic cruising, the best engine must be more like a turbojet. With its low bypass ratio, the F119 engine is almost a pure turbojet, with only enough air sent down the bypass duct to provide for the cooling and combustion (oxygen) requirements of the afterburner. During test runs in 1990 and 1991, the F-22 was able to sustain Mach 1.58 at altitude, without using its afterburner. The tremendous advantage of maintaining supersonic speeds without the afterburner, coupled with thrust-vectored exhaust nozzles, will provide the F-22 with significantly enhanced maneuvering characteristics over even the nimble F-16 Block 50/52, equipped with the -229 version of the F100. Thrust vectoring is the use of steerable nozzles or vanes to deflect part of the engine exhaust in a desired direction. This allows the aircraft to change its direction, or flight attitude, with less use of its control surfaces (ailerons, rudder), which induce a lot of drag. The Rolls-Royce Pegasus engine, which enables the AV-8 Harrier to land and take off from a tennis court, is the best known example of thrust vectoring.

Where engine technology will go from here is anyone's guess. One of the major challenges that have faced designers for decades is to produce powerplants that can make Short Takeoff/Vertical Landing (STOVL) tactical aircraft a practical reality. The AV-8B Harrier II is a wonderful tool for the U.S. Marines, but the weight of its Pegasus powerplant limits it to short-range, subsonic flights. Perhaps the next-generation engine that is being developed under the Joint Advanced Strike Technology (JAST) program will provide the answer for this quest. Whatever happens, though, engine designers will always hold the key to those who "feel the need for speed . . ."

Stealth

Stealth is a good Anglo-Saxon word, derived from the same root as the verb "steal," in the sense of "stealing" up on your foe to surprise him. When a good set of eyes and ears were the only sensors, camouflage and careful, muffled steps (don't break any twigs, and I'll flog the first legionary whose armor clanks!) were the way to sneak up on the enemy. The ninja warriors of medieval Japan were masters of stealth, using the cover of night, black suits, and silent methods of infiltrating castles and killing sentries to earn a legendary reputation for mystical invisibility. Submarines use the ocean to conceal their movements, and no high-technology sensor has yet managed to render the ocean transparent.

For aircraft, radar and infrared are the sensors that represent the greatest threat. Let's consider radar first. The acronym RADAR first came into the military vocabulary during World War II. The term stands for Radio Detection and Ranging, and this significantly enhanced the ability of a land-based warning outpost, ship, or aircraft to detect enemy units. A transmitter generates a pulse of electromagnetic energy, which is fed to an antenna via a switching circuit. The antenna forms the pulse into a concentrated beam which can be steered by the antenna. If a target lies within the beam, some is absorbed, and a very small amount is reflected back to the radar antenna. The switching circuit then takes the returning pulse from the antenna and sends it to a receiver which amplifies the signal and extracts the important tactical information (target bearing and range). This information is displayed on a screen, where a human can see the target's position, guess where it is going, and try to make tactical decisions. A big object that reflects lots of energy back toward the antenna shows up as a big, bright blip on the screen. A very small object that reflects very little energy may not show up at all.

There are two stealth techniques to defeat radar: shaping, to reduce an object's "radar cross section," and coating the object with radar-absorbing materials (RAM). When radar was in its infancy in World War II, both sides experimented with these techniques. The Germans were particularly successful. By 1943, the Germans were applying two different types of RAM coatings, called *Jaumann* and *Wesch* absorbers, to their U-boat snorkel masts to reduce detectability to aircraft radar. Although the RAM reduced the radar-detection range of a snorkel mast from about 8 miles/14.6 km. to 1 mile/1.8 km., the coatings didn't adhere well to the snorkel masts after prolonged immersion in seawater. Meanwhile, the *Luftwaffe* was investigating radar-defeating airframe shapes. In 1943, two German brothers named Horten designed a jet-propelled flying wing, quite similar in appearance to the USAF B-2 bomber. Tail surfaces and sharp breaks between wing and fuselage increase a plane's radar cross section, so an all-wing airplane is an ideal stealth shape, as well as an efficient design. A prototype aircraft, designated the Ho IX V-2, first flew in 1944, but crashed in the spring of 1945 after a test flight. Due to Allied advances on both fronts, the program was stopped. The remarkable work on reducing various aircraft signatures that was done by German engineers in the early-to-mid 1940s would not be reproduced in an operational aircraft until 1958 when Lockheed's Skunk Works started working on the A-12, the forerunner to the SR-71 Blackbird.

As with any other active sensor, a radar's performance is highly dependent on how much of the transmitted energy is reflected by the target back towards the receiving antenna. A lot of energy, and the operator sees a big blip. Less energy, and the operator sees a small blip. The amount of the reflected energy, the radar cross section (RCS) of the target, is expressed as an area, usually in square meters (about 10.8 square feet). This measurement is, however, somewhat misleading: RCS can't be determined by simply calculating the target area facing the radar. RCS is a complex characteristic that depends on the cross-sectional area of that target (geometric cross section), how well the target reflects radar energy (material reflectivity), and how much of the reflected energy travels back toward the radar antenna (directivity). To lower an aircraft's RCS, designers must reduce these factors as much as they can without degrading the aircraft's ability to carry out its mission. It should be said that

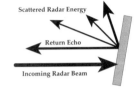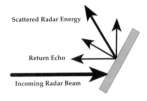

| 90° Angle of Incidence | 80° Angle of Incidence | 60° Angle of Incidence |

A comparison of the radar reflectivity of three angled surfaces. *Jack Ryan Enterprises, Ltd., by Laura Alpher*

such design features are not easily slapped onto an existing design, but in fact are fundamental to the plane's design. Thus the need for designed-to-purpose stealth structures.

Of the three factors that determine RCS, geometric cross section is the least worrisome to designers. Compare the RCS of the B-2 bomber with your average duck. A duck is physically much, much smaller than a stealth bomber. However, to a long-range search radar, a duck is actually *five times larger* than the B-2A! The common sparrow or finch would be a closer match from a search radar's perspective. Since physical size isn't critical for RCS reduction, designers are mainly concerned with the reflectivity and directivity, and as we will see, a *lot* can be done with these.

And of the two, directivity is by far the part of the RCS equation that has the greatest effect. Reducing the directivity component is why the F-117A and the B-2 have shapes that make them look so odd. Shaping can lower the directivity component by orienting target surfaces and edges so that the incoming radar energy is deflected away from the radar antenna, like the many mirrored faces of a dance club "disco ball." The F-117A is "faceted" into a series of flat plates, while the smoothly contoured B-2 uses a technique called planform shaping. Both techniques present surfaces that are angled about 30° away from the incoming radar signals. Smaller angles, however, can also have a significant effect on RCS. Consider three metal plates with different angles with respect to the radar beam. If the first plate is perpendicular (90°) to the radar beam, most of the energy is reflected back towards the radar antenna, maximizing the plate's RCS with respect to the radar. Now, imagine a second plate that is tilted back by 10°. About 97% of the energy is deflected away from the direction of the radar. This is better. Now, think about a third plate, tilted back by 30°. Almost 99.9% of the incoming radar energy is deflected away from the radar!

Even though shaping is the best way to reduce RCS, it is virtually impossible to eliminate all the surfaces or edges which reflect radar energy. Examples of such reflectors are engine inlets, leading edges of wings, canopy rails, or even access-panel join lines on the aircraft's fuselage. These trouble spots are taken care of by reducing their reflectivity through the use of RAM coatings and radar-absorbing structures (RAS). RAM materials absorb radar energy and convert it into heat or small magnetic fields. The physical mechanism that accomplishes this is very complex: The material resonates with the incoming radar energy and then changes it by vibration into heat or by electrical induction into weak magnetic fields. RAM can absorb about 90% to 95% of the incident radar energy, depending on composition and thickness. For existing non-stealth aircraft designs, like the F-15 or F-16, RAM coatings (the U.S. Air Force reportedly has a radar-absorbing paint called "Iron Ball") can cut their RCS by as much as 70% to 80%.

Radar-absorbing structures, on the other hand, are only used by aircraft designed specifically to be stealthy, as they must be carefully built into the aircraft's framework. Modern RAS designs use strong, radar-transparent composites to build a rigid hollow structure which is then filled with RAM. Because the RAM can be quite thick under the composite shell, most of the radar beam's energy is absorbed before it hits one of the metallic components of the aircraft's structure. Older RAS structure designs, like those on the SR-71, are made of radar-reflective metals in a triangular shape, with a RAM filling in the triangle cavity. When a radar beam hits such a structure, it is reflected back and forth between the reflector plates. With each bounce, the radar beam passes through the RAM, and more of the energy is absorbed. Eventually, the radar signal becomes too weak to show up on a radar screen, and that is that! On stealth aircraft like the B-2 and F-22, radar-absorbing structures are used extensively on hard-to-shape spots like the leading and trailing edges of the wings, control surfaces, and the inlets to the engines. A well-designed RAS can absorb up to 99.9% of an incoming radar beam's energy.

Consider a hypothetical air-search radar with a detection range of 200 nm./365.7 km. against a B-52, which looks like the broad side of a barn to a radar. With extensive use of stealth technologies, the B-2A's RCS is 1/10,000 that of the B-52, and the detection range drops to less than 20 nm./36.6 km.! This reduction in a radar's range leaves massive gaps in a hostile nation's early warning net, which an aircraft like the B-2 can easily fly through.

In sum, the B-2A, or for that matter the F-117A or the F-22A, isn't invisible to a radar; but the effective range against these aircraft is so short that they can fly around radar warning sites with relative impunity. And this is exactly what the F-117s of the 37th Tactical Fighter Wing (Provisional) did to Iraq during Desert Storm.

While radar is the primary sensor used to detect aircraft, infrared (IR) sensors are becoming increasingly sensitive. The frequency of the IR portion of the electromagnetic spectrum is just below that of visible light and well above that of radar. Since most infrared energy is absorbed by water vapor and carbon dioxide gas in the atmosphere, there are only two "windows" in the infrared band where detection of an aircraft is likely. One window ("mid-IR") occurs at a wavelength of 2 to 5 microns. Mid-IR is used by current IR-homing air-to-air missiles like the AIM-9 Sidewinder series. Infrared radiation from the heat of an aircraft's engine parts and exhaust falls in this mid-IR region. The other window is in the long IR band, at a wavelength of 8 to 15 microns. The long IR signature of an aircraft is caused by solar heating or by air friction on the fuselage of the aircraft. Modern Infrared Search and Track (IRST) and Forward-Looking Infrared (FLIR) systems (which have become more significant as air-to-air sensors since radar-stealthy aircraft became operational) can look for targets in both windows.

To decrease an aircraft's IR signature, the designer must find ways to cool the engine exhaust, where most of the IR radiation is generated. A good start is eliminating the afterburner, which creates a large IR bright spot or "bloom." Though this reduces the aircraft's flight performance, if high speed is not a requirement (as in the design of the F-117A and the B-2A), then the afterburner can be discarded. Both the F-117A and the B-2A have non-afterburning versions of turbofan engines used on other aircraft. The next step in IR suppression is to design the engine inlet so that cool ambient air goes around the engine and mixes with the hot exhaust gases before they are expelled from the aircraft. Cooling the exhaust by even 100° or 200°F significantly reduces the aircraft's IR signature.

Since it is impossible to completely cool the engine exhaust to ambient air temperature, the aircraft designer must reduce the detectability of the hot exhaust. Wide, thin nozzles can flatten out the exhaust plume so it mixes more rapidly with the ambient air. This rapid mixing quickly dissipates the exhaust plume, reducing its detectability by IR sensors. Both the F-117A and B-2 have exotic nozzles that not only rapidly dissipate the exhaust plume, but also block the line of sight to the hotter parts of the engine itself. In the case of the F-117A, the nozzles were coated with a ceramic material, similar to that used on the Space Shuttle, to help deal with the heat erosion of the hot exhaust.

Although a lot can be done to reduce the medium IR band signature from the engines, little can be done about solar or friction heating of the aircraft's outer skin. At best, one could make greater use of carbon-carbon composite materials, which have good IR-dissipation qualities, in the aircraft's fuselage and wing surfaces. Some special paints have modest effects on the long IR signature, but this is a limited modification at best. Short of an expensive and complex active cooling system, this exhausts the limited list of useful options. Fortunately, current IRSTs do not provide greater detection ranges than radar, even against a stealth aircraft, though this could change in the future.

Detection technologies are moving forward rapidly, and today's stealth jet could be tomorrow's sitting duck if designers remain complacent. My friend Steve Coonts used a concept of "active" stealth in his novel *The Minotaur* a few years ago. Computer-controlled "cloaking" systems are just science fiction right now, but with the continuing improvements in computer and signal-processing technology, we may be only a generation away from an aircraft with the ability to hide behind an electronic cloak of its own making. Millions of years ago, natural selection taught a little reptile called the chameleon that the way to become invisible to a predator is to look exactly like your background.

Avionics

In *Submarine* and *Armored Cav,* we saw how advances in computer hardware and software revolutionized a fighting machine's ability to find and kill targets. Because the crew is often made up of only one person, modern high-performance aircraft place heavier than ever requirements on fast, high-data-rate computers. You can think of sensors as the eyes and ears of an aircraft, computers as its brain, and displays as its voice—the way it communicates with the human in the cockpit. Sensors, computers, and displays are all components of the aircraft's electronic nervous system or "avionics."

In older aircraft, such as the F-15A Eagle, the only search sensor available was a radar, and almost all of the system indicators were analog gauges. In combat, the pilot of an early-model Eagle had a first-generation Heads-Up Display (HUD) which showed him what he needed to fly and fight the aircraft. When you are through counting everything, the F-15A pilot still had over a hundred dials, switches, and screens to worry about. As computer technology improved, and as more capable sensors were added, the amount of data that became available to the pilot increased dramatically. To avoid overloading the pilot, multi-function displays (which look like small computer monitors surrounded by buttons) started replacing many of the single-purpose displays and gauges. In some aircraft, such as the F-15E Strike Eagle, there was now so much data available that to employ the aircraft to its full potential, both a pilot and a weapon systems officer (WSO) had to man it. The Air Force's new F-22 fighter will incorporate even greater advances in sensor and computer capabilities. In comparison to the F-15E Strike Eagle, which has, at best, the equivalent of two or three IBM PC-AT computers (based on Intel 80286 microprocessors), the F-22 will take to the skies with the equivalent of two Cray mainframe supercomputers in her belly, and there is room for a third! To keep up with this vast increase in processing power, data rates on the network or "bus" connecting various aircraft subsystems have increased from one million characters per second (1 Mb/sec.) to over 50 Mb/sec. There has been a similar increase in computer memory and data-storage capacity.

A pilot simply cannot fly the F-22 without the assistance of a computer. In fact, all U.S. combat aircraft produced since the F-16 have been designed with inherently unstable flight characteristics. The only way for such a machine to stay in the air is for a computer-controlled flight-control system, with reaction time and agility measured in milliseconds, to control things (human reaction times are typically measured in tenths of seconds, a hundred times longer). Usually the automated systems process and filter the pilot's "stick and rudder" control inputs, preventing any "pilot-induced oscillations" that might cause the aircraft to "depart controlled flight." A nightmarish phrase sometimes occurs in accident reports: "controlled flight into terrain." The English translation is that some poor bastard drilled a crater right into the ground and never knew it. The dream of every flight-control avionics designer and programmer is to make that impossible.

To help the pilot make practical use of all this greatly expanded tactical information, the F-22 will incorporate decision-aid and management software which will help him or her to drive and fight the aircraft to its limits. In essence, the functions of the human WSO of the F-15E have been delegated to electronic systems rather than flesh and blood. But whether the extra help is human or machine, there is no doubt future pilots will need plenty of it to handle all of the information collected by integrated sensor suites and multiple off-board assets while still flying the plane. Automation is an absolute necessity if future combat aircraft are going to be manned by just one person. It costs over a million dollars to train a pilot or WSO, and personnel costs are the biggest single factor in the defense budget, so it is easy to understand the desire to minimize the aircrew required. The trick is to figure out just what the machines are capable of doing on their own, and what requires the pilot's human judgment. The key to this relationship is a cockpit design that lets the pilot glance at no more than four or five display panels to know exactly what's going on inside and outside the cockpit ("situational awareness").

An overview of recent advances in computer technology is beyond the scope of this book, but two areas are critical to our understanding of how an aircraft finds its target, destroys it, and leaves before the enemy can do anything about it. These areas are sensors and "man-machine interfaces" or displays. In sensors, we'll look at the advances in the performance of radar, IR, and electronic-support-measures (ESM) systems made possible by the massive number-crunching power of today's computers. In displays, we'll look at how information is conveyed to the pilot so that he or she can use it to make better tactical decisions under the stress of combat.

Sensors

Radar has been the most important sensor for fighter and ground-attack aircraft since the Korean War. And the operating principles of airborne systems haven't changed fundamentally since World War II. Until the 1970s, airborne radar systems were mostly single-purpose air-intercept or ground-mapping/navigation systems. In 1975 the F-15A Eagle, equipped with the powerful Hughes APG-63, introduced a new era of multi-mode radars.

The APG-63 radar was the first all-weather, programmable, multi-mode, Pulse-Doppler radar designed to be used by a single pilot. Pulse-Doppler radars rely on the principle that the frequency of waves reflected from a moving object will be slightly shifted upward or downward, depending on whether the object is moving toward or away from the observer. Precise measurement of this Doppler shift allows the radar's signal-processing computer to determine the target's relative speed and direction with great precision. With a detection range of greater than 100 nm./182.8 km. against a large RCS target (like a Tu-95 BEAR bomber), the APG-63 combined long range with features such as automatic detection and lock-on. By allowing a digital computer to control most radar operations, the pilot was left free to concentrate on getting into position to make an effective attack. This computer, by the way, was just slightly more powerful than your standard first generation IBM PC (equipped with an Intel 8-Bit 8086/8088 processor; today many home appliances like refrigerators use a more powerful computer chip!). The most impressive aspect of the APG-63 radar system was the first-generation programmable signal processor (PSP), which effectively filtered out ground clutter, giving the radar "look-down, shoot-down" capability. This meant that in broken terrain the pilot could successfully track and engage targets flying at low altitude, which previously were able to "hide" amid the clutter of returns from trees, hills, rocks, and buildings. With some modifications to the PSP's hardware and software, the APG-63 could also provide real-time, high-resolution ground maps, allowing navigation in poor weather or at night. The radar ground maps were good enough for an experienced pilot to pick out vehicles, bunkers, and other targets. This ability would be further enhanced in the F-15E Strike Eagle fighter-bomber variant. Finally, the APG-63 can track one target while searching for others (track-while-scan or TWS).

The hardware of the APG-63 was as revolutionary as its software. The antenna is a flat, circular planar array, gimbaled in two axes so that it can maintain target lock-on during high-G maneuvers. This means that the F-15 can launch an air-to-air missile, turn up to 60° away from the target (called off-boresight), and still maintain the track, even while the target pulls evasive maneuvers. The APG-63's subsystems, such as the power supply, transmitter, and signal processor, are packaged as individual line-replaceable units (LRUs), which reduces maintenance and repair time. An LRU is a box

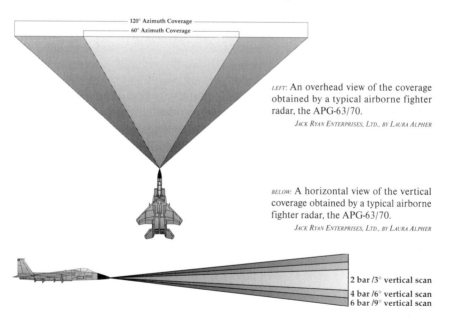

LEFT: An overhead view of the coverage obtained by a typical airborne fighter radar, the APG-63/70.
JACK RYAN ENTERPRISES, LTD., BY LAURA ALPHER

BELOW: A horizontal view of the vertical coverage obtained by a typical airborne fighter radar, the APG-63/70.
JACK RYAN ENTERPRISES, LTD., BY LAURA ALPHER

of system electronics (usually small enough to be handled, removed, and rapidly replaced by a single mechanic) that contains a major electronic or mechanical subsystem of an aircraft. When something inside an LRU fails, the entire box is sent back to the factory or a base/depot-level maintenance facility for repair.

The radar's horizontal or azimuth scan has three selectable arcs, 30°, 60°, or 120°, centered directly in front of the aircraft. The vertical or elevation scan has three selectable "bars" (a bar is a slice of airspace with a vertical depth of 1 1/2° per bar)–2 bar (3°), 4 bar (6°), or 6 bar (90°)–for varying vertical coverage. To cover a specific search pattern, the gimbaled antenna scans from left to right over the selected arc. At the end of the arc, the radar beam drops down one bar and scans back right to left. This continues until the entire bar scan is completed. With an antenna sweep speed of around 70°/sec./bar, the largest search pattern (a 120°, 6-bar scan) can take up to fourteen seconds to complete. Early Eagle drivers were very happy with their new aircraft's radar because, after years of peering into fuzzy, cluttered radar screens as if they were crystal balls, struggling to glean target data, the APG-63 was a revelation. But the ultimate proof of a system only comes in combat. The USAF F-15Cs in Desert Storm, as well as those in Saudi and Israeli service, have proved the value of the APG-63 radar system. The F-15 has at least 96.5 "kills" of enemy aircraft to its credit, with no losses.

As good as the APG-63 was, the follow-on radar system for the dual-role F-15E Strike Eagle had to be even better. Hughes engineers used the APG-63 as the basis for the new APG-70 radar. When it was tested in 1983 on a modified two-seat F-15B, it was obvious that the Eagle's eyes had gotten even sharper. To keep costs and airframe modifications to a minimum, the APG-70 used the same antenna, power supply, and transmitter as its predecessor. But the brains of the system were all new. A new radar data processor, PSP, and other modules replaced older APG-63 LRUs. The software package was completely new, with greater flexibility, making future modifications even easier. The APG-70 can simultaneously track and engage *multiple* airborne targets with the new AIM-120 AMRAAM air-to-air missile. To support the F-15E's ground-attack mission, there is a high-resolution ground-mapping mode (crews tell us it can routinely pick up high-tension power lines), and an even finer synthetic-aperture-radar (SAR) mode, which produces in just seconds a black-and-white photographic-quality picture of the ground for use by the WSO. SARs use a processing technique that uses the aircraft's horizontal motion to "fool" the radar system into "believing" the antenna is actually much larger than it really is. By overlapping multiple return echoes from several scans, and matching them up with the Doppler shift from the various objects in each individual scan, a very high resolution image can be created. Objects as small as 8.5 feet/2.6 meters can be clearly seen in the SAR mode at a range of around 15 nm./27.4 km. The ability to clearly pick out buildings or even vehicles from the radar image at long ranges and in almost any weather greatly simplifies the targeting problem for an aircrew.

Another remarkable feature of the APG-70 is called Non-Cooperative Target Recognition (NCTR). "Cooperative" target recognition depends on the transponders carried by friendly aircraft, which return the proper coded reply when they are "interrogated" by an IFF system. The relatively low reliability of this method has led to very restrictive rules of engagement (ROE) that require several independent means of verifying that a target is really, truly an enemy before a pilot is allowed to shoot it. All air commanders live in fear of "fratricide" or "blue-on-blue" accidents, and the tragic shootdown of two Army helicopters in Northern Iraq in 1994 by F-15Cs suggests that this fear is well-founded. NCTR, which is quickly becoming standard on many U.S.-designed radars, is the ability to classify a target by type while it is still beyond visual range. How this is done is highly classified; and even mentioning NCTR around an Air Force or contractor site is likely to raise eyebrows and tighten lips. Nevertheless, NCTR was used in Desert Storm. One possible means discussed in open sources is to focus a high-resolution radar beam on a head-on target and count the number of blades in the opposing aircraft's engine fan or compressor. Knowing the blade count tells you the type of engine and can give you a good idea as to whether the target is hostile.

The APG-70 also has a Low Probability of Intercept (LPI) mode, designed to defeat the Radar Warning Receivers (RWRs) and Electronic Support Measure (ESM) detectors on enemy aircraft, by using techniques like frequency-hopping and power regulation.

The key to the APG-70's capabilities is raw computer power. Compared to earlier F-15s, the Strike Eagle has a five-fold increase in computer processing capability, a ten-fold increase in system memory and storage, and software which is easier to reprogram and use. Troubleshooting is simplified by Built-In Test (BIT) software that routinely checks on the health and well-being of major systems and can isolate a fault to a particular LRU. These capabilities make the F-15E Strike Eagle the most dangerous bird of prey in the air today. Yet even as the "Mud Hen" (as the early crews called the F-15E) was finishing up its testing in 1990, the U.S. Department of Defense was already looking into ways to shorten the time it took to get advanced computer technology into military systems.

In 1980, the Pave Pillar program was initiated by the USAF, with the goal of developing an advanced avionics architecture that could be built out of standard modules containing next-generation digital integrated circuits. With this approach, all of the sensors, communications, navigation, and weapon systems management subsystems will talk to each other over a local area network (LAN), and processed information will be presented to the crew as needed or requested. This significantly reduces pilot workload, allowing him or her to concentrate on flying the plane—a must if future aircraft are to have only one human on board. The new F-22 is the first aircraft to benefit from the Pave Pillar program, and the increase in computer power will make the avionics system of the F-15E Strike Eagle look like a pocket calculator by comparison.

The F-22 carries two Hughes Common Integrated Processors (CIPs). They give the new fighter a hundred-fold increase in computer-processing power over the Strike Eagle. When new sensors or other systems become available, there is room for a third CIP, if required. To accommodate this increase in processing capability, the F-22 data bus bandwidth has been increased to 50 Mb/sec. By comparison the F-15E's data bus carries only 1 Mb/sec. Since the F-22's APG-77 radar is no longer a stand-alone system, the radar antenna will be just one of a number of sensor arrays, including the electronic-warfare and the threat-warning systems. Data from all of these sensors will be fused together, processed by the CIPs, and displayed to the pilot on one or more color flat-panel multi-function displays (MFDs). Now let's take a look at what the F-22's new APG-77 radar will do.

The APG-77 is nothing like older radar systems. The antenna is a fixed, elliptical, active array which contains about 1,500 radar Transmit/Receive (T/R) modules. Each T/R module is about the size of an adult's finger and is a complete radar system in its own right. The AN/APG-77 T/R module is the result of a massive technology development program by Texas Instruments and the DoD. As planned, each module will cost about $500 per unit (depending on the quantity ordered), a price that was set when the program was first begun almost a decade ago. The APG-77 has no motors or mechanical linkages to aim the antenna. Even though the antenna doesn't move, the APG-77 is still able to sweep a 120° multiple-bar search pattern. However, instead of taking fourteen seconds to sweep a 120°, six-bar search pattern like the APG-70, the APG-77 will search the equivalent volume almost instantaneously. This is because the active array can form multiple radar beams to rapidly scan an area.

The most impressive capability of the APG-77 radar is LPI (low probability of intercept) search. LPI radar pulses are very difficult to detect with conventional RWR and ESM systems. This means the F-22 can conduct an active search with its APG-77 radar, and RWR/ESM-equipped aircraft will probably be none the wiser. Conventional radars emit high-energy pulses in a narrow frequency band, then listen for relatively high-energy returns. A good warning set, however, can pick up these high-energy pulses at over two times the radar's effective range. LPI radars, on the other hand, transmit low-energy pulses over a wide band of frequencies (this is called "spread spectrum" transmission). When the multiple echoes are received from the target, the radar's signal processor integrates all the individual pulses back together, and the amount of reflected EM energy is about the same as a normal radar's high-energy pulse. But because each individual LPI pulse has significantly less energy, and since they do not necessarily fit the normal frequency pattern used by air-search radars, an enemy's warning system will be hard-pressed to detect the pulses long before the LPI radar has detected the target. This will give the F-22 a tremendous advantage in any long-range engagement, as the pilot doesn't have to establish a lock-on when firing AMRAAM missiles. Thus, the first indication that a hostile aircraft will have of an attack by an F-22 will be the screams from his radar-warning receiver telling him that the AMRAAM's radar has lit off, locked on, and is in the final stages of intercept. By that time it's probably too late for him to do anything except eject.

Finally, the APG-77 has an improved capability to conduct NCTR. Since it can form incredibly fine beams, the signal processor can generate a high-resolution radar image of an aircraft through Inverse Synthetic Aperture Radar (ISAR) mode processing. An ISAR-capable radar uses the Doppler shifts caused by rotational changes in the target's position with respect to the radar antenna to create a 3-D map of its target. Thus, where ISAR processing is used, it is the target that provides the Doppler shift, and not the aircraft that the radar is mounted on, which is the case in SAR processing. With a good 3-D radar image, an integrated aircraft-combat system could conceivably identify the target by comparing the image to a stored data base. The computer would then pass its best guess to the pilot, who could, if desired, check for himself by calling up the radar image on one of the multi-function displays. If this sounds like a scene from a *Star Trek* movie, remember that it's all done by software in the F-22s CIPs, and additional capabilities are only a software upgrade away.

Although radar will continue to be the main sensor of combat aircraft for decades to come, infrared sensors are increasingly important for both air superiority and ground-attack missions. In Desert Storm, FLIR-equipped aircraft (such as F-117A, F-111F, F-15E, and F-16C) made precision bombing attacks around the clock. For the air-superiority mission, an aircraft needs an IRST system, while a specialized ground-attack aircraft needs a FLIR system. The differences between these two IR sensors stem from different mission requirements.

IRSTs are wide field-of-view sensors that look for targets in both the middle and long IR bands. IRSTs use automated detection and track routines, designed to find targets in highly cluttered backgrounds. Modern IRSTs are stabilized, gimbaled staring arrays that can scan large areas and detect aircraft at ranges out to 10 to 15 nm./18.2 to 27.4 km.—although 5 to 8 nm./9.1 to 14.6 km. is a more reasonable range against a non-afterburning, non-IR stealthy aircraft. Stabilized means that the sensor automatically compensates for the motion of the aircraft. Gimbals are the supporting bearings that make this possible by allowing the sensor head to rotate on multiple axes. A staring array is like an insect's eye—it consists of many independent detector elements arranged more or less hemispherically rather than a single element that must be mechanically driven to sweep the whole field of view.

FLIRs can be either wide or narrow field-of-view sensors. However, image quality is not particularly good with a wide field-of-view FLIR, and such systems are usually for navigation purposes only. Because FLIRs are designed to provide a higher-resolution picture than an IRST, they have a higher data rate and do not undergo as much signal processing. Essentially, FLIRs are IR television cameras, which must provide a clear image so that an operator can identify the picture with the world's smartest sensor, a Mark 1 human eyeball. Most ground-attack FLIR systems are mounted in external pods or turrets. The Low-Altitude Navigation and Targeting Infrared Night (LANTIRN) system used on the F-15E and F-16C consists of two such pods. The AAQ-13 Navigation pod is equipped with a wide field-of-view FLIR for navigation and a terrain-following radar for all-weather navigation. The AAQ-14 Targeting pod has a narrow field-of-view FLIR for precise target recognition, along with a bore-sighted laser designator. The FLIR systems used by F-15Es and F-111s in Desert Storm were the cameras that brought you some of the amazing nighttime footage of laser-guided bombs going down Iraqi command post ventilation shafts.

Only a few years ago, radar-warning receivers were widely regarded as noisy and unreliable nuisances in the cockpit. Today, however, no sane combat pilot wants to fly in harm's way without a good RWR/ESM suite. Most combat aircraft have RWRs which are tuned to provide a warning only when an enemy fire control radar has established a lock-on. That means they work about as effectively as smoke alarms do when you are in the same room with the fire. With the greatly increased computer power available to the F-22A, a fully integrated ESM and electronic-warfare (EW) system is now finally possible. ESM is basically a wide frequency band passive radar receiver. It is designed to find radar signals, analyze them, and classify the type of radar that is producing the emissions. This has already been done on specialized EW aircraft such as the EF-111A Raven, which are packed with so many electronic black boxes and festooned with so many antennas that they have little direct combat capability.

In addition to the standard ESM package, dedicated missile-warning systems are being investigated for installation on the F-22. Historically, 80% of all aircraft shot down never saw the opponent that killed them. With a missile-warning receiver providing 360° spherical coverage, a pilot will know when an enemy missile has been fired at him. Based on data from the missile-warning receiver, other aircraft systems could automatically deploy expendable counter-measures (chaff and flares) and sound an aural warning to the pilot. This will improve the pilot's reaction time to an incoming missile, reducing aircraft losses in high-threat environments.

A drawing of a notional Heads-Up Display (HUD), showing the symbology that a pilot would typically see.
Jack Ryan Enterprises, Ltd., by Laura Alpher

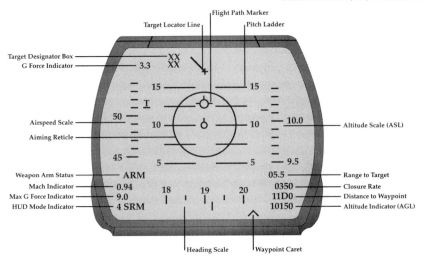

Displays

Human senses set a limit to how much data pilots can handle before they become overloaded. The key to managing this flood of data is to give the pilot only processed information relevant to the current situation. In other words, we need "pilot friendly" cockpits: If you don't get the message, it doesn't matter if the computer had the right answer or not. Earlier, we noted the sheer number of gauges, switches, and screens that an early F-15 pilot had to be aware of in order to fly the plane. However, once he went into combat, all he needed to do was put the wide-angle HUD onto the enemy aircraft, which allowed him to keep his eyes out of the cockpit.

The HUD displays all relevant tactical and aircraft-systems information in a clear and concise manner—once you understand what all the numbers and symbols mean. The HUD is tied to and controlled by a series of switches mounted on the engine throttle and control stick. Called Hands On Throttle and Stick (HOTAS), this system allows a pilot to avoid having to go "head down" into the cockpit while in a combat situation. On the Vietnam-era F-4E Phantom, the pilot had to reach below his seat to find the selector switch for the 20mm cannon! Today, the pilot of an F-15 or F-16 has only to flip a selector switch to control everything from radar modes to weapons selection.

A lot of important data is crammed onto the HUD. For example, a pilot can tell that he is on a course of 191° at an airspeed of 510 knots, that the aircraft is in a 10° climb, and that the target is up and to the left of the plane's present course. A short range IR-homing missile can be selected to engage the target, once the pilot is in a proper position to shoot. Unfortunately, when pilots take their eyes off the HUD to look around (and a good pilot will do that often to check his "six"—the sky behind him), all that data is lost to them until they look forward again. The HUD is just an image projected onto a glass screen mounted above the instrument panel. Since it is a fixed display, it can't follow the pilot's eyes when they look around.

Or can it? Right now, helmet-mounted HUDs are under development in the U.S. and Great Britain (and Israel and Russia both have operational systems). The helmet-mounted HUD supplements the standard HUD, providing enhanced situational awareness. If the aircraft carries air-to-air missiles with slewable seekers (called high off-boresight seekers), like the Russian AA-11 Archer or the Israeli Python-4, the pilot can attack targets that are offset from the aircraft's nose. You can attack a crossing target without wasting time or energy maneuvering for position, which gives you a tremendous advantage in a high-speed, multi-aircraft dogfight or "furball."

Future possibilities include virtual-reality (VR) displays, voice-command recognition (remember the book and movie *Firefox*?), VR control gloves, VR body suits, or eye motion command controls. In skies filled with stealthy, silent attacks, there is no time to waste.

The "Edge": Coming USAF Aircraft

So what about the "edge"? What's the next step in combat aircraft design?

Two new combat aircraft will be arriving at USAF bases in the next decade or so; both incorporate elements of the technologies we have talked about. Each is a state-of-the-art solution to some problem that USAF planners identified over the last decade or two, and thus represents the thinking of the late stages of the Cold War. This fact alone has made some folks question their utility and affordability, given the changes in the world scene in the last five years. Nevertheless, given the lessons of the 1991 Persian Gulf War, as well as the general acceptance that the U.S. military in the 21st century will be a "home-based" force, these systems will be vital to maintaining the credibility of the USAF.

Northrop Grumman B-2A Spirit

> Two B-2s, without escorts or tankers, could have performed the same mission as a package of thirty-two strike aircraft, sixteen fighters, twelve air-defense suppression aircraft, and fifteen tankers.
>
> General Chuck Horner, USAF (Ret.)

The most expensive airplane ever built is a hard sell to taxpayers and legislators who are increasingly cynical about defense contractors and increasingly skeptical about military procurement. But to understand the B-2, you have to understand the threat that it was designed to overcome and the almost unimaginable mission it was created to perform. One of the things that helped to bankrupt the Soviet Union was an obsessive, forty-year attempt to build an impenetrable air-defense system. The National Air Defense Force (known by its Russian initials, PVO) was a separate service, co-equal with the Soviet Army, Navy, Air Force, and Strategic Rocket Forces. It was designed to keep the U.S. Air Force and the few strategic bombers of the other Western allies from penetrating the Russian heartland and decapitating the highly centralized Soviet command and control system, as well as their top military and political leadership. Ultimately, the only Western plan for defeating the system was the Doomsday scenario, using nuclear missiles to "roll back" the successive layers of air defense so the bombers could get through to their targets.

In the 1970s, the Russians began to develop mobile ICBM systems that could shuttle around the vast spaces of the Soviet Union on special railroad trains or giant wheeled vehicles. The Soviets knew that every fixed missile silo could be pinpointed by satellite imagery and targeted for destruction; every Soviet ballistic missile submarine could be tracked by sonar arrays and trailed by a U.S./NATO attack boat; but what could you do to kill a mobile missile complex? The proposed U.S. solution was to hunt down the mobile missiles with an aircraft so revolutionary that nothing in the Soviet arsenal could touch it.

The first pre-production B-2A Spirit stealth bomber in front of its hanger at the Northrop Grumman factory at Palmdale, California. *CRAIG E. KASTON*

An invisible airplane that traveled at the speed of light, armed with precision "death ray" weapons, would have been ideal. But a subsonic airplane which was almost invisible to radar and IR sensors, carrying a few nuclear-tipped missiles, was sufficient if (and it was a big if) its development could be kept so secret that the other side would have no time, and no data, to develop effective countermeasures. Thus was born the B-2A Spirit. The origins of the B-2 design date back to experimental aircraft of the 1920s, when the visionary Horten brothers of Germany designed their first "flying wing" aircraft, without conventional tail surfaces and with a cockpit smoothly blended into the thickened wing section. Their goal was low drag (they were unaware as yet of the advantages of a low radar cross section). The problem with all-wing aircraft is that they are inherently less stable than the more normal kind with fuselages and tail sections; and crashes of various prototypes led to the shelving of the Hortens' project (although a very ambitious twin-jet-powered version was under development at the end of the Second World War). In the 1940s, the brilliant and eccentric American engineer Jack Northrop designed the XB-35 heavy bomber, a propeller-driven flying wing, and later the YB-49, a promising eight-engined turbojet bomber (which compromised the purity of the design by adding four small vertical fins). Unfortunately, the manual flight controls of the time were inadequate to solve the inherent stability problems of pure flying wing designs, and the Air Force canceled the project. Despite the problems inherent in the flying wing design, it does have one undeniable characteristic: It is tough to see on radar. Thus, the stage was set for the development of the B-2.

Originally called the Advanced Technology Bomber (ATB), the B-2 began development in 1978 as a black program, which means that it was not published in the Air Force budget and its existence was revealed only to a limited circle of legislators. In 1981 the Northrop/Boeing team's proposal was selected, and full-scale development of the new bomber followed. It took seven years, including a major redesign in the mid-1980s, when the USAF changed the original B-2 specification to include a low-level penetration capability. (Shortly before his death, under a special security dispensation, Jack Northrop was allowed to see a model of the B-2—the vindication of the idea he had championed four decades earlier.)

The first B-2 pre-production aircraft (known as Air Vehicle #1) was rolled out at Palmdale, California, on November 22nd, 1988, and the first flight was on July 17th, 1989. The first B-2A squadron (of eight aircraft) of the 509th Bombardment Wing at Whiteman AFB, Missouri, are scheduled to reach IOC (initial operation capability) in 1996. Given the official Air Force designation of Spirit, each aircraft will be named for a state; the first five are "Spirit of California," "Spirit of Missouri," "Spirit of Texas," "Spirit of Washington," and "Spirit of South Carolina." General Mike Loh, the ACC commander, likes the designation because, like a ghost, the B-2 will be able to come and go without being seen.

A combination of several advanced technologies made the B-2 possible. Foremost among these was computer-aided design/computer-aided manufacturing, known as CAD/CAM in the aircraft industry. The F-117A had to employ awkwardly faceted flat surfaces, because this was the only solution available in the mid-1970s to the earlier-generation computer hardware and software on which it was designed (millions of radar cross section calculations were necessary to validate the design). The B-2, designed on vastly more powerful computer systems, could have smoothly contoured aerodynamic surfaces because, by that time, the billions of necessary calculations could be performed relatively quickly.

Moreover, the B-2 was the first modern aircraft to go into production without requiring a prototype, or even a development fixture. Designed with advanced three-dimensional CAD/CAM systems, which are used to fix parts, the B-2's virtual development fixture allowed every component to be fit-checked before it was manufactured. As a result, when the first B-2s were assembled, something happened that was unprecedented in aviation history, possibly in the entire history of engineering development and manufacturing. Every part fit perfectly the first time, and the finished aircraft precisely matched its designed dimensions within a few millimeters over a span of 172 feet/52.4 meters.

The B-2's flight-control surfaces are unique. The outboard trailing edge of each wing tip consists of a pair of hinged "drag rudders," moved by hydraulic actuators, with another set called "elevons" inboard of those. These surfaces take the place of the rudder, elevators, and ailerons on a conventional aircraft.

The B-2's crew consists of a mission commander and pilot, who sit side by side on conventional ejection seats beneath blow-out panels overhead. The

The first pre-production B-2A Spirit bomber flies over Edwards AFB, California. Note the control surfaces (elevons and flaperons) along the trailing edge of the wing. *CRAIG E. KASTON*

commander is in the right-hand (starboard) position, with the pilot on the left (port). Each crew station has four color multi-function displays and fighter-type control sticks, rather than the control yokes commonly used on large multi-engined aircraft. These controls feed into the quad-redundant fly-by-wire flight control system, which makes the Spirit very stable, but highly agile. (According to the test pilots, the B-2 flies "like a fighter" thanks to the agility of the fly-by-wire system.) The communications systems consist of a full array of HF/UHF/VHF radios, as well as a satellite communications terminal, all of which are controlled from a single data entry panel. Eventually, this will be fully compatible with the new MILSTAR communications satellites that are now coming on-line. The wraparound windows are very large, but there is no visibility aft, so the crew must rely on sophisticated tail-warning sensors to "check six." The crew enters through a floor hatch with a retractable ladder that is just aft of the nose landing gear well. The traditional "alert" button is on the nose gear, though most experts agree that it will probably never be used by a B-2 crew.

The four General Electric F118-100 turbofan engines buried inside the wing are non-afterburning versions of the F101 used in the B-1B. Each engine is rated at 19,000 lb./8,600 kg. of thrust. To dissipate heat and hide the hot section from hostile IR tracking systems, the complex air intakes receive incoming air through an S-shaped turn, which shields the fan sections from the view of any hostile radar; then the unique V-shaped exhaust slots pass the exhaust gases across a long, wide, trough-shaped section of the upper wing.

While many details of the structure and materials of the B-2 will remain closely guarded secrets for years to come, published sources suggest that graphite-epoxy composites are used extensively. Even the paint requires unique new technology. Antennas are mounted flush with the skin; even the air-data sensors which stick out prominently on most fly-by-wire aircraft are flush-mounted on the leading edge of the B-2. The most conventional equipment is the main landing gear, derived from the Boeing 767 airliner, and the nose gear, from the Boeing 757.

With only one air-to-air refueling, a range of more than 10,000 nm./18,280 km. is possible. Endurance is thus limited only by crew fatigue, which is exceptionally low due to the high degree of onboard automation. In effect, with a minimum of tanker support, the B-2 can strike any target in the world and return to a base in the continental United States. The in-flight refueling receptacle on top of the crew compartment is concealed behind a retractable door of radar-absorbing material, and according to pilot reports, the B-2 is quite stable and has very pleasant flying qualities around tankers.

All weapons will be carried internally—an absolute requirement for any stealthy aircraft, since ordnance dangling on pylons increases the radar cross section dramatically. The two bomb bays, aft of the crew compartment, are designed to each accommodate an eight-round rotary launcher, or a conventional munitions module similar to those on the B-1B.

The Air Force plans to buy twenty B-2s by 1998 for $44 billion from Northrop Grumman Corp. of Los Angeles. Originally the service wanted 132 B-2s, but because of the plane's high purchase price and the end of the Cold War, Congress limited the program. Though Northrop Grumman has proposed constructing an additional twenty aircraft by 2008 at a guaranteed fixed price of about $570 million each, the future of the program is highly uncertain. Nevertheless, the B-2A Spirit is the state of the art in strike aircraft, and probably will be well into the middle of the next century.

Lockheed Martin-Boeing F-22

It has been over twenty years since the current USAF air superiority fighter, the F-15 Eagle, first took wing in 1972. Those two decades have seen massive changes, both in the political makeup of the world and the nature of aviation technology. Thus, it is in that context that the Air Force is betting billions of dollars and the future of manned fighter aircraft on the Lockheed Martin-Boeing F-22 and its new Pratt & Whitney F119 engines. In 1984, the ATF specification called for a 50,000 lb./22,700 kg., $35 million aircraft (that's in 1985 U.S. dollars) incorporating the latest advances in low-observable technologies and able to cruise at supersonic speed (the YF-22A demonstrated the ability to cruise at Mach 1.58 during the competitive fly-off, and to do so at altitudes in excess of 50,000 feet) to a combat radius of more than 800 nm./1,200 km. By 1986 the competition narrowed down to two teams, each of which would build and fly a pair of prototypes: the Lockheed-Boeing-General Dynamics YF-22 and the Northrop-McDonnell Douglas YF-23. Although the YF-23 had excellent performance, the Air Force decided in April 1991 to go with the superior agility of the YF-22. Under current plans, the Air Force will now buy 442 aircraft, with a first production aircraft flight scheduled early in 1997 and initial operational capability by 2004. Planned production will continue

One of the two YF-22 prototype aircraft flying over Edwards AFB during the advanced tactical fighter "fly-off." *LOCKHEED MARTIN*

through 2011, with follow-on versions such as strike, SEAD (Suppression of Enemy Air Defenses), and reconnaissance coming afterwards as required.

The Air Force views the mission of air superiority as instrumental for the success of other types of missions (deep strike, battlefield, interdiction, close air support, etc.). With the wide variety of current-generation fighters in the air forces of potential adversaries, as well as the potential sales of new-generation aircraft, the USAF will require a fighter able to engage and destroy any potential opponent at times and places of *their* choosing. The F-22 is designed to take the basic weapons/sensor load of the F-15C and repackage it into a stealthy platform capable of supersonic cruise. This combination of stealth and high cruise speed is designed to allow the F-22 to rapidly enter an area, establish air superiority, avoid enemy detection/engagement, and basically act like Ridley Scott's *Alien,* so that the bad guys are too scared to even come up.

Lockheed Martin indicates that the F-22A/B will be a true stealth design, in the same class as the F-117A and the B-2A. Although the F-22 is essentially the same size as the F-15, over the frontal aspect its radar cross section is reportedly over one hundred times smaller! The structure of the F-22 will be composed of the following: 28% composites (carbon-carbon, thermoplastics, etc.), 37% titanium, 20% metal (aluminum and steel), and 15% "other" materials (kryptonite?). To reduce the weight of the aircraft and still provide strength,

An F119 turbofan engine in a test stand, running at full afterburner. A pair of F119 engines will power the new F-22 fighter in the 21st century.
PRATT & WHITNEY-UNITED TECHNOLOGIES

the structural members of the F-22 are of a mixed metal/composite design that minimizes the total RCS of the package. For example, two of every three wing spars are of composite construction, while every third one is titanium. Also, watch for a new paint which may have RAM properties as well. By the way, the "notch" in the leading edge of the wing is supposed to be a radar "trap" to catch and dissipate radar waves around the wing roots.

Even the engines are stealthy. Since the twin F119 power plants deliver enough dry thrust (i.e. without use of the afterburner) to allow the F-22 to cruise at supersonic speeds, its IR signature is significantly reduced over a conventional fighter aircraft traveling at the same speed. The Pratt and Whitney F119 (35,000 lb./15,909.1 kg. of thrust each) provides the F-22 with the performance of the F-15C (with the F100-PW-220 engine in full afterburner) while in military (dry) power. All this is done without a variable inlet ramp (to reduce the aircraft's RCS) and with an engine that is stealthy by itself, unlike those on the F-117A, which require inlet screens. The inlet ducts are curved to hide the fan section of the engine from enemy radar, with RAM and other engineering tricks to further reduce this traditional radar trap. On most jet aircraft the exhaust nozzles are round; on the F-22 they are rectangular slots, with movable vanes that can deflect the exhaust—in effect "steering" the thrust vector. These "2-D" nozzles (up to +/-20° of vertical displacement from centerline) of the F119 improve aircraft agility and give the F-22 superb short-field takeoff-and-landing performance.

The cockpit will be an almost totally "glass" design (i.e., only MFDs), with only three analog instruments as emergency backups. No less than six multi-function displays of three sizes are arrayed for the pilot to configure as he

A mockup of the "glass" cockpit design of the new F-22 fighter. Note the use of computer-style multi-function displays instead of traditional dial or "strip" instruments. *LOCKHEED MARTIN*

or she pleases. The cockpit is a classic HOTAS design, with a wide-field-of-view holographic HUD. Also, a helmet-mounted sight for helping the pilots get weapons onto their targets is a likely upgrade. If the design for the F-22 works as planned, its flight envelope will vastly exceed that of any existing U.S. fighter, or even the MiG-29 or Su-27/35. Acceleration, rate of roll, and other control parameters are also planned to be superior on the F-22 when compared to existing designs. The quad-redundant, fly-by-wire flight control system is going to make the F-22 a true sustained 9-G airplane, able to rapidly turn and hold that load for as long as the pilot can stand it.

The F-22A/B will have the first fully integrated avionics suite ever flown on a combat aircraft. The Common Integrated Processor (CIP—the F-22 has two CIP bays, with room for a third) built by GM-Hughes is the core of the system and supports the Westinghouse-Texas Instruments APG-77 radar, the Lockheed Martin electronic warfare suite, and the TRW communications/navigation/IFF subsystems. The electronics will be liquid-cooled, and they will run over one million lines of computer code. Total processing power for the F-22A/B with two CIP bays will be in the area of 700 Mips (700 million operations/sec—equivalent to four Cray supercomputers), with an expansion potential of something over 100% already planned into the design.

As for sensors, the new Westinghouse APG-77 radar is a wide-field-of-view (over 120°) fixed phased array, which is virtually undetectable with conventional RWR systems. In fact, the APG-77 can probably be programmed to do virtually any kind of operation that a radar is capable of doing just by programming it with additional software and adding the necessary processor/memory capacity to the CIPs. Also, the F-22A/B will have an integrated countermeasures suite tied to the CIP bays. This will allow for rapid systems reprogramming in the event of a crisis, and should allow modifications to be handled quickly. The jammer/RWR antennas are contained in "smart skins" on the wing tips, with the communications, navigation, and IFF antennas in the leading edges of the wings.

The basic weapons package of the F-22 will be roughly similar to that of the F-15C, though it will develop in stages. The missiles will be fired off hydraulically extensible rail launchers out of three internal weapons bays (one on either side, and one in the belly). Since opening a door to launch or fire a weapon may suddenly increase the RCS of the aircraft from certain angles, the designers have provided actuators that rapidly open and shut those doors, so that the exposure time is minimized. As an added stealth feature, the 20mm gun is buried deep in the right mid-fuselage area, and fires through a door that snaps open at the time of firing, then closes immediately after the last bullet passes. Also, in a non-stealth configuration, an additional eight air-to-air missiles can be carried on four wing pylons.

The F-22 has been designed so that most of the access panels are at ground level, and require only eight more tools than are already in the standard kit of the F-15C. Also, the F-22 will require a bare minimum of ground support equipment, such as service carts and workstands. For example, the F-22 has its own onboard oxygen and inert-gas generators to supply the environmental control system for the pilot and to provide pressurization for the fuel system. Thus, maintenance hours per flight hour should be even less than the F-16 or A-10. There also will be a portable electronic maintenance aid, based around a hand-held computer, which will plug into the aircraft, and a maintenance laptop computer, which will do all the diagnostic work on what needs to be replaced, filled, or whatever. One of the design goals was to increase sortie rates by achieving a fifteen-minute combat turnaround time—that's to both refuel and re-arm!

While the final production number is still in flux, a figure of about $100 million is a fair estimate of what each F-22 will cost the taxpayers. In spite of this, the F-22 remains just about the highest-priority acquisition program that the USAF has today. It should keep the Air Force pushing the edge well into the next century.

Desert Storm: Planning the Air Campaign

Recently, the anniversary of Operation Desert Storm brought back memories of those incredible hours we spent glued to our televisions back in January of 1991 and the vivid images we saw: F-15s launching from Saudi runways; bombs dropping through windows; massed tanks crossing the desert; soldiers digging in on terrain that looked like Mars; ragged, dispirited Iraqi POWs trudging down roads littered with the wreckage of their army; those extraordinary sights of AAA bursts at night over Baghdad; and so much more. The media coverage of the war against Iraq was splendid. Yet when you think about it, for most of us the impression that remains is scattered, fragmented. Something is missing. What? *That there was a plan. On the ground. And in the air.* The war against Iraq was no "Hey, kids, let's put on a show" kind of affair. It took time, and the work of not a few brilliant minds.

The plan for the air war, for instance, grew out of three decades of intellectual and spiritual growth by the USAF officers who command combat aviators. In *Armored Cav,* we talked with two of the men who helped win the ground victory, General Fred Franks and Major H.R. McMaster. Now we're going to talk with two men who helped win the air war.

Now, I have to emphasize that many airmen from many services, from many countries, contributed to the victory in Desert Storm. Nevertheless, the plan for the air war against Iraq was uniquely U.S. Air Force.

USAF officers spent years trying to build a new vision of air power—a vision that was *not* based on traditional roles and missions, such as nuclear deterrence against the Soviet Union or bombing a bridge in North Vietnam, but on the deep-rooted belief that airpower can be a decisive tool at the operational or theater level of warfare. According to this new vision, it wasn't enough to know how to fly planes, shoot missiles, and drop bombs; you also had to know how to plan and lead an air campaign.

Different men came to these ideas by different routes. Some saw the vision as they were being shot at by MiGs, SAMs, and AAA guns while trying futilely to bomb worthless suspected targets in North Vietnam, targets picked by politicians with no coherent goal in mind. Others followed the lure and seduction that airpower has always held for true believers in the magic of flight. Commonly called airpower zealots, they dedicated decades of hard work and sacrifice to the single-minded goal of giving the United States the greatest concentration of that oh-so-intangible force.

You have to have a plan. You have to have leadership.

The air bombardment campaigns against Germany and Japan in World War II were costly failures until the introduction of escorting fighters and the identification of targets that truly could affect the final outcome of a war. Later, when the 8th AF acquired long-range P-51 escort fighters and began to *methodically* strike the German petrochemical and transportation industries, the effects were felt almost immediately in every theater of the war. It should have been obvious to anyone who understood airpower that the key is the right mix of forces, hitting the right combination of targets, at the right time. In short, the right *plan*. Such a plan would require packaging the proper aircraft, ordnance, and personnel into forces capable of destroying the right targets to do maximum damage to an enemy's war effort. It would also require officers trained and experienced in leading such an effort. Not just from USAF units, but from the other services, as well as allies from other nations. Such leaders would have to be credible flyers, and also diplomats, logisticians, and even public-relations experts.

Naturally, though it seemed logical to the airpower supporters that the U.S. Air Force should recruit, train, and control these forces, the other services in the U.S. military had their own ideas. Many USN and USMC aviation officers felt, with some justification, that turning over de facto control of their aviation assets would be tantamount to giving the USAF a stranglehold on the use of airpower in future operations.

So the vision remained just that, a vision, until several well-known failures in air operations during the 1980s (notably the bungled hostage-rescue mission to Iran) led to changes in how airpower would be used in the 1990s. Foremost among these changes was the Goldwater-Nichols Military Reform Act, which redefined the military chain of command. It also recognized that different kinds of fighting forces (naval, ground, air) should be organized and headed by appropriate professionals. Airpower would be run by an airman known as a Joint Forces Air Component Commander (JFACC). At the theater level, the JFACC is a USAF lieutenant general (0-9-three star), directly responsible to the unified Commander in Chief (CinC). A "theater" of operations is a distinct geographical area in which air, land, and naval forces are coordinated usually against a single enemy. In World War II the European and Pacific theaters were virtually separate wars.

During Desert Shield and Desert Storm, the JFACC for CENTCOM was Lieutenant General Charles A. Horner, USAF. In August 1990, just prior to the invasion of Kuwait, he was the commander of the U.S. 9th Air Force based out of Shaw AFB, South Carolina. One of four numbered air force commanders based in the United States, he had a secondary responsibility as commander of the Central Command Air Forces (CENTAF). CENTCOM—U.S. Central Command—is the unified command responsible for most of the Middle East (Southwest Asia). CENTCOM, which replaced the Rapid Deployment Force created during the Iranian hostage crisis, is a command without forces. These are assigned to CENTCOM's operational control only in event of a crisis. As commander of the CENTCOM air forces,

Horner led the staff that would eventually plan and execute the air war against Iraq.

Born in 1936 in Davenport, Iowa, Chuck Horner (as he prefers to be called) is a graduate of the University of Iowa. After graduation, he entered the Air Force in the early 1960s and flew two tours in Southeast Asia, with some 111 missions on the second tour alone. His particular specialty was the hunting of Surface-to-Air (SAM) and Anti-Aircraft Artillery (AAA) radars. Known as "Wild Weasel" missions, they were (and are) very hazardous, with casualties running high among the crews. Like so many other young USAF officers, he lost much of his faith in the Air Force "system" in the skies over North Vietnam.

Tom Clancy: You fought in Vietnam. What did it teach you?

Gen. Horner: All fighter pilots feel they are invulnerable until they get shot down. The day they get shot down, and jump out of the cocoon that's their cockpit, then you really see a change in them. Having never been shot down, I really can't speculate on that. But I can say there is nothing better than to come back and not be killed. You really feel good.

More to the point, I just sort of became fascinated by ground fire, SAMs, and stuff like that. I thought that was interesting. The thing is, I'm a practical person, I'm a farmer; so when we were sent up to hit some dumb target and there was a great target available, I made a mental note that this would *never* happen if I was running things. Sometimes it *didn't* happen, because there were no policemen up there [in North Vietnam] to check on what we were bombing.

When you have the people in Washington who think they are running the war, and the people over the battlefield who are fighting the war, and they are not on the same emotional and psychological level, and you don't have trust, you've got *nothing*. Unfortunately, integrity was the first casualty in the Vietnam War.

While Chuck Horner was flying combat missions in Vietnam, a new generation of USAF officers was emerging, with a new set of ideas and values. Among these was an intellectual young officer named John A. Warden III. Born in 1943 in McKinney, Texas, he came from a family with a long record of military service. Fascinated by military history and technology, he was one of the earliest graduates of the new Air Force Academy at Colorado Springs, Colorado, in the 1960s. While he did his share of flying in fighters such as the OV-10 Bronco and F-4 Phantom in Southeast Asia, his real passion throughout his career has been planning doctrine for the successful execution of air campaigns.

Tom Clancy: In the post-Vietnam era, what was the vision of the Air Force and the other services as they came out of Southeast Asia into the late 1970s?

Col. Warden: In Vietnam, the Navy did well at a tactical level; and afterward it was generally pleased with itself, but realized it needed to rethink its force structure. And so it developed its "Maritime Strategy," which focused on taking the Soviet Navy out of the picture and then attacking the "bastion" areas of the Soviet homeland waters. It was a pretty good set of ideas, and gave the Navy a good vehicle for training and force building. The Air Force, though, came out with some wildly different ideas. On the one hand, people like me believed we had done well *tactically* with the tools at our disposal, but that those tools had been used for the wrong purposes *strategically.* In other words, I was disgusted that we had squandered our men and machines for the wrong reasons in the wrong way. And my resolution was never to have anything to do with a war that didn't have identified political objectives and a coherent way to engage them. For example, the idea of gradual escalation seemed to me to be really stupid.

On the other hand, many Air Force officers learned an entirely different set of lessons. To them, the strategic side of the war was irrelevant. What was important was the *way* it was fought, so their lessons were at a different level. And then later, after the war, the fighter officers rapidly took control of the Air Force from the officers who had grown up in Strategic Air Command. Many of these new Air Force fighter leaders, having spent the majority of their Vietnam tours doing close air support in South Vietnam, came out of the war believing that the future of the Air Force was in supporting the Army. Now, there is nothing wrong with supporting the Army or the Navy—or the other way around—but making this the sole function severely circumscribed the potential of airpower, because it was all focused on tactical events.

John Warden, like other airpower supporters, advocated the inherent virtues of airpower. In his view, in order to realize airpower's unfulfilled promise, new ways of using it would have to be devised. Though there was much debate about these new ways, no consensus about them was reached. Then in 1988, Warden published a little book called *The Air Campaign: Planning for Combat.* It was the first new book on air operations to be published since the end of World War II, and the first to deal specifically with the issue of planning an entire air campaign. Thus it was an instant must-read among officers and systems analysts. It also caused a storm of controversy, since it argued that airpower should be treated as more than just a supporting arm in a ground campaign. Let Colonel Warden tell the story.

Tom Clancy: Will you tell us about *The Air Campaign: Planning for Combat?*

Col. Warden: I was a grad student at National War College, and I decided I wanted to do three things: write a book, learn to use a computer, and run a marathon. For the book, I had two possibilities: modern applications of the ideas of Alexander the Great, or something on operational-level airpower. My academic advisor told me I would probably get more out of the operational-airpower subject, so I chose that one. I worked on the book for about six months, in between attending classes. General Perry Smith, who was the commandant then, read an early draft, liked it, and sent copies to some key USAF generals. When the book finally worked its way through the publishing process and came out in 1988, it already had a fair amount of circulation around the USAF in its draft form. As for the book itself, the fundamentals are as valid today as they were when I wrote it. However, now I have a far better understanding of war and airpower, so I would like to write a couple of more books on a higher level.

In 1988, John Warden, now a colonel, moved over to the Office of the USAF Directorate of Plans in the Pentagon as its Deputy Director for Strategy, Doctrine, and Warfighting. While there, he had responsibility for the team that would develop Instant Thunder, the basic plan for the air war against Iraq some three years later.

Tom Clancy: In 1988 you moved to the USAF Plans Directorate in the Pentagon. Tell us about that.

Col. Warden: My new boss, General Mike Dugan, then Deputy Chief of Staff for Plans and Operations (the future USAF Chief of Staff), had given me the job helping to change the Air Force mindset. I had about a hundred officers in the Plans Directorate under my command, and we began by giving them some operational and strategic-level airpower concepts. Then, we all spent a lot of time debating and refining the ideas. Our weekly staff meetings would run three or four hours—not because we were discussing administrative trivia, but because we were dealing with large operational or strategic topics that would force all the divisional and other people to work these things hard. By and by, we were ready to start turning our ideas into action, and we rewrote the AFM 1-1 [the Air Force Basic Operations] manual, and put together a program to reform the USAF professional military education program. We had literally dozens of projects going on, with all of them having the common thread of, "Let's start thinking seriously about airpower at the operational and strategic levels."

Here's an example of a project we ran at Checkmate [one of the organizations in the plans division]: Let's start out with the hypothesis that fuel is the "center of gravity" [a vital necessity for operations] for the Soviet Army. So we talk to the intelligence people, and they say, "You're wasting your time—the Soviets have a one-hundred-eighty-day supply of fuel buried in hardened storage tanks under East Germany. You only have about fourteen days before the war goes 'nuke,' or before the Soviets achieve their objectives. There simply isn't enough time to destroy that amount of fuel in hardened storage tanks."

Well, this doesn't make sense to the Checkmate officers. So they ask another question: "How does the fuel get from the underground storage to the main battle tanks that actually use it up on the front?" It's a simple question about *distribution*. So we went back and found out that the Soviets had established about twenty-five operational-level fuel depots that stretched from the Baltic (in the north) to the Alps (in the south). They were designed to bring bulk fuel in from the East, and then "push" it out farther to the West. Now, number one, there were no north-south cross-connections between these depots. And number two, although the hardened underground storage of this stuff was done very well, each depot had only about three output manifolds. It was like a filling station with only three gas islands. A fuel truck would drive up, fill up, then head west to the next lower echelon, where it would off-load and then return for more. There was also a manifold for tactical pipelines [field fuel lines laid by battlefield engineers following the forward echelons into combat]. So all the fuel from these great big depots ended up flowing through three or four very fragile output manifolds.

Now, what happens if we shut those down? We decided to look a little further, and it turned out that the depot units were undermanned and didn't have the allotted number of trucks required to meet the established doctrinal movement rates of their tank units. There was no "elasticity" in the Soviet system, so if we stop the flow of fuel [by bombing the depot fuel manifolds], in four or five days they run out.

Now, imagine you're a Soviet tactical commander, and you know that your fuel has been cut off. Although you might not physically run out of the last drop of gas you're carrying with you for three to five days, you're probably going to stop, dig in, and wait for more supplies. The way their system was designed, work-arounds were almost impossible, so the Soviet-style corps which was dependent on a particular depot to its east was simply out of luck until someone fixed the problem—and it couldn't be fixed in a few days. We learned from this exercise that a handful of fighter-bomber sorties properly employed against operational centers of gravity could have a hugely disproportionate effect on fighting at the front itself. We used these lessons to good stead in planning for the Gulf War. Everyone we briefed liked the concept, except the intelligence people.

When they look at a problem, analysts like to use what they call a "model." This is a concept or simulation which can be used as a method of testing or expressing ideas. Colonel Warden's model of the enemy as an array of strategic targets envisions five concentric rings, with the military/civil leadership at the center, then key production facilities, transportation infrastructure, civilian morale/popular support, and in the outermost circle deployed military forces. Let's hear his views on it.

Tom Clancy: Through these studies, had you established a process of analysis that would serve you when you started to look at Iraq?

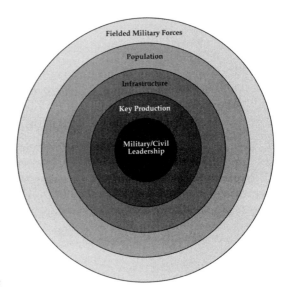

An illustration of Colonel John Warden's "Five Rings" strategic targeting model. The enemy's fielded forces are on the outside, the national/military leadership in the center.

Jack Ryan Enterprises, Ltd., by Laura Alpher

Col. Warden: Yes, the overarching system we used was the one I developed for General Dugan in the spring of 1988. This was what became known as the "Five Rings" model. In essence, it tells you to start your thinking at the highest system-level possible, that your goal is to make the enemy system become what you want it to become, and do what you want it to do. The Five Rings show how all systems are organized—they are fractal in nature. For example, an army corps has a pattern of organization very similar to a nation or an air force. Every system has centers of gravity, which, when attacked, tend to drive the whole system into lower energy states, or into actual paralysis. In the Deputy Directorate for Operations, we had been discussing this concept for almost two years; so it was easy to apply it quickly after the Iraqi invasion of Kuwait.

While Colonel Warden had been working to change the Air Force intellectually, officers like General Chuck Horner had been doing the routine work to keep the force going and improve it. Then, in 1987, General Horner was given command of the U.S. 9th-Air Force, headquartered at Shaw AFB, South Carolina. As commander, his mission was to act as the JFAAC for any air operations that might be conducted by CENTCOM, as well as commander of any air forces that might be assigned to CENTCOM. Let's hear his thoughts on the appointment.

Tom Clancy: Would you please talk about your assignment to command of 9th Air Force?

Then-Major General Charles Horner while commander of the U.S. 9th Air Force and U.S. Air Forces Central Command (CENTAF).

OFFICIAL U.S. AIR FORCE PHOTO

Gen. Horner: 9th Air Force was at its best during World War II. Then it became a training command back in the United States. Then in 1980, along came the Rapid Deployment Joint Task Force [RDJTF], the predecessor of the present CENTCOM organization. Larry Welch was the Director of Operations in TAC then, and the RDJTF was the hottest thing going. It had to do with the Carter Doctrine to make the Middle East an area of vital national interest to the United States.

Later, when RDJTF became CENTCOM, 9th AF was to be the air component. The next 9th AF commander, General Bill Kirk, was probably the best tactician the Air Force has ever produced. I wound up replacing him. So from Larry Welch, with his tremendous intellectual capability, and Bill Kirk, with his tremendous tactical capability, I inherited a staff that was war-oriented and really working the problem day in and day out. I also was one of the first to benefit from the Goldwater-Nichols Act. Now, one thing Goldwater-Nichols did was free me from a lot of administrative responsibility. I got to spend a lot of time as commander of ten combat wings, visiting those wings. What I *didn't* have to do was a lot of administrative things. And since General Wilber Creech [the commander of TAC] had taken care of maintenance, I didn't have to worry about maintenance. Also, General Creech had fixed operations; so I didn't have to worry about operations. All I had to do was give the wing commanders another set of experienced eyes, chew them out or give them a pat on the back, hand out medals, and fly with them to know what they were doing. So I really could spend eighty percent of my time on CENTCOM's problems. The system was working pretty well at that time.

Tom Clancy: You had this new responsibility as a JFACC—joint forces air component commander. As you understood it, what did it all mean to you at the time?

Gen. Horner: It meant that if we went to war, all the air forces would function under the overall structure and guidance of the JFACC. I never used the word "command," because that just irritated the Marines [whose air units were independent of the JFACC's command, but operated under his "guidance"]. The big thing we had going for us was an exercise called Blue Flag. Whenever we would run the CENTAF Blue Flag, I would bring in the Navy and Marine Corps. In addition, the Army was always willing to come. However, the Navy and Marines would always drag their feet, but they did come. Eventually, these were the same guys I went to war with.

Tom Clancy: You were there a long time, five years, so you got to see the shift from the Cold War to the post–Cold War period. Talk a little about this.

Gen. Horner: We were still fighting the Russians in our training scenarios until Norman Schwarzkopf came in as the CENTCOM CinC in November of 1989. He reviewed the existing plans and said, "Put them on the shelf, we are never going to use them. We will *never* fight the Russians." He knew the Cold War was over.

Tom Clancy: Prior to the invasion in 1990, what were your people doing with regard to campaign and operations planning?

Gen. Horner: A variety of things. We had been exercising a *lot*. This was not unusual, though; and we were also running exercises in the Middle East. Also, there was the material pre-positioning program, which is a good program, a product of the Cold War. Those supplies were available for any kind of regional contingency in the Persian Gulf area. What really jump-started our planning for Iraq was the Internal Look exercise, which was conducted in July of 1990. Meanwhile, General Schwarzkopf had already defined the threat there as Iraq invading Kuwait and Saudi Arabia.

With Iraq's invasion of Kuwait in August 1990, all the ideas that had been put down on paper were dusted off and put to use. For General Horner, this meant a trip to Saudi Arabia to assist Secretary of Defense Richard Cheney and General H. Norman Schwarzkopf in briefing the Saudi Arabian leadership and securing permission to deploy U.S. forces to the region. This done, General Schwarzkopf left Chuck Horner to act as "CENTCOM Forward" for several weeks, so that he might return to CENTCOM headquarters in Tampa, Florida, and more rapidly push forward the forces needed to deter further Iraqi aggression in the region.

Tom Clancy: During your visit to Jedda, Saudi Arabia, you and General Schwarzkopf had a little talk about building an air campaign. Please talk about that.

Gen. Horner: In April of 1990, I went down to Tampa to brief Schwarzkopf in preparation for the July Internal Look exercise, because I did not want to go off on a tangent and show up with the "wrong" plan. There I gave him an overview on a number of things, one of them being the concept of a "strategic air campaign" in the region. He liked the briefing and the idea; he bought everything all the way.

Later, when we were finishing up our briefings in Jedda, just before he got on the airplane to Tampa, he decided that when he got home, he should investigate having someone develop such a campaign plan. I could have hugged him! Let me tell you, the greatest thing in the world is when you boss looks at you and says, "Now Horner, the *first* thing I want you to do is get air superiority."

When General Schwarzkopf returned to the United States, one of his first actions was to contact the USAF Air Staff to ask for support in the development of a strategic air campaign plan. The assignment wound up on Colonel Warden's desk, and was assigned to the Checkmate team. There were a few interesting diversions along the way, though.

Tom Clancy: What was your first involvement with the planning process for the air war?

Col. Warden: On Monday morning, the 6th of August, I brought a dozen or so officers together into Checkmate to start serious planning in the hope that we would figure out some way to sell our plan. I told my boss my ideas, and he told the Vice-Chief, Lieutenant General Mike Loh, and the Chief of Staff [General Mike Dugan]. On Wednesday morning, August 8th, General Schwarzkopf called General Dugan on the phone, but spoke to General Loh instead, as General Dugan was out of town at the time. General Schwarzkopf told General Loh that he needed some help in building a strategic air campaign plan, and could the Air Staff do anything for him. General Loh told him that we already had some people working on it, and would have something to him as quickly as possible. General Loh asked us when he could see a draft of the plan. We told him that afternoon—and we delivered.

From that first draft, we started refining our ideas with more in-depth intelligence data and analysis. After a short period of time, we were able to start asking the intelligence agencies [Air Force Intelligence, CIA, National Security Agency, Defense Intelligence Agency, etc.] to start giving us information to fill in the blanks. We knew what to ask for, because of our understanding of how nation states, military units, and other entities are organized. This allowed us to understand how Iraq worked at the highest levels, and it was merely a matter of getting down a couple of layers through the available information to find out the specifics. It was only because we had a "systems" view of the world that we were able to move very quickly.

With their mission defined, the Checkmate staff worked on. Using a pair of joint targeting lists from CENTAF (218 targets) and CENTCOM (256 targets), they developed a series of targeting plans (known as Instant Thunder) to attack targets inside Iraq and Kuwait. It was almost two hundred pages long, and took advantage of the full range of new aircraft, weapons, sensors, and other technologies.

Tom Clancy: Would you please tell us about your Instant Thunder briefing with General Schwarzkopf?

Col. Warden: General Alexander went down with us in a C-21 [the military version of the Learjet]. Also accompanying us were Lieutenant Colonel Ben Harvey, Lieutenant Colonel Dave Deptula, and one or two other guys. When we got there, General Alexander and I went into the office of the CENTCOM Director of Operations [Major General Bert Moore]. Shortly thereafter, General Schwarzkopf joined us with his deputy commander. We sat around a table, and I showed paper copies of our briefing viewgraphs to General Schwarzkopf. This was the first iteration for what we called Instant Thunder. It went over very well. Schwarzkopf said, "You guys have restored my faith in the Air Force." He was a good listener and had no negative observations. He did give us some additional tasking. At the conclusion of our session with General Schwarzkopf, he told us to brief the Chairman of the Joint Chiefs of Staff, General Colin Powell, as soon as possible.

The purpose of Instant Thunder was to impose strategic paralysis on Iraq, so that it would be incapable of providing support to its army in Kuwait, so that it would be put in an impossible position. Beyond that, it was designed to reduce the overall power of Iraq as a player in the Persian Gulf, so that there would be a more appropriate balance of power in the region after the war. One of the big debates we had with many individuals in the Air Force, but not with General Schwarzkopf, was this: The original Instant Thunder plan was to go right to the heart of Iraq and shut it down. Many senior USAF officers thought that the Iraqi Army in Kuwait would then march south [into Saudi Arabia]. At the time, I said logistically it was too hard. In all of history, no army ever marched forward offensively when its strategic homeland was collapsing.

At our session with General Powell, I had made the comment about inducing Iraq to withdraw from Kuwait. He replied that he didn't want it to withdraw; he wanted to destroy it in place. I told him we could do that too. So shortly thereafter, we began to develop Phases II and III of the Instant Thunder plan to destroy the Iraqi Army. By mid-October, we had a good plan worked out, which we faxed to Dave Deptula, who by this time was in Riyadh. We also sent it in hard copy via Major Buck Rogers when he went over to relieve Dave for a month or so.

Tom Clancy: What happened next?

Col. Warden: A little less than a week after our briefing to General Powell, I went back to Tampa under the auspices of the Joint Staff to give General Schwarzkopf the full briefing, complete with the logistics assessments, concepts of operation, deception, and psychological warfare plans, etc. After this presentation, which included most of his senior staff, he asked me to take the plan to General Horner, who was then serving as Central Command's forward commander. The next day, we left for Riyadh. Late on Sunday evening, August 20th, we briefed the CENTAF staff in Riyadh. The trouble began with the briefing to General Horner the next day. We just failed to communicate.

The problem, I feel, was General Horner's view of how ground forces move. His view also was that the only way to stop ground forces was with other ground forces, aided by airpower. So in his mind, he had an impossible problem as CENTCOM Forward. At that time, he had no significant ground forces to stop enemy ground forces. Now, here's this "armchair colonel" coming in from Washington with a plan that's got funny words in it like "offense" and "strategic targets," and they just didn't make sense to General Horner.

Colonel Warden returned home following the briefing, but not all that he said to Chuck Horner fell on deaf ears. On the contrary, much of what he had said fitted exactly into what General Horner had in mind for the coming air campaign. He also kept three of Warden's briefers for his own staff to start the planning for the coming war. Let's hear it in his own words.

Tom Clancy: Would you tell us about your perceptions of Colonel Warden's briefing of the proposed Instant Thunder plan?

Gen. Horner: Colonel Warden and his planning team showed up in Riyadh, and I was struck by the brilliance of the plan. He is a *very* intelligent guy. But it was *not* a campaign plan; it was a *really* insightful listing of targets. He and his staff had accessed information that we never had access to. We had had good briefings from the Navy about two weeks before, so we knew how to take out the Iraqi air defense control system. But he had *good* stuff on nuclear weapons production, chemical and biological weapons storage that we did not have. Where the briefing fell down is that it did not address to my satisfaction, the theater aspects of the war—hitting the Iraqi Army. When I questioned him about it, he said, "Don't worry about it; it's not important." Now, *he* may not have thought it was important, *but I did;* and that's where it broke down. Nevertheless, I said, "These guys are good," and I needed additional planning staff team members to do the offensive air plan, so I kept the three lieutenant colonels from Colonel Warden's briefing team to work with me, as my staff was overloaded with the day-in-and-day-out things we were already tasked with during Desert Shield.

This regular workload was already starting to pile up, so I said, "Who am I going to get to do this offensive air campaign and run this outfit?" My answer was Major General "Buster" Glosson. Buster had been exiled down to the Gulf to Rear Admiral Bill Fogerty aboard the flagship USS *LaSalle,* and was dying to get out of there and get up to Riyadh. So I just called him and said, "Buster, go AWOL and get up here." And he did. Now, Buster gets things done in a hurry. As soon as he arrived, I sat down with him and said, "You are going to go in and get this briefing [from the three remaining briefers]. You will find a lot of great things in it and I want those kept in, but you have to make this a practical plan. We have to make it something we can put into an Air Tasking Order [ATO]."

Of course, the planning staff continued to grow. In fact, as new people came in to CENTAF headquarters, if they showed any reasonable planning skills at all, we would put them to work under Buster. This was all going on in a conference room [called the Black Hole] right next to my office, because we didn't want anyone to know that we were planning offensive operations. Schwarzkopf wanted all this kept secret, because we were still trying to negotiate the Iraqis out of Kuwait. So, whenever a person signed onto the Black Hole team, they would have to swear that they would not talk to anyone else except the team. The team worked eighteen hours a day. It must have smelled like hell in there . . . .

Back home at the Pentagon, Colonel Warden had returned without his three lieutenant colonel briefers, but still with some hope of supporting the growing planning effort in Riyadh. Let's let him pick up the story from there.

Colonel John Warden outlines the basics of the Instant Thunder campaign plan to the Checkmate staff in early August 1990.

Tom Clancy: The briefing with General Horner doesn't go well, but he asks to keep three of your guys, as well as your viewgraphs and plans. He has felt your presence and has kept your men. How were you feeling?

Col. Warden: I decided then that we would keep the Checkmate planning operation going and continue to develop plans to support future operations—in the hope that they would find some application at CENTAF headquarters. My idea was to do everything possible to make sure we fought the right kind of air war. It was clear to me at this point that we had resources in Washington which the Riyadh planning staffs would be unable to tap. Also, it was clear that Dave Deptula could not hope to find enough of the right kind of people to help him finish off the plan we had begun in Washington. Thus, I committed the Checkmate team to feeding plans and information to Dave. We put as little identification as possible on the products we sent, so as not to irritate the leadership in Saudi Arabia.

Tom Clancy: What is your view of the CENTAF staff and how the Instant Thunder plan developed?

Col. Warden: The CENTAF staff at that time really had to be thought of as two different groups. The overwhelming majority was associated with the traditional Tactical Air Control Center operations staff that up until three or four days before the war actually started thought that their only job was to work on the defensive plan for Saudi Arabia. Then, there was a relatively small group that was operating in the Black Hole—fifteen to twenty people maximum, working under "compartmented" security conditions. It was those folks working in the Black Hole planning center—Glosson, Deptula, etc.—that we were trying to support by pushing data and ideas forward. The intelligence bureaucracy was putting out megabytes of data also, but the problem with their institutional products was a lack of correlation. So, we sent over processed data in the form of target coordinates, specifications, and strike/targeting plans. Buster and Dave were under no compulsion to use it, but they found most of it pretty good and did end up using it. What we were doing was putting it into something as close as possible to an executable plan. In many cases, all you had to do was put a tail number [i.e. assign aircraft] to it, and say what time it was supposed to happen.

In November 1990, with diplomatic options running out, President George Bush ordered the reinforcement of the existing forces assigned to Desert Shield, with additional units designed to provide "an offensive option," should it be required. General Horner picks up the story at this point.

Tom Clancy: November 1990 comes, and the President decides that if Iraq doesn't get out of Kuwait, the U.S.-led coalition will use force to get them out. Where are your people in the planning process now?

Gen. Horner: I think we had an offensive air campaign laid out pretty well in October 1990. Then, when President Bush made that decision, the Army was told it needed more forces. So of course, the Air Force needed more forces to support the Army. We basically doubled the size of the overall Air Force in-theater, being intelligent about where we could base more airplanes. This was because at that point, ramp space [for parking and servicing coalition aircraft] was becoming the driving limitation on adding more aircraft to our force.

As for the strategic air campaign plan itself, I would only let them plan the first two days. Another problem was that a multi-national coalition force was forming. As you can imagine, respecting the various host countries' laws, and ensuring that the host nations knew what was going on, was of vital import. Thus, if you wanted to fly, you had to be in the ATO. The Saudis wanted that, because then they knew what was going on, and could say, "No you can't fly here." Or ask, "Who owned those planes that sonic-boomed that camel herd?"

January 1991 came in like a lion, and with it came the war. General Horner remembers his surprise at the successes of the early moments of Desert Storm, and his reservations about the inevitable costs ahead.

Tom Clancy: If you were to summarize the objectives of the air campaign plan that became Desert Storm, how would you characterize them?

Gen. Horner: First, to control the air (Phase I). Secondly, cripple the Iraqi offensive capabilities, in particular the SCUDs and nuclear, biological, and chemical weapons to the extent we could (Phase II). Then, isolate the battlefield (Phase III), and prepare it for the ground war (Phase IV).

Tom Clancy: The first night of the war (January 16th/17th, 1991), did you have any idea of how well things were going?

Gen. Horner: No. Partly because—along with the rest of the USAF; I represented twenty five years of pessimism. I guess I had started believing the stuff that we heard all these years—that we were no good. As a society, we thought our military forces were a bunch of dummies.

That kind of pessimism is useful in my profession, because it's much better to be surprised the way we were than the way the Lancers were in the Crimea [the famous "Charge of the Light Brigade"]. The highlights of that first night were how the F-117As were able to penetrate Baghdad, and the fact that we lost just one airplane [a Navy F-18 Hornet]. A tragedy, but not the thirty or forty lost aircraft that some had predicted.

Tom Clancy: Talk about "Poobah's Party."

Gen. Horner: "Poobah's Party." That was planned by Larry "Poobah" Henry, probably one of the best planners we ever had. He was the only navigator [backseater] who was a wing commander in the Gulf. He looks mediocre, he's got navigator wings, but he's an incredible genius. The man's an absolute fiend when it comes to hunting SAMs. He arranged to have a mass of air- and ground-launched decoys, and *one hundred* HARM missiles all in the air at the same time. It was devastating to the Iraqis, something they never recovered from during the war.

While General Horner and his staff were launching the aerial assault on Iraq, back at the Pentagon in Washington, D.C., Colonel Warden and the Checkmate staff were watching it on CNN, just like the rest of us. Nevertheless, the events of that night are worth his recollection.

Tom Clancy: What was it that the CENTAF units were actually hitting at the first bang, H-Hour (0300 hours local time)?

Col. Warden: The national command authority, centers of operations, any place that we knew was serving as a command post; the two principal communication facilities in downtown Baghdad, as well as the electrical power grid and the key nodes in the KARI [Iraq in French, spelled backwards] air-defense system. These are the things that were being hit in a matter of a couple of minutes or so at H-Hour [0300L, January 17th, 1991]. Essentially, at this point, Iraq was unable to respond, due to the breakdown of its systems.

Back in Riyadh, General Horner and his staff were trying to deal with the inevitable changes and difficulties that come with trying to execute any sort of complex plan. The worst of these was the threat posed by the Iraq ballistic missile systems, generically known as SCUDs.

Tom Clancy: Did the Iraqis do *anything* smart in their conduct of the war?

Gen. Horner: Well, they did the command and control of the SCUDs pretty well, using motorcycle couriers; and they hid the SCUDs well. Their COMSEC [communications security] was *awesome*. We had the impression that Saddam had orders out that *anyone* who used a radio would be shot.

Tom Clancy: Talk about the underestimation of the SCUDs.

Gen. Horner: Being a military person, I tend to do my pluses and minuses in military terms. Civilians just don't exist in the mind of a military man until you get into a war; then you are surrounded by them. What happened was the SCUDs started coming at us. Now, the Saudi society handled it pretty well. On the other hand, the Israelis went into shock, and that surprised me. The SCUDs would hit their cities, and the Israelis would go into panic; people literally died from *fear*.

Tom Clancy: How did you feel about the performance of the Patriot SAM missiles in intercepting the SCUDs?

Gen. Horner: Good. Let's put it this way, though. Who cares if they ever really intercepted a SCUD? The perception was that they did. The SCUD is not a military weapon, it's a terror weapon. So if you have an anti-terror weapon that people *perceive* works, then it works.

Colonel Warden had his own set of perceptions on the SCUD threat, and the measures taken to deal with it.

Tom Clancy: How about the attacks on the SCUD missile sites?

Col. Warden: There are two ways of looking at the results of the air attacks on the mobile SCUDs. The popular view is that we failed to destroy a single launcher. But the Iraqis had a preferred firing rate of about ten to twelve missiles a day, based on what they were doing before the counter-SCUD operations got underway. Almost instantaneously, as these missiles and their launchers were being hunted, the firing rate dropped to about two a day, except for some spasmodic firings at the very end of the war; and the Patriot SAMs were not encountering too many incoming missiles. That was the real result of the anti-SCUD effort—perhaps a tactical failure but an operational and strategic success. And it is at the operational and strategic level where wars are won or lost.

One of the more interesting problems faced by General Horner and his staff was that after the first few days of Desert Storm, the Iraqi Air Force decided not to fly anymore. They had apparently decided to go into their hardened shelters at their airbases and "ride out" the attacks, just as the various air forces had done in the 1973 Yom Kippur War. It was a good idea that did not work out well for the Iraqis.

Tom Clancy: Whose idea was it to go after the shelters and were you confident that the BLU-109 warheads on the GBU-24 and -27 LGBs could do the job on the shelters?

Gen. Horner: Buster Glosson was the guy that did all the thinking on that. And when the first films came back to us, yes, we were confident. The shelters that we were concerned about were the Yugoslav-built ones. They were massive. They looked like big cow-dung heaps. When we saw they were being destroyed on the films, we knew that the rest would not be a problem.

Bomb damage assessment [BDA] was something we were not worried about. It really didn't matter; we were just trying to keep up the pressure on the Iraqis. Knowing when to start the ground war really didn't matter to me, because at some point the Iraqis were going to tell us that they were tired. You'd know that from defections, etc. Thus we were looking for outcome more than input.

As days moved into weeks, the campaign plan moved on towards its goals. Some of General Horner's thoughts at this time are interesting, for they begin to give you some idea of what running the air war was like for him personally. Not all his thoughts were happy.

Tom Clancy: By the end of the first week, did you have the feeling that you had won air supremacy?

Gen. Horner: Yes. The only thing we were worried about was how efficient we were. Quite frankly, the stuff we did in the strategic war was interesting, but when you get right down to it, the only thing that seemed to matter to the Iraqi Army was killing tanks. We didn't know about some of the nuclear facilities, and there was no way we were going to get all the chemical weapons—we knew that. He [Saddam Hussein] just had more than could possibly be attacked. We did a poor job of taking battlefield intelligence and reacting rapidly to it—we just didn't have the setup. Also, my Air Force guys weren't allowed to interrogate the prisoners, because the Army Special Forces thought that was their job.

Khafji is a small Saudi coastal town just south of the Kuwaiti border. On January 16, 1991, before the start of the air war, the civilian population was evacuated. And on January 29-30, 1991, the Iraqis moved into the town. This was partly a "reconnaissance in force," to test how the Coalition would react; partly a "spoiling attack," to disrupt Coalition preparations for the ground war in this area; and partly a political gesture of defiance. Let's hear General Horner's impressions of the battle:

Tom Clancy: Talk about the Khafji offensive.

Gen. Horner: Jack Liede, CENTCOM's J-2 [intelligence officer] gave us a heads-up that the Iraqi 3rd Armored Division commander was up to something. I did not know what it was, or who it was, but we started watching with the E-8 JSTARS radar aircraft that had arrived in-theater just prior to the war. All the action took place at night. The thing that cinched it was a

Marine unmanned aerial vehicle [UAV] came back with pictures of armored personnel carriers close to the berm between Kuwait and Saudi Arabia. I remember saying, "Hey, the ground fight is on!" We had beaten on them quite a bit before their deployment, and it showed when the Saudis, Qataris, and U.S. Marines finished beating on them.

General Horner was also dealing with the day-in, day-out problems inherent to the war effort. Losses and schedules were key on his mind.

Tom Clancy: How were you feeling about losses at this point?

Gen. Horner: Every loss was a tragedy. In fact, every day I would try and take a nap about four to seven in the morning. And upon returning to the Tactical Air Control Center, the first place I would stop was the rescue desk to see just how many we had lost. I can't really explain it other than it's very difficult. I got my former aide into the F-15Es of the 4th Wing; and when he was killed up near Basra, I felt as if I had killed him myself.

Tom Clancy: Talk more about your day-to-day routine.

Gen. Horner: The key players running the TACC were four colonels— Crigger, Reavy, Volman, and Harr. When I would come in the morning, I would stop and discuss with Dave Deptula the overnight updates on the Baghdad targets, and then I would go and see the Army guys. I would generally have a routine of checking on targeting, that we were getting the ATO out on time, that sort of thing. I sometimes did some paperwork, read messages, ate lunch, talked with people about what they thought was going on, slept a little, and then got ready for the evening briefing. Buster and I would then go to General Schwarzkopf's daily meeting, and he would always change the Army targets that we were assigned to hit. And then around 11:00 or 12:00 PM, the action would heat up. SCUD things, JSTARS would be up, and we'd get some movers [moving ground targets], etc. I slept about two hours a night, along with some naps during the day. I did have to get hold of myself, though, because after the first few days of the war, I was too "wired" to sleep.

Back at Checkmate in the Pentagon, Colonel Warden was busy supporting the operations in the Persian Gulf, as well as dealing with the other situations unique to a capitol city at war.

Tom Clancy: At this busy point in the war, what were you and the Checkmate team doing?

Col. Warden: All kinds of things were going on, one of them being that we were trying to give the Secretary of Defense and the White House a true picture of what was going on . . . because much of the analysis of the war coming out of the traditional DIA and CIA bureaucracies was "Newtonian" [static] analysis of what was a "quantum" [dynamic] situation. By that I mean that we had entered into an entirely new epoch of war—a military technological revolution, if you will. So the methods the old-line intelligence bureaucracies were using were the equivalent of trying to use a vacuum tube tester to see how well a microchip was working. The tester would say that it wasn't—and the conclusion would be completely irrelevant.

Tom Clancy: How important were the space satellite systems to operations in the Gulf?

Col. Warden: I like to think of the Gulf War as the first *genuine* "World War." Things were going on all around the globe, with real-time effects on the combat theater. World War II was not a true global war—it was a series of campaigns that took place in scattered places. Satellite systems are what made genuine world war possible and real during Desert Storm.

Tom Clancy: Could you please talk a little about the conditions that the aircrews were having to deal with during the war?

Col. Warden: Keep in mind that we were having a terrible time with the weather. Historically it was the worst weather since they began keeping records in that area, which went back to about 1947. A significant number of F-117 sorties simply could not drive home their attacks, given the rules of engagement [ROE], which essentially said: If you're not sure you're going to hit the target, don't drop. The F-16s and F/A-18s were not doing so well either, because by the second day, they were flying at a medium altitude [from 12,000 to 20,000 feet/3,657 to 6,096 meters] to reduce losses. So they're trying to drop dumb bombs from there. This does not mean that they would never hit a particular target, just that it would take many more sorties than with laser guided bombs from an F-111F or F-117A.

Tom Clancy:	Let's talk about the transition to Phase II.
Col. Warden:	Well, it's important to understand that rather than transitioning from phase to phase, what really happened was a merging of Phases I, II, and III. We had originally planned distinct phases, but that was when we had a limited number of aircraft available. We had wanted to concentrate every ounce of our strength against the strategic centers of gravity within the Iraqi war machine in Phase I. We simply did not feel that we could do anything in Kuwait until we had completed the operation in Iraq.

Phase II, though, was originally designed to be a one day operation, where we would finish off the air superiority problem in Kuwait. This meant knocking out some missile [SAM] sites, as there was no evidence of Iraqi aircraft being based in Kuwait. The next phase, Phase III, was to destroy the Iraqi Army in Kuwait. The Army wanted to call this "battlefield preparation." But Dave Deptula had it right when he told General Horner, "We're not preparing the battlefield, we're destroying it!"

The intention of Phase III was to reduce the Iraqi Army to fifty percent of its pre-war strength. This would make it operationally ineffective. If necessary, we could have gone beyond that and literally destroyed it. We were absolutely confident that if we imposed a fifty percent attrition rate on units in the Iraqi Army, and it didn't become operationally ineffective, then it would be the first army in history not to do so. After a lot of discussion in the fall of 1990, we based the Phase III plan on eliminating the Republican Guard units first, followed next with the regular and conscript army near the Saudi border. |
| Tom Clancy: | Talk about the Bomb Damage Assessment [BDA] controversy. |
| Col. Warden: | The BDA problem goes back to World War II. The intelligence guys are somewhat conservative, since they don't want to say something is destroyed if it really isn't. It's a reasonable presumption that if it's rubble it's destroyed. If there's a wall knocked down, it's damaged. Otherwise it's undamaged. But with targets hit by precision weapons, there may be little or no evidence of damage or destruction that fits any of the standard intelligence criteria. The majority of the analysts were going by the rules they had been taught. So the Air Force says, "We're out there blowing up things." And the CIA says, "No, you're not." Here's a good example. We had |

an overhead picture of a tank that the CIA said was undamaged. Then somebody got an oblique shot [picture] from a reconnaissance aircraft, and you saw the turret was shifted about a foot, and the gun tube was drooping into the sand. Destroyed tank.

This sort of thing led Buster Glosson to come up with "tank plinking," where we used small LGBs to destroy armored vehicles. The common wisdom was that it was ridiculous to use an expensive [$12,000] precision LGB against a tank. But when you send four planes out with four bombs each and they come back with an average of twelve kills, that's *cheap.*

As February 1991 moved on, a greater percentage of the sorties generated by CENTAF were being dedicated to supporting the planned ground operations that would evict the Iraqi forces from Kuwait. Despite what others were judging from the daily results, General Horner had his own criteria for success.

Tom Clancy: Preparing the way for the ground war to start, did you have the feeling that your people were effective? What factors were limiting what you were doing?

Gen. Horner: Quite frankly, we had all the time we wanted. I was not overly concerned about *when* the ground war would start. I never really worried about "how effective" we were, because we knew by things like Iraqi desertions. If you think about it, we were going to get them all. The weather was really not a factor, because if we didn't get it today, I was confident we would get it tomorrow. They [the Iraqis] weren't going anywhere. Where we really started making money was when Buster thought up "tank plinking." That worked great!

On February 24th, the ground war started, and the air campaign against Iraq began to wind down.

Tom Clancy: What were your impressions of the situation when Desert Storm was completed at the end of February 1991?

Gen. Horner: I was glad to see the ground war go so quickly and so well. I tell you, we were tired of war, really tired of killing people. I guess we all would have liked it if Saddam had gone; but Saddam was *not* a target, the command and control system was. The Iraqi Army would hold staff meetings, we would confirm the location by "other sources," and we would bomb the location, destroying the notes from the meeting.

The last few days of the war we were really working hard to find things to hit. My general impressions of the air campaign? I was pleased with it. You're never totally satisfied, but the overall loss rate was good, the munitions worked better than anticipated. But because of my personality, I was never completely satisfied with it.

Colonel Warden spent the end of the war watching the ground war from the Checkmate center in the Pentagon, and then went home for a well-deserved couple of days of sleep. Afterwards, though:

Tom Clancy: What happened to Checkmate after the war ended?

Col. Warden: Right after the war we had an absolutely marvelous party. Cases and cases of champagne. Our friends from CIA, DIA, and NSA came down. The Secretary of the Air Force [Donald Rice] and the Under Secretary of Defense for Policy spent the afternoon with us.

Soon after that, we became a "politically incorrect" organization that seemed counter to Goldwater-Nichols. And so Checkmate was shut down a couple months or so after the war. However, it was eventually reborn. Today, it does a lot of contingency planning for the Air Force Chief of Staff. As for me personally, I left the Pentagon about two months after the war ended, and went to the White House to work as a special assistant to Vice President Quayle. I worked exclusively on non-military things, ironically.

Tom Clancy: Today, the effects of the Gulf War are clear. The plan was executed well in your opinion?

Col. Warden: Yes. On balance, I think we achieved just about exactly what we wanted. For me, though, the really gratifying thing is that we achieved such momentous results with so little blood shed on *either* side. I am not aware of any war on this scale where so much happened at so little cost in blood. In addition, it also seems to me a demonstration of what you can accomplish with airpower when you use it correctly. I just hope that we continue the revolution and don't fall back into the old ways of doing things because of bureaucratic pressures in the Department of Defense, and in the Congress.

Today, both General Horner and Colonel Warden are looking forward to their lives after military service. After the war, Chuck Horner was promoted to general (four stars), and took over the unified U.S. Space Command at Colorado Springs, Colorado. There, he handled a variety of tasks, including the direction of the North American Air Defense Command, as well as working on ballistic missile defenses. Following his retirement in the summer of 1994, he and his wife Mary Jo have settled in Florida, where he is writing his own memoirs of the 1990/1991 Persian Gulf Crisis/War. Colonel Warden has finished his career with one of the most satisfying appointments he could have imagined, commandant of the Air Command and Staff College at the USAF Air University, located at Maxwell AFB, Alabama. There he has transformed the curriculum, emphasizing air campaign planning for joint service and international students from all over the world. He will retire from the Air Force in the summer of 1995. Arguably, he has become the Clausewitz or Alfred Thayer Mahan of airpower, having codified the use of airpower in *The Air Campaign: Planning for Combat*. Both Horner and Warden have undeniably made their marks in the USAF and the history of airpower.

Combat Aircraft

hat is a "classic"? The term has become overused, its meaning fuzzy. Perhaps the best definition I've heard goes something like this; "I can't tell you what it is, but I know it when I see it." When you talk to the people who fly and maintain today's fleet of U.S. Air Force aircraft, they use the word classic a lot. There's a reason: Every USAF fighter, bomber, and support aircraft in service is a classic, because it has to be. It takes so much time, money, and effort to produce a combat aircraft these days, anything less than a roaring success is going to be a disaster for everyone concerned. Every new combat aircraft must be an instant classic, capable of vastly outperforming the plane or planes it was designed to replace. This chapter will help you get to know some of the classic aircraft programs of recent years.

Today, when a military service commits to fund an aircraft program, and a company chooses to jump in and build that airplane, both are literally "betting the farm," with severe consequences for both if the program fails. Given the risks involved, it is amazing that anyone wants to be in the aircraft business at all—but the payoffs of a successful program can be immense for a company, its stockholders, the surrounding communities, and the military service that takes delivery of the final product.

In order to spread their cost over as long a period as possible, modern aircraft tend to have extremely long service lives. For example, the Boeing KC-135 first came into USAF service in the late 1950s, and is planned to be retired in the later 2020s, a run of over sixty years! Even longer lived is the truly classic C-130 Hercules, which first flew just after the Korean War. A new version (the C-130J) is being built right now for use into the middle of the next century by the USAF, as well as by Great Britain and Australia.

The gestation period of a modern aircraft may take as long as fifteen years from first specification to squadron service. And there may be several generations of production models built, with up to twenty-five years of total production. If this period seems long, consider the McDonnell Douglas F-15 Eagle. It was first designed in the late 1960s, went into production in the mid-1970s, and has remained in continuous production ever since. Given the current backlog of orders to Saudi Arabia and Israel, and other possible production orders, the third-generation Eagle variants will be in production and in service for over twenty-five years, until approximately 2015 to 2020. So read on, and get to know some of the classic aircraft being flown by the USAF, now and in the future.

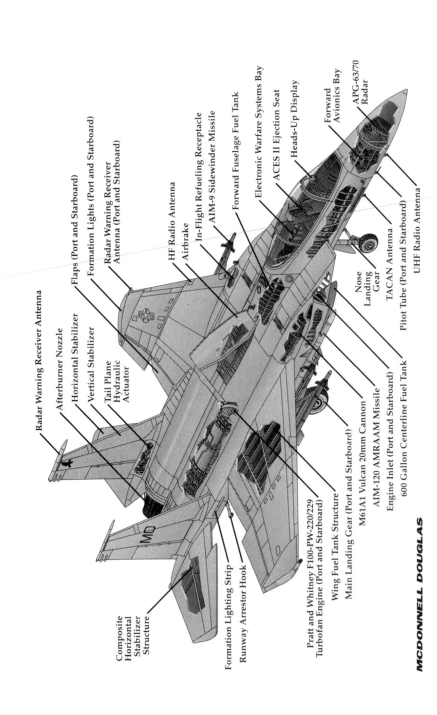

Radar Warning Receiver Antenna

Afterburner Nozzle

Horizontal Stabilizer

Vertical Stabilizer

Tail Plane Hydraulic Actuator

Flaps (Port and Starboard)

Formation Lights (Port and Starboard)

Radar Warning Receiver Antenna (Port and Starboard)

HF Radio Antenna

Airbrake

In-Flight Refueling Receptacle

AIM-9 Sidewinder Missile

Forward Fuselage Fuel Tank

Electronic Warfare Systems Bay

ACES II Ejection Seat

Heads-Up Display

Forward Avionics Bay

APG-63/70 Radar

Composite Horizontal Stabilizer Structure

Formation Lighting Strip

Runway Arrestor Hook

Pratt and Whitney F100-PW-220/229 Turbofan Engine (Port and Starboard)

Wing Fuel Tank Structure

Main Landing Gear (Port and Starboard)

M61A1 Vulcan 20mm Cannon

AIM-120 AMRAAM Missile

Engine Inlet (Port and Starboard)

600 Gallon Centerline Fuel Tank

Nose Landing Gear

TACAN Antenna

Pitot Tube (Port and Starboard)

UHF Radio Antenna

MCDONNELL DOUGLAS

A cutaway drawing of the McDonnell Douglas F-15C Eagle.

McDonnell Douglas F-15 Eagle

In July 1967 at Domodedevo Airport, outside Moscow, the Soviet Air Force proudly unveiled a new aircraft to the world press, the Ye-266/MiG-25. Nomenclature rules used by Western intelligence agencies specified that all "threat" fighter types got names starting with the letter F; so the MiG-25 was called "Foxbat." Like its namesake, the world's largest flying mammal, this new plane was a beast with remarkable sensors, sharp teeth, and impressive performance. It quickly established several new world records for altitude, speed, rate-of-climb, and time-to-altitude, all important measures of a fighter's capability in combat. The best contemporary American fighter of the time, the McDonnell F-4 Phantom was clearly outclassed; and the U.S. Air Force launched a competition to design a plane that could surpass the Russian achievement. This program became even more vital when you consider that the same airshow had seen the rollout of the MiG-23/27 Flogger-series aircraft, and a number of other impressive Soviet fighters as well. Quickly, the USAF produced a specification for what they called the Fighter Experimental (FX). Several manufacturers competed for the FX contract, which eventually went to McDonnell Douglas in St. Louis. The contract was awarded in December 1969, and the first F-15, dubbed the "Eagle," was rolled out on June 26th, 1972. By the end of 1975, operations of the first F-15 training squadron at Luke AFB, the famous 555th "Triple Nickel," were in full swing; and the 1st Tactical Fighter Wing (TFW) at Langley AFB, Virginia, was fully equipped with its cadre of the new birds. There were 361 F-15A fighters and 58 combat-capable F-15B trainers produced before the improved -C and -D models went into production in 1979. In early 1995 the Air Force operated about twenty squadrons of F-15s, including five Reserve and National Guard squadrons.

The designers at McDonnell Aircraft produced a 40,000 lb./18,181 kg., "no-compromise" air superiority fighter that, superficially, resembled the Foxbat, with huge, boxy air intakes, large wing area, and tall twin tail fins. The exterior is covered with access panels, most at shoulder level for easy access without the need for work stands. The structure made extensive use of titanium (stronger than steel) for the wing spars and engine bay, and limited use of advanced boron fiber (non-metallic) composite materials in the tail surfaces. Stainless steel is found mainly in the landing gear struts, and the skin is primarily made of aircraft-grade aluminum. By comparison, the Foxbat used heavy steel alloys throughout the airframe. This imposed a huge weight penalty on the Soviet machine. In case you wonder about the strength of the American bird, consider that McDonnell Douglas's F-15 test airframe has completed over eighteen thousand hours of simulated flight, which represents a potential service life of fifty-three years, based on a flight schedule of three hundred hours per year.

According to the original FX design guidelines, the aircraft was to be a pure air-superiority fighter—"not a pound for air-to-ground." Earlier designs like the F-4 Phantom and F-105 Thunderchief had traded off air-to-air performance

An F-15C of the 366th Wing/390th Fighter Squadron on the flight line of Nellis AFB during Green Flag 94-3. It carries the standard load of three 610 gallon/2,301.9 liter fuel tanks and eight air-to-air missiles.

CRAIG E. KASTON

for a multi-role "fighter-bomber" capability, and this often put them at a fatal disadvantage against the more agile Soviet MiGs, such as those that they encountered over North Vietnam. (Later, as it happened, the Strike Eagle derivative of the F-15 became one of the great air-to-ground combat aircraft of all time.)

The F-15 used the very advanced Pratt and Whitney F100-PW-100 turbofan, which pushed then-existing technology to the limits. The 17,600 lb./8,000 kg. thrust J-79 engine, for example, two of which powered the F-4 Phantom, had a turbine inlet temperature of 2,035°F/1,113°C, while the F-100-PW-100 turbine inlet can sustain a hellish 2,460°F/1,349°C. In full afterburner, the basic F100 produces 25,000 lb./11,340 kg. of thrust—nearly eight times its own weight! A skilled ground crew can remove and replace an engine in thirty minutes; just try that on your Oldsmobile! In service, F100 engines have worn out much faster than expected, principally because the Eagle's advanced airframe allowed pilots to fly on the "edge of the envelope" at throttle settings and angles of attack that stress the engines severely. But the edge of the envelope is where pilots win air battles, so the price has been paid to maintain the awesome capability that the F100 delivers.

One of the realities of modern jet fighters is that they burn gas faster than teenagers drink diet soda—a lot faster. While the F100 turbofan is more efficient than the older turbojet fighter engines, they still burn a huge load of fuel, especially in afterburner. To feed the two big turbofans, the Eagle carries a huge load of fuel internally, in the fuselage and wings. In addition, all F-15s can carry up to three external 610 gallon/2,309 liter drop tanks, one on the centerline and one under each wing. To extend the Eagle's unrefueled range even further, McDonnell Douglas developed the Fuel and Sensors, Tactical (FAST) Pack, a pair of bulging "conformal" fuel tanks (CFTs) that fit tightly against the sides of the fuselage below the wings. These are designed to minimize drag and actually generate some lift, so the Eagle's performance is only slightly affected. Holding 750 gallons/2,839 liters of fuel, each CFT can be installed or removed in fifteen minutes. In addition, there are fittings on each CFT for mounting bomb racks or missile rails. CFTs are not carried on the current fighter version of the Eagle, the F-15C, because the normal internal fuel load, as well as that in the drop tanks, is usually adequate for the missions the Eagle drivers fly.

The business end of the Eagle is the cockpit, which is topped with a large bubble canopy. It provides exceptional panoramic visibility, which is critical to survival in a dogfight. F-15 pilots talk about a feeling of riding "on" the aircraft rather than "in" it. By slightly extending the canopy, the design left sufficient room behind the pilot for a second seat, making it relatively simple to build the F-15B/D operational trainer, and ultimately the F-15E Strike Eagle.

The pilot sits in a McDonnell Douglas ACES II ejection seat, which is one of the best in the world. When you sit in one, you are held by a lap belt and shoulder-harness system, and the cushions contain the parachute and rescue packs that deploy when the seat separates. All you need to do to escape from a stricken aircraft is to pull one of the two sets of ejection handles (one on either side of the seat) while sitting firmly in the seat, and you are on your way. Pyrotechnic charges blow off the canopy, and then a rocket motor fires and blasts you free. At that point, everything, including the parachute deployment, is handled automatically. Even the release of the parachute in the event of a water landing is handled by sensors that detect the presence of water and cut the riser lines loose to keep the survivor from fouling the chute and drowning.

While the instrument panel directly in front of the pilot is crammed with a mix of dial gauges, most of what he actually uses centers around just three things, the Head-Up Display (HUD), the control stick, and the throttles.

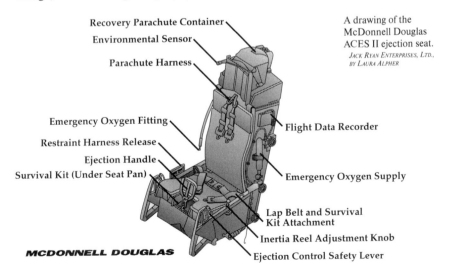

Recovery Parachute Container
Environmental Sensor
Parachute Harness
Emergency Oxygen Fitting
Restraint Harness Release
Ejection Handle
Survival Kit (Under Seat Pan)
MCDONNELL DOUGLAS

Flight Data Recorder
Emergency Oxygen Supply
Lap Belt and Survival Kit Attachment
Inertia Reel Adjustment Knob
Ejection Control Safety Lever

A drawing of the McDonnell Douglas ACES II ejection seat.
JACK RYAN ENTERPRISES, LTD., BY LAURA ALPHER

Earlier we saw how the HUD presents the most vital flight and sensor data to the pilot, without the pilot having to move his gaze down into the cockpit. This is critical, because the last thing you want to do in a dogfight is take your eyes off the target. Most of the controls that an F-15 pilot needs for fighting in the Eagle are located on the control stick; engine throttles are on the left side of the cockpit. Both are studded with small switches and buttons, each shaped and textured differently, so that after a short time, a pilot can rapidly identify a particular switch just by feel. This system—known as Hands on Throttle and Stick (HOTAS)—was developed by a brilliant McDonnell Douglas engineer named Eugene Adam, who is a legend in the business of cockpit design, having also been behind the "glass" (using computer MFDs instead of dials and gauges) cockpits in the F-15E Strike Eagle, the F/A-18 Hornet, and many other combat aircraft in service today. The HOTAS switches control almost everything a pilot needs in a fight—the radar mode, radio-transmit switch, decoy launchers, and of course the weapons release, which can be controlled by the movement of a finger and a flip of a switch.

While I've never flown in the front seat of an actual Eagle, I spent some time on the domed full-motion simulators operated by McDonnell Douglas at their St. Louis facility. When you sit down in the seat of an Eagle, the first thing you notice is that your hands just naturally move to the HOTAS controls and your eyes to the HUD. It takes a while to sort out all the switches and buttons, though you rapidly identify the really important ones. When they start it up and you're actually "flying," the first thing you notice is that your aircraft seems to wobble all over the sky, because the controls are so sensitive. You quickly learn that the trick to maintaining a smooth flight path is to loosen your grip on the control stick and let your right hand just "kiss" it with a light touch. When you start maneuvering the Eagle, the control system is just so quick and responsive to even the smallest control inputs that you feel you're "behind" the airplane. Even the twin F100 power plants are quick to accelerate and idle, thanks to the digital engine control system.

I mentioned earlier that the Hughes-built radar of the Eagle has been a standard for air intercept (AI) radars since it came into service in 1975. Originally designated the APG-63, it has been updated to the APG-70 standard in the F-15E and the last block of F-15C Eagles. The reason for having a radar so powerful and agile (i.e. able to discriminate and hold lock even on small targets during the high-G maneuvers of a dogfight) on the Eagle was that the designers wanted to be able to scan and attack targets in a vast volume of airspace in front of the new fighter. This requires a *lot* of power. The brute power of a radar is determined mainly by two factors, the amount of electrical current the aircraft can supply and the space available for the antenna. The sophistication of a modern radar is determined largely by the state-of-the-art in digital signal processing, an arcane branch of computer science. The original APG-63 radar had three main operating modes: low pulse-rate (frequency) for ground mapping, medium pulse rate for close-range maneuvering targets, and high pulse rate for long-range detection at ranges of 100 nm./183 km. or more. Since the most important radar controls are located on the throttle column and control stick, they are easy to use in combat. The most important of these are the switches for selecting where the radar is pointed in elevation and the various radar modes. This system has been continually upgraded to keep pace with advances in technology, and is now designated the APG-70, with a programmable signal processor (PSP). The PSP was added to the APG-63 in later F-15A/B model aircraft; and later -C/D/E models got the APG-70 with the PSP already built in. The upgrade included a variety of new operating modes, such as Synthetic Aperture Radar (SAR) precision ground mapping in the F-15E model.

Another important part of the Eagle's avionics is the communications suite. In addition to the new Have Quick II radios (jam and intercept resistant), there is one of the new Joint Tactical Information Data System (JTIDS) terminals, which allows the "linking" of any aircraft so equipped to an aerial local area network. This secure (i.e., unjammable and untappable) data link allows the sharing of information from a plane's sensors and other systems with other aircraft, ships, and ground units. JTIDS terminals are currently on the E-3 Sentry AWACS, as well as new E-8 Joint-STARS ground surveillance aircraft. Even U.S. Army Patriot SAM batteries, U.S. Navy Aegis cruisers and destroyers, and NATO units have the capability to tap into the JTIDS data link system. Now, while data links are nothing new, what makes JTIDS special is that it transmits a full situational report, including radar contacts, sending aircraft position, altitude, and heading, and even fuel and armament status (counting gun, bomb, and missile rounds onboard) to anyone with a terminal equipped to receive it. The major problem with the early JTIDS terminals was that they were extremely expensive; but later versions have been re-engineered to reduce their size, cost, and complexity. Luckily, the rapid march of technology has made this both possible and reasonable, and the new terminals should be in service within a year or two. Currently, only the F-15Cs assigned to the 391st Fighter Squadron of the 366th Wing at Mountain Home AFB, Idaho, are equipped with JTIDS.

It is always vitally important that the pilot know where he or she is; thus the inclusion of a highly accurate inertial navigation system (INS) in the Eagle's avionics suite. The Litton ASN-109 INS is a "black box" that uses laser beams moving in opposite directions in rings of fiber-optic cable. Any motion of the aircraft causes tiny shifts in the wavelength of the light, which is sensed and analyzed to determine position, velocity, and acceleration. Before takeoff, the system is "aligned" and fed the geographic coordinates of the starting point (usually the aircraft parking ramp, where a sign is posted with the surveyed coordinates) and a series of "waypoints." Since INS positional fixes tend to "drift" over the course of a mission several hours long, there are provisions to update the navigational fix with inputs from ground-based aids such as the TACAN system (a series of ground-based electronic navigation stations), as well as visual and radar map fixes. A future avionics upgrade for the -C will add a super-accurate Honeywell system combining a GPS receiver with a ring laser gyro in a single box.

Another system directed from the pilot's HOTAS controls is the defensive countermeasures system. To survive today in a high-threat environment, you need a radar jammer. In the Eagle, this system is the internally mounted Northrop ALQ-135(V), which operates automatically, requiring only that the pilot turn it on. To alert the pilot to electronic (i.e., radar guided) threats, there is a Loral ALR-56C Radar Warning Receiver (RWR), with the display mounted just below and to the right of the HUD. This display shows both the type of threat and the bearing to the enemy radar. It also can tell the pilot whether the enemy radar is just scanning, or if it has actually fired a SAM. As might be imagined, this information is vital for a pilot to survive in the modern aerial battlefield. Antennas for the ECM and RWR systems are mounted in pods on top of the twin tail fins. Should the ECM system fail and there's an incoming missile on your tail, the pilot also has a Tracor ALE-45/47 chaff and flare decoy dispenser, with the release button mounted on the left side of the throttle column.

The only reason for the existence of a combat aircraft is to deliver (or at least threaten to deliver) ordnance (the technical term for weapons) onto an enemy target. As we stated earlier, the original design of the Eagle was for a no-compromise air-to-air (the USAF term for this is "air superiority") fighter. Thus, the F-15C weapons suite was optimized for taking on and rapidly defeating a large number of air-to-air targets. For the designers of the Eagle, their starting point was the original weapons loadout of the aircraft that it replaced, the eight air-to-air missiles of the F-4 Phantom. In addition, they decided to add a gun to the package, since the lack of such a weapon had cost American pilots so many MiG kills over North Vietnam. Unlike guided missiles, guns have no minimum range, and can also be used against ground targets, should that be required. While originally it was planned to fit the F-15 with the new Philco Ford (now Loral Aeronutronic) 25mm GAU-7, it was eventually decided that the F-15 would be equipped with the older, more dependable General Electric M-61 Vulcan 20mm six-barreled rotary cannon. Used on USAF aircraft since the mid-1950s, it is something of a classic on its own, and is on every air superiority fighter currently in the U.S. inventory. The cannon muzzle is located in the starboard wing root, well behind the engine intake, so there is no risk of ingesting gun gas, causing an engine flameout. A drum magazine behind the cockpit holds 940 rounds, but you better fire short bursts, since this is just enough for 9.4 seconds of firing. (The M61 fires over six thousand rounds per minute!) Today, the big news about the Vulcan is that there is a new kind of ammunition for it to fire—the PGU-28, which has armor piercing, explosive fragmentation, and incendiary effects, all in a single round. This new bullet has greatly improved the capabilities of the M-61, which is still one of the finest airborne cannons in the world. In the F-15C, the gun is angled up about 2°, so that it "lofts" the rounds towards the target, allowing a better view before you lose sight of the target under the nose of the aircraft. There also is a new gunsight—or more properly, gunsight symbology for the HUD—which greatly eases the task of aiming. When the GUN mode is selected (from a switch on the throttle), what looks like a funnel appears on the HUD. Once you have the enemy aircraft centered between the two lines of the funnel, a squeeze of the trigger on the front of the control stick sends a stream of cannon shells toward the target. According to F-15 pilots, the new sight symbology has radically improved gunnery accuracy and makes the gun a much more dangerous weapon.

Good as the gun is, the most powerful weapons on the Eagle are its eight air-to-air missiles (AAMs). Originally, the F-15's primary AAM was the Raytheon AIM-7 Sparrow, four of which could be carried on racks tucked neatly on the underside of the fuselage. These have since been replaced by the Hughes AIM-120 Advanced Medium Range Air-to-Air Missile (AMRAAM), which is known as the "Slammer" by pilots. Underwing pylons also can carry up to four AIM-9 Sidewinder AAMs or AMRAAMs.

All these systems and weaponry have made the Eagle the most powerful air superiority fighter in the world for over two decades now. This has translated to a modest degree of success in the export market, despite the relatively high cost of the Eagle compared to the F-16 Fighting Falcon, the Mirage F-1 and -2000, and the MiG-29. Several generations of Russian, British, and French fighters have tried to get the better of the Eagle, but regular upgrades and the superb training of the USAF pilots have kept the F-15 at the top of the worldwide fighter hierachy. Currently, there are more than 1,300 F-15s of all models in service with the U.S. Air Force, the Israeli Air Force (F-15A/B/I models), the Japanese Air Self-Defense Force (F-15J), and the Royal Saudi Air Force (F-15A/B/S models). The Japanese F-15J is built by Mitsubishi on license from McDonnell Douglas.

The ultimate test of any military aircraft is combat, and the Eagle has an undefeated record. The Israelis scored the Eagle's first kill, a Syrian MiG-21 in June of 1979. Later on, in February 1981, they provided the ultimate proof of the Eagle's superiority by downing a Syrian MiG-25 Foxbat, the very aircraft it had been designed to defeat. Israeli F-15s also escorted the force of F-16s that destroyed an unfinished Iraqi nuclear reactor outside Baghdad in 1981. The Saudis also have scored with their force of Eagles, with at least one kill of an Iranian Phantom over the Persian Gulf in 1988, and two kills by one pilot of a pair of Iraqi Mirage F-1Qs armed with AM-39 Exocet anti-shipping missiles during Desert Storm. In fact, Eagles shot down at least thirty-five of the forty-one aircraft that Iraq lost in air-to-air combat during the 1991 conflict. The record book currently credits the F-15 with a career total of 96.5 confirmed air-to-air kills for no losses.

With the coming of the F-15's designated replacement, the Lockheed F-22, further production of the Eagle for the USAF and a few foreign governments will be limited to the Strike version. The remaining USAF -C and -E model aircraft will all be fitted with GPS receivers, as well as the follow-on version of the JTIDS data link terminal. There is also a radar upgrade program, designed to replace some of the "black box" components of the APG-63/70 system with newer units from the APG-73 radar used on the F/A-18 Hornet fighters now being delivered to the U.S. Navy. This upgrade will allow for faster processing of information, as well as a larger memory module. It is also likely that before it goes out of service, the new model of the venerable Sidewinder AAM, the AIM-9X with its helmet-mounted sighting system, will be integrated into the Eagle. Whatever happens to the Eagle fleet, the taxpayers of the United States can be pleased with the value that they received for their investment in the Eagle, which held the line in the air for the last years of the Cold War and the beginning of the new world order.

McDonnell Douglas F-15E Strike Eagle

I had never flown an eighty-one-thousand-pound jet before, and we were surprised when we started taxiing. We felt a thump, thump, thump underneath us, and we were concerned until we realized that all that weight standing on the tires had molded a temporary flat spot on them.

F-15E Pilot, Desert Storm, January 17th, 1991

The F-15E Strike Eagle is an almost perfect balance of structure, power plant, sensors, weapons, and avionics, controlled by the finest cockpit design in the world today. Now you might wonder why I'm describing it separately from the air-to-air version of the Eagle. The truth is that while the two birds share a common heritage, they really are different aircraft, both inside and out. In fact, the crews that fly this powerful beast say there are two kinds of USAF crews: those

A McDonnell Douglas F-15E Strike Eagle of the 366th Wing's 391st Fighter Squadron flies over the Nevada desert during Green Flag 94-3. It is armed with training versions of Sidewinder and AMRAAM air-to-air and Maverick air-to-ground missiles. *Craig E. Kaston*

that fly the Strike Eagle, and those who wish they did. Given what I've learned about this machine, they may be right.

It is surprising that an aircraft originally designed as a pure air superiority machine should give rise to one of the greatest fighter-bombers in aviation history. Nevertheless, by the early 1980s, with the fleet of F-111 fighter bombers aging rapidly, and the F-117As just coming into service, there was a severe shortage of all-weather strike aircraft in USAF service. Thus, the USAF leadership began to kick around the idea of an interim strike aircraft, which could bridge the gap between the older F-111 and the new stealth types that were being planned.

The F-15E was not a plane the Air Force requested directly per se; it began as a private venture funded by McDonnell Douglas. This is because the contracting rules of the U.S. Department of Defense (DoD) do not allow the services to "ask" a contractor directly to make them something. They can, however, "suggest" that a company put together an "unsolicited proposal" to offer certain goods and services. Such dialogues are common, and were apparently conducted by General Wilber Creech, USAF, then commander of the Tactical Air Command, and several aircraft companies concerning strike variants of existing fighter designs. Thus, General Creech might well be considered the USAF "father" of the Strike Eagle. The effort began when a production F-15B (originally a two-seat trainer version) was converted for ground attack by adding extra underwing pylons and bomb racks on CFTs. Demonstrations of the prototype at Edwards and Eglin AFBs in 1982 and 1983 were sufficiently impressive that the Air Force decided to hold a competition between the F-15 and an improved version of the General Dynamics (now Lockheed) F-16 with a cranked delta wing, the F-16XL. The McDonnell Douglas entry won the competition, and in 1984 they were awarded a contract to begin full-scale development, with an original goal of 392 production aircraft. But budget cuts at the end of the Cold War chopped this number down to two hundred by 1994, plus a few replacements for aircraft lost in Desert Storm and training mishaps.

The first flight of the Strike Eagle was on December 11th, 1986, with deliveries to the Air Force beginning on December 29th, 1988. The 4th TFW, with three squadrons, reached an initial operational capability (IOC—first squadron service) in October 1989 at Seymour Johnson AFB, North Carolina.

That change was more than just cosmetic. Although the F-15E is externally very similar to the F-15D (the two-seat trainer model of the F-15C), about 60% of the F-15's structure was redesigned to accommodate its new role as a strike aircraft. These changes were designed to strengthen the airframe, extending the certified fatigue life to sixteen thousand hours, and allowing sustained 9-G maneuvers, like its smaller partner, the F-16. The extra strength is important, because the huge fixed-geometry wing of the F-15 can make for a rough ride at low altitude for both the airframe and the crew, even when nobody is trying to kill you. Also, since low-altitude, high-speed flight can be a dangerous thing, the F-15E's windshield is specially strengthened against bird-strikes,

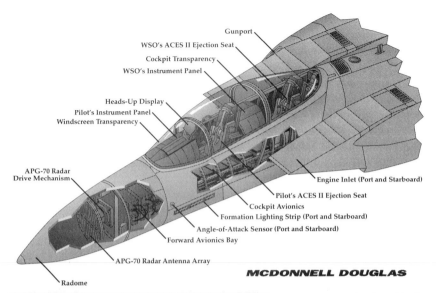

Gunport

WSO's ACES II Ejection Seat

Cockpit Transparency

WSO's Instrument Panel

Heads-Up Display

Pilot's Instrument Panel

Windscreen Transparency

APG-70 Radar Drive Mechanism

Engine Inlet (Port and Starboard)

Pilot's ACES II Ejection Seat

Cockpit Avionics

Formation Lighting Strip (Port and Starboard)

Angle-of-Attack Sensor (Port and Starboard)

Forward Avionics Bay

APG-70 Radar Antenna Array

Radome

MCDONNELL DOUGLAS

ABOVE: A cutaway drawing of the forward fuselage of the McDonnell Douglas F-15E Strike Eagle. *JACK RYAN ENTERPRISES, LTD., BY LAURA ALPHER*

LEFT: The two-man cockpit of this McDonnell Douglas F-15E Strike Eagle is shown to advantage, with the wide-field-of-view Heads-Up Display (HUD) at the bottom, in front of the pilot. *CRAIG E. KASTON*

which are more common than you might think. The basic F-15 is an enormously tough airplane—after a midair collision, one F-15 pilot safely landed his craft with only 14 in./35 cm. of wing remaining on one side—and the modifications to the -E model have only made it tougher. Maximum takeoff weight was increased from 68,000 lb./30,845 kg. to an astounding 81,000 lb./36741 kg.! Of this total, up to 24,500 lb./11,100 kg. can be ordnance, in almost any mix of air-to-air and air-to-ground weapons imaginable.

The greatest strength of the Strike Eagle is the two-man cockpit, which allows for the increased workloads of low-level, day and night strike missions. Historically, two-seat fighters have usually gained the advantage in combat against single-seat types, because the situational awareness benefit of an extra set of eyes and brains is greater than the weight penalty of the extra ejection seat. The benefit is even greater in ground attack missions, because the backseater can concentrate on precise delivery of weapons and managing the defensive-counter-measures systems (jamming, chaff, and flares), while the pilot concentrates on flying the plane. Though Weapons Systems Officers (WSOs) are not trained as pilots, they do tend to become skilled at flying and "staying" the pilot; and both crew positions have a full set of flight controls.

The division of labor in the Strike Eagle between the pilot (in the front seat) and WSO (or "wizzo," in the backseat) is nearly perfect, thanks to

The pilot's instrument panel in the McDonnell Douglas F-15E Strike Eagle. The three computer-style Multi-Function Displays are clearly shown, as well as the Data Entry Panel (top center).
McDonnell Douglas Aeronautical Systems

another excellent design effort by Eugene Adam and his team at McDonnell Douglas. In the front seat, the pilot has a wide field-of-view HUD and three Multi-Function Displays (MFDs), two monochrome/green and one full-color, in addition to the normal controls you would encounter in an F-15C. Each MFD functions like a computer monitor that can show data clearly even in bright daylight, and has an array of selection buttons mounted on all four sides of the bezel. The HOTAS controls have been upgraded to support the extra capabilities of the -E model's APG-70 radar, as well as the Low Altitude Navigation and Targeting Infrared for Night (LANTIRN) system pods (which we will look at later). To the right of the HUD is the display for the Improved Data Modem (IDM), a sort of low-speed data link which is tied to the onboard Have Quick II radios and the weapons delivery system. It is designed to be part of the joint-service Automatic Target Hand-Off System (ATHS), which allows the F-15E to automatically send and receive targeting coordinates to and from a number of other U.S. Army, Marine, and Air Force systems, including the F-16C, the OH-58D Kiowa Warrior, the AV-8V Harrier II, the AH-64A Apache, and the Army's TACFIRE artillery control system. In lieu of a JTIDS terminal (which is planned for installation later), it is a capable little device for getting targeting information from a variety of sources. In the rear cockpit, delivery of air-to-ground ordnance is the WSO's main job, and the best tool for this is the same Hughes APG-70 radar that is on -C model Eagle, though it has a number of added features unique to the Strike Eagle. The radar data, as well as data from the onboard LANTIRN pods, are displayed on four MFDs—two color and two monochrome/green—in the rear cockpit. An onboard videotape recorder serves as the "gun camera," recording whatever appears in the HUD, or on any of the selected MFDs.

Along with the radar, the WSO also controls the same ALQ-135 internal jammer package, ALE-45/47 decoy launchers, ALR-56M RWR, APX-101 IFF

A heads-on view of a McDonnell Douglas F-15E Strike Eagle from the 366th Wing's 391st Fighter Squadron. The two Lockheed Martin Low Altitude Navigation and Targeting Infrared for Night (LANTIRN) system pods are mounted on pylons under the engine inlets, with a pair of Mk 84 general-purpose bombs mounted on hard points under the two Conformal Fuel Tanks (CFTs). There is also a Sidewinder air-to-missile training round on the port wing weapons pylon. *JOHN D. GRESHAM*

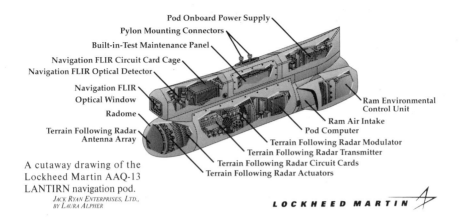

Pod Onboard Power Supply
Pylon Mounting Connectors
Built-in-Test Maintenance Panel
Navigation FLIR Circuit Card Cage
Navigation FLIR Optical Detector
Navigation FLIR
Optical Window
Radome
Terrain Following Radar
Antenna Array

Ram Environmental
Control Unit
Ram Air Intake
Pod Computer
Terrain Following Radar Modulator
Terrain Following Radar Transmitter
Terrain Following Radar Circuit Cards
Terrain Following Radar Actuators

A cutaway drawing of the
Lockheed Martin AAQ-13
LANTIRN navigation pod.
Jack Ryan Enterprises, Ltd.,
by Laura Alpher

LOCKHEED MARTIN

system, as on the -C model Eagle, along with the other avionics. Provisions are currently being made in the F-15Es flight software and on the data bus for a GPS receiver and the JTIDS secure data link, which will be added later in the 1990s. Another planned upgrade may be a satellite communications system, which would allow ground-based commanders to stay in contact with aircraft on the most distant missions.

The engine bays of the F-15E were designed with a common interface to accommodate either the standard Pratt & Whitney F100-PW-220 turbofan or the more powerful F100-PW-229, which can deliver up to 29,000 lb./13,181 kg. of thrust. All this thrust means that in "clean" configuration at high altitude, the F-15E's maximum speed is Mach 2.5. At low altitude, with a maximum bomb load, the weapons impose a practical limit around 490 knots/564 mph./908 kph. The maximum unrefueled combat radius of the F-15E depends very much on the flight profile, but a typical figure is about 790 nm./1,445 km. using 3,475 gallons/13,100 liters of internal fuel (including that in the CFT packs) and three 610 gallon/2,300 liter external tanks. For truly long-range missions, tanker support is essential to the Strike Eagle, though the F-15E needs less of this than other strike aircraft.

Lockheed Martin AAQ-13/14 LANTIRN System

I commented on how close our wing tip was to the trees. [The pilot] responded, "It's worse in the daytime. You can see every chipmunk...."

Aviation Week Pilot Report, F16/LANTIRN
April 25, 1988

The Lockheed Martin (formerly Martin Marietta) Low Altitude Navigation and Targeting Infrared for Night (LANTIRN) system consists of a pair of cylindrical pods that fit on stubby pylons under the forward fuselage of the F-15E and selected F-16s. The AAQ-13 navigation pod weighs 430 lb./195 kg.;

the AAQ-14 targeting pod weighs 540 lb./245 kg.; and the software that integrates them with the aircraft flight controls and weapons weighs nothing at all. LANTIRN combines a host of electro-optical and computer technologies to do something quite simple: turn night into day for the crew of a strike fighter. Under a $2.9 billion contract awarded in 1985, Martin Marietta delivered 561 navigation pods and 506 targeting pods, plus support equipment, to the U.S. Air Force. At one time, there were plans to integrate the system on the A-10, and possibly the B-1B, but this is now unlikely, due to budget constraints. The complete LANTIRN system adds about $4 million to the cost of the aircraft; not a high price for turning night into day.

The AAQ-13 navigation pod includes a Texas Instruments Ku-band terrain-following radar (TFR) and forward-looking infrared (FLIR) sensor that turns heat emitted by objects into a visible image. The pod generates video imagery and symbology for the pilot's Heads-Up Display (HUD) for a field-of-view of 21° by 28°. The image is grainy, but the sense of depth is good enough to fly by in total darkness or the smoke of a battlefield. Rain, fog, or snow, however, degrade the performance of the system, since infrared energy is attenuated by aerosols or water vapor. The TFR in the AAQ-13 pod can be linked directly to the aircraft's autopilot to automatically maintain a preset altitude down to 100 feet/30.5 meters while flying over virtually any kind of terrain. For manual operations it projects a "fly-to box" on the HUD, so that all the pilot needs to do is keep the plane's centerline aimed at the "fly-to box" to safely clear obstacles. It is even possible to land the plane safely at night without runway lights, simply by viewing the different infrared signatures of the painted strips on the runway surface! By flicking a HOTAS switch on the control stick, the pilot can "snap look" left, right, up, or down, either in level flight or in a banked turn. Another switch selects "black hot" or "white hot," allowing the pilot to choose whichever mode provides the best image contrast.

The AAQ-14 targeting pod includes another FLIR in a two-axis turret, with a selectable wide or narrow field-of-view, and a laser designator/

A cutaway drawing of the Lockheed Martin AAQ-14 LANTIRN Targeting Pod.

JACK RYAN ENTERPRISES, LTD., BY LAURA ALPHER

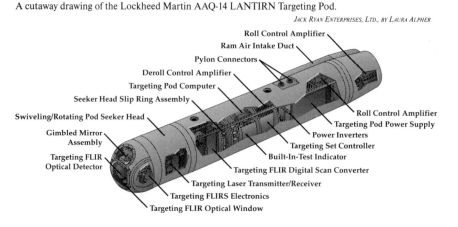

Roll Control Amplifier
Ram Air Intake Duct
Pylon Connectors
Deroll Control Amplifier
Targeting Pod Computer
Seeker Head Slip Ring Assembly
Swiveling/Rotating Pod Seeker Head
Gimbled Mirror Assembly
Targeting FLIR Optical Detector
Roll Control Amplifier
Targeting Pod Power Supply
Power Inverters
Targeting Set Controller
Built-In-Test Indicator
Targeting FLIR Digital Scan Converter
Targeting Laser Transmitter/Receiver
Targeting FLIRS Electronics
Targeting FLIR Optical Window

rangefinder. The targeting pod FLIR displays its imagery on a small video screen in the cockpit; it can be aimed independently of the navigation pod FLIR and used like a telescope to identify terrain features or targets at fairly long ranges. The targeting pod's laser designator can then "illuminate" targets for laser-guided bombs like the Paveway III-series (described later). It can also lock on to moving targets and track them automatically, as well as designate ground targets for AGM-65 Maverick missiles (which use either TV or imaging infrared guidance). In fact, it is possible to designate targets for multiple Maverick shots in a single pass. The laser can also be used to determine the exact range to a landmark in order to update the aircraft's inertial navigation system; this is critical for the accurate delivery of all kinds of ordnance (guided and unguided) without visual references. For training, the targeting pod laser has a special low-energy "eye-safe" mode, which suggests that the full power of the AAQ-14's laser could potentially blind ground troops. Although LANTIRN targeting was designed for air-to-ground weapons delivery, there is nothing to prevent the crew from using the capabilities of the system in air-to-air combat. Modern Russian aircraft like the MiG-29 and Su-27 have an Infrared Search and Track System (IRST) mounted in a small hemispherical fairing forward of the cockpit that allows for detection and targeting of enemy aircraft without radar emissions that might alert the potential victim. It is likely that AAQ-14 pod has a similar potential, although it is not certain how well this is supported by the current software.

Despite delays in the LANTIRN program, one wing of seventy-two F-16s (out of some 249 deployed) was equipped for LANTIRN during Desert Storm, with the AAQ-13 navigation pod. Forty-eight F-15Es deployed to the Persian Gulf; all of these had the navigation pod, and about a dozen received AAQ-14 targeting pods, rushed into service directly from the factory. LANTIRN made it possible to fly safely, at low level, at night, across featureless desert terrain, without the need for high-powered navigation aids, such as the APG-70 ground-mapping radar, which might have alerted enemy sensors. Many of the LANTIRN combat sorties flown by the F-15Es and F-16Cs were devoted to the "Great SCUD Hunt" in the western desert of Iraq.

Flying the F-15E Strike Eagle

The first time they go to an airshow featuring the USAF Thunderbirds, the USN Blue Angels, or perhaps the RAF Red Arrows, many boys and girls dream of flying the kind of high performance aircraft they see there. When we went out to visit the 366th Wing at Mountain Home AFB, there was an invitation waiting for just such a ride, in the aircraft of our choice—F-15 Eagle, F-15E Strike Eagle, or F-16 Fighting Falcon. Now, it's no secret that I'm not much of a fan of powered flight, much less sitting on top of an explosive ejection seat ready to launch me from the airplane! I've turned down a number of such offers over the years, the most tempting of these being an F-16 ride from my old friend Brigadier General "Tony" Tolin, who once commanded the F-117 Wing out in

Nevada. Luckily, my researcher John Gresham has no such qualms, and all but left tread marks on the ground when he was informed of the opportunity.

His first choice of aircraft was something of a "no-brainer," being one of the powerful F-15E Strike Eagles flown by the 391st FS, the "Bold Tigers." Thus, several days before we flew down to Nellis AFB, Nevada, for Green Flag 94-3, we all went down to the 391st FS headquarters building to watch him suit up and go on his flight. The first stop was to meet Lieutenant Colonel Frank W. "Claw" Clawson, the 391st's commanding officer, who gave John the opportunity to choose who would chauffeur him around the sky this day. John, no fool, asked for one of the senior pilots in the squadron, and got one of the best, Lieutenant Colonel Roger "Boom-Boom" Turcott, the squadron's operations officer. This decided, we were shuttled off to get ready for his adventure.

First stop was a quick check from the squadron flight surgeon. After a look with a stethoscope and blood pressure cuff, he was pronounced fit for "limited, low-altitude flight." This is because he does not have a current altitude chamber card (issued after an annual pressure chamber test to certify a flyer's tolerance to the low pressures above 15,000 feet/4,572 meters altitude), or a centrifuge certification (similar to the chamber card) which would allow him to pull the maximum Gs that the modern USAF is capable of pulling. Not that any of this was going to be a limitation, for the flight he was going on was to be an actual low-altitude training flight, practicing bomb and missile deliveries on the 366th's range at Saylor Creek, some twenty miles from the base. As the medical officer was finishing, he smiled and said he would see John afterwards, just in case he needed something for nausea or anything else.

The next stop was the cockpit simulator, which is kept in a small room in the headquarters building. Here, we were met by Captain Rob Evans, who ran us through what John would be doing in the backseat of Boom-Boom's aircraft. Evans then demonstrated what not to touch unless directed to by the pilot (the stick, throttles, and ejection seat handles being key items!), and how to use the ACES II ejection seat in the event of an emergency. It is incredibly simple actually. All you have to do is straighten yourself up in the seat and pull one of the two yellow ejection-seat handles. The canopy transparency is then jettisoned, and the seats eject, the WSO's first, followed by the pilot's. From that point on, everything happens pretty much automatically, including seat separation and parachute deployment.

Now it was time for the preflight briefing. Moving over to the squadron briefing room, John sat down with Boom-Boom, Claw, and the other five crewmen who would be on the flight. One thing that was made clear to us was that with training dollars as scarce as hen's teeth these days, this mission was going to run exactly like any other training sortie. Every part of the planned flight was discussed, and then loaded from a planning computer onto a 32K data transfer module (DTM) cartridges. All Boom-Boom would have to do is stick the DTM into a small slot in the front cockpit of the F-15E, and the bird would pretty much know where to go, what to do, and how to do it. Flight and equipment safety rules were restated and reinforced. Finally, as the meeting broke up, each of the other aircrews wished John a hearty "good luck," and then we headed down to the 391st Life Support Shop.

The Life Support Shop is so named because its equipment is absolutely vital to sustaining life in the variety of conditions that a combat pilot may encounter. These can range from the freezing temperatures and oxygen starvation of high altitudes to staying afloat in the water following an ejection. The technicians in the Life Support Shop tend to take a holistic approach to fitting gear to a particular individual, and watching them fit John with his gear was like seeing a turtle getting fitted with a new custom-made shell. You start with underwear, which can just be what you wear normally. While some pilots do wear Nomex (a fire-resistant fabric produced by Dupont) long underwear, especially in cold weather, the bulk of them wear normal "jockey-style" briefs and undershirts, though the new crop of female tactical aviators also usually wear a firm sports bra to help ward off the effects of Gs on those sensitive areas. Aircrews also like to wear thick socks to help their boots fit well and to keep their feet warm in the event of a cockpit heater failure. Next to go on is an olive-drab CWU-27/P flight suit, which is really comfortable and sharp-looking, considering that it is designed to resist flame for a period of time. It seems to have a million pockets for "stuff" all over the sleeves and legs, which John promptly began to fill with things needed for the coming flight. Most important of these were several small manila envelopes, containing plastic bags in case he suffered from the in-flight nausea and airsickness that is more common among flight crews than you might think. Stuffed in one of the leg pockets went another vital piece of survival gear, a "piddle pack." The male version of this item is basically a plastic zip-lock bag with a strip of dry sponge inside to soak up and hold the urine, while the female version is essentially a diaper which is donned before flight. Currently, the USAF is working hard to improve both models, which are vital on long missions and overseas deployments. Next come flight boots, the choice of which is left to the individual aircrews. For additional warmth, you can also add a Nomex CWU-36/P "summer" flight jacket, or even a rubberized "poopy suit" (the name is derived from the fact that when you sweat in one, there is nowhere for the moisture and odors to go!) for flying in arctic conditions over water. Along with the suit go a set of GS/FRP Nomex flying gloves, with leather palms, which are wonderfully comfortable.

On your head goes a cotton skull cap to help absorb sweat and keep your head cool, followed by one of the new USAF HGU-55 lightweight helmets. Weighing only about 30 oz./.85 kg., these are lighter and smaller than the older HGU-33, and are easier on the neck muscles during high-G maneuvers. The HGU-55 is equipped with the new MBU-12/P oxygen mask, which fits quite nicely, though John later wished that he had shaved his beard to get a tighter seal on his face. Once John's helmet was fitted, on came the G-suit, a girdle for the abdomen and legs. It is composed of a system of pneumatic bladders, which inflate to squeeze the lower body and keep blood from pooling there. This helps aircrews to better tolerate the G forces of high-performance aircraft

Series researcher John D. Gresham just prior to his ride in a McDonnell Douglas F-15E Strike Eagle of the 366th Wing's 391st Fighter Squadron. He is wearing a standard USAF issue HGU-55 lightweight flight helmet with an MBU-12/P oxygen mask and a CWU-27/U Nomex flight suit.

OFFICIAL U.S. AIR FORCE PHOTO

that can lead to a blackout.

At 1320 hours (1:20 PM), clad in what seemed like a mountain of clothing and equipment, Boom-Boom, John, and the rest of the training-flight aircrews boarded a blue step van to ride out the flight-line. Carrying his helmet and knee board in a green bag, and waddling out of the van with a decided stoop, John was helped into the rear cockpit. Meanwhile Boom-Boom completed a walka-round of the aircraft, an early-production F-15E, equipped with F100-PW-220 engines, which appears to have flown in the 1991 Persian Gulf War with the 4th Wing. While Boom-Boom completed his check, several technicians were strapping John in, making sure the various oxygen and telecommunications lines were properly hooked up. Both cockpits of the Strike Eagle are roomy and spacious, with lots of room for people who are John's size (he's over 6 feet 3 inches/1.9 meters tall). There's plenty of room to store personal gear, maps, and other things in a small compartment on the left, slightly behind the seat. On either side of the seat are the hand controllers for the sensor/weapons systems, with the control stick and throttle column exactly as they are in the front seat. The instrument panel is dominated by the four MFDs, the two outside screens being smaller color displays, while the two inner ones are larger monochrome "green" screens. What makes these MFDs unique is that unlike normal computer displays, they function perfectly well in bright daylight. The whole cockpit is laid out in an incredibly efficient manner. It just makes logical sense to do things that way.

By 1340 hours, Boom-Boom, John, and the rest of the crews were strapped in and ready to go. Boom-Boom then yelled to John to get ready for engine start, as the crew chief plugged in a special microphone/headset designed for use in areas with high noise levels. When he was ready, Boom-Boom fired up the engines with a whine and a roar and began to get the avionics spun up and settled. This took several minutes, as the navigation system aligned itself and the rest of the systems warmed up. In the cockpit, the ear-splitting noise is muffled by the helmets, headsets, and the aircraft structure, although you can feel the power almost immediately through your butt. It is something more than you feel with a powerful V-8 automobile engine...more like a motorcycle engine at full tilt. Both John and Boom-Boom snapped in the bayonet clips on their oxygen masks, and Boom-Boom turned up the air-conditioning system to keep a flow of cool air going into the rear cockpit to help keep John comfortable.

Around the cockpit, the various strip indicators and warning enunciators all switched to a "green" condition, and Boom-Boom called over the radio to ground control for permission to taxi down to the east end of the ramp. This done, at 1355 they followed the other three F-15Es down to the arming pit, where they parked for a time. There, the ordnance technicians removed the last of the safety arming pins from the BDU-33 practice bomb dispensers; and Claw Flight got ready to roll onto the runway. Sharing the pit were several F-16s from the 389th FS which were going out on their own training hop. Mountain Home is a busy place year-round, and this day was no exception. After about a ten minute wait, the final clearance for takeoff from the tower was received, and at 1415, Lieutenant Colonel Clawson rolled Claw-1 out to takeoff position. Pushing his engines to afterburner for takeoff, he was off the ground in a few thousand feet, and headed out over the south side of the base to wait for the rest of the flight to form up.

When their turn came, Boom-Boom and John in Claw-2 taxied to takeoff position, and Boom-Boom dropped the flaps and told John to grab the handlebar above the instrument panel and hang on. As Boom-Boom slid the throttles all the way forward, the twin F100 engines roared. Boom-Boom released the brakes, the afterburners belched flame, and the Strike Eagle literally leaped down the runway. Unlike airliners, which seem to take forever to accelerate to takeoff speed, the Strike Eagle seems to fling itself off of the earth. At 130 knots/241 kph., Boom-Boom rotated the aircraft upwards, and just seconds later, as they passed 166 knots/307 kph., they took off. As soon as they were off the ground, Boom-Boom retracted the landing gear and flaps, getting the Strike Eagle cleaned up for their flight to Saylor Creek Bombing Range; then he retarded the throttles to a more civil "dry" setting, to save fuel as well as wear and tear on the precious engines.

The feelings of flying in a high-performance fighter are fundamentally different from an airliner, even the supersonic Concorde. It's a raw, almost wild experience, like a ride on a Harley-Davidson motorcycle. The view out of the bubble transparency is simply amazing. You feel exposed, sitting as you do with your shoulders well above the canopy rails, almost sitting on top of the jet. And since low-level flight is where the Strike Eagle earns its pay, the feeling of the world going by in a hurry is more like a super-fast helicopter than any airliner you have ever ridden. It also needs to be said that flying the Strike Eagle is something like riding a wild horse: The older-style controls of the F-15E are a bit "twitchy" and require a delicate, almost "kissing" touch on the stick to keep the big bird from wallowing around the sky.

Boom-Boom Turcott has that soft touch, and he needed it this day; the air over the Idaho desert was decidedly unpleasant. While the base was under bright sunshine and a hard but steady wind, the range was under a heavy cloud cover, with intermittent snow and rain falling. This is a rough combination, and Boom-Boom was working hard to keep John from having to use one of the vomit bags in the pocket of his flight suit. In fact, several of the other WSOs in the flight were also having problems with motion sickness, and eyeing the bags in those little manila envelopes. Despite the popular notion that aircrews have cast-iron stomachs, almost every flier has occasional bouts of airsickness and vertigo. In fact, the ability to rapidly recover from such maladies is greatly respected among aircrews.

Meanwhile, as the flight transited out to the Saylor Creek Range, Boom-Boom took the opportunity to show John a few things about the territory, and about the F-15E. As they flew just a few thousand feet over the canyon of the Snake River, he had him power up and unstow the FLIR turret on the AAQ-14 targeting pod under the belly of the fighter. The crews of LANTIRN-equipped aircraft usually keep the targeting FLIR turrets in the stowed position, since dust and sand tend to pit and erode the optical windows. The targeting FLIR is normally controlled by the right-hand controller, and is aimed via a small dish-shaped switch which uses the WSO's finger movement, much like a mouse on a computer. There are also two other controls in this cluster, one called a "coolie hat" and the other the "rook" or "castle" controller, because of their shape and feel. These two manipulate the two right-hand displays, which show the FLIR video, radar displays, and other sensor and weapons-related data. There is an identical controller on the left side of the cockpit, which mostly controls the ring laser gyro-based INS. The INS drives the most noticeable and dynamic display, the left-side color MFD, called the moving-map display. This MFD displays a full-color navigational chart of where you are, where you are going, and how you are oriented.

Moving back to the right-hand controller, you find that with a little practice, the targeting FLIR is quite easy to use, and has a field-of-view that can see almost everything in the lower hemisphere of the Strike Eagle. There are also several magnification settings, which can easily allow you to determine what you are looking at from a considerable range. Once you get an object centered up in the scope, you can lock it up and the FLIR will track it, no matter what maneuvers the pilot chooses to lay onto the bird. This proved useful, as John found when Boom-Boom gave him a mild demonstration of the Strike Eagle's maneuvering capabilities by pulling some hard turns at one of the navigational waypoints; the FLIR stayed steady on a telephone pole on the desert floor below.

Even though they only pulled about 3 1/2 Gs in these maneuvers, it was a telling experience for John, who is a big, burly sort of man. It felt like everything on his body began to head towards his feet, and he found the movement of his lips and cheeks towards the bottom of his face particularly eerie. As soon as Boom-Boom would start a run and the Gs came on, the G-suit around his waist and legs inflated to keep the blood from pooling in his abdomen, thus avoiding a blackout. Despite the stresses of the Gs, John found that he still could work the controllers and continue doing the tasks Boom-Boom asked him to perform. In fact, one of the surprises was that despite his relative lack of experience with the LANTIRN system (and rising nausea), he was easily able to learn the routine with the controllers, and he even managed to fire up the APG-70 radar and lock up Colonel Clawson and his WSO (callsign "Fuzz") in Claw-1. He also managed to take a couple of SAR radar maps with the APG-70.

By then they were at the Saylor Creek Bombing Range, which was experiencing a series of intermittent snow/hail/rain showers. These made the air fairly rough during the runs that followed. Boom-Boom again followed Claw-1, and set up the arming panel to drop one BDU-33 practice bomb on each run. John's job on each run was to lock up the aiming point, so the video recorder could evaluate the accuracy of the run. This involved slewing the FLIR turret around until the desired target in the array was centered in the screen, and then selecting the lock button to start the system autotracking. At the same time, the ground-based television optical scoring system (TOSS) would score each bomb dropped. What followed was a pinwheel of F-15Es, with each making a run about every thirty seconds. Boom-Boom and John started each run by lining up the target array on the nose of Claw-2 and putting the aircraft into a shallow 15° dive. As soon as John would lock up the target with the targeting FLIR (or the APG-70 radar), the weapons delivery system would begin computing the proper course to the target. This was displayed to Boom-Boom as a steering cue on the HUD; all he had to do was aim the "fly to" box at the steering cue, and the computers did the rest. Despite the high crosswind in the target area, the crews of all four Strike Eagles were easily scoring "shacks" (direct hits) on their desired targets. The idea of this exercise was to see how accurately each crew could place a "dumb" bomb on the target, with the assistance of the Strike Eagle's weapons delivery systems. Despite the popular public notion that Desert Storm was a war won with "smart" munitions, the vast majority of the bombs dropped were unguided, and this will be the case for some time to come. Thus the need to stay in practice with the older-style weapons. After each run, Boom-Boom would pull Claw-2 off to the right and climb back to several thousand feet AGL to set up for the next run. Each time, as they banked overhead, Boom-Boom and John could see the runs of Claw-3 and -4 off to their right as they hit the ring of targets on the TOSS range.

When their supply of BDU-33s was expended, Claw Flight moved over to the Maverick missile target array a few miles away. The first of these was a circular array of oil drums (called Target 101). These showed up nicely on the targeting FLIR when warmed by the sun, which was breaking through the clouds from time to time. The 391st is the only Strike Eagle unit in the USAF equipped with the IIR Maverick missile, and they are quite skilled with it. Their tactic is to make side-by-side runs at the targets, two at a time, starting at 11 nm./20.1 km. with a 30° split and a 10° climb to the pushover at about 8 nm./14.6 km., then a 30° merge with a 5° dive at the weapons release point, and an egress (pilot talk for leaving) at about 2 nm./3.7 km. They then make a right-hand turn, with the number-two aircraft falling in behind the leader. This gives them time to acquire multiple targets, if desired, and hit them all on the same pass. Boom-Boom and John in Claw-2 made their first pass on the left side of the circular array, locking up three of the barrels and delivering three simulated missiles fairly successfully. It struck John then that less than an hour before, he had never touched an F-15E. Now he was delivering ordnance well enough to actually hit things.

Once Claw-3 and -4 had made their run on Target 101, the flight moved over to the Owyhee Pumping Station, which is also used as a target for the simulated missiles (the seeker heads are real, but do not fire). This time the WSOs of Claw-1 and -2, John and Fuzz, worked to lock up specific points on the pump house for the missiles to hit, thus producing a true precision strike, despite the rough air over the Idaho desert.

With the weapons practice finished, the flight headed back to land at Mountain Home AFB, some miles to the west. As they headed home, Boom-Boom was trying to coach John on some more procedures with the radar, but by this time the rough air had taken its toll, and John began to reach for the little manila envelope with the plastic bag in it. Boom-Boom was kind enough to keep the Strike Eagle level while John relieved himself—and felt better immediately. A few minutes later, they were in the Mountain Home AFB traffic pattern, preparing to land. With just a handful of aircraft in the pattern at this time of day, it took just a few minutes to contact the tower, gain clearance, drop into the landing pattern, and set up for landing.

The runway of a modern military airfield seems huge when you are approaching it in an aircraft the size of a fighter, and the vast tarmac almost seems wasted upon you, though as a passenger, you appreciate every square yard/meter of area to land upon. Boom-Boom made his approach with a practiced grace, in spite of a stiff crosswind that was crabbing the Strike Eagle to one side. As he flared the F-15E for touchdown, he extended the large airbrake, which acted like a drag parachute, rapidly slowing the jet to taxi speed. When you are taxiing one of the Eagle family, you almost feel as if you are up on stilts, and you wonder if you're going to fall over. It should be said, though, that the landing gear struts and brakes of the Strike Eagle are the toughest ever installed on a USAF tactical aircraft, and they work just fine!

After taxiing back to the 391st ramp, the crews of the four jets—including a somewhat wobbly and green-around-the-gills John Gresham—exited the aircraft. They immediately proceeded back to the Life Support Shop and turned in their gear for repair and maintenance. Though still a bit nauseous, John, smiling from ear-to-ear, proclaimed, "God can take an arm or leg or whatever he wants. I've done what I always wanted to do!" As if on cue, the 391st flight surgeon showed up and asked if he wanted something for his nausea. When John replied in the affirmative, the flight surgeon handed him a small pill bottle of Phenergan, which settles the stomach and the inner ears. Later that day, after a nap and a shower, he was up and around, enthusiastically describing his adventure.

When we asked what he thought about flying in the big bird, this was his answer: "If I had to go to a war and didn't know where or against whom, I'd want to take that plane with Boom-Boom as the driver!"

Lockheed Martin F-16C Fighting Falcon

The F-16 was the workhorse of this war. It did the baseline bombing, the body punching. It hauled the iron.

General Chuck Horner, USAF (Ret.)

Officially it's the Fighting Falcon, but to its pilots it's the Viper (after the fighters in the TV series *Battlestar Galactica*) or the "Electric Jet" (because of its digital flight-control system). To millions of Americans who attend airshows, however, it's one of the Thunderbirds: six F-16Cs with some of the finest aerobatic flight crews in the world (a statement that is sure to start a debate if any Naval aviators are reading this). It is the Lockheed (formerly General Dynamics) F-16, the most successful fighter design—at least in terms of production numbers—in the last quarter century. Its existence came about when the USAF leadership realized in the 1970s that America no longer had unlimited funds to spend on airplanes and that a compromise between cost and capability was needed. For many years, military planners have known that the cost of combat aircraft is roughly proportional to their weight. If you want to buy more aircraft for the same budget, the solution seems obvious—design a lightweight fighter. "Light" and "heavy" are relative terms; the typical standard for comparing aircraft is maximum gross takeoff weight.

A lightweight fighter might not have all the "bells and whistles" that engineers can think up, but a no-frills aircraft is better than no aircraft at all; and for the cost of one heavyweight fighter you might buy two no-frills aircraft that together should be able to outfly and outfight one heavy one. This became the central dogma of the "Lightweight Fighter Mafia," a group of Air Force and Pentagon officials gathered around the charismatic John Boyd, an Air Force colonel who codified the original concept of energy maneuvering (using power and speed in the vertical dimension to outmaneuver another aircraft) and had been a prime mover in the F-15 program office. During the Vietnam War, lightweight enemy aircraft like the MiG-17 and MiG-21 were often able to outmaneuver and kill heavy multi-role U.S. fighters like the F-4 Phantom and F-105, despite the Americans' advantages of speed, sensors, and weaponry. Though these losses were in great part caused by the restrictive ROE that were set by politicians, the Air Force was determined to stop that from happening again. Thus, while the new USAF lightweight fighter might not have ultra-long range or super-sophisticated electronics, it would for damn sure be more agile than any MiG flying.

The lightweight fighter competition came down to a flyoff between two excellent designs, the General Dynamics Model 401, and the Northrop YF-17;

TOP: A Lockheed Martin Block 52F-16C assigned to the 366th Wing's 389th Fighter squadron cruises over the Nevada desert during Green Flag 94-3. It carries a simulated Sidewinder air-to-air missile and a range instrumentation pod on the wingtips, an ALQ-131 electronic jamming pod on the centerline, as well as fuel tanks and Mk 82 general-purpose bombs on the wing pylons.

JOHN D. GRESHAM

BELOW: A head-on view of a Lockheed Martin Block 52 F-16C Fighting Falcon. The large engine inlet and bubble canopy are clearly shown, as well as the two large 370 gallon/1,396.2 liter external fuel tanks.

JOHN D. GRESHAM

NEXT PAGE: A cutaway drawing of the Lockheed Martin F-16C Block 50/52 Fighting Falcon.

JACK RYAN ENTERPRISES, LTD., BY LAURA ALPHER

Tail Warning Antenna
Anti-Collision Light

Vertical Stabilizer
Rudder
Rudder Servo Actuator
Afterburner Nozzle
Split Airbrake
(Port and Starboard)
Horizontal Stabilizer
(Port and Starboard)
Static Dischargers

Rudder Servo Actuator

F100-PW-220/229 or
F110-GE-120/129 Turbofan Engine

Mk 82 500 lb./227 kg. Bombs
on a Triple Ejection Rack
(Port and Starboard)

Static Dischargers
Trailing Edge Flaps
(Port and Starboard)

370 Gallon/1,700 Liter Fuel Tanks (Port and Starboard)
M61 20mm Vulcan Cannon
20mm Cannon
Ammunition Feed

Ventral Fins (Port and Starboard)
AIM-9M Sidewinders
(Port and Starboard)
In-Flight Refueling Receptacle
Hydraulic System
20mm Cannon Ammunition
Drum (500 Rounds)

Cannon
Nozzle
Engine Inlet
Port Instrument Panel

ACES II Ejection Seat
Cockpit Transparency
Heads-Up Display
Instrument Panel
Radar Warning
Receiver Antennas
Radome

Weapons Control Avionics
APG-68 Radar Electronics
APG-68 Radar Antenna Array

Radome

and in February 1974, General Dynamics's entry won. The design was a slightly enlarged Model 401, and the prototype was designated YF-16. The competing twin-engined YF-17 ultimately became the basis for the McDonnell Douglas F/A-18 Hornet.

One key design element of the Model 401 was accepting the risk of only one engine—you have to have a lot of confidence in that engine. At the same time, one reason the YF-16 was the winner against the Northrop entry was the matter of that single engine. GD made the decision early to use the same Pratt & Whitney F100-series engine that was on the F-15 Eagle, thus providing a great deal of risk reduction and savings for the Air Force. Risk reduction because it was using an already proven engine design that was in USAF service, and savings because of the economies of greater production numbers and a wider user base.

The first production F-16, officially named the "Fighting Falcon," was delivered to the Air Force in August 1978, and the first full wing, the 388th TFW at Hill AFB, Utah, became operational in October 1980. Meanwhile, by eliminating some 17% of the internal fuel capacity, General Dynamics was able to squeeze in a second seat under an enlarged canopy, creating the F-16B operational trainer (later replaced by the more advanced F-16D). The U.S. Air Force eventually ordered some 121 F-16Bs, and 206 F-16Ds.

One advantage of a small fighter is that you are a small target: hard to spot visually and on radar, as well as hard to hit. The blended wing-body of the F-16 helps to reduce its radar cross section, but the gaping air intake, large vertical tail fin, and the need to carry weapons and pods externally mean that it is by no means a stealth aircraft. About 95% of the structure is made up of conventional aircraft aluminum alloys in order to simplify manufacturing and keep costs down. Production of the F-16A and -B models for the USAF ended in 1985, when the F-16C/D models began to roll off the mile-long assembly line at Fort Worth, Texas. In addition to the letters that designate major F-16 variants (like the F-16C), there are "Block" numbers that describe particular production batches. The current version (since October 1991) is the Block 50/52. In 1994, General Dynamics sold its Ft. Worth, Texas, aircraft factory to Lockheed, which will continue to produce the F-16 through at least 1999. When production ends, over four thousand F-16s will have been delivered.

One reason the F-16 has been so successful is its fly-by-wire flight control system. On most aircraft, when you move the stick or rudder pedals, you are working mechanical linkages tied to a series of hydraulic actuators that move the control surfaces of the wings and tail. This is similar to the brakes on a car. When you hit the brake pedal, you are not directly applying pressure to the wheels; you are opening a hydraulic valve (the master cylinder) that allows stored mechanical energy to apply a lot more force to the brake pads than your foot could ever deliver. Just as the feel of the brake pedal, when integrated with the perception of deceleration (or the lack of it), conveys important information to a driver, the feel of the control stick provides vital feedback to the pilot. In fly-by-wire the mechanical linkages in the flight-control system are replaced

The cockpit of a Lockheed Martin Block 50/52 F-16C Fighting Falcon. Just above the pilot's knees are the two Multi-Function Displays (MFDs), with the Heads-Up Display (HUD) mounted on top of the Data Entry Panel. *LOCKHEED MARTIN*

with a tightly integrated set of electro-mechanical force sensors and computer software that translates the pilot's movement of the stick into precisely regulated electronic commands. These are sent over a quad-redundant (i.e. four-channel) data bus to the hydraulic actuators that move the control surfaces, causing the plane to pitch, roll, or yaw as desired. The flight computer software regulates all this without allowing dangerous or excessive excursions that might cause the plane to "depart controlled flight." All F-16A/B aircraft and F-16C/Ds before Block 40 had an analog flight control system; subsequent aircraft have an improved digital system.

One major benefit of fly-by-wire is weight reduction, since mechanical cables and pulleys can now be replaced by slim electrical signal lines, and even fiber optical cable ("fly-by-light") in newer systems. Another benefit has been a dream of aircraft designers ever since the Wrights flew their first airplanes—the creation of aerodynamically unstable aircraft. Prior to fly-by-wire systems, all aircraft were designed to be neutrally stable or balanced in the air, so that only a small trimming was required to keep it flying. While this is fine for an airliner or transport aircraft, it is not necessarily what is desired for a combat aircraft like a fighter. Ideally, you want a fighter to be quick and agile—right on the edge of disaster—so that it can react more quickly than other aircraft. With the coming of fly-by-wire control systems, aircraft designers can actually make an aircraft so dynamically unstable that a human being cannot even fly it. The flight software of the system can make adjustments to the attitude and trim of an unstable aircraft many times a second, thus rendering it stable through sheer quickness on the part of the computer.

The unique characteristics of the fly-by-wire flight control system allowed the General Dynamics engineers to do a number of new things to the cockpit of the F-16. The ACES II ejection seat, for example, is reclined at an angle of 30°, since this helps to reduce the frontal cross section of the aircraft, which cuts drag and is also more comfortable, especially when pulling high-G maneuvers. The single-piece bubble canopy provides better all-around visibility than any modern fighter aircraft in the world. Remember that most planes shot down in combat never see their opponent sneaking up from behind or below. The lack of normal hydraulic runs means that the control stick can be mounted on the right side of the cockpit, instead of the usual position between the pilot's legs, which eases the strain on the pilot during maneuvers. Mounted on the right armrest, the "side stick" controller is a force-sensing device which requires only light pressure to execute large and rapid maneuvers.

The throttle column is on the left armrest, and both it and the side stick are studded with the same kind of HOTAS radar, weapon, and communications switches as the F-15, and are optimized for operations in high-G maneuvers. In front of the pilot is a small but busy control panel, with the HUD mounted on top, the display for the RWR to its left, and the IDM display (called a Data Entry Display) on the right. Below this is a center pedestal that runs between the pilot's legs. It contains most of the analog flight instruments (artificial horizon, airspeed indicator, etc.), the data keypad (called an Integrated Control Panel), and a pair of MFDs, one on either side of the pedestal.

You can hang a lot of weaponry—up to ten tons of it—on an F-16, if you're willing to pay the costs. These include increased drag, which translates into decreased range, endurance, speed, and agility. However, even when heavily loaded, an F-16 is a dangerous opponent, as a number of Iraqi and Serbian pilots have found out the hard way. On the wing tips are launch rails for AIM-9 Sidewinder AAM or AIM-120 AMRAAM. About 270 F-16s assigned to Air Defense units of the Air National Guard also have the software and radar modifications needed to launch the AIM-7 Sparrow, though this older AAM is rapidly being phased out of service in favor of the newer AIM-120. Under each wing are three hard points where pylons can be installed to carry additional missiles, bombs, pods, or fuel tanks.

Another station under the centerline of the fuselage usually carries a fuel tank, but can also be fitted with an electronic jamming pod (the ALQ-131 or ALQ-184) or (in the future) a reconnaissance pod. All F-16s have an M61 Vulcan 20mm cannon located inside the port strake, with over five hundred rounds of ammunition in a drum magazine just behind the cockpit. The muzzle exhaust of the gun is well clear of the engine air intake to avoid any ingestion of gun gasses.

The F-16's sharply pointed nose provides limited space for a radar antenna, so the designers of the Westinghouse APG-66 radar had to use cleverness rather than brute force to get the performance that was required. This included the ability to launch air-to-air missiles, aim the gun, drop bombs, and deliver air-to-ground missiles. When it was finished, the entire APG-66 installation weighed only 260 lb./115 kg., and it was one of the first airborne radars to use a digital signal processor, translating the stream of analog data from the X-band pulse-Doppler receiver, filtering out clutter, and displaying simplified symbology in the pilot's HUD or one of the display panels. In the "look down" mode, the new radar could scan the ground 23 to 35 nm./45.7 to 64 km. ahead, while in "look up" mode it could search the air as far as 29 to 46 nm./53 to 84.1 km.; the higher figures represent performance under ideal conditions, while the lower figures are worst-case maximums. The solid reliability and modular design of this radar has allowed it to be modified for installation on a wide variety of aircraft and other platforms, including the Rockwell B-1B bomber, and the tethered "aerostat" balloons that scan the skies of the U.S. southern borders for drug-smuggling aircraft.

Even as the early-model Fighting Falcons were going into general service, improvements were already being contemplated for the F-16. These became the F-16C and -D (the two-seat trainer), which had a number of sub-variants or Blocks which first came into series production in 1985. The first major set of upgrades were incorporated into the Block 25 F-16Cs, which had an improved cockpit, a new wide-angle HUD, and the new APG-68 radar system. The following year, the Block 30/32-series birds appeared with a bigger computer memory, new fuel tanks, and the same kind of common engine bay that's on the F-15E. This means that either the General Electric F110-GE-100 (Block 30) or the Pratt & Whitney F100-PW-220 (Block 32) engine can be fitted, with only minor changes between the two variants. The biggest of these is a larger engine inlet for the F110-powered variant, which can be easily changed. In addition, the inlet of both variants, always a major contributor to the F-16's RCS, has been specially treated with several radar absorbing material (RAM) coatings, which radically reduces its detectability. The next major variant (it appeared in 1989) was the Block 40 (F110)/42 (F100) version, which had the new enhanced enveloped gunsight (like the F-15C/E), APG-68V5 radar and ALE-47 decoy launchers, a GPS receiver, and provisions for a higher gross weight (42,300 lb./19,227.3 kg.). Following this (in 1991) was the Block 50/52 version, which made use of a pair of new technology, higher thrust engines (29,000 lb./13,182 kg.), the General Electric F-110-GE-129 installed in Block 50 birds, and the Pratt & Whitney F100-PW-229 in the Block 52s. In addition to the new engines, the Block 50/52 F-16s were equipped with a new ALR-56M RWR and a MIL-STD-1760 data bus for programming new-generation PGMs. The latest, and probably final, production variant is the Block 50D/52D version, equipped with a new 128K DLD cartridge, a ring laser gyro INS, an improved data modem (IDM) like the F-15E, and the ability to fire the latest versions of the AGM-65 Maverick and AGM-88 HARM missiles.

On the Block 15 and later models of the F-16, there are two special mounting points on either "cheek" of the air intake that can support sensors such as the LANTIRN system pods (targeting on one side, navigation on the other), the ASQ-213 HARM targeting system (HTS) pod, the Atlis II targeting pod, the Pave Penny laser tracking pod, or future precision targeting devices. The HTS pod has opened up a whole new mission for the Viper. Only 8 in./20 cm. in diameter, 56 in./142 cm. long, and weighing 85 lb./36 kg., it fits on the right-side cheek mount (Station 5 as it is called), where the AAQ-14 LANTIRN pod would normally hang. Originally developed by Texas Instruments under a program to provide new modular targeting systems for USAF aircraft, it is the key to USAF's effort to hold onto some kind of SAM hunting capability in the 21st century. This is particularly vital, given the age of the F-4G Wild Weasel fleet, which is rapidly drawing down. The HTS pod allows the pilot of a single-seat F-16C to do just about everything a two-seat F-4G can do with its APR-47 RWR system. Most important of these is the ability to rapidly generate ranges to target radars, as well as to provide greater discretion between different types of enemy radars. Lockheed is even working on a new version of the F-16 flight software which will allow two or more F-16s with HTS pods, GPS receivers, and IDMs (acting as data links) to work together so they can generate more accurate targeting solutions, and even feed them to other HARM-equipped aircraft with IDMs. This matter of establishing ranges to target radars is vitally important since standoff range for an AGM-88 can be roughly doubled if you know this before launch and can program it into the HARM. It also reduces the time of flight for a HARM, by allowing the missile to fly a more direct path. About a hundred of the HTS pods were manufactured and delivered by Texas Instruments (who also manufacture the AGM-88 HARM), and have been assigned to several F-16 units within ACC and overseas units.

Beginning with the -C and -D models of the F-16, a new radar, the Westinghouse APG-68, has been installed, with higher reliability (very low false alarm rate, and up to 250 hours' mean time between failure), much greater computer capacity, increased range out to 80 nm./146.3 km., improved countermeasures against enemy jamming, and a special sea search mode for operation against naval targets. The radar can scan a 120° arc horizontally and 2, 4, or 6 "bars" in elevation (each bar being about 1.5° in elevation). These enhancements came at the cost of increased weight—an extra 116 lb./53 kg. The APG-68 offers a lot of choices for a single hard-working pilot, especially in the stress of combat. Fortunately for the pilot, their favorite radar mode presets (along with many other system settings) can be programmed on a mission-planning computer and stored in a DTU cartridge (Data Transfer Unit, much like the DTD on the F-15E Strike Eagle) which snaps into a socket in the cockpit. Designed for continuous upgrading, the APG-68 will eventually provide automatic terrain following, integrated with the aircraft flight control system, a high-resolution synthetic aperture mode (SAR) like the APG-70 on the F-15E, and perhaps even NCTR capabilities. Another possibility is the retrofitting of a radar with an electronically scanned antenna like the APG-77 planned for the F-22 (the present antenna is mechanically scanned in azimuth and elevation by electric motors). All of this translates into a radar as capable as anything flying today, at relatively low cost, volume, and weight.

Because a large number of Fighting Falcons have been sold overseas, an early trial in combat for the little jet was virtually guaranteed. In July 1980, the Israeli Air Force (Hel Avir) received its first F-16s, after an eleven-hour, six-thousand-mile ferry flight from New Hampshire. Within months, the new birds had gone into combat. The highlights of these early actions were the raid on the Osiris nuclear reactor complex near Baghdad in 1981, and the huge air-to-air victory over the Syrian Air Force in what has come to be called the "Bekka Valley Turkey Shoot" over Lebanon. And Pakistani Air Force F-16s scored more than a dozen air-to-air victories against Soviet and Afghan aircraft during the war in Afghanistan.

And then there was "the Storm." During Desert Storm, the performance of the F-16 was something of a disappointment, despite some 13,500 combat sorties that delivered over twenty thousand tons of ordnance. Part of the problem was the rotten weather, for the F-16 is optimized as a clear-weather day fighter. Another part of the problem was the reluctance of the Iraqi Air Force to come out and get killed in air-to-air duels (the F-16 is very capable as an air superiority machine). But the greatest problem was the lack of LANTIRN precision targeting pods. Only seventy-two of the 249 F-16s in the theater had this vital system, and they only had the AAQ-13 navigation pod, and not the AAQ-14 targeting pod. The F-16's bomb delivery software and the training of the pilots had been optimized for low-level attacks, where even the dumbest bombs can be delivered with some accuracy. But the volume of Iraqi ground fire led Coalition air commanders to decree that bombing runs would be made from medium altitude (12,000 to 15,000 feet/3,657.6 to 4,572 meters), an environment where the F-16 was at that time definitely *not* optimized. Reportedly, software modifications to the weapons delivery system have overcome these shortcomings. However, since that time the F-16 has shined, obtaining six air-to-air kills over Iraqi and Serbian aircraft trying to operate in United Nations mandated no-fly zones, as well as gaining the capabilities inherent to the LANTIRN and ASQ-213 HTS pods.

One criticism of the F-16, compared to its competitors, is its relatively short unrefueled range. The Israelis use six-hundred-gallon external fuel tanks, which extend typical mission range 25 to 35%; but the U.S. Air Force has stuck with the standard 370 gallon tanks. Lockheed has recently developed a pair of conformal fuel tanks which hug the upper surface of the fuselage. To cope with the increased weight, the landing gear and brakes are being strengthened. This "enhanced strategic" version will reportedly be able to fly deep penetration missions like the F-15E.

There are other ideas to keep the F-16 alive. In the life cycle of any combat aircraft program, weight growth is almost inevitable, leading to a gradual loss of agility. Considerable research and development has gone into finding ways to compensate for this in the F-16. One experimental variant was the F-16XL, with a greatly enlarged "cranked arrow" delta wing. Another experiment was the Multi-Axis Thrust Vectoring (MATV) engine nozzle, which uses hydraulic actuators to deflect the exhaust up to 17° in any direction. A very promising future enhancement is an enlarged wing which could be the basis for a third generation of production Vipers.

The ultimate replacement for the F-16 is already evolving, under the acronym JAST, which stands for Joint Advanced Strike Technology. This is likely to be a single-seat, single-engine aircraft that may come into service sometime around 2010, if the Navy, Marines, and Air Force can manage to cooperate enough to impress Congress with the need for a new generation of manned combat aircraft. It will probably incorporate low-observables technologies, but not the super-stealthy features of the F-117, B-2, or F-22. Also, it may wind up using vectored thrust to achieve short takeoff and vertical landing.

Rockwell International B-1B Lancer

It may seem perverse to describe a bomber as sexy, but when you get up close to the B-1B, the sinuous curves and sculptural form of the airframe radiate an almost erotic energy, looking like smooth flawless skin over warm pulsing muscles rather than aluminum and composite panels riveted to steel and aluminum ribs. Pilots like to say that if a plane looks good, it flies good, and the B-1B proves the point. The plane holds most of the world records for time-to-altitude with heavy payloads, and it has flight characteristics more like a fighter plane than a bomber with twice the weight-carrying capacity of the classic B-52 Stratofortress which it was designed to replace.

Few modern aircraft programs have involved such bitter and protracted political battles as the B-1—or so many radical redesigns—and still made it into squadron service. The B-1 story began with the cancellation of the North American Rockwell XB-70 Valkyrie in 1964. This huge dart-shaped aircraft was designed to fly nuclear strike and reconnaissance missions at Mach 3 above 80,000 feet/24,384 meters. The growing effectiveness of American ICBMs and the Soviet development of surface-to-air missiles (as demonstrated by the downing of the U-2 flown by Francis Gary Powers in 1960) and high-speed, high-altitude interceptors like the MiG-25 threatened, it seemed, to make the manned bomber as obsolete as horse cavalry.

But there was still life in bombers. If there was no safety in high altitude, then a high-speed, low-level penetrator might still get through the thick wall of the Soviet air defense network, but only if a thicket of technical problems could be solved. Low-level means from 50 to 500 feet/15.2 to 152.4 meters above the ground, where the air is dense and you need a lot of power to push it aside. Simple enough over the Nevada salt flats perhaps; but in rough terrain, the mountains and hills are much denser, and you can't push them aside. You have to go up and over them, hugging the contours but avoiding the violent roller-coaster excursions that leave both crew and airframe overstressed, and fatigued.

Moreover, fuel considerations make it impossible for an aircraft to fly a low-level dash at supersonic speeds while still carrying a useful payload to a strategically meaningful range, say 7,500 nm./13,716 km. For reasonable fuel economy and fast transit to the enemy border, any new bomber would have to cruise at high subsonic speed above 25,000 feet/7,620 meters, before descending for the run in to the target. One way to achieve this goal is to use "variable geometry" wings. That is, you change the sweep angle of the wings to optimize lift and minimize drag under a wide range of flight conditions. Variable geometry has been successfully implemented on fighter-sized aircraft like the MiG-23 Flogger, F-111, F-14 Tomcat, and Panavia Tornado, but on a big bomber it requires actuators of enormous power and a pivot bearing of immense strength.

In 1970, the Air Force chose Rockwell International (formerly North American Aviation) to develop the "Advanced Manned Strategic Aircraft." It would be powered by four GE F101 turbofan engines, each rated at 30,000 lb./13,600 kg. thrust with afterburner. The first B-1A was rolled out on October 26th, 1974, and the Strategic Air Command (SAC) hoped to procure a total force of 240 of the new bombers to replace the B-52s that had worn themselves out over Vietnam. In those years of runaway inflation, the cost of the plane escalated rapidly, and the complex software-driven avionics system was plagued with the usual development problems inherent in the early systems of this type. Then in 1977, President Jimmy Carter canceled the program in favor of long-range cruise missiles launched from the existing fleet of B-52s. The four completed prototypes were nevertheless retained in service for testing, though one was eventually lost due to a crew error in regulating the aircraft's fuel supply and center-of-gravity, and another as a result of a collision with a pelican. Bird strikes are a major hazard to low flying aircraft. Like most tactical aircraft, the B-1 is designed to withstand high-speed collision with a 4-lb./1.8-kg. bird, even on the windscreen transparency. Unfortunately, at 600 knots/1,097.8 kph., the 15 lb./6.8 kg. pelican that hit the Test B-1 was a lethal projectile, taking out a significant part of the hydraulic system and causing the loss of the aircraft.

Meanwhile, by the end of the 1970s, the B-52s weren't getting any younger, and the SAC bomber force, with no follow-on replacement program, was facing obsolescence. As might be imagined, the SAC leadership lobbied hard to get the B-1 program back on track, with lots of support from Rockwell and those who believed in the continued importance and viability of the manned strategic bomber as part of the American nuclear triad (bombers, ICBM, and SLBMs). And in 1981 President Ronald Reagan announced the decision to build one hundred B-1B bombers—externally similar to the B-1A but radically redesigned in many respects. The production of those one hundred aircraft had been at the heart of his presidential campaign promise to rebuild the American military force to face down the Soviet Union in the 1980s. The first production bomber, christened the B-1B Lancer (after a

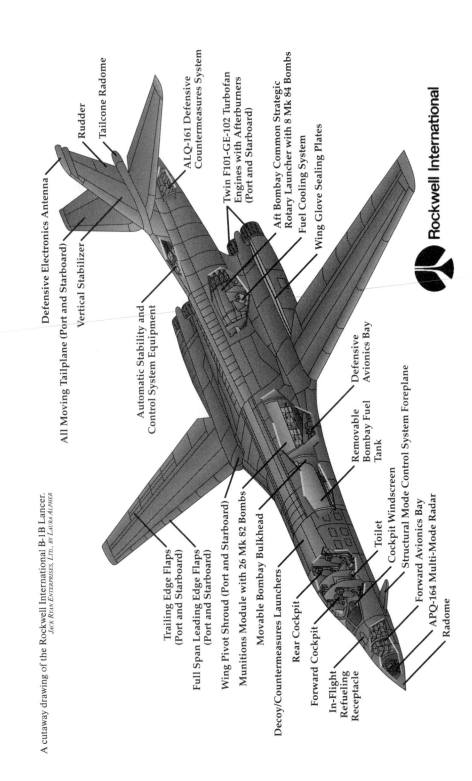

A cutaway drawing of the Rockwell International B-1B Lancer.
JACK RYAN ENTERPRISES, LTD., BY LAURA ALPHER

Defensive Electronics Antenna

All Moving Tailplane (Port and Starboard)

Rudder

Tailcone Radome

Vertical Stabilizer

ALQ-161 Defensive
Countermeasures System

Automatic Stability and
Control System Equipment

Twin F101-GE-102 Turbofan
Engines with Afterburners
(Port and Starboard)

Aft Bombay Common Strategic
Rotary Launcher with 8 Mk 84 Bombs

Fuel Cooling System

Wing Glove Sealing Plates

Trailing Edge Flaps
(Port and Starboard)

Full Span Leading Edge Flaps
(Port and Starboard)

Wing Pivot Shroud (Port and Starboard)

Munitions Module with 26 Mk 82 Bombs

Movable Bombay Bulkhead

Decoy/Countermeasures Launchers

Rear Cockpit

Forward Cockpit

In-Flight
Refueling
Receptacle

Removable
Bombay Fuel
Tank

Defensive
Avionics Bay

Toilet

Cockpit Windscreen

Structural Mode Control System Foreplane

Forward Avionics Bay

APQ-164 Multi-Mode Radar

Radome

Rockwell International

famous pre-World War II interceptor), rolled out of Rockwell's Palmdale, California, plant on September 4th, 1984, with the IOC of the first squadron being achieved on October 1st, 1986.

While it is officially designated the "Lancer," the B-1B's crews call it "the Bone." Currently, B-1B squadrons are based at Dyess AFB, Texas; Ellsworth AFB, South Dakota; and McConnell AFB, Kansas. In addition, the six B-1Bs of Ellsworth's 34th Bomb Squadron, now attached to the 366th Composite Wing, are hopefully scheduled to move to Mountain Home AFB in 1998, when expanded facilities are completed. Finally, two aircraft are permanently based at Edwards AFB, California, for continuing testing and evaluation of new B-1B weapons and systems. The B-1B force did not participate in Desert Storm, since it was then dedicated mainly to the nuclear deterrent role, crew training and software modifications for delivering conventional weapons were incomplete, and it was not really needed in the Gulf.

The place to explore a B-1B is the flightline of Ellsworth AFB near Rapid City, South Dakota, which is the home of the 28th Bombardment Wing, as well as the 34th Bombardment Squadron, which is assigned to the 366th Wing at Mountain Home AFB, Idaho. When you see a B-1B on the flight line at Ellsworth, the first thing you feel is speed. The Bone seems to be moving—and fast—just standing still on the ramp. Then there are the sensuous curves. As you get closer, the details that show the quality of the B-1B's workmanship begin to show, and you begin to notice that the join lines between panels and access doors are almost impossible to see without knowing exactly where to look. Part of the reason for this has to do with the desire of the USAF and Rockwell to make the B-1B as small to enemy radars as possible. While technically not a stealth aircraft, it is considered a "low-observable" airframe, which does give it some penetration capabilities that even small fighters like the F-16 lack. The four afterburning F101 engines are mounted in underwing gondolas, with the two bomb bays located in the fuselage aft of the crew compartment. Except for a pattern of white markings around the in-flight refueling receptacle, B-1s are currently painted the same uniform dark gray as the F-111 and F-15E fleets, with small, low-visibility national markings. In peacetime, B-1 crews have applied some of the most creative nose artwork in the Air Force, but the rampaging animals and well-endowed young ladies would probably be painted over for combat missions, to reduce the visual signature. Moreover, the coming of women to the flight crews of USAF combat aircraft has imposed certain limits of taste upon such decorations, probably to the advantage of all concerned, but to the detriment of a highly cherished tradition of airmen around the world.

The crew enters the Bone by climbing a retractable ladder built into the nose wheel well. An interesting feature here is the "alert start" button. Since SAC originally expected to launch under conditions of nuclear attack, a single big red "bang" button on the nose wheel strut can start all four engines and begin alignment of the inertial navigation system, so that the aircraft would be ready to roll as soon as the crew was strapped in. Now that the B-1Bs no longer operate in the nuclear deterrent role, nobody uses the panic start button anymore, and there's time to work through the preflight checklist methodically. You have to be a bit careful going up the ladder, because the aisle is narrow and the headroom is limited. The flight crew consists of a pilot and copilot, who sit side-by-side in the front, with an offensive avionics operator (who fills the role of bombardier/navigator) and defensive avionics operator in a separate compartment behind them. The backseaters have small side windows, but their attention is dominated by large electronic consoles. The original B-1A design incorporated a complex crew "escape capsule"; the entire cockpit compartment would separate from the aircraft and deploy stabilizing fins and a parachute. But on the B-1B this was replaced by simpler, lighter, and more reliable ACES II ejection seats. Blow-out panels above each crew position are triggered by the ejection mechanism, which has a surprisingly good record for crew survival in emergencies. The in-flight refueling receptacle is built into the nose, just forward of the windshield; flight crews with B-52 experience find this a bit disorienting at first.

The controls, while not quite as advanced as those on the F-15E or F-16C, are quite easy to use, and very functional. You sit in the pilot's seat, with the fighter-style control stick fitting in a nice, neutral position that is designed to reduce crew fatigue. While there is no HUD, the mission data is easily read from several MFDs located on the instrument panels. The throttle quadrant is located on a pedestal between the pilot and copilot positions, with other common controls like navigation and flight management systems being positioned there for easy access from either position. Engine, fuel, and other indicators are of the "strip" type, much like an old-style mercury thermometer. These visual readouts make it easy to see if an engine or some other system is operating within "green" (safe) parameters or in a "red" (danger) situation. There is also a small panel of enunciators, which show system status and warning lights for things like engine fires or low hydraulic pressure.

B-1s prefer to operate as lone wolves. Any escorting fighter that is not stealthy is likely to increase the risk of enemy detection. In low-level penetration missions, when the autopilot is coupled to the TFR mode of the APQ-164, speed is life. At 500 feet/152.4 meters altitude, the B-1's cruising speed is about 550 knots/1,006 kph., and at full afterburner it can be cranked up to just a hair over the speed of sound. Maximum takeoff weight is 477,000 lb./216,365 kg., with a maximum altitude of over 50,000 feet/15,240 meters.

No fighter in the world can overtake a B-1B operating at low altitudes. Over rough terrain, any fighter pilot who tries to stay on the B-1's tail is likely to have a highly detrimental intersection with the ground. In addition to the APQ-164's TFR radar mode, what makes this possible is a pair of small downward-slanted vanes on the nose, just forward of the cockpit. (From some angles, they make the plane look like a catfish.) Everything on an aircraft gets an acronym, and these little fins are part of the SMCS: Structural Mode Control System. Flying at low altitude means an aircraft is going to encounter turbulence even in good weather. This can make the aircraft dangerously hard to control, fatigues the crew, and causes flexing of the airframe that drastically shortens its service life. To reduce this problem, a set of accelerometers mounted in the aircraft sense the turbulence, and a computer rapidly moves the fins to compensate. The effect is to limit the vertical accelerations felt by the crew to no more than three Gs.

Just behind the pilot's position is a space, about the size of a large packing carton, which pretends to be a toilet. This is not of the flush variety, but simply a canned chemical "pack" which allows a crew of four to function for about twenty hours. For the longer "Global Power/Global Reach" missions, which can last more than thirty hours, a second toilet pack is kept in the stowage compartment just behind the copilot's position. Also kept here are things like food, water, coffee, personal equipment, engine inlet covers, and anything else that can be crammed into the space. For crews used to the relatively roominess of the old B-52s, the B-1B can be somewhat confining and spartan. In fact, where the B-52 had crew rest bunks, B-1 crews tend to just lay a couple of engine covers in the aisle between the front and rear compartments and snatch catnaps as time and events allow. Mission endurance is, in fact, virtually unlimited. With aerial refueling, B-1s have flown completely around the Earth in thirty-hour marathons.

In the after part of the crew compartment, on either side of the crew entry hatch, are the positions for the offensive avionics operator (bombardier/navigator) and defensive avionics operator (electronic warfare officer). Sitting in their own ejection seats, they each face a large vertical panel which controls the various sensor and electronic warfare systems. The electronic systems of the B-1B are tied together by a quadruple-redundant MIL-STD-1553 data bus. The health and status of all systems are continuously monitored and recorded by a central integrated test system, which greatly simplifies troubleshooting for ground-based mechanics. There are a number of IBM AP-101F computers, based on the 1960s-vintage computers, installed in the B-52G; two are dedicated to terrain following, one is for navigation, one for controls and displays, one for weapons control, and one for backup. By modern standards these computers are pretty feeble—they share a total mass memory unit with only 512K of magnetic core memory (less than the cheapest portable computer you could buy today); but these systems are hardened against the electromagnetic effects of a nearby nuclear explosion. Just try that trick with your desktop PC or Macintosh. Continuing upgrades of the computers and software are likely, if government policies do not cripple the highly specialized radiation-hardened chip industry.

On the right is the position for the offensive avionics operator, who controls the radar, navigational, and weapons-delivery systems of the B-1B. The nose-mounted Westinghouse APQ-164 radar of the Bone is derived from the APG-66 used on the F-16A. Actually composed of two radars (one to control the terrain-following autopilot, the other to provide an attack sensor) stacked one on top of the other, the APQ-164 has matured a great deal since coming into service ten years ago. Updated software provides for up to thirteen different radar modes to provide ground mapping, navigation, weapons targeting, and all-weather terrain following. The APQ-164 can also operate in an SAR mode, to take the same kind of target-mapping photos that can be obtained from the APG-68 on the F-16C, and the APG-70 on the F-15E. Recent software improvements in SAR mapping radar mode are dramatic. "You could pick out fence posts before; now you can practically see the wire," said one Rockwell executive in a recent trade journal interview, and the crews from the 34th BS confirmed this claim. One of them told us that with the attack system he could resolve the structural legs of high-tension power towers, and deliver 500 lb./227.1 kg. iron bombs *between* the legs. And that's the whole point of keeping the big bombers—their ability to deliver vast amounts of ordnance with a single sortie.

One thing that B-1B crews have desperately needed is an improved navigation system, preferably one based around the NAVSTAR GPS satellite constellation, which was recently completed. Composed of 24 satellites, it provides super-accurate navigation and timing information to users equipped with relatively cheap, small, and lightweight GPS receivers. Unfortunately, unlike fighters like the F-16C, which were among the first to get the Rockwell Collins MAGR, the B-1B bomber force has languished without this badly needed black box. While there are future plans to add the MAGR to the Bone's avionics fit, the crews decided to take matters into their own hands, and thus are the roots of a story. Several years ago, when faced with exactly the same problem, the crews of U-2 reconnaissance aircraft, whose navigation must by nature be extremely accurate, began to get impatient for their own GPS upgrade, and started to look at some commercial options. This led them to our old friends at Trimble Navigation, the makers of the famous SLGR GPS receiver which was used extensively during Desert Storm. (See my previous book *Armored Cav* for a description of the SLGR.) Makers of a whole line of military and commercial GPS receivers, they had taken the basic technology elements of the SLGR, which was packaged into a case about the size of a car stereo, and repackaged it into a smaller, lighter, and cheaper form factor called the Scout-M. Looking for all the world like an olive-drab phaser from the TV series *Star Trek: The Next Generation*, the Scout-M provided similar functionality to the SLGR, at less than one fifth the weight, volume, and cost. The little green machine has proven quite popular with military personnel and sportsmen around the world, despite the lack of a more accurate PY-code military model, and it is here that we start our story. Trimble's aviation version of the Scout-M contained an additional read-only-memory (ROM) chip, which stores additional flight-related data. Known as the Flightmate Pro, its special ROM is loaded with some 12,000 positions for airfields, airbases, and other important navigational landmarks of concern to aviators. Originally designed to provide private pilots with an inexpensive way of taking advantage of the benefits of the GPS system, it is in fact a highly sophisticated self-contained navigation system which can be had for less than $1,000, and then clipped to the control wheel of your Cessna, Piper, or Beechcraft. Packaged in an attractive gray case, it is equipped with a socket for an external antenna, as well as an interface connector to connect it to a

A Rockwell International B-1B Lancer bomber assigned to the 366th Wing's 34th Bombardment Squadron on the ramp at Ellsworth AFB. *John D. Gresham*

personal computer for route and flight planning. First sold in 1993, it has sold thousands of units to pilots worldwide, and has become something of a best-seller in the world of general aviation.

Now enter the U-2 crews of the 9th Reconnaissance Wing, who, as we previously mentioned, were desperately in need of a GPS-type navigational system. Soon after the Flightmate Pro's introduction, the U-2 pilots pressured their procurement office to make a request for a commercial buy of the little GPS receivers. To keep the Powers-That-Be from figuring out just what they were doing, they claimed that the Flightmates were going to be used as a search-and-rescue (SAR) aid, to help SAR forces to find them, and in fact, they are quite useful for that task. If it had been bought as a piece of navigation gear, it would have been treated as an avionic system by the folks who manage the procurement programs, and taken years to get approval. As a commercial buy though, it could be done in a matter of days. Almost immediately, the U-2 pilots began to strap them to their kneeboards, and use them without modifications, since the GPS satellite signals could be easily read by the receiver right through the aircraft's bubble canopy. The U-2 drivers loved it, and have kept their Flightmate Pros well after their aircraft have finally received their scheduled MAGR GPS receiver installation. Word of the nifty little GPS receiver has gotten around, and numerous other units have made "commercial orders" of Flightmate Pros as a "SAR aid." Many of these have come from the B-1B community, including the 34th Bombardment Squadron (BS) of the 366th Wing. The 34th BS maintenance technicians have rigged a GPS antenna on top of the fuselage, and then run antenna connections to each of the crew positions, so that each one can plug in their own personal Flightmate Pro to assist them in their tasks. For the pilot and copilot, this usually means assisting them

The Trimble Flightmate, a hand-held GPS receiver being used by USAF crews, including those who fly the B-1B Lancer. *Trimble Navigation*

with route planning, execution, and timing. For the folks in the rear seats, it can be used to assist in planning weapons deliveries and avoiding the envelopes of threat systems like SAM sites. The young B-1 crews are always finding new ways to use their laptop computers to program the Flightmate Pro, and I have to imagine that they will continue to in the future. Even though it is only accurate to about 100 yards-meters of ground truth, this is usually accurate enough to make a considerable difference in a crew's performance of a particular task. And while the Flightmate may lack some of the accuracy of the PY-code MAGR (which is accurate to within about 10 yards/meters), it is a vast improvement over their existing systems, and may have to do until the coming B-1B GPS installation in the late 1990s. In any case, it's another example of how this fast-moving technology can do almost impossible things for absurdly low prices, and you can even buy one for yourself to boot!

On the left side of the compartment is the position for the defensive avionics operator, whose job it is to manage and operate the defensive countermeasure systems of the Lancer. These include a variety of different sensor, jammer, and decoy systems. But the B-1B's best defense lies in its ability to avoid being seen and caught. As a result, the B-1's designers dispensed with the traditional tail gun, relying on elaborate electronic countermeasures for protection and the aircraft's inherent low radar cross section (RCS).

All of the offensive weapons are carried internally—and I mean a lot of weapons. The maximum ordnance load is 125,000 lb./56,700 kg.—twice the capacity of a B-52. But a more typical combat load would be about half that much. There are two bomb bays: The forward bay is twice the length of the aft bay, and has a movable bulkhead that allows the fitting of one or two optional extra fuel tanks in place of bombs. Up to eighty-four Mk 82 500-pound bombs

A Conventional Munitions Module (CMM) is loaded into the forward bomb bay of a B-1B Lancer bomber. The B-1B can carry up to three CMMs, each of which can be loaded with up to twenty-six 500 lb/227.3 kg Mk 82 general-purpose bombs. *John D. Gresham*

can be carried in special dispensers called conventional munitions modules (CMMs) that can drop the entire bomb load in just two seconds—about 3,000 feet/914.4 meters of horizontal flight. This is the equivalent of the maximum combat load of seven F-15Es delivered by just one aircraft! Back in the Cold War when the Lancer flew in the strategic deterrent role, it carried up to three removable eight-round rotary launchers, loaded with nuclear gravity bombs or AGM-69 Short Range Attack Missiles. The launchers have been retained and can be fitted with adapters for up to eight Mk 84 2,000 pound bombs, BLU-109, or other weapons, including the AGM-86 ALCM-C air-launched cruise missile with a conventional warhead. (See Chapter 4 for a fuller description of these.) Strangely, because the B-1B is no longer being counted as a nuclear-capable platform under the SALT and START treaties, the entire force is now unable to drop nuclear weapons.

Weapons deliveries of the Mk 82 500 lb./227.1 kg. bombs tend to be made in "strings" or "sticks" of bombs, usually in multiples of six, though as few as one at a time can be dropped. Until the new Precision Guided Munitions (PGMs) come on-line later in the 1990s, the B-1 will run a string of bombs across or along the line of a target, insuring that at least one of the deadly projectiles hits it. Precision targeting was not a big concern back in the days of nuclear deterrence. During the Cold War, target aim points were planned years in advance, and crews trained and drilled endlessly for specific missions until the target area was as familiar as their own neighborhoods. When you're dropping 500 kiloton thermonuclear weapons, an error of a few meters one way or the other is not significant. But in the conventional role, the B-1's current lack of PGMs is a crippling handicap.

With only 500 lb./227 kg. bombs to drop, you might wonder why the USAF has not grounded the B-1B fleet and scheduled it for decommissioning. The reason is that while it has some shortcomings in the area of weapons and communications, the Bone represents a potential to rapidly deliver a vast load of precision ordnance over intercontinental distances. Thus, the Bone is at the core of the new "Bomber Roadmap" program that has new communications and weapons systems being installed to support ACC's current and projected conventional missions. Where the B-1B is concerned, this will be a phased upgrade program running over the next five years or so.

In 1996, the active squadrons of B-1Bs will begin to receive the Conventional Munitions Upgrade Program (CMUP) that will provide modified bomb racks bombs (called "Tactical Munitions Dispensers") for delivering CBU-87/89/97 cluster bombs. By 2001, a more ambitious second phase of the CMUP will begin equipping the fleet with the new Joint Direct Attack Munition (JDAM) system. This will require installation of a GPS receiver, an upgraded mission computer, and wiring the bomb bay for the high-speed MIL-STD-1760 data bus, which transfers GPS time, position, and velocity data from the aircraft to the smart bombs.

After many delays and configuration hassles, the NAVSTAR/GPS system, with a suitable low-profile antenna, is finally being integrated onto the B-1's data bus. This Rockwell Collins MAGR unit will supplement or replace the outdated inertial navigation system currently installed on the Bone.

One thing that will have to be upgraded is the communications systems, which are currently oriented towards the old Doomsday mission of the Cold War (largely limited to receiving and authenticating the "Go" codes). Thus, the priority is to install the new Have Quick radios and JTIDS terminals in the bombers' communications bays, so that they will be able to work with the other combat aircraft in the ACC force. Thus, the CMUP will also provide new Rockwell Collins ARC-210 Have Quick II jam-resistant tactical radios. Also likely is a mid-life upgrade for the ALQ-161 jammer, and better integration of advanced missile-warning and radar-warning systems into the defensive avionics suite. Because of the perceived lack of sophisticated threats, money for electronic countermeasures is very scarce in the budget right now. But with the planned decommissioning of the EF-111A Ravens in 1996, the B-1B's onboard jammer will probably be the most capable airborne jammer in the USAF inventory, and may well be required to fill in that role for a time.

The B-1B is an airframe and a community in transition, with much potential that will have to be realized if it is to perform useful work into the 21st century. Doing this will not be cheap, but ACC will need these bombers if they are to succeed in their goal of supporting two major regional conflicts at one time.

Boeing KC-135R Stratotanker

Where once a trip to Europe was considered an adventure, today a trip to the Middle East elicits a travel-weary reaction. "I don't want to go to Saudi Arabia again; I've been there five times, [and] I've got enough souvenirs," one KC-135 pilot said.

Quoted in *Air Force Times*, February 6, 1995

It is a hard fact that much of the "Global Reach" of the U.S. Air Force depends on a fleet of aerial refueling tankers that are, in many cases, now older than their crews. The first KC-135 made its maiden flight on August 21, 1956, and the aircraft entered service in January 1957. A total of 798 KC-135 Stratotankers were built between 1956 and 1966. Their original, highly critical mission was to refuel the SAC fleet of B-52 nuclear bombers on their way to Doomsday (and back). Many of these planes spent decades standing alert duty, enjoying the fanatically meticulous maintenance that SAC enforced. Because the aircraft spent so little time under the stresses of flying, the -135 fleet is in surprisingly good condition. In fact, the fleet average on flight hours per airframes is something less than fifteen thousand hours, which is amazing when you consider that most of them were built in the early 1960s, and an equivalent commercial Boeing 707 might have over 120,000 flight hours! Now equipped with new engines, new wing skins, strengthened landing gear, and modernized avionics, the 552 remaining KC-135s will continue to give many years of good service. They will have to, because there is currently nothing on the drawing boards, or in the Air Force budget, to replace them.

Throughout the history of aerial warfare, the single most limiting factor has been the fuel capacity—and thus the range—of the aircraft flying the combat missions. The lack of a long-range escort fighter cost the Germans the Battle of Britain in 1940. Conversely, the P-51 Mustang, with its "seven-league boots," was the deciding factor in the success of the 8th Air Force in their operations over Germany. Thus, the idea of extending an aircraft's range by aerial refueling is such a simple idea, it is surprising that it took so long to catch on.

The first known attempt to do so occurred in 1921, when an aviator named Wesley May climbed from one flying biplane to another with a 5 gallon/18.9-liter can of gas strapped to his back. Later, daring young officers like Major Henry H. "Hap" Arnold and Major Carl A. Spaatz (both became generals in World War II) experimented with simple hose and gravity-feed or pump arrangements for passing fuel from one aircraft to another. At the time, this was regarded more as a stunt to set flight endurance records than a realistic operational option; but it was a start on the road to the airborne tankers of today. World War II passed without any known use of aerial refueling by any of the combatants, though it would be the last major conflict where the technique would not be used.

After World War II, two different technologies for aerial refueling were developed in the United States. The first of these, the probe-and-drogue method, required the tanker aircraft to reel out a hose with a cone-shaped receptacle (the drogue), that could then be "speared" by a fixed or extensible probe on the receiving aircraft. This method is preferred by the U.S. Navy, the Royal Air Force, and a number of NATO countries. The other method, Boeing's Flying Boom, required a trained boom operator with nerves of steel to guide a telescoping boom with twin steering fins into a locking receptacle on a receiving aircraft, which meanwhile is trying to maintain precise formation in the tanker's turbulent wake. This technique appealed to the USAF, who felt that the actual hookup between the aircraft should be controlled by a professional who did this odd task for a living. Tanker "boomers," as they are known, are usually sergeants who double as the aircraft's crew chief.

The first operational tankers, the KB-29, the KB-50, and the KC-97, were derived from the Boeing B-29 bomber. Their shortcomings were obvious. Because of their four piston engines, the early tankers simply could not keep up with the new generation of jet fighters and bombers that were quickly becoming the primary customers for these aerial gas stations. The solution, clearly, was going to be a jet tanker capable of integrating itself with the new jet combat force of the USAF.

The problem was that until someone developed a jet transport with sufficient payload capacity, this idea was going to stay just that—an idea. Fortunately, in the early 1950s there was an international race to produce the first commercially viable jet transport, and the USAF was able to pick their new tanker from the winners. The British Comet was first into service, but an unforeseen problem with metal fatigue around the window frames led to the loss of several aircraft in flight through explosive decompression. In the United States, Boeing's long experience with designing pressurized high-altitude aircraft like the B-29 paid off in the design of a tremendously strong airframe that would become the basis for both the military C-135 transport and the 707 commercial passenger liner. In 1954, soon after the first flight of Boeing's first jet transport prototype, the Model 367-80, the Air Force ordered a fleet of Boeing tankers to support the bomber force of the then-Strategic Air Command.

Boeing's project number for what became known as the Stratotanker was Model 717. It differed from the basic 707 airliner in having smaller overall dimensions, a somewhat narrower fuselage, no cabin windows, and, of course, an extendible, finned refueling boom and tiny compartment for the boom operator under the tail. The tankers, constructed more simply, to military standards, than their commercial cousins, actually went into service before the Boeing 707 completed final commercial certification.

Now, you should understand that if the whole fuselage barrel section were filled with fuel, the plane would be too heavy to take off. Thus, the fuel carried is actually contained in a relatively small volume, leaving the inside of the cabin available for other uses. All of the tanker-related equipment is below the main deck, leaving seating space for passengers or an equivalent volume of cargo—up to 83,000 lb./37,650 kg.

Over the years, more than two dozen variants of this versatile airframe have been built, including a bewildering collection of "deep black" intelligence collection platforms, going by such names as Rivet Joint and Cobra Ball. A small number of all-cargo versions were built as C-135 Stratolifters. The -135 has also enjoyed some modest success in the export market; a dozen C-135F models were sold to France in 1964 to support that country's tiny but potent nuclear strike force of Mirage IV bombers. Canada and Israel also purchased tanker/cargo aircraft from the 707/KC-135 family, and continue to operate them today.

If you take a walk around one of the big tankers, the first thing that strikes you is how much it looks like an old Boeing 707, but with fewer windows. This absence of viewports is one of the reasons for the Stratotankers' longevity, since each hole that you put in a pressurized airframe is just another place for structural fatigue cracks to start.

The entire KC-135 fleet was originally equipped with the noisy and fuel-guzzling Pratt & Whitney J-57 engine, which also put out a lot of smoke on takeoff. Fortunately, most of the aircraft remaining in service have been re-engined with more efficient and powerful or General Electric/SNECMA CFM-56 turbofans, creating the KC-135R variant. The engine change reduces noise by 85% and pollutant emissions by 90%, and the increased power allows for a much shorter takeoff run. The biggest benefit, though, is the vastly improved fuel efficiency, which allows a KC-135R to offload up to 50% more fuel than one of the earlier J-57-equipped birds. While most aircraft in the USAF fleet are equipped to take fuel from tankers, most KC-135s are not themselves equipped with flight-refueling receptacles. The few that are so equipped are known as KC-135RTs, and are highly coveted assets by the new Air Mobility Command (AMC), which controls most of their operations, maintenance, and use. Thus, unlike the small fleet of McDonnell Douglas KC-10 Extenders (the newest USAF tanker, based on the commercial DC-10), most KC-135s can only be refueled on the ground. This makes for an interesting set of decisions for the operators of the -135. Unlike the Extender, they can either off-load fuel or deploy to an overseas area, but not both at the same time.

You get into the KC-135 through an entry hatch in the bottom of the fuselage, on the left side of the nose. It requires a bit of a climb to get up the ladder and into the cockpit, something like the climb into the conning tower of a submarine. Once there, the first thing you will probably notice is that by the standards of current commercial airliner cockpits, the -135 is decidedly ancient. The four-person flight crew usually includes three officers (aircraft commander, pilot, and navigator/radar operator) and one enlisted airman (the crew chief/boom operator), each with a seat in the tight little workspace up front. Very little of the modern computer age is evident, other than a digital flight management system and the throttle controls for the four CFM-56 engines. The fit of communications and navigation gear enables the tanker to maintain station precisely and talk to its customers, though the navigation gear is also a bit dated. Until the planned installation of a GPS receiver later in the 1990s, the navigator has to depend on the old standbys of shooting the sun and stars with a sextant, and the old-style LORAN and TACAN navigation beacon systems. The nose-mounted radar is a Texas Instruments APQ-122(V) weather and ground-mapping radar, which is capable of assisting in the navigator's tasks. All USAF tankers are unarmed; and indeed, they are not even equipped with basic self-protection radar warning receivers, chaff or flare dispensers, or jamming pods. As a result, they can only survive and operate under conditions of total local air supremacy. It is not hard to understand why, when you consider that a tanker is nothing but a relatively slow and unmaneuverable bag of fuel, requiring just one cannon shell or "hot" warhead fragment from an AAM to turn it into a *very* large fireball.

As you move aft, you encounter the lavatory compartment on the left side, just aft of the cockpit. You are struck again by the rather spartan nature of this most necessary of aerial conveniences; it does not even flush! Instead, they use the same kind of chemical toilet "packs" found on the B-1B. Also, for the male crew members, there is a "whiz tube" urinal. While convenient, this can be *deadly* during rough flights, as the spring loaded lid tends to snap shut when "bumped." Just across from the lavatory is the galley—or more precisely, the place where box lunches and the thermos bottles for coffee and water are kept. There are no microwave ovens or refrigerators, just a bare aluminum rack, looking for all the world like an airline food/drink cart with no wheels. Just aft of the lavatory compartment on the aircraft's left side is a large pressurized cargo door, big enough to load large items like bulk cargo, duffel bags, or other personal equipment. These can be strapped down or placed in large crate bins tied to the floors. The original floors are made of impregnated plywood, and are kept lovingly cleaned and painted by the ground crews. Other than the planned GPS receiver upgrade, these floors are the next major planned upgrade for the -135 fleet. The plan, if money is available, is to replace the existing floors with hardened metal Roll-On/Roll-Off (Ro/Ro) floors, so that items like palletized cargo and small wheeled vehicles like ramp service carts can be loaded and tied down. This should help alleviate some of the airlift problems Air Mobility Command (AMC) has been having with their fleet of heavy airlift aircraft.

Along the side walls of the KC-135 are passenger seats made of aluminum tubing and synthetic webbing. These are surprisingly comfortable, if you aren't packed in too tightly. That means eighty people can travel in mild discomfort, and 160 in total unpleasantness! Except during actual deployment, most tankers fly with few passengers, and are actually quite comfortable. While I'm always a reluctant flier, other people I know generally enjoy their time in the -135s, and even find that the webbing seats make passable bunks if there is enough room to spread out. In fact, the main cargo compartment is large and open. You feel like you're in a wide-body commercial jet, with none of the annoying overhead bins or narrow seat aisles to bump yourself on.

In the rear of the compartment is the environmental control system, with large green bottles of oxygen mounted to the after bulkhead. Just above these are several very comfortable bunks, though a pair of severely lettered signs make it clear that these are for members of the crew to rest in, and not for mere passengers. Overall, the pressurized cabin of the KC-135 is quite comfortable, though the heating system, which occupies a large part of the after cabin, is somewhat inadequate to warm the entire interior. Thus, it is advisable on long flights to wear something warm, preferably a leather flight jacket, which also has the advantage of looking good around the officers' club!

At the far after end of the cargo compartment, on either side of the environmental control system, are the entrances to the refueling pod. To get into this, the business end of the KC-135, pick one side or another, step down onto what looks like a very comfortable cushion, and lie on your stomach. At this point, you are on one side or another (observers' stations actually) of the "boomer" position, so named because this is where the refueling boom is actually "flown" and mated to other aircraft. The boomer lies on a similar couch between the two observers' stations and faces a thick window (with two smaller side windows) with a small control panel below it. This position is a favorite of aerial photographers who want to take really spectacular pictures; you never forget the view. Just below the boomer's couch is a control stick, which flies the boom. This stick controls a pair of fins on the telescoping refueling boom just in front of the boomer's window, and these respond to control inputs from the operator. The stick is surprisingly simple to use. To conduct a refueling, the boomer flips a switch which deploys the boom from its stowed position up against the KC-135's tailcone down into its "flying" position. The boomer then sets the telescoping boom to a "neutral" length position and alerts the flight crew that he is ready to have an aircraft take on fuel. What happens next borders on the bizarre if you are not familiar with it.

From behind will come a small formation of aircraft, having flown to the tanker track in complete radio and emissions silence (which limits the ability of an enemy to read whether something is coming at them or not). Even in peacetime, this is a skill practiced whenever the restrictions of weather and the exercise rules allow. After establishing formation on the tanker (either on the wing or behind), the first recipient moves up behind the KC-135, aligns itself with a series of colored position lights located under the tail of the tanker, and opens its refueling receptacle door. Most aircraft designs have this placed behind the flight crew position, over their shoulder and to the left side. Once the boomer sees that the receiving aircraft is stable and in its proper refueling position (this varies with different aircraft types), the real fun begins.

Using the control stick to fly the refueling boom into position over the receiving aircraft's receptacle, the boomer activates a switch which stabs the refueling probe of the boom into the receptacle, causing it to "hard latch." This last part of the operation can be tough, especially in rough air, and may require several attempts to get it right. The two aircraft are now joined, flying just a few yards/meters apart, and the boomer relays this fact to the flight deck, where the flying crew actually controls the pumping of fuel down the boom to the receiving aircraft. Though the pumping is fairly rapid, fully refueling a tactical aircraft like the F-15E Strike Eagle or the F-16 Fighting Falcon does take a few minutes. Meanwhile, both aircraft are flying an oval "racetrack" course at about 300 knots/545.5 kph. at an altitude of 20,000 to 25,000 feet/6,060.1 to 7575.8 meters. One of the more interesting features of this aerial dance is that once the two aircraft are hooked up, they can talk plane-to-plane over a special intercom link, which allows the pilot of the receiving aircraft to report battle damage or other problems, and to receive updates on targeting and scheduling changes. For many pilots during the early hours of Desert Storm in 1991, the last thing they heard before going into combat was the reassuring voice of a Boomer on the intercom, wishing them well and a safe return. Since the two aircraft are only about 35 feet/10 meters apart, the receiving aircraft can take a severe buffeting from the tanker's wake turbulence. It's tough to maintain a position, even for a skilled pilot, especially at night, in bad weather, when you are low on gas.

To the aircrews of combat aircraft returning to base, shot full of holes and leaking fuel all over the sky, every drop on a tanker is precious. Happily, the KC-135R tanker can carry a lot of fuel—some 203,288 lb./92,210 kg., which translates to a capacity of about 25,411 gallons/95,890.6 liters. Since an airborne tanker can do two things with the fuel, burn it or off load it to another aircraft, there is a tradeoff between the range and endurance of the tanker on the one hand and the amount of fuel available for off load. For example, with 120,000 lb./54,545 kg. of transfer fuel, the range of the KC-135R is 1,150 nm./2,090.1 km. On the other hand, with 24,000 lb./10,909.1 kg. of transfer fuel, the range is 3,450 nm./6,309.4 km.

So, how does all of this come together in the real world of combat operations? In an intervention scenario, a KC-135R tanker can either deploy to an overseas base (carrying high-priority personnel and cargo), or support the deployment of other aircraft by tanking them—it can't do both. This means that planners have to be careful to make sure that enough tankers are available to do both. Unfortunately, this is getting tougher all the time. During 1994, the tanker force took a 25% personnel cut and moved almost three quarters of its U.S.-based tankers and people from former SAC bases to three main AMC bases, as well as reassigning many aircraft to USAF Reserve and Air National Guard units. Tankers also are increasingly used to transport cargo, because metal fatigue and other problems with the C-141B Starlifter fleet have forced planners to assign cargo missions to the hard-working tankers.

As long as combat aircraft need to burn fuel, there will be a requirement for tankers. Eventually the KC-135s and the force of about sixty wide-body KC-10 Extenders will have to be replaced. To some extent, the tanker mission can be performed by tactical aircraft fitted with extra fuel tanks and refueling gear mounted in removable "buddy packs." But for really long hauls, there is no substitute for specialized and dedicated aerial tankers, based on economical, standardized commercial airframes. Just what that replacement will be exactly is anyone's guess, but rest assured that when fuel is low and tensions are running high, the tanker crews will the most popular folks in the skies.

Boeing E-3C Sentry Airborne Warning and Control System

Ever since our simian ancestors learned to climb trees, we have known instinctively that the higher you climb, the farther you can see. Later, many ancient cultures devoted considerable labor to building hilltop watchtowers. Spotting an approaching enemy even a few minutes sooner can make the critical difference between victory and defeat. The development of radar in the 1930s provided proof that nature is consistent. Generally speaking, radar works much like light—it travels in straight lines and usually cannot bend to peer over the local horizon. While a mountaintop is a good spot for a radar station, a mountain is rarely located where you need it, and it's hard to move. However, if you could put a big radar antenna on a high-flying airplane, your radar horizon could theoretically reach out to two or three hundred miles. Also, if you put an air battle control staff on the same airplane and provide them with powerful computers, situation displays, and secure communications, you have what is called an Airborne Warning and Control System (AWACS)—the king on the chessboard of the modern air battle. Its status also makes it the most prized target in the sky, making the Sentry the sort of high value airborne asset that will normally be protected by a hefty escort of fighters.

AWACS aircraft had their start at the end of World War II, when the U.S. Navy was desperately trying to fight off the hordes of Japanese Kamikaze suicide aircraft that were trying to stop the invasion and battle fleets of the Americans. The Navy's solution to the relative vulnerability of their surface ships was to convert TBM Avenger torpedo bombers into primitive AWACS aircraft. These early AWACS aircraft would have been available for the invasion of Japan in late 1945, had it taken place. Later, purpose-built AWACS aircraft were built by both the Air Force and Navy to their specific needs, usually on transport or airliner airframes. For many years, the USAF birds were based upon the classic Lockheed C-121 Super Constellation airliner/transport. Called the EC-121 Warning Star, it served in the AWACS mission for over twenty years before being replaced by the current AWACS aircraft, the E-3 Sentry, in the later 1970s.

The Boeing E-3C Sentry AWACS looks like a large jet airliner being attacked by a small flying saucer. The airliner is the old reliable Boeing 707-320B airframe, with a flight deck crew of four (pilot, copilot, navigator, and flight engineer) and a "mission crew" of thirteen to eighteen controllers, supervisors, and technicians back in the main cabin. Using an airframe similar to the venerable KC-135 and all the other Boeing Model 320 derivatives has proven quite popular with the U.S. military, and quite practical for the taxpayers. The saucer, or "rotodome," is 30 feet/9.1 meters in diameter, 6 feet/1.8 meters thick at the

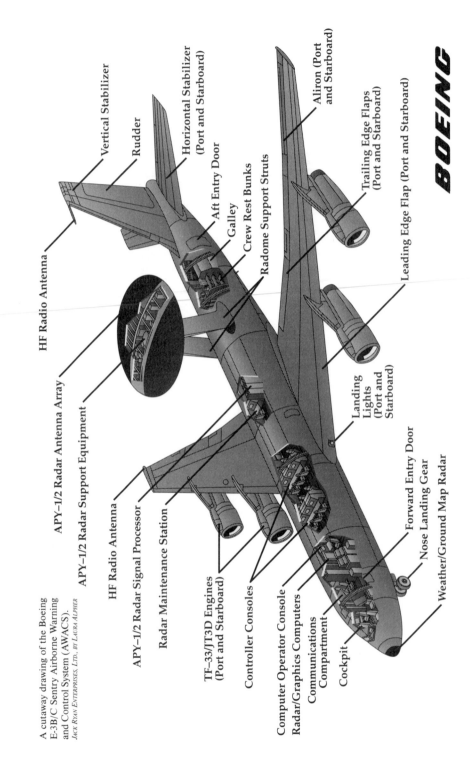

A cutaway drawing of the Boeing E-3B/C Sentry Airborne Warning and Control System (AWACS).
Jack Ryan Enterprises, Ltd., by Laura Alpher.

HF Radio Antenna

Vertical Stabilizer

Rudder

Horizontal Stabilizer (Port and Starboard)

Aft Entry Door

Galley

Crew Rest Bunks

Radome Support Struts

Aliron (Port and Starboard)

Trailing Edge Flaps (Port and Starboard)

Leading Edge Flap (Port and Starboard)

Landing Lights (Port and Starboard)

Forward Entry Door

Nose Landing Gear

Weather/Ground Map Radar

Cockpit

Communications Compartment

Radar/Graphics Computers

Computer Operator Console

Controller Consoles

TF–33/JT3D Engines (Port and Starboard)

Radar Maintenance Station

APY–1/2 Radar Signal Processor

HF Radio Antenna

APY–1/2 Radar Support Equipment

APY–1/2 Radar Antenna Array

BOEING

A USAF Boeing E-3 Sentry Airborne Warning and Control System (AWACS) aircraft arrives in Saudi Arabia during Operation Desert Shield. Fourteen of these valuable aircraft, as well as E-3s from the Royal Saudi Air Force and NATO, provided airborne radar support during Desert Shield and Desert Storm.

OFFICIAL U.S. AIR FORCE PHOTO BY JIM CURTIS

center, and is supported 11 feet/3.35 meters above the fuselage on two stream-lined struts just aft of the trailing edge of the wings. It is designed to generate enough aerodynamic lift to support itself, and does not place any stress, other than drag, on the wings or airframe. Mounted back-to-back with the main APY-2 radar antenna (upgraded from the original APY-1 version) inside the rotodome is an antenna array for the APX-103 IFF/Tactical Digital Data Link (IFF/TADIL-C) system. This is a highly sophisticated IFF system, capable of interrogating virtually any IFF transponder in the world within 200 nm./365.7 km. (It reportedly has some sort of NCTR capabilities as well.) When transmitting, the rotodome, powered by hydraulic motors, makes one complete revolution every ten seconds. When it is not transmitting, it makes one revolution every four minutes, to keep the bearings lubricated. Considering the flight stresses it has to support and the complex of wave guides, power cables, and signal lines that must pass through it, the saucer's rotary slip joint is a marvel of mechanical engineering. The radar transmitters and their elaborate power supplies and cooling equipment are located under the floor of the aft cabin, where conventional 707s stow the passengers' luggage.

All of this is packaged inside a standard Boeing Model 707-320B/VC-137 airframe with four Pratt & Whitney JT3D/TF33 turbofan engines. It is also quite expensive, having originally cost something like $270 million a copy.

Getting into an E-3 is roughly the same as a KC-135, through a normal passenger hatch on the left side of the aircraft, where the cargo door is on the tanker. The first thing that strikes you is that the interior is much more comfortably appointed than the -135s. The interior is covered with the same kinds of sound-deadening walls as a conventional airliner, mainly to ensure the comfort of the mission crew. Along with all the display consoles and other electronic gear, they are crammed into the cabin for missions that can last most of a day (though twelve to sixteen hours is normal). The tops of all the consoles in the main cabin are covered with blue indoor/outdoor carpet, which is actually quite nice to lean on! The flight deck is roughly similar to that of the Stratotanker, though some of the controls and displays are a bit more modern than the 1960s-vintage instruments on the -135.

As you move back through the main cabin, there are any number of large cabinets and consoles scattered throughout, which can make moving about somewhat tight. These include the main computers for the radar system, as well as the symbology/display generator systems for the controller consoles. Towards the mid-cabin area over the wings are the radar control consoles. There are fourteen of these in back-to-back rows, with a flight seat (complete with shoulder harnesses and seat belts) in front of each position. Each console is configurable by the user, and can be set up for a controller, supervisor, or mission commander. Everyone is linked by a thirteen-channel intercom system, which feeds into a bank of secure Have Quick II radios, as well as other sets capable of UHF, VHF, and HF communications. In addition, the E-3 is equipped with a JTIDS data link terminal, which does much to reduce the burden on the radio channels.

Obviously, the primary reason for this aircraft's existence is the radar system it is designed to carry. The original AWACS radar system, designated APY-1, was designed by Westinghouse after a 1972 competition with Hughes.

The interior of a USAF Boeing E-3 Sentry Airborne Warning and Control System (AWACS) aircraft looking aft. Visible are the consoles, where the controllers sort out airborne contacts and supervise flight operations. *Boeing Aerospace*

The AWACS radar operates in the E/F band, meaning that it generates radar waves in the 2-to-4-Gigahertz (GHz) range, with a wavelength of from 7.5 to 15 cm./2.95 to 5.9 in. The radar uses the pulse-Doppler principle, relying on precise measurement of the tiny frequency shift in energy reflected from a moving target to distinguish flying aircraft from background ground clutter. This gives the radar the ability to "look down" and detect low-flying targets, as long as they are moving faster than 80 knots/148 kph.

The normal E-3 mission crew consists of separate surveillance and control sections, each typically commanded by a senior captain. In the surveillance section, three to five technicians monitor the air traffic in a huge volume of airspace and pass on information to the control section. This is composed of two to five weapons controllers sitting at multi-purpose consoles, guiding friendly aircraft to intercept enemy or unidentified contacts. Depending on its particular mission, an AWACS also may carry senior staff officers, radar technicians, radio operators, a communications technician, and a computer technician.

While the E-3 displays are a great improvement over the "bogey dope" screens of the old EC-121s, which required almost mystical powers to interpret, they are rapidly becoming dated. The symbology is somewhat hard to interpret, and the screens can easily become cluttered. On the positive side, the trackball "mouse" used to select or "hook" targets on the screens is quite easy to use, and once you get used to the idea that a small symbol with a track number is an aircraft, you do quite well.

Aft from the console area are more electronics cabinets, as well as an area reserved for passengers and off-duty personnel. While the seats are not terribly comfortable, they are an improvement over the maximum-stress environment of being "on the scope." There is also a tiny galley, as well as several small bunks which are usually reserved for spare flight crew personnel (pilots, navigators, etc.). Combat AWACS missions in excess of eighteen hours during Desert Storm were not uncommon, and spare personnel were often necessary. At the very back of the cabin is a rack of parachutes, and there's a bail-out door in the floor of the forward cabin. This, fortunately, has never had to be used, since no E-3 Sentry has ever been lost.

The key to making this system work is the need for steady, consistent flying. Sentry pilots are trained to fly a precise, wide oval racetrack course, straight and level, avoiding any sharp banking turns that might disrupt the radar beam's normal sweep. Typical cruising altitude for an operation mission is 29,000 feet/8,840 meters (just about the height of Mt. Everest), at a maximum cruising speed of 443 knots/510 mph./860 kph. Unrefueled, the E-3 has an endurance of more than eleven hours, and the aircraft has a receptacle for in-flight refueling which can stretch the endurance to twenty-two hours, a limit set by the supply of lube oil for the four JT3D/TF33 engines. On these marathon aerial-surveillance missions, the endurance of both the flight crews and mission personnel is stretched to the limit. This has been pointed to as one of the weaknesses of the AWACS community. In the past, there have frequently been difficulties with flight personnel getting adequate rest between missions, as well as with the excessive number of "on-the-road" days that have been a hallmark of the AWACS lifestyle for almost twenty years. Unfortunately, since AWACS aircraft are a favorite instrument of politicians trying to find out what's happening in a trouble spot, the lifestyle of the AWACS crews is unlikely to change much.

Most of the thirty-four E-3s in USAF service are assigned to three operational Airborne Air Control squadrons (the 963rd, 964th, and 965th), and one training squadron (the 966th) of the 552nd Air Control Wing based at Tinker AFB, Oklahoma. One aircraft is assigned to continuing research and development work at the Boeing plant in Seattle, and a few are permanently stationed in Alaska, assigned to the Pacific Air Force (PACAF) commander. Detachments have been, and continue to be, deployed to trouble spots all over the world. These started with a movement by the Administration of President Jimmy Carter of a three-aircraft detachment of E-3s to Saudi Arabia to keep an eye on the Iran/Iraq War. It was called ELF-1, and what was planned as a deployment of several months eventually wound up lasting over eleven years. It seems to be the lot of the AWACS community to spend their lives on the road, keeping watch on the world's trouble spots.

Even though some of the E-3's systems are getting to be a bit dated right now, the E-3s of the AWACS fleet are the crown jewels of the USAF fleet, and represent the most valuable aircraft that an aerial commander can be assigned. Their presence on the aerial battlefield greatly improves the efficiency of any force that they support, thus explaining why USAF leaders call the AWACS fleet a "force multiplier." This may explain the tolerance for the high costs of developing, operating, and maintaining such a force. The technical problems of developing a reliable and effective airborne warning and control system are so great that only one other nation has ever really managed it—Russia, with its A-50 Mainstay AWACS, based on an IL-76 heavy transport airframe. Meanwhile, NATO, Saudi Arabia, and a few other very friendly nations have bought versions of the E-3.

As the E-3 fleet heads into its twentieth year of service, there are strong plans to upgrade the system so that it will be ready to continue its valuable service into the 21st century. The major points of the planned E-3 upgrade program include:

- **GPS**—It has taken a while, but the E-3 is finally going to get a GPS receiver to help improve both navigational accuracy of the AWACS aircraft itself, as well as the quality of the information it supplies.
- **Radar System Improvement Program (RSIP)**—The RSIP upgrade is a long-overdue series of improvements to the APY-1/2 radar systems that includes an improved radar computer, a more modern graphics processor for the radar operators' consoles, as well as upgrades to the radar system itself. All of these should

allow the AWACS controllers to handle more targets with less clutter on the displays. In addition, the software rewrite that is included with RSIP will allow for things like "windowing" (display-within-a-display) capabilities, as well as the ability to detect low-observable/first-generation stealth aircraft. While the technology behind this last capability is highly classified, it probably centers around the same kind of "broad band" processing technology that is used on submarines. Westinghouse is the prime contractor on the RSIP upgrade, and will begin installation in the late 1990s.

As the E-3 completes its second decade of service, it is time for the Air Force to start thinking about a Sentry replacement. The problem, of course, is finding the money, as well as deciding what kind of aircraft the USAF wants to base it on. As with the other models of first-generation American jet transports, the 707 was designed to very conservative 1950s engineering standards; and after forty years of steadily advancing technology, it's too heavy, it's a fuel hog, and it's too hard to update with modern digital flight control systems. When Japan decided to join the AWACS club, the Japanese ordered the basic E-3 mission package on a modern airframe, the wide-body, twin-turbofan Boeing 767. With a two-person flight crew and better fuel economy, operational costs should be lower, but this is still going to be a very costly aircraft.

In the future (around 2010 to 2020), it should become possible to do away with the radar rotodome and rely on conformal phased-array and synthetic aperture antennas to integrate the AWACS air surveillance mission and the Joint-Stars ground-surveillance mission onto a single platform. This could well be a very high-flying stealthy aircraft, with most of the crew replaced by advanced computers. AWACS, with a top speed of only Mach .78 and a radar cross section somewhat greater than the broad side of an average office building, has been fortunate in its long operational career, since it has never faced an enemy with long-range, high-speed anti-radiation missiles. Right now, though, with the E-3 in the prime of its service life, such a solution is several decades away from fruition, and the Sentry is still the undisputed king on the aerial chessboard.

Ordnance:
How Bombs Got "Smart"

If you read analyses of military aviation, especially in the mass media, you might get the impression that air forces are concerned with aircraft, not with weapons. The guy who flies a plane into the wild blue yonder is a steely-eyed, heroic officer and gentleman. The guy who tinkers with missile guidance systems at a workbench is an enlisted nerd. Aircraft are more glamorous than ordnance. But without ordnance to deliver on targets, the only thing airplanes can do is watch. And while we have seen that reconnaissance is a valued and important mission for aircraft, it is the delivery of ordnance on enemy targets that makes airpower a credible combat force.

The story of today's ordnance is the story of how bombs and bullets got "smart." Since the end of World War II, most of the developmental money for new conventional (i.e., not nuclear, chemical, or biological) weapons has gone into guided systems that have held the promise of "one round, one hit." Some systems, like the Sidewinder air-to-air missile and the Paveway laser-guided bombs, have almost fulfilled that promise. Others have not done so well. Nevertheless, after the 1991 Persian Gulf War, when the 10% of the weapons dropped that were smart did something like 90% of the damage to critical strategic targets, you can count on all types of weapons getting smarter. While the use of the unguided rocket or "dumb" bomb may not yet be over, their days are clearly numbered.

Meanwhile, the variety of weapons that a modern combat aircraft can carry simply boggles the mind. Recently, another defense writer contacted me to ask about Air Force munitions programs. So confusing was the variety of the programs we discussed, that we decided this book would try to explain as many of the different things that U.S. Air Force aircraft can shoot at, launch at, or drop on our enemies as possible.

Air-to-Air Missiles

Though rapid-firing cannons are a vital part of the weapons mix that make fighters both dangerous and effective, bullets aren't smart. Once they leave the muzzle of a gun, they can only follow a ballistic path determined by the laws of physics, no matter what the target does. A *guided* missile, on the other hand, can alter its flight path after it is launched, which greatly increases the probability of a hit. If you look at the world record books since the end of the Korean

War, the vast majority of air-to-air kills have been achieved by guided air-to-air missiles (AAMs). Maybe not as righteous as a gun kill, but as any fighter jock will tell you, "A kill's a kill!"

AIM-9 Sidewinder Missile

The first experiments with guided AAMs were done in Nazi Germany during World War II. In an attempt to keep their fighters out of range of the defensive machine guns of the massed air fleets of bombers and fighters attacking their homeland, the Germans developed a series of air-to-air missiles. Luckily for the Allied air forces, the Ruhrstahl X-4 came too late to make it into service. This compact, wire-guided missile was designed to be "flown" by the pilot of the firing aircraft using a small joystick. It was a halting step on the way to the AAMs of today, but it was a first step nevertheless.

Following the war, a number of nations began to develop SAM and AAM designs, hoping to knock down the fleets of nuclear bombers that were expected to dominate the next major conflict. Most were designed to use the new technology of radar that had matured during World War II. The problem with radar-guided missiles was that they were relatively heavy, vastly complex, and required the firing aircraft/battery to track the target with its own radar. In order to allow the missile to get within lethal range of the target aircraft, you had to either "illuminate" the target with a radar beam (called a fire-control radar), or track the outgoing missile in flight and radio flight commands (called command guidance or "beam riding"). Early fighters equipped with these bulky systems had to be large, placing aircraft designers of the day under great pressure to build aircraft with performance equal to their smaller, gun-armed competitors. It seemed for a time that designers of missile-armed fighters would just have to grit their teeth and wait for technical advances in power plants, electronics, airframes, and computers to make the promise of air-to-air missiles a reality.

Then suddenly, out of a brilliant, unorthodox scientist's garage laboratory in the high desert of California, came an elegantly simple solution to the problem of missile guidance. The scientist was Dr. William B. McLean, at the Naval Ordnance Test Station (NOTS) at Inyokern, California (today the Michelson Laboratory of the U.S. Naval Weapons Center at China Lake, California). In the late 1940s, in his home garage workshop and on his own time, he built a simple device that could track an aircraft by the heat emissions from its power plant. This meant that a missile seeker could be developed to track a target without any sort of radar guidance from the firing battery or aircraft.

The key was a small electronic detector, called a photovoltaic cell, which was capable of detecting heat—or infrared radiation emissions in the short-wavelength region of the electromagnetic spectrum. The early infrared seekers used detectors based on lead sulfide, a material whose electronic characteristics are altered when it becomes saturated by infrared radiation. These seekers were *not* looking for the heat given off by the exhaust gases of a jet engine (as mistakenly reported for decades). On the contrary, what the tracking elements of the first-generation heat-seeking missiles were looking for was hot metal, or more specifically, the infrared radiation given off by the hot metal of jet or piston engine exhaust ports. The major technical advantage of infrared seekers is that they can be more compact, lighter, and cheaper than radar missile seekers. This allowed Dr. McLean and the engineers at NOTS to design a missile, initially known as Local Project (LP) 612, that only weighed about 155 lb./70.45 kg., in a tubular body only 5 in./12.7 cm. in diameter. To save money (which he did not have anyway), McLean used airframes from unguided 5 in./12.7 cm. High Velocity Artillery Rockets (HVARs), into which he packed the motors, warheads, and electronics. At the rear of each of the fixed tail fins is a small device that looks like a metal pinwheel. This is called a rolleron, and is used to stabilize the weapon while it is in flight. It's one of the tricks thought up by Dr. McLean and his team to help keep the Sidewinder on a stable course, and uses the missile's own slipstream through the air to generate gyroscopic motion to dampen any oscillations induced by the guidance system. The rolleron was on the first missile, and is still there today. LP612 also had the advantage of being a "fire-and-forget" weapon—the pilot does not guide the weapon after firing. Tactically, this means the firing aircraft is free to maneuver or evade once the weapon is launched.

When the first test launches of what would become the Aerial Intercept Missile Nine (AIM-9) were conducted in 1953, the missile's snakelike flight path towards the test targets provided the name it would carry for the next half century of service, the Sidewinder. From its first tests against target drones, it was a favorite of the pilots at China Lake, because of its high reliability and deadly accuracy. In addition, it could be rapidly and cheaply retrofitted on older aircraft, so a whole generation of existing fighters could enjoy the benefits of AAMs, without the weight penalty of a massive air-intercept (AI) radar for guidance. Sidewinder was quickly adopted by the Navy and U.S. Marine Corps as the standard short-range AAM of the day.

The effectiveness of the little AIM-9 missile was demonstrated in 1958, when the Eisenhower Administration supplied the Republic of China (ROC)/Taiwan, with Sidewinder AAMs and launchers to equip its F-86 Sabrejets. The ROC Air Force was fighting daily air battles with MiG-17s of the People's Republic of China, over two small islands in the Formosa Straits, Quemoy and Matsu. While the AIM-9s were responsible for shooting down only a small percentage of the MiGs destroyed in the battles (most were still shot down by the .50-caliber machine guns of the ROC F-86s), their impact was immense, and the word quickly spread around the fighter world about the deadly little AAM named after a rattlesnake.

Over the next ten years or so, the early models of the AIM-9 (usually the AIM-9B variant) fought in theaters all over the world. In the skies over the Indian subcontinent (the 1965 India-Pakistan War), North Vietnam (1965 to 1973), and the Middle East (the June 1967 Six Day War), the Sidewinder was the most effective AAM in service. It shot down more enemy aircraft than any other AAM of the period, and put the longer-range, heavier, and more costly radar homing AAMs like the AIM-7 Sparrow to shame. So effective was the early AIM-9, that when several fell into Communist hands in the late-1950s and early 1960s, the Soviet Union produced an exact copy, the R-13/AA-2 Atoll, for use on its own fighter aircraft.

For all its successes, the Sidewinder had some significant limitations and shortcomings. Many of these became evident in Vietnam. For instance, the early-model AIM-9B Sidewinder was a relatively short-range (about 2.6 nm./4.75 km.) missile, and its seeker could only "acquire" a target and "lock" onto it if the firing aircraft was behind the target (within a 90° arc centered on the target's line of flight). It also was susceptible to being decoyed by flares, infrared jammers, and even the sun. (If you fired at a target within about 20° of the sun, the missile would ignore the target and lock onto the sun.) The biggest problem, though, was the pilots' lack of in-depth understanding of the missile's performance "envelope" (aviator jargon for things like, "How fast can it turn, climb, or dive at different altitudes and velocities?"). In addition, the early electronics technology of the day (vacuum tubes) simply lacked the reliability to survive the shock of aircraft carrier landings and the tropical heat and humidity of Southeast Asia. As a result, several efforts were initiated by the U.S. military to improve the Sidewinder and other air-to-air missiles.

In 1968, a U.S. Navy study, the "Ault Report," examined the poor performance of U.S. fighter, radar, and missile systems in Southeast Asia. One of the first results of this study was better training of U.S. pilots, to teach them how to maneuver their aircraft into the "heart" of the missile's lethal envelope, thus maximizing the chances of a kill. The development of Dissimilar Air Combat Training courses (DACT, practice dogfights against fighters with different flying characteristics from your own aircraft, using electronic scoring systems that simulate the performance of real missiles) in the USAF and USN, particularly the Navy's famous Top Gun school, did much to improve the performance of U.S. pilots in combat. As for the Sidewinder, there already was a series of product improvement programs in the works to remake the little AAM.

The first of these programs produced versions of the missile for the USAF (the AIM-9E) and the USN/USMC (the AIM-9D). Both versions, fielded in the mid-1960s, featured improved seekers that were cooled (thermoelectrically in the case of the AIM-9E, gas cooled for the AIM-9D). The -E models were converted from earlier AIM-9B-model Sidewinders, and provided better low-altitude performance than the -B model. In addition, the -D had a more powerful rocket motor for greater range (up to 11 nm./20.11 km.) and an improved warhead. Later, the USAF further modified the -E model Sidewinder to the AIM-9J configuration, with improved aerodynamic surfaces and control for greater maneuverability and range (about 9 nm./16.46 km.). This second generation gradually expanded the launch envelope, range, and performance of the various Sidewinder versions, so that a pilot could launch from anywhere aft of an enemy aircraft's wings (the rear 180° hemisphere), from a fairly high off-angle (from the target aircraft's centerline), and from maximum and minimum

Loral Aeronutronic AIM-9L/M Sidewinder air-to-air missiles loaded onto their launch rails. The seeker is contained in the rounded nose of the missile, and the fins are designed to provide good maneuvering control and minimize drag. *LORAL AERONUTRONIC*

ranges. These versions of the Sidewinder helped the USN and USAF fighter forces decimate the North Vietnamese MiGs in 1972, and they were the backbone of the Free World's short-range AAM inventory for the rest of the 1970s. A third generation, the AIM-9L, saw service in the 1980s.

The final, and currently deployed, third-generation version of the Sidewinder is the AIM-9M. Like the earlier AIM-9L variant, the "Mike" as it is called, is used by the fighter forces of the USN, USMC, and USAF on virtually every combat aircraft with an air-to-air capability. The Air Force normally deploys the "Mike" on fighters such as the F-15 Eagle and F-16 Fighting Falcon. Its dominant feature is the tubular airframe, 5 in./12.7 cm. in diameter, to which the forward (guidance) and aft cruciform fins are attached. At the front of the missile is a tapered nose section with a hemispherical seeker window at the tip. The 5 in./12.7 cm. dimension has been one of the little missile's great virtues, as well as its biggest vice. On the plus side, it has meant that the basic missile and interface has remained relatively unchanged for over forty years. This has allowed aircraft designers to find a variety of inventive ways of adding Sidewinder to the weapons suite of fighters. In the case of the F-16 and F-18, the primary AIM-9 launchers were placed on the wingtips. The down side is that packing improvements into a 5 in./12.7 cm. tube can be difficult. For example,

Israeli and Soviet/Russian AAM designers long ago abandoned the small diameter airframe, so they could pack larger motors and warheads inside.

It's what is inside that airframe tube that counts, and the Sidewinder does as much with the limited space available as any missile in the world. The current -M version is some 113 in./287 cm. long, with a forward canard (BSU-32/B) wingspan of 15 in./38.1 cm., and a rear stabilizer (Mk 1) wingspan of 24.8 in./63 cm. Weighing in at 194 lb./88.2 kg., it was first produced in fiscal year 1981. At the front of the missile is the WGU-4A/B Guidance Control Section (GCS). Inside the GCS is the seeker, which is the ultimate in single-element infrared sensitivity. Composed of an indium-antimonide (InSb) detector element, cooled by an open-cycle Joule-Thompson cryostat, it is mounted on a gimbaled "head" behind a magnesium-fluoride (MgF_2, a fragile material, but selectively transparent to infrared radiation in the seeker's particular wavelengths) seeker dome/window. The seeker element feeds into a signal processor, which generates the commands for the missile's four guidance fins, which are mounted on the side of the seeker-guidance section. The real beauty of the current system is that it scans in two different wavelengths or "colors." This means that it is looking at both short- and middle-wavelength (infrared) light as well as the long wavelength (ultraviolet) spectrum. It is a deadly combination.

Just forward of the rocket motor is the WDU-17 Annular Blast Fragmentation (ABF) warhead section. Previously, there had been a great deal of criticism over the relatively puny size of the Sidewinder's warhead. Thus, when development of the third-generation AIM-9 began, the designers decided to enhance the destructive power of the 25 lb./11.36 kg. warhead. The previous versions had provided a mixed bag of weapons effects. The solution was a new kind of proximity fuse that would detect when a target aircraft got into lethal range and detonate in such a way that the force (and fragments) of the warhead would impact directly into the target aircraft. Composed of a ring of four pairs of laser emitting diodes (somewhat like the IR emitter/detectors on your TV/VCR remote controls) and laser detectors, the DSU-15/B Active Optical Target Detector uses the laser detector ring as a way of determining when a target aircraft is within range. If the missile should miss the target (a rare occasion due to the accuracy of the guidance system), the warhead is designed to detonate and spew its fragmentation pattern at the target aircraft. This is a particularly effective kill mechanism, since the second- and third-generation Soviet fighters that the AIM-9L/M was designed to attack had no self-sealing fuel tanks or fuel bladders. In fact, Soviet designs like the MiG-23/27 Flogger and the MiG-25 Foxbat usually had only a thin skin of aircraft-grade aluminum or stainless steel between their fuel supply and the open sky. This meant that if so much as a single hot fragment penetrated a fuel tank, the Soviet aircraft was probably going to be headed down in a ball of flames.

At the rear part of the airframe is the rocket motor. Over the years, the USAF and USN have differed over what they want from the propulsion system of the Sidewinder. In fact, this has been the basic philosophical difference between USAF and USN since the first of the improved Sidewinders began to roll off the lines in the 1960s. The Mk 36 rocket motor in the AIM-9M favors the USAF point-of-view. With the Mk 36, an M-model Sidewinder can theoretically fly out to a range of up to 11 nm./20.1 km. with a maximum flight time of one minute.

What does all of this mean when it comes to real-world combat? Well, consider the performance of AIM-9L/M-series AAMs in U.S. service over a ten year period from 1981 to 1991. In that time, some twenty-two missiles were fired, with sixteen guiding to hits, resulting in some thirteen "kills." During the same period, foreign clients have scored an even better record, with two kills going to Saudi pilots, twenty-five to Royal Navy Sea Harrier pilots in the Falklands, sixteen to Pakistani aircrew, and probably several dozen more to the Israelis. This run of success may never be duplicated by any future model of AAM.

For all the high technology and old-fashioned ingenuity that have gone into making Sidewinder so successful, it is still among the easiest of missiles to use. When the pilot of an F-16C wants to launch an AIM-9M at a target, all that is required is to select AAM from the stores control panel. At this point, the seeker in the nose of the missile begins to look for a target in front of the fighter. If the radar is already locked onto a target, the seeker head can be slaved to the radar, and the seeker will lock onto the desired target. The pilot is informed of the lock-on through an audio tone in his/her headset. When the tone becomes a solid "growl," the missile is ready to launch. At this point, all the pilot has to do is squeeze the trigger gently, and the missile is on the way. The pilot of the F-16 is now free to fire another missile, seek another target, or just "get the hell out of Dodge City," should that be necessary.

AIM-120 AMRAAM

The pilots call it the "Slammer," and it is the fastest, smartest, most deadly AAM in the world today. It works so well that an F-15 pilot compared shooting down enemy aircraft with the AIM-120 to "clubbing baby seals, one after the other . . . whomp . . . whomp . . . WHOMP!" It is a telling statement, even more telling when you consider that the AIM-120 Advanced Medium Range Air-to-Air Missile (AMRAAM) program was nearly still-born because of development problems and Congressional opposition. Its long and painful gestation, particularly in software and production engineering, came close to killing it repeatedly in the 1980s. Yet just four years into its service life, the initial model, the AIM-120A, is the most feared missile in the history of air warfare. In spite of that, AMRAAM would never have been needed if its predecessor, the AIM-7 Sparrow III, had not been such a terrible disappointment.

The AIM-7 Sparrow was born as the Sperry XAAM-N-2 Sparrow I out of a 1946 Navy program called Project Hot Shot. Hot Shot sought to find an airborne solution to the kinds of jet and kamikaze aircraft encountered at the end of World War II. While it went into production in 1951, the first Sparrow

AAM did not intercept a test target until 1953 at Inyokern in California, and finally went into USN fleet service in 1956. That first radar homing AAM utilized a "beam riding" radar guidance system that was really only capable of hitting large, bomber-sized targets flying straight and level. Realizing the limitations of the Sparrow I, in the late 1950s, the Navy began a program to improve the missile into a weapon with greater tactical capability. Out of this effort came the AIM-7C Sparrow III, produced by Raytheon in Massachusetts. This new version retained the basic airframe and propulsion package, but used a new guidance scheme known as "semi-active" homing, in which the radar of the firing aircraft "illuminates" a target aircraft with its radar, and the missile seeker homes in on the reflected radar energy. This puts the burden of the intercept problem on the aircraft's radar, allowing the missile to be smaller, lighter, and supposedly simpler. If it were only that easy!

When the Sparrow system was conceived just after World War II, the electronic technologies that make guided missiles effective and reliable just weren't there. Early airborne radar/missile designers had to make do with vacuum tubes, early analog computers, and complex, bulky logic circuit boards. Thus Sparrow has spent its long service life hamstrung by primitive technology. For example, keeping the target illuminated throughout the flight of the missile required the launching aircraft to remain in a tactically disadvantageous position—flying straight and level instead of maneuvering aggressively. This became particularly evident in Vietnam, when unrealistic ROE were politically determined at the Presidential level. The ROE prohibited use of the Sparrow at medium/Beyond-Visual-Range (BVR), distances where it was capable of destroying an enemy target with little risk to the launching aircraft. (BVR meant greater than 20 nm./36 km. Pilots prefer to think in terms of a missile's "no escape zone," an ever-changing teardrop-shaped volume of space with dimensions that are classified.) This forced crews of the heavy F-4 Phantoms that used the Sparrow to close to visual range with the more agile North Vietnamese MiGs, making it nearly impossible to maneuver the big fighter's radar onto the nimble enemy interceptors.

And then the firing sequence was a nightmare. The AIM-7E2 version of the Sparrow III, used throughout the Vietnam War, had over ninety electrical, pyrotechnic, and pneumatic functions that had to work perfectly in the proper order, and took over three seconds just to get out of the launch well and on its way to the target. If that was not bad enough, the AWG-10 radar system on the U.S. Navy F-4J was roughly comparable in parts count and design complexity to the Surveyor-series of unmanned moon probes launched in 1966. And the lunar probe only had to function in the relatively benign vacuum environment of the moon for a month or two. The AWG-10 had to function after being slammed around repeatedly by catapult takeoffs and carrier landings in tropical conditions. As a result, the Sparrow III, as well as the radar systems of the various models of F-4s, had severe reliability problems. The Project Hot Shot engineers had never anticipated the possibility that AIM-7 missiles and their associated black boxes might be catapulted off aircraft carriers and do arrested landings three times a day in the steaming heat of Southeast Asia for weeks on end. In short, nobody had anticipated the nature of air warfare in the real world, and the Sparrow AAM was one of the victims of that lack of vision.

In short, it would be nice to say that the radar guided Sparrow has been as successful as its heat-seeking cousin, the AIM-9 Sidewinder. But it would be a lie. The AIM-7 has been a disappointment, despite tens of billions of dollars spent on it and its fire control radars. When it is used properly, and the breaks go its way, it can be the most deadly of AAMs. But its designers promised a "silver bullet," and it never delivered, proving that no matter how much money you throw at a program, basic design limitations cannot be overcome. Some of the technologies the AIM-7 was based on were just fundamentally flawed. Nevertheless, the Sparrow has served for five decades, and continues to soldier on, periodically improved and updated. It became a primary weapon of the F-15 Eagle, and is carried on most other U.S. and NATO fighters capable of air-to-air operations (such as the U.S. F-14 Tomcat and F-18 Hornet). Slowly and painfully, shortcomings and problems were overcome, at a cost of billions of taxpayer dollars. Finally, some forty-five years after it was conceived, the Sparrow III got its day in the sun during Operation Desert Storm. The good news was that the final major version of the missile, the AIM-7M, shot down more Iraqi aircraft (twenty-four) than all other weapons combined, and that it was over four times as effective as it was in Vietnam. (In Vietnam, the AIM-7 had a success rate of about 9%, while in Desert Storm, depending how you interpret the data, it was about 36%.) The bad news was that almost half the AIM-7s launched failed to function properly, and only about one Sparrow in three actually hit and killed anything. Out of seventy-one AIM-7Ms fired in Desert Storm, only twenty-six hit their targets, for twenty-three kills. It was as good a performance as the Sparrow ever gave, and it stank. Luckily, there was already a replacement on the way.

Vietnam was a wake-up call for the fighter community. They didn't have the right weapons for the job; and that stung them. Then it took several more years, and more proposed Sparrow variants, for the truth to finally hit home. They needed a new BVR missile. The argument for a radically new missile was simple. If an enemy fighter force with an all-aspect, IR missile faced off against a U.S. fighter force using Sparrow, the U.S. force might barely break even in the critical kill/loss ratio that separates victory from defeat.

Thus came a specification for a new kind of BVR missile: It would have the same fire-and-forget capabilities as Sidewinder, but much greater reliability and speed; it could be carried on much smaller fighters than the Sparrow; and it would throw away the concept of "maximum range" for a more useful and deadly measuring stick—the no-escape zone. No-escape means that any target aircraft inside the new missile's performance "envelope" would be unable to get away, no matter how hard and fast it punched the afterburner or how violently it maneuvered. Because the AIM-7 series had neither the brains nor the energy for such sophisticated maneuvering, it was relatively easy for a skilled pilot to evade, especially with the warning that even a primitive RWR provided.

Five different manufacturers vied for the opportunity to build the Advanced Medium Range Air-to-Air Missile or AMRAAM. In 1979, the competition was whittled down to just two contractors: Raytheon Corporation and Hughes Missile Systems. After two years of development and competition, Hughes won the biggest AAM contract of the century in 1981. The contract was for twenty-four developmental missiles with options for production of an additional 924, and plans for up to 24,000. The missile, designated as the AIM-120, would take almost a decade to bring into service.

Hughes brought strong credentials and a wealth of experience to the problem of developing AMRAAM. They were builders of the long-serving AIM-4 Falcon series of AAM, and the most powerful AAM in history, the mighty AIM-54 Phoenix. Phoenix, which came into service in 1974 on the Navy F-14 Tomcat fighter, was the first true "fire-and-forget" radar homing AAM, and has been the airborne shield for the fleet for over two decades. Known as "the buffalo" by the fleet aircrews for its impressive size and weight, Phoenix has a range of up to 100 nm./182.9 km. and the ability to engage multiple targets with multiple missiles at the same time. One of the key objectives of the AMRAAM program was to give pilots of single-seat fighters like the F-15 and F-16 the same kind of firepower and tactical capabilities as the F-14 Tomcat, with its two-man crew and powerful AWG-9 radar/fire control system. It would be a technical challenge to pack so much performance into a much smaller airframe.

Unfortunately, the AMRAAM program ran into terrible technical problems. For years, AMRAAM development and testing failed to go smoothly, mostly because everything in the AIM-120 was generations ahead of the best technology on the Sparrow. The advanced electronics, structures, and rocket motor were difficult to design, qualify, and produce. The real hang-up, though, was the software. The AIM-120 is driven by microprocessors running hundreds of thousands of lines of computer code—more than any AAM in history. After each line of code is written, it has to be validated through rigorous testing. Any faults or problems have to be isolated and fixed, and then the process begins again. This cycle continues until the code is ready to be loaded on tape cassettes for delivery to units equipped with AMRAAM. If this sounds frustrating, try to remember the last time a commercial software program "bombed" on your computer. You probably lost an hour or two of work, rebooted, and drove on, muttering a curse on the programming "geeks" who left the bug in the code. But in a system like an AAM, the software has to be *perfect*. If it is not, you've just thrown $300,000 of the taxpayers' money into the toilet, and potentially put an aircraft and crew at risk. This was the problem the AMRAAM program faced as the 1980s wore on. Schedules slipped, and the project ran over budget. Hostile members of Congress repeatedly tried to kill the program; and several critical General Accounting Office reports raised doubts that the program could ever "get well." Finally, Congress threw down the gauntlet, mandating a series of successful live-fire tests before full production of the missile would be authorized. Things started to look grim.

An F-16C launches a Hughes AIM-120 Advanced Medium Range Air-to-Missile (AMRAM) during testing. The fighter also caries AIM-9 Sidewinder missiles on the wingtips. *Hughes Missile Systems*

Then, some good things began happening. Fully validated software tapes began to arrive at test sites, and missiles began to fly straight and true against their drone targets. To some of the missile's critics, it appeared that a miracle had happened. In fact, AMRAAM had followed the normal path of a system controlled by computers and software. It is a hallmark of software driven systems that they are virtually useless until a valid version of the software is available. But when the day comes that a technician plugs in the final release version of the software, it usually works exactly as promised. Like the Army's Patriot SAM and Navy's Aegis Combat System, AIM-120 came of age when its software was finally ready. The final validation of AMRAAM came at the White Sands Missile Range when an F-15C ripple-fired four test AIM-120s at four jammer-equipped QF-100 target drones, maneuvering aggressively and kicking out flares and chaff decoys. Dubbed the "World War III Shot" by test directors, it resulted in all four drones going down in flames. All of the Congressionally mandated tests were passed.

With the problems of testing behind, the first production missiles began to be delivered in late 1988, becoming operational in 1991 when 52 AIM-120As deployed with the F-15Cs 58th Tactical Fighter Squadron (TFS) of the 33rd Tactical Fighter Wing (TFW) to the Persian Gulf, in time for the end of Desert Storm. As it turned out, the missile did not get a chance to shoot at anything before the end of hostilities, but did acquire plenty of "captive carry" flight time, which is critical to "wringing out" the problems of any new airborne weapons system. The new missile's chance for combat finally came on the morning of December 27th, 1992, when a USAF F-16C assigned to the 33rd TFS of the 363rd TFW, patrolling a no-fly zone in Iraq, shot down an Iraqi Air Force MiG-25 Foxbat with a single, front aspect, "in-your-face" AIM-120A shot. This also was the first USAF kill for the F-16. Three weeks later, on January 17th, 1993, the AMRAAM/"Viper" combination scored again, when a

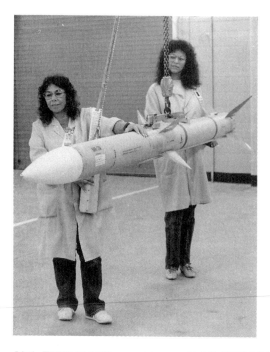

Two Hughes Missile Systems technicians move an AIM-120A Advanced Medium Range Air-to-Air Missile from the assembly line to the shipping area.

50th TFW F-16C escorting an F-4G "Wild Weasel" encountered an Iraqi MiG-23 Flogger in one of the no-fly zones. After sparring with the MiG for several minutes, it launched a single AIM-120A from the outer edge of the missile's no-escape zone. The missile guided true, downing the MiG as it tried to escape. Later, as the missile was rapidly acquiring the nickname of Slammer from the aircrews, the AIM-120A/F-16C combination scored again over Bosnia. A single AMRAAM scored a kill against a Serbian attack aircraft, this time hugging the ground, dodging through mountainous terrain (three other kills in this engagement went to AIM-9M Sidewinders). The Slammer had silenced its critics, downing three enemy aircraft with three shots—a perfect combat record. No other missile in history, even the legendary AIM-9 Sidewinder or AGM-84 Harpoon, did so well during its combat introduction. This amazing performance deserves a closer look.

If you walk up to an AMRAAM at the factory, the first thing you notice is that it looks a lot like the old AIM-7 Sparrow: a pointed nose cone on a cylindrical airframe with two sets of cruciform guidance/stabilization fins. On the surface, nothing special. As you look closer, subtle differences begin to appear. The AIM-120 is considerably smaller than the Sparrow, based on a 7 in./17.8 cm.-diameter airframe tube, as opposed to the 8 in./20.3 cm. barrel section on an AIM-7. It is shorter, measuring 12 feet/3.7 meters, with a center (stabilizing) fin span of 21 in./53.3 cm., and a rear (guidance) fin span of 25 in./63.5 cm. And it weighs in at a modest 335 lb./152 kg., compared to the hefty 500 lb./227.3 kg. of the AIM-7. This weight difference makes it possible to mount the AIM-120 on launch rails designed for the smaller AIM-9

Sidewinder. In fact, F-16s often carry two AIM-120s on the wing-tip missile launchers. The smooth integration of the F-16 and the AIM-120 makes the missile a favorite among Viper drivers, who claim that they can now shoot anything the larger F-15 can.

At the front of the missile is the seeker section with its electronics, antenna, and batteries. Under the nose radome is the gimbaled radar antenna of the missile. Unlike Sparrow, AMRAAM does not depend on the AI radar of the launching aircraft to illuminate the target to provide guidance for the missile. Instead, the Hughes engineers have built a complete AI radar system into the nose of the AIM-120. The missile can hit a fast-moving airborne target all by itself. All the radar of the launching aircraft has to do is send the missile the three-dimensional position, course, heading, and speed of the target. The missile then flies out to a point where it switches on its own radar. If the target is anywhere inside the radar "cone" of the AMRAAM's seeker, it locks up the enemy aircraft, interrogates it with IFF to make sure that it is not a "friendly," then initiates the endgame and streaks in to the kill.

Because it does things that were previously limited to missiles over three times its size and weight, the seeker of the AIM-120 is where the magic happens. The radar antenna of the seeker (produced by Microwave Associates) looks just like a miniature of the dish on the APG-63 and functions in exactly the same way. Just aft of the gimbaled mounting for the radar is the seeker/guidance electronics package. Here are mounted the circuit cards for the Watkins-Johnson signal processor, transmitter, receiver, the digital autopilot, and the battery array. All of this is contained in a series of modules about 24 in./61 cm. long and about 6 in./15.2 cm. in diameter—a marvel of packaging and miniaturization. At the rear of this package is the Northrop strapdown Inertial Reference Unit (IRU), which is the heart of the guidance system. It contains three small gyros (one each for the roll, pitch, and yaw axes), and senses the movement of the missile along its flight path. This allows the AMRAAM's guidance electronics to calculate any deviations from the programmed flight path and generate course corrections.

Since all of the AIM-120's electronics are microprocessor-controlled modules, they are easily upgraded by adding new software (uploaded through the aircraft data bus, or inserted on new Programmable Read Only Memory chips). In addition, as the circuits resulting from Pave Pillar and other programs come on-line in the 1990s and beyond, it will be possible to keep the missile up to date, including software upgrades rapidly produced during wartime. There are already plans to replace the mechanical gyros in the AMRAAM's IRU with much more accurate ring-laser gyros. There are even studies to evaluate fitting AIM-120 with a GPS receiver, to enhance its navigational accuracy.

Just aft of the seeker guidance section is the AMRAAM's armament section, which contains the warhead and target-detection device. The warhead is an ABF-type warhead built by Chamberlain Manufacturing which weighs in at a hefty 50.6 lb./23 kg., using a ring of contact plus/laser proximity fuses, just like the AIM-9M. While not as powerful as the big warhead on the AIM-7M, it can down virtually any aircraft in the world today.

Just behind the armament package, and taking up fully half the AIM-120's length, is the single-grain, ducted rocket motor built by Hercules. It is a fine compromise between a fast burning, high impulse motor and one which burns with lower thrust for a longer time. What makes this possible is the small size and low aerodynamic drag of the AIM-120 airframe. The missile rapidly accelerates to about Mach 4 (plus the speed of the launch aircraft), and can sustain this with an intelligent autopilot designed to conserve the vital "smash" energy that creates the no-escape zone. The result is a missile with the ability to virtually guarantee a kill against an approaching head-on target out to something like 40 nm./73.2 km. In a "tail chase" engagement, which requires the missile to overtake the target, this range drops to probably around 12 nm./21.9 km. These numbers should be considered approximate, because DoD is very sensitive about the precise no-escape range at various points of the AMRAAM envelope. At the rear of the missile are the maneuvering fins. Hughes found that rear-mounted maneuvering fins enhance the ability to turn rapidly during the terminal endgame.

So how do you launch an AMRAAM missile shot? If you are flying an F-16C, you select an air-to-air mode for the radar such as BORE (Boresight—i.e., where the radar is sighted down the centerline of the aircraft) or TWS, DOGFIGHT (where the radar is in a mode useful for close-in dogfighting). Then you thumb the missile selection switch on the control stick for AIM-120, and select either SLAVE or BORE to program the missile radar to accept commands from the F-16's onboard APG-68 radar. The SLAVE option locks the missile seeker onto whatever target the aircraft's radar is currently tracking, while BORE simply points the aircraft's radar straight ahead along your line of flight—the first target it sees will be locked. Once a radar contact is established, the onboard weapons computer establishes a fire control solution, including elapsed time from missile launch until the AMRAAM's radar goes active. At this point, the F-16's Heads Up Display will begin to give you steering cues to bring the aircraft into range to fire. Once the HUD gives you an IN RANGE indicator, you press the weapons release ("pickle" switch) on the control stick. At this point, the missile is launched and will accept updates from the radar (if you have selected a FIRE AND UPDATE mode) until either you break radar contract from maneuvering or the missile hits the target. At this point, you are ready to either select another target or evade. Total time for the engagement? Well, on my first try in the F-16 simulator at Lockheed's Fort Worth Plant, I was able to do it in about eight seconds. It is that simple, just like playing the computer game *Falcon*.

So, what is the future for AMRAAM? For starters, there are exports. Great Britain, Norway, Sweden, and Germany have already become customers for the AIM-120. Additional nations will certainly be added to this list. New versions of the missile are on the drawing board, getting ready for test and production. The most important of these will be the AIM-120C, designed for internal carriage on the Lockheed F-22A stealth fighter, which will enter service early in the 21st century. This new version of the AIM-120, with smaller control surfaces and a much smaller stowage profile, will give the F-22 lethal air-to-air firepower without compromising its ultra-smooth low-observable profile. AMRAAM is really a flying computer with a big bang attached. With continuous software improvements, it will be a cornerstone of the U.S. AAM arsenal well into the middle of the 21st century

Future Developments: The AIM-9X

Once upon a time in the 1980s, there was a master plan for future U.S. AAM development. This plan included the introduction of AMRAAM, as well as the replacement of both the AIM-9L/M Sidewinder and the AIM-54 Phoenix. Unfortunately, with Congressional restrictions and budget cuts, the end of the Cold War, and some badly managed programs, this master plan fell apart before it could be implemented. The AIM-54 replacement, known as the Advanced Air-to-Air Missile (AAAM), was stillborn when the requirement died with the Soviet Union in the late 1980s. But the most painful loss for fighter crews was the Sidewinder replacement.

Originally, the AIM-9's successor was to be a European-built system known as the AIM-132 Advanced Short Range Air-to-Air Missile (ASRAAM), built by a consortium of British Aerospace and Bodenseewerk Technik Geraete (BGT) of Germany. Under a multi-national Memorandum of Understanding (MOU) signed in 1981 by the United States and a number of NATO nations, all agreed to adopt AMRAAM and ASRAAM as their standard AAMs. Unfortunately, the United States and Germany dropped out of the program. While the AIM-132 has continued development, and will go into service with the Royal Air Force in the late 90s, the result was disarray in Western AAM procurement.

Today the next generation of American short-range AAMs is being conceived in the halls of the Pentagon and the engineering design shops of Hughes and Raytheon. The missile is tentatively called the AIM-9X, and if it goes into production, it should put the United States back into the game of short-range dogfighting in the 21st century. In January 1995, Hughes Missile Systems and Raytheon Corporation won a competition to develop separate proposals for the new model of Sidewinder. Final selection of a prime contractor will happen in 1996, with service introduction sometime in the early years of the 21st century. While the exact configurations that the two contract teams will submit to the AIM-9X JPO are proprietary, there are probably many common features. These include:

- **Seeker**—The seeker will probably be a staring (constantly viewing the target) IIR array with many detector-array elements, each one sensitive enough to track a target at all aspects. It will be backed up by an advanced signal processor, designed to actually look for the signature of a particular aircraft configuration (such as a Mirage 2000 or a MiG-29), providing it with a basic NCTR function. Also, it will be capable of tracking targets from a high "off-boresight" mode (the ability to lock up a target well off the launch aircraft's centerline—maybe more than 60°—and then fly directly off the launch rail to a hit).

- **Helmet Mounted Sight (HMS)**—The Navy and Air Force have finally accepted the inevitability of the HMS as the visual sighting system for future manned combat aircraft. The big advance planned for the U.S. HMS will be that HUD symbology will be superimposed on the sight glass, directly in front of the user's right eye. Studies indicate that this will provide a two-to-four second improvement in overall reaction time to launch an AIM-9X, and will also make AMRAAM shots more rapid and accurate.

- **Warhead**—The current generation of ABF warheads, while quite adequate for killing a MiG-23 Flogger or MiG-25 Foxbat, may not perform as well against newer Russian and Western designs. These blast-fragmentation warheads were designed to perforate the target's fuel tanks, igniting catastrophic fires on any plane not equipped with self-sealing fuel tanks and fire suppression systems. Plans are afoot to design warheads that specifically target other aircraft systems like the engines or the crew. This will keep the AIM-9X a highly lethal contender in the endless contest between the warhead engineers and the "vulnerability engineers" who design aircraft protective systems for use well into the middle of the 21st century.

- **Propulsion/Guidance**—For the first time in a Western AAM, the AIM-9X will utilize an active thrust vectoring propulsion system, which will radically improve maneuverability. It appears that whatever design team wins the competition, the winner will make use of a Raytheon-designed and -developed fin control system known as Box Office. Composed of four tail-mounted maneuvering fins (there are no mid-body guidance fins as in AMRAAM), Box Office will make 60-G maneuvers possible for the first time on a U.S. AAM.

When all these components are integrated and the inevitable software bugs are eventually tracked down and stamped out, the AIM-9X will carry the proud Sidewinder tradition into a new century. With the will, the money, and an efficient management team, Dr. McLean's vision of an agile, lightweight, intelligent, and deadly missile will take to the skies on wings he could never have imagined back in that desert garage lab. Let's hope it works out; for without it, tomorrow's U.S. fighter pilots could be outgunned as well as outnumbered by systems made elsewhere.

Air-to-Ground Ordnance

On the third day of the Persian Gulf War in 1991, General Charles A. Horner held a press conference in Riyadh, Saudi Arabia, to discuss how things were going. Known as the "four o'clock follies," these daily briefings were rather dull until General Horner started showing gun camera film (videotape actually) from the various strikes of the first night of the Desert Storm. A stunned hush, punctuated by an occasional grim chuckle or curse, fell over the "newsies" as they became the first witnesses of the revolution in the accuracy, range, and precision of modern airborne munitions. In clip after clip, the taped footage showed Iraqi command and control centers, bunkers, aircraft shelters, and other targets blowing up under a hail of guided bombs and other ordnance. Perhaps the most impressive demonstration of modern precision guided munitions (PGMs) were a pair of clips from two F-117A Nighthawks. The target was the central communications and switching center in downtown Baghdad, known by Coalition planners as the "AT&T Building." Heavily overbuilt, it had a reinforced concrete roof designed to resist penetration and blast by normal general purpose (GP) bombs. It did not last long, though. The first F-117A arrived over the target and dropped a 2,000 lb./909.1 kg. laser-guided bomb (LGB) with a special penetrating warhead, blowing a huge hole in the reinforced roof of the building. Several minutes later, to allow time for the dust and other debris to settle (and thus not block the Nighthawk's thermal targeting system), another F-117, sighting on the edges of the hole in the roof, dropped two laser guided bombs of its own into the hole from the first bomb and into the building's core shaft. Armed with GP warheads (blast and fragmentation), they blew out all four sides of the building, leaving it incapable of operations for the duration of the conflict. So specific are the characteristics of individual types of weapons that you now use one kind to blow open a hole and another type to fly through the hole to kill what you *really* want to be dead inside.

> Fighter pilots make movies. Bomber pilots make history!
>
> *Old Bomber Pilot Barroom Chant*

That statement expresses a great truth about airpower. Nobody has ever won, or ever will win, a war by shooting down MiGs, Mirages, or whatever else the enemy may be flying against you. Airpower only helps win wars when you destroy things that are critically important to an enemy on the ground. Airpower's inherent limitation is staying power. Deadly machines like F-16s and B-1Bs simply cannot stay over a piece of battlefield forever. Therefore, it is vital that when a Joint Forces Air Component Commander (JFACC) commits his expensive and limited air resources, he must make them capable of delivering a "bolt from the blue." Not just deadly to what or who you want to destroy, but shocking and frightening to the survivors to the point where their morale is broken and their ability to fight effectively is destroyed. There is a story from

Operation Desert Storm, about the commander of an Iraqi ground unit who surrendered with his entire unit several weeks into the aerial bombardment. When asked by his interrogator why he had surrendered, he responded, "It was the B-52s." When the interrogator pointed out that his unit had never been bombed by B-52s, the Iraqi officer replied, "That's true. But we saw units that had been." That is the ultimate goal of anyone using airpower: to so demoralize the survivors of bombing raids they don't even want to fight. They just give up. That's how you *really* make history.

Now it needs to be said that much of the effectiveness of the Desert Storm bombing campaign was due not only to dropping an overwhelming weight of ordnance on the targets in Iraq and Kuwait, but also to making sure that the *right* targets were getting hit by the *right* aircraft with the *right* munitions for *those* targets. For example, it would have been counterproductive for the huge B-52s, loaded with "dumb," unguided, general purpose bombs, to hit targets in downtown Baghdad. City blocks of buildings would have been flattened, causing thousands of civilian casualties, and the real targets, Saddam Hussein's hardened command bunkers, would have survived without harm. Moreover, because of the heavy air defense over Baghdad, we would have lost many aircraft just making the attempt. Colonel John Warden of the Air Command and Staff College is fond of saying, "Every bomb is a political bomb, with political costs, political benefits, and political effects." It is therefore doubtful that such a campaign would have ever been attempted by the Bush Administration given the political considerations of Coalition warfare and the sensibilities of the domestic media.

What actually happened was that Major General "Buster" Glosson and his "Black Hole" team developed a plan by which only aircraft capable of delivering precision guided munitions (PGMs) would be allowed to bomb targets within the Baghdad metroplex. Downtown Baghdad was limited to weapons deliveries from F-117As and BGM-109 Tomahawk cruise missiles. As a result, while individual buildings and systems were demolished, the city of Baghdad was little touched by the campaign designed to help eject the Iraqis from Kuwait. This is the new face of airpower, where the right weapons are put on the right targets at the right time with the correctly planned weapons effects.

General Purpose Bombs

History tells us that the first time aircraft were used to attack enemy forces on the ground was in January 1912, when an Italian second lieutenant named Giulio Gavotti, assigned to the *Squadriglia di Tripoli* and flying a crude biplane armed with four small improvised bombs, attacked Bedouin tribesmen in the towns of Taguira and Ain Zara in Libya. Since that time, the basic destructive mechanism of the general purpose (GP) bomb has changed relatively little: a tubular metal case, filled with explosive, fuzed to go off when it hits the ground, with some sort of stabilizing fins to make its fall to the target reasonably straight. Today, the USAF uses GP bombs that are true to that basic design, though there have been some recent changes of note.

The basic family of GP bombs used by the U.S. military (including the U.S. Navy and U.S. Marine Corps) is known as the Mark (Mk) 80 series. Though some of the World War II-vintage Mk 117 (a 750 lb./340.9 kg. weapon) and Mk 118 (a 3,000 lb./1,63.6 kg. weapon) bombs are still in use on platforms such as the B-52, the standard family of weapons used on U.S. aircraft today are the 80-series GP bombs. Designed in the 1950s by the famous Ed Heinemann, the Mk 80 series are what is called low-drag, general purpose (LDGP) bombs. Previously, the designers of GP bombs which were carried internally, or on subsonic aircraft, gave little thought to how much parasitic drag they added to an aircraft in flight. This became a major issue, though, with the design of Heinemann's classic A-4 Skyhawk attack bomber, which carried all of its ordnance externally on pylons. Thus, he and his design team began with a clean sheet of paper, and came up with the LDGP shape so familiar to military enthusiasts around the world. The cases are made from cast steel, with relatively thin (less than 1 in./2.5 cm.) walls. This provides one of the bomb's primary damage mechanisms: fragmentation. Being relatively brittle, the steel case expands into a shower of fragments, deadly out to a certain radius. As for the explosive, the current generation of 80-series weapons uses an explosive called Tritonal 80/20. It is composed of an 80% mix of TNT with 20% of the volume of an aluminum binder/inhibitor. The result is an explosive with slightly less explosive power than TNT but extremely stable in storage conditions such as ships and tropical sites. Also, it has a relatively high "cook-off" temperature, which makes the 80-series bombs able to survive for a time in conditions of flame, such as a shipboard fire. Just for added insurance against a cook-off, the U.S. Navy coats their bombs with an ablative coating to buy extra time to suppress the fire and "safe" the bombs.

About 50% of the weight of an 80-series LDGP bomb is explosive, with the rest being taken up by the bomb case, mounting/attachment lugs, fin group, and fuze(s).

Fuzes are more important than you might think, since most modern explosives require a sequence of deliberate actions to detonate. Fuzes have evolved a great deal since the delicate glass/fulminate-of-mercury devices used in the American Civil War to detonate ground and naval mines. Today, you

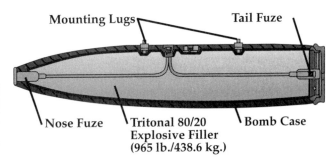

A cutaway drawing of the Mk 84 2,000 lb./909.1 kg. General Purpose Bomb warhead.
Jack Ryan Enterprises, Ltd., by Laura Alpher

Mounting Lugs   Tail Fuze

Nose Fuze   Tritonal 80/20
Explosive Filler
(965 lb./438.6 kg.)   Bomb Case

choose a specific fuze based upon how and when you want a weapon to blow up. The current generation of fuzes are notable because of the variety of conditions that they can be adapted to function in and their ever-increasing reliability. This issue of reliability is critical. If you lug a bomb into defended enemy airspace and drop it with pinpoint precision on an enemy target, and it does not explode because of a fuze failure, then you have just wasted fuel, time, and maybe a multi-million dollar aircraft (as well as your life) for nothing. Some of the more common fuzes include:

Fuze Type	Activation Mode	Function Mode	Mounting	Warheads Used On
FMU-81	Impact	Instantaneous/ Short Delay	Nose/Tail	Paveway LGBs
FMU-113	Radar Proximity	Proximity	Nose	Mk 80-Series
FMU-124A/B	Impact	Instantaneous/ Delay	Tail	Mk 80-Series/ BLU-109
FMU-139	Impact	Instantaneous/ Short Delay	Nose/Tail	Mk 80-Series
FMU-143	Impact	Instantaneous/ Short Delay	Tail	BLU-109/113

Another item critical to successful employment of bombs is making sure that bomb fragments do not hit the attacking aircraft. This can happen to an aircraft doing low-altitude drops with LDGP bombs in a "slick" configuration. To avoid such accidents, "hi-drag" kits were developed to slow the bomb down and provide enough separation for the launching aircraft to safely escape the effects of the weapons it has just delivered. In World War II, these kits took the form of an attached parachute. During the Vietnam War, the spring-loaded fins of the Mk 15 "Snakeye" kit were used on the Mk 82. Today, the standard hi-drag or retard kit is an air inflated bag, or "ballute," mounted in a special fin-group assembly attached to the rear of the bomb. There are two varieties: the BSU-49/B for the Mk 82 and the BSU-50/B for the Mk 84. After launch, the ballute kits channel the slipstream surrounding the bomb into the ballute, inflating it from the incoming rush of air. Their big advantage is their vastly greater reliability over the Mk 15 units, as air moving at hundreds of knots/kph. tends to be a more consistent mechanical medium than folded springs.

Penetration Bombs

A constant of warfare in the 20th century is that concrete has been one of the great equalizers among combatants. Cheap, available, and relatively easy to work with, it can be fashioned into a variety of structures which can protect

LEFT: The interior of an Iraqi hardened aircraft shelter showing the effects of a laser-guided BLU-109/B penetrating warhead following Operation Desert Storm. The pile in the middle of the floor is the concrete and filler from the ceiling, and what appears to be spaghetti is the steel reinforcement bars blown in by the force of the warhead.
OFFICIAL U.S. AIR FORCE PHOTO

BELOW: A cutaway drawing of the BLU-109/B Penetrating Bomb warhead.
JACK RYAN ENTERPRISES, LTD., BY LAURA ALPHER

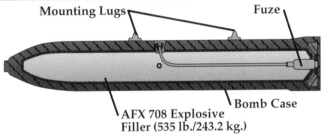

Mounting Lugs **Fuze**

AFX 708 Explosive **Bomb Case**
Filler (535 lb./243.2 kg.)

even delicate, high-value items like aircraft and dictators from the ravages of the elements and the forces of modern warfare.

Ever since the end of the Vietnam War, the USAF wanted a bomb that could penetrate bunkers, runways, and other reinforced concrete structures—a bomb that didn't weigh 3,000 to 4,000 lb./1,363.6 to 1,818 kg., and wasn't nuclear. In 1984, the Air Force Armament Division initiated Project Have Void and awarded a contract to Lockheed Missile and Space's Austin (Texas) Division to develop the new bomb, to be known as the BLU-109/B. Forged out of hardened 4340 steel, the BLU-109/B is essentially a large "masonry nail," shaped to plow through concrete, earth, and armor plate, and then explode on the other side of the protection. Weighing in at 1,925.5 lb./875.3 kg., it has a specially shaped nose that is designed to help it "dig in" to flat concrete at high grazing angles. While the BLU-109/B can be dropped as a "dumb" bomb, when married to a Paveway III-series or GBU-15 guidance kit, it becomes a killing machine of incredible power and accuracy.

With its capability of destroying, or "holding at risk," something like 99% of all the hardened targets in the world, the BLU-109/B has transformed the nature of air warfare. Saddam Hussein found this out the hard way back in 1991, when these bombs blew up virtually every hardened target in his country.

When the Iraqi Air Force tried to take refuge in Yugoslav and European-built hardened aircraft shelters that were thought proof against even near-misses by tactical nuclear weapons, they were opened up like tin cans to the penetrating power of the BLU-109/B. After a couple of days of such pounding, the remnants of the Iraqi Air Force ran for Iran.

Cluster Bombs

Early in the Vietnam War, American airmen began to encounter more and more targets that were spread out—so-called "area" targets made up of "soft," unarmored vehicles, supply dumps, and lightly built structures. What was needed was a weapon which would spread its effects over a known area, with a well understood set of weapons effects. Rather than try to smear flaming napalm onto all of these things, something more modern was needed. That something was the cluster munition. Cluster bombs were not new. The idea dates back to World War II, when both fragmentation and incendiary cluster bombs were used for many purposes, but suffered from restrictive delivery profiles and the lack of predictable dispersal patterns for the small bombs (called "bomblets" or submunitions) carried in the cluster. To overcome these limitations, the U.S. Navy developed a new concept—the munitions dispenser.

The dispenser would be a "truck" for the load of submunitions, which would be be dropped like a normal GP bomb onto the target area. At a preplanned altitude, the fuze (proximity or time delay from aircraft launch) would activate, causing the outer skin panels of the dispenser to break loose. Then another charge (usually compressed air or a small pyrotechnic charge) blasted the load of bomblets loose into a preplanned pattern, which would then fall onto the target.

The Navy's first effort, which began in 1963, centered around a dispenser called the Mk 7. When activated by a Mk 339 time delay fuze, the dispersion charge has the effect of scattering the submunitions in an elongated, doughnut-shaped pattern whose size is controlled by the release height of the bomblets. Each submunition has its own fuze, which detonates upon contact with a target or the ground. When the whole package was put together, it was known as the Mk 20 Rockeye II Mod. 2. It carried a load of 247 M118 anti-tank munitions that looked for all the world like sadistic hypodermic syringes, weighed in at some 490 lb./222.7 kg., and was an instant success with American aircrews when it reached Vietnam in 1967. Adopted by both the Navy and Air Force, it was particularly welcomed by aircrews tasked with attacking SAM sites and AAA gun emplacements, which were particularly vulnerable to the deadly rain of cluster munitions. This classic piece of aircraft ordnance has been so effective that some 27,987 Rockeye IIs were dropped on targets during Desert Storm, more than any other cluster munition used. At only $3,449.00 a copy (in 1991 dollars), it is quite a bargain by current standards.

With the early success of the Rockeye, the Air Force quickly jumped on the bandwagon and started development of its own cluster bomb dispenser, the

Suspension Underwing Unit (SUU -30H/B). A total of 17,831 SUU-30-series weapons were delivered by U.S. aircraft during Desert Storm. This dispenser became the basis for a whole family of USAF CBUs. Some of the versions currently in use include:

Designation	Weight	Payload	Weapon Function
CBU-52B	790 lb./359.1 kg.	217 BLU-61 Bomblets	Anti-Personnel/ Fragmentation
CBU-58	810 lb./368.2 kg.	650 BLU-63 Bomblets	Anti-Personnel/ Fragmentation
CBU-58A	820 lb./372.3 kg.	650 BLU-63A Bomblets	Anti-Personnel/ Incendiary
CBU-71	810 lb./368.2 kg.	650 BLU-86 Bomblets	Anti-Personnel (Time Delay)
CBU-71A	820 lb./372.3 kg.	650 BLU-68 Bomblets	Anti-Personnel/ Incendiary (Time Delay)

As you can see, the variety of submunitions and weapons effects is numbing. Again, fuzing is as critical to successful employment of the SUU-30 family as it is for the 80-series GP bombs. If the dispenser opens too soon, then the density of submunitions will not be high enough to ensure destruction of the target. Similarly, if the canister opens too late, then the bomblets will not spread out enough to cover the whole target. As might be imagined, it is a challenge for planners, ordnance technicians, and loaders to figure out the proper dispenser/submunition/fuze combination.

As good as the early CBUs were, they still imposed a number of restrictions upon fliers trying to deliver them. By the early 1980s the Air Force was beginning to realize that the early CBUs were shackled by a number of limitations in high-threat target areas. Most especially, the aircraft delivering them had to actually overfly the target in "laydown" delivery profiles, exposing them to ground fire. Thus, a new series of submunitions was developed by the Air Force, with a larger dispenser that would get enough of them onto a target array to be useful. And so was born the SUU-64/65 Tactical Munitions Dispenser (TMD).

The TMD is a 1,000 lb./454.5 kg.-class weapon, with three versions currently in service with the USAF. All three share the basic TMD dispenser components, with only the submunition load and other minor details differentiating them. Starting at the front is the optional FZU-39/B proximity fuze, which is designed to tell the TMD its exact altitude at all times. There is also a time delay fuze, which can be used by itself, or in conjunction with the FZU-39/B. Just aft of the nose/fuze section is the cargo section where the submunitions are packed. This is a tubular body section, with equipment designed to cut the body into thirds when the submunitions are ready to be deployed.

This is topped by a structure called a strongback, where the mounting lugs are attached. At the rear is a tail assembly, with spring loaded guidance fins designed to stabilize the entire TMD assembly.

The three different variants of the TMD are shown in the table below:

Designation	Weight	Payload	Weapon Function
CBU-87/B	960 lb./ 436.3 kg.	214 BLU-97/B CEMs	Anti-Tank/ Anti-Personnel/Incendiary
CBU-89/B	700 lb./ 318.2 kg.	72 BLU-91/ 24 BLU-92 Mines	Anti-Personnel/ Anti-Tank
CBU-97/B	920 lb./ 418.2 kg.	BLU-108/B "Skeet" Submunitions	"Smart" Anti-Armor/ Anti-Vehicle

On the CBU-87/B, the SUU-65 dispenser is loaded with 214 BLU-97/B Combined Effects Munitions (CEMs), and is planned to replace almost every type of CBU. About the size and shape of a beer can, each CEM is equipped with its own ballute, making each a tiny high-drag bomb. It is designed to have excellent weapons effects against armored vehicles and exposed infantry, as well as superb incendiary effects against targets like fuel and ammunition dumps. The BLU-97/B accomplishes this through the use of a unique triple-function pyrotechnic package. Its anti-armor capability comes from a shaped charge capable of penetrating the top armor of virtually any tank or armored vehicle in the world. Surrounding the shaped charge is a serrated steel case, which fragments into hundreds of 30-grain size (about 1/4 in./6 mm.) fragments. Finally, at the rear of the CEM is a ring of zirconium. When fragmented and heated to incandescence by the explosive of the shaped charge, it ignites violently as soon as it hits the oxygen of air.

Armed with the finest general purpose submunition in the world, the CBU-87/B functions by delivering its load more accurately than any other

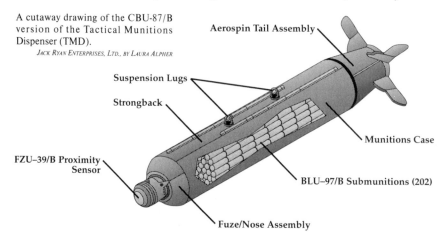

A cutaway drawing of the CBU-87/B version of the Tactical Munitions Dispenser (TMD).
Jack Ryan Enterprises, Ltd., by Laura Alpher

Aerospin Tail Assembly

Suspension Lugs

Strongback

FZU–39/B Proximity Sensor

Munitions Case

BLU–97/B Submunitions (202)

Fuze/Nose Assembly

dispenser in the inventory. Also, the CBU-87/B can be dropped from as low as 400 feet/121.9 meters, and as high as 40,000 feet/12,192 meters. This means that in addition to making tactical aircraft more survivable in high-threat environments, the CBU-97/B can now be used from bombers like the B-52, B-1B, and B-2. Some 10,035 CBU-87/Bs were dropped during Desert Storm, and in time, it will become the primary CBU in the USAF inventory.

The second TMD derivative to be fielded is the CBU-89/B, which is designed to replace the earlier CBU-78/B in the mine deployment role. Composed of a SUU-64/B TMD, it is loaded with seventy-two BLU-91/B anti-personnel mines, and twenty-four BLU-92/B Gator anti-tank mines. The BLU-92/B Gator is an anti-vehicle mine with a highly sophisticated fusing system, including the deployment of wire "feelers" to detonate the warhead. Once activated, the Gator fires a self-forging projectile or "spoon" into the belly of the target vehicle at a speed of over Mach 3, destroying the target. There were 1,105 CBU-89/Bs used during Desert Storm with great success.

The newest TMD variant to make it into the field is the CBU-97B, which is equipped with the new BLU-108/B anti-armor submunition. First fielded in 1992, each CBU-97/B is composed of an SUU-64/B TMD, loaded with ten of the BLU-108/Bs. Known as a "sensor fused weapon," the BLU-108/B looks like an oversized coffee can when it is ejected from the TMD. Once clear of the TMD, each BLU-108/B ejects four small devices called "skeets." The skeets, which look a lot like jumbo-sized hockey pucks, are flung spinning from the BLU-108/B in four different directions to maximize their coverage. Once armed, each skeet scans the ground with a sensitive infrared seeker, tuned to look for the heat signature of an internal combustion engine. Should the skeet sensor detect the heat of a vehicle below, it fires a self-forging projectile or "spoon" down into the engine compartment of the vehicle at a speed of roughly Mach 5! The projectile has so much energy, that it just punches through the vehicle, even if it is a tank, usually destroying whatever it hits.

With the coming of the SUU-64/65 TMD, most of the tactical limitations of previous types of CBUs have been eliminated. There is also a program, called the Wind Corrected Munition (WCM), which is designed to add a small, cheap, strapdown INS guidance system to the back of the TMD, along with guidance fins. The idea is that the inertial system would detect any course deviations resulting from crosswinds and correct for the wind drift. Given the hyper-accurate weapons delivery systems on various U.S. aircraft, particularly bombers like the B-1B and B-2, this would make truly accurate high altitude CBU drops a reality.

Electro-Optical Bombs: The GBU-15/AGM-130 Series

Airpower enthusiasts have long dreamed of a munition which would drop a bridge or destroy a building with only one round. This has been the promise of airpower for over seventy-five years, and it has taken a long time to even get close to that. Like the AAM, the first real successes in the area of precision-guided munitions came from Nazi Germany in World War II. In 1943, the *Luftwaffe* deployed a pair of guided bombs, the FRITZ-X and the HS-293, for use as standoff precision strike weapons. Though they were quite primitive, they terrorized Allied shipping, and even sank an Italian battleship, the *Roma,* as it was on its way to surrender to Allied forces. After World War II, such efforts took a backseat to nuclear weapons development. Then, with the coming of the Vietnam War, the Air Force was forced to realize that there were a number of international situations where nukes were just not appropriate. Thus, the USAF went into Vietnam completely unequipped for the war they would spend the next decade trying to win.

Immediately, the air units involved in the war began to find that they had been the victims of an unanticipated paradigm shift. Where in the past the flattening of a town with a carpet of GP bombs was a politically acceptable option, in Vietnam, it was a war crime. The politics of appearance were taking over in the 1960s, with the result that politicians now wanted the "surgical" air strikes that airpower zealots had promised for decades. Unfortunately, such promises by the visionaries who had created airpower as a weapon had never anticipated flying into an integrated air defense system (IADS) of fighters, SAMs, and AAA guns all tied together with a computerized sensor network of radars and observation posts. No one had anticipated that crews of tactical aircraft would be trying to drop their loads of munitions while violently "jinking" and fighting for their lives against coordinated multiple threats such as American pilots and crews saw in the skies over North Vietnam. Worse than that was where some of those bombs fell after they were dropped. Collateral damage is a serious concern in any war, but even more so when the enemy is showing American newsmen the destruction wrought by errant bombs and contrasting it with the stories of "precision strikes" coming out of official channels in Washington, D.C.

In an effort to overcome the political problems of collateral damage, as well as the tactical problems of fighting in an IADS environment to precisely deliver ordnance onto a target, the USN and USAF initiated a series of programs known as Precision Avionics Vectoring Equipment (PAVE), designed to provide aviators with weapons that could hit high-value targets with some sort of standoff and precision. One promising technology was television electo-optics (TV E/O). This means that the guidance electronics package looks at the TV camera picture and locks onto the contrast "edge" or line between a dark and light zone on the picture. Integrated circuits and microprocessors were years away, and the early history of what we now call electro-optically (E/O) guided bombs was riddled with problems as a result.

The Air Force E/O guided bomb program, known as the Glide Bomb Unit (GBU) -8 (also known by its program nickname of HOBOS, which stands for Homing Bomb System), was designed to be what is called a "modular" bomb. This means that the guidance kit (the seeker and guidance fin sections) would be literally bolted onto a standard -80 series bomb, which would act as the warhead. This meant that the warhead could be tailored for any kind of target that was required, be it heavy demolition (where a 2,000 lb./909.1 kg. Mk 84 would be appropriate), or area suppression (where a cluster bomb dispenser would be best). The GBU-8 was designed and built by Rockwell International in Columbus. Unfortunately, the USAF HOBOS had a poor combat career in Vietnam. There were a lot of single-point failures in various subsystems that made proper development of E/O bomb delivery tactics nearly impossible. But the worst of the problems revolved around the GBU-8 seeker itself. Because they had to actually see the target, the E/O bombs of the period could not be used in times of darkness or reduced visibility. In anything but "perfect" conditions, the WSOs had to take manual control of the HOBOS through the data links and try to fly the bombs on the targets. Frequently, they did not have time to make the necessary corrections before bomb impact.

By 1972, the shortcomings of the first-generation HOBOS were well understood, and the Air Force initiated a program to develop an improved family of E/O guided bombs. Now known officially as the Modular Glide Bomb System, the new program was designed to overcome the problems that had plagued the early HOBOS. Following a design competition under the Pave Strike program, the USAF selected Rockwell International as the winner to build what would now be called the GBU-15. The major improvements that the GBU-15 was designed to have over the earlier GBU-8 included:

- A longer standoff range to allow the launch aircraft to stay out of the range of SAMs and AAA guns.
- More maneuverability and cross-range performance, to provide greater tactical flexibility, and to improve endgame accuracy during approach to the target.
- An improved data link system, to allow greater control of the weapon during the terminal phase, the approach to the target.
- A greatly improved seeker system, with greater resolution and target discrimination capabilities.
- Options for improved seekers, including an infrared imaging (IIR) variant.

With these ideas in mind, the Rockwell International engineers got to work. Though they started fresh with the new design, Rockwell kept most of the good things that the GBU-8 had offered, starting with a standard Mk 84 2,000 lb./909.1 kg. bomb body as the warhead. This time, though, with the emerging miracle of integrated circuitry and microprocessors, Rockwell was able to do a much better job. Rockwell also added Hughes Missile Systems to the GBU-15 team; they produced the TV seeker from technology based on their highly successful AGM-65 Maverick air-to-ground missile. As an added bonus, a version of the seeker based on technology from the Imaging Infrared (IIR) version of the Maverick was designed and eventually fielded.

The basic GBU-15 is composed of a guidance/fin section, a bomb warhead, and a cruciform wing group (with steering fins) at the rear of the weapon. The following table shows the details of the various GBU-15 variants:

Designation	Guidance Group	Warhead	Fin Group	Weight
GBU-15(V)-1	DSU-27 E/O	Mk 84	MXU-724	2,510 lb./ 1,149.9 kg.
GBU-15(V)-2	WGU-10 IIR	Mk 84	MXU-724	2,560 lb./ 1,163.6 kg.
GBU-15(V)-32	DSU-27 E/O	BLU-109/B	MXU-787	2,450 lb./ 1,113.6 kg.
GBU-15(V)-31	WGU-10 IIR	BLU-109/B	MXU-787	2,500 lb./ 1,136.4 kg.
AGM-130A	DSU-27 E/O or WGU-10 IIR	Mk 84	MXU-787	2,980 lb./ 1,354.5 kg.
AGM-130C	DSU-27 E/O or WGU-10 IIR	BLU-109/B	MXU-787	3,026 lb./ 1,375.5 kg.

The initial E/O version was known as the GBU-15(V)-1. Originally operational in 1977 with the Israeli Air Force (the USAF spent five more years testing and developing it), it is currently cleared for use on the F-111F and the F-15E Strike Eagle. It was followed by the IIR version, designated GBU-15(V)-2, and is favored by crews and planners. Some seventy of the GBU-15(V)-2s were expended in the Persian Gulf during Desert Storm in 1991. Like the earlier HOBOS, it is equipped with a two-way data link, with the instructions and seeker video data being fed through a pod, designated AN/AXQ-14. This allows the WSO of the launching aircraft, or another controlling aircraft, to actually fly the bomb onto a target with truly stunning precision. In addition, the data link system allows the seeker video to be recorded; this assists in bomb damage assessment (BDA), as well as providing CNN with exciting videos!

All the basic GBU-15s can be launched from a maximum range of 8 miles/14.6 km. at low altitude, and up to 20 miles/36.6 km. at higher altitudes. The key to this relatively long range are the lift capabilities of the cruciform wings at the front and rear of the GBU-15; these make the bomb an unpowered glider, with much greater maneuverability than previous HOBOS.

Following Desert Storm, several new variants, called the GBU-15I series, came into service with the Air Force. But at a FY-1991 cost of $227,000 per copy, a GBU-15 is anything but cheap, and further development is unlikely. There is, however, one GBU-15I variant which is rapidly gaining momentum, the Air-to-Ground Missile (AGM)-130. The AGM-130 is basically a GBU-15I with a small rocket motor strapped to its belly. This has the effect of extending the AGM-130's range to 16 nm./30 km. at low altitudes, and up to 40 nm./45.7 km. at higher release altitudes. It's an impressive set of capabilities for one family of weapons, though it places a great burden of responsibility on its operators. WSOs assigned to operate the GBU-15/AGM-130-series weapons have to be carefully trained, and have a delicate touch, to get the most out of this most accurate of PGMs.

Laser Guided Bombs: The Paveway Series

Once there were two bridges that were the stuff of nightmares to U.S. pilots who flew over North Vietnam. The Paul Doumer Bridge over the Red River in Hanoi and the Dragon's Jaw Bridge (Ham Rung in Vietnamese) near Thanh Hoa were the toughest targets in a war full of tough targets. Prior to 1972, despite the efforts of thousands of U.S. Air Force, Navy, and Marine strike sorties, millions of pounds of bombs, and dozens of lost airplanes and killed and/or imprisoned aircrews, the Paul Doumer was only dropped for a few weeks at a time. Then it would quickly be repaired, to carry rail traffic south, laden with supplies for the ground war in South Vietnam. Even worse, despite every effort that the Department of Defense could devise in the 1960s, the Thanh Hoa bridge was *never* dropped.

Then, in just four days of May 1972, both targets went down for good, the most visible sign of a new weapons technology which saw its first use in 1967— the laser-guided bomb (LGB). On May 10th, 1972, sixteen F-4Ds from the 8th Tactical Fighter Wing (TFW) at the RTAFB at Ubon, Thailand, roared down on the Paul Doumer Bridge. Twelve of them were each armed with a pair of the new 2,000 lb./909.1 kg. LGBs. When the smoke and spray from the exploding bombs subsided, the bridge was heavily damaged and closed to all traffic. Amazingly, not one of the strike aircraft was damaged.

Then, the next day, four more 8th TFW F-4Ds again attacked the Doumer Bridge with LGBs, this time dropping several spans. After several more applications of LGBs, the bridge would not be rebuilt until after the cease-fire in 1973. As an added bonus, the control bunker for the entire North Vietnamese air defense system at Gia Lam airfield was destroyed by four more LGB-armed F-4Ds from Ubon.

The crowning achievement came two days later when the laser bombers of the 8th TFW went after the big one: the Dragon's Jaw. It took everything the ordnance shop and contractor techreps at Ubon could put together, including some specially built 3,000 lb./1,363 kg. LGBs; but when the smoke and limestone dust cleared, one whole end of the bridge had been lifted off of its abutment and heaved into the river.

The weapons that did this amazing job were certainly not the most advanced or sophisticated ever deployed by the U.S. to Southeast Asia. On the contrary, first-generation LGBs were extremely simple in concept and execution, yet they have been the most successful type of PGM in history. Like the ubiquitous AIM-9 Sidewinder, a simple concept behind the LGB paid massive dividends when it got to war.

If you are over forty, you probably remember when the magic of the laser beam was first touted by its inventors at Bell Labs. Laser stands for Light Amplification by Stimulated Emission of Radiation. What it means is that a coherent (composed of only one primary wavelength) beam of light with a very high amplitude (bright in the extreme) can be produced and manipulated. The first lasers relied upon solid materials like synthetic ruby to provide a medium to produce the laser light. Today, most lasers are based on gases like carbon dioxide (CO_2) or argon (AR). At the time of their introduction, lasers promised to become the "death beams" envisioned by science fiction authors like Jules Verne and H.G. Wells. But the truth was somewhat more modest, for the lasers of the 1960s had nothing like the power required to burn through the solid metal of a rocket or aircraft at tactical engagement ranges.

Then in 1965, a simple idea for using the laser in a weapons system came to a small engineering team at Texas Instruments (TI). Weldon Word, the brilliant engineer who led the team, decided that instead of using the laser *as a weapon,* he would use the laser as a way to *guide a weapon.* Laser light, because it is coherent and tends to stay in a tight beam, has the ability to mark a very small target from a long distance. This means that a seeker could be devised that would "see" only a specific (coherent) frequency of laser light and guide onto it, much as the AIM-9M seeker looks for specific "colors" of light to home on. It's like shining a flashlight in a completely dark room. If you are human, all you can see is the target illuminated by the flashlight.

Simple as this sounds, it posed daunting technical and financial problems for Weldon Word and his TI team. As a starter, there was not much money to develop this new strike technology. In the mid-1960s, DoD was offering $100,000 for ideas that could be put to winning use in Vietnam. But *only* $100,000 until the ideas had been tested and proven. For Word and his team, this meant the entire system—the seeker/guidance package, the laser "flashlight" (designator), and the warhead—had to be made for that $100,000, and not one penny more. Even in 1965, this would buy only a few thousand man-hours of TI engineering and technical talent, and a small amount of technical hardware for testing the concept. With only a short time available for development, the team made some important decisions. One of the first was that the warhead sections of the new guided bombs, now called Paveway, would be composed of normal 80-series LDGP bombs. The seeker and guidance sections would literally be "screwed" onto the LDGP bombs, providing a solid airframe for the whole package. This meant that the warheads, fuses, and assorted other equipment could be supplied, at no cost to TI, as government furnished equipment (GFE). Then, rather than building the laser designator from scratch, they adapted a design from a scientist in Alabama. Finally, the team obtained their parts for the laser seeker from a West German salvage firm. Wind-tunnel testing of the proposed bomb package was found to be too expensive, so Weldon Word had his team test the bomb shapes with subscale models in a swimming pool.

In spite of the "low ball" approach to the problem, the result was successful beyond the wildest dreams of anyone at TI or in the Air Force, even though the first Paveway laser designator (called Paveway I) was about the size of an old sheet-film camera, was bolted to the canopy rails of an F-4 Phantom, and manually aimed through a telescopic lens by the backseater. Once this was done, then another aircraft had to fly over the target and drop the bomb. As might be imagined, this made the designating aircraft highly vulnerable to AAA guns and SAMs. Nevertheless, the results of the Vietnam combat tests held in 1967 were good enough for the Air Force to order the Paveway guidance kits into limited production. Eventually, the "limited" production wound up totaling over 25,000 units (each virtually hand-built) that were dropped during the Vietnam War. And amazingly, some seventeen thousand hits were scored, for an overall combat success record of some 68%.

But maybe even more amazing was the way Paveway bombs redefined the word *hit*. With LGBs frequently generating average circular error probability (CEP) miss distances under 10 feet/3.05 meters (a typical Vietnam-era F-4D CEP with "dumb" LDGP bombs was commonly 150 feet/45.7 meters), it frequently only took a single bomb from one plane to destroy a target which previously took a whole squadron of fighter bombers to hit. Quickly, the cry of "one bomb, one target" became a hallmark of LGB performance around Southeast Asia. As if to highlight the economy of the LGB effort further, a Paveway I guidance kit cost only about $2,700 in 1972 dollars—cheap compared to over $20,000 for a GBU-8 E/O guidance kit.

Paveway caused a revolution in aerial warfare, and it showed during the final U.S. air campaigns of the war, Linebacker I/II. During these efforts, which ran from May 1972 until January 1973, Paveway LGBs were the "magic bullets" of the American arsenal. They were everywhere, doing everything. In the south, LGBs from the 8th TFW (the only unit equipped with them at the time) helped stop the armored drive of the North Vietnamese at An Loc with an early demonstration of what would become known as "tank plinking" during the 1991 Persian Gulf War. In the north, they were dropping every vital bridge between the Chinese border and Vinh, as well as a variety of other vital targets.

Now, with all this success, there also came problems. While the LGB seeker would guide the bomb to an almost perfect bull's-eye every time, the bomb had to be dropped within a fairly narrow "basket" in the sky (within a few thousand feet of a "perfect" ballistic launch point) for the bomb to have the necessary energy or "smash" to reach the target. This meant that in Vietnam, the Paveway I-series bombs had to be dropped from medium to high altitude (above 10,000 feet/3,048 meters); low-level drops (less than 10,000 feet/3,048 meters) were completely out of the question. In addition, clear visibility in daylight was a must, because the early Paveway I designators did not have low-light or thermal imaging systems. In fact, until the introduction of the AAQ-26 Pave Tack targeting and designation pod in the late-1970s, the designators were the major limitation in the use of LGBs.

The first designation system that made LGB drops in high-threat areas viable was the Pave Knife built by Ford Aeronutronic (now Loral Aeronutronic). Hand-built and fielded by a team led by the legendary optical engineer Reno Perotti, the six prototype Pave Knife pods that were available became one of the single most important factors to the continued success of the Linebacker campaigns in 1972.

In the late 1970s, DoD began fielding a new version of the bomb-guidance kit, the Paveway II. Essentially a production version of the hand-built Paveway I-series kits, they provided the USAF, USN, and USMC with their primary PGM capability well into the 1980s. They have even enjoyed a measure of export success, including use by the British in Desert Storm. In fact, Paveway II-series kits are still in the U.S. and NATO inventory, and will continue to soldier on well into the 21st century.

The Paveway II kits come in three varieties, broken down by the following bomb configurations:

Designation	Guidance Group	Warhead	Airfoil Group
GBU-10E/B	MAU-169E/B	Mk 84	MXU-651/B
GBU-12D/B	MAU-169E/B	Mk 82	MXU-650/B
GBU-16B/B	MAU-169E/B	Mk 83	MXU-667/B

The Paveway II-series bombs proved to be extremely successful, and have enjoyed a long and useful career. The first attempted combat use of Paveway II appears to have occurred in October 1983, when an A-6E from the USS *John F. Kennedy* (CV-67) dropped several LGBs on targets in the Beirut area. Unfortunately, problems with the ground-based laser designator caused them to miss their assigned targets. They saw their first really successful combat trials during Operation Prairie Fire in 1986, a series of confrontations between the U.S. Navy and Libya in the Gulf of Sidra. During the famous "Line of Death" confrontations, USN A-6Es used Paveway II-series bombs to help destroy/disable several Libyan patrol boats. Later, they were used during Operation Eldorado Canyon, the joint April 1986 USAF/USN/USMC raid on Benghazi and Tripoli.

One of the Paveway II configurations, the diminutive 500 lb./227.3 kg. GBU-12, proved to be one of the most important weapons of the 1991 Persian Gulf War. In late January and early February of 1991, CENTAF BDA teams showed that the "battlefield preparation" in the KTO (Kuwaiti Theater of Operations) was not destroying enough armored vehicles and artillery pieces with standard LDGP bombs to meet the proposed attrition target of 50% prior to the start of the ground war.

To help overcome this problem, Major General Buster Glosson, the CENTAF Director of Operations, came up with an idea called "tank plinking." General Charles A. Horner, the commander of CENTAF during the war, is said to have been told by the commander of CENTCOM, General H. Norman Schwartzkopf, to *never* call this tactic "tank plinking." General Horner, always the obedient fighter pilot, promptly ordered his staff to make sure that everyone *always* called it "tank plinking."

Here is how tank plinking worked. A flight of F-111Fs or F-15Es would fly over an Iraqi artillery or armored unit shortly after sunset. Since the sand of the desert cooled faster than the military equipment dug in among the dunes, the vehicles and artillery tended to show up as "hot spots" in the aircraft's FLIR targeting systems. They would then drop one of the "old" GBU-12s on the desired target, and the results were, in a word, spectacular. Despite what you might think, even a main battle tank cannot have armor everywhere, especially on top. Thus, when one of the "little" LGBs hit one, the target would go up in flames, and the BDA assessments were quite positive. The fact that an F-111F might carry four GBU-12s, and an F-15E up to eight, meant that tank plinking was a surprisingly economical way of killing targets up in the KTO. Every night, for several weeks in early February 1991, the 4th and 48th TFWs would send pairs of F-15Es and four ship flights of F-111Fs into the KTO to hunt artillery and armor targets. The results were spectacular. Often, the small formations would come home with anything from twelve and sixteen targets killed per mission.

Combined with the capabilities of an integrated thermal imaging/laser designation/weapons delivery system, the Paveway II-series LGB was a formidable weapon when properly employed. Formidable, but very limited. Paveway II still had a very small launch "basket," which diminished its utility in high-threat environments. In particular, its low-level capabilities were highly restrictive, making its utility in that mode marginal. Even with drops from 20,000 feet/6,096 meters, the favored altitude for Paveway II drops, there were challenges for the crews.

Even before Paveway II went into combat, the Air Force and TI had begun to develop the replacement for the Paveway II under a program called the Low-Level Laser Guided Bomb (LLLGB). Begun in 1981, it was designed to overcome the shortcomings inherent in the previous Paveway-II bombs and take full advantage of the new series of laser designator systems being deployed worldwide. The result was The Paveway III series of bombs, which came into service in the mid-1980s.

The key was to be an all-new guidance section, which would be equipped with a microprocessor-controlled digital autopilot adaptive to the flight and release conditions. There are a variety of settings for delivery aircraft, flight mode, warhead configuration, laser coding, and delivery profile. Even more important, with a change of the Programmable Read Only Memory (PROM) chips which hold the autopilot software, the basic guidance package can be adapted to a variety of bomb configurations and capabilities. The changes to Paveway III start at the front of the seeker with the seeker dome, which is made of Lexan plastic with a fine wire mesh. Inside this dome is an optics housing containing a four-quadrant laser sensor and optics to focus the spot of laser light from the laser designator. The simple four quadrant detector in the seeker is touchstone of the Paveway program's simplicity, and is one of the keys of its success. And the sensitivity of the seeker itself has also been improved, so that even low-power laser designators (or standard designators degraded by weather) can be used. The seeker housing is gimbaled in two axes, and can scan in a bar (horizontally, back and forth), box (rectangular), or conical (circular) mode. Aft of the seeker is the guidance electronics section, which contains the autopilot, laser decoding, and signal processing circuitry, as well as the rotary switches for programming the bomb. The control setting switches are mounted flush with the exterior of the airframe, and can be set with almost any flathead tool, though the "ordies" (ordnance technicians) from the 391st Fighter Squadron at Mountain Home AFB (they fly the F-15E Strike Eagle) tell me that a quarter works best for this job.

The laser seeker, guidance electronics, and control section form what is termed the Guidance and Control Unit (GCU), which is attached to the front of the selected warhead. Paveway LGBs have always made use of standard USAF munitions as the warhead; and Paveway III is no exception. It can be attached to any of the 80-series bombs, as well as the BLU-109/B penetrating warhead. At the rear of the warhead is mounted the cruciform airfoil group. This is a tail section equipped with four pop-out wings to help stabilize the weapon during its flight. Along with mounting lugs for the bomb rack on top of the weapon, this is the makeup of a complete Paveway III LGB.

Designation	Guidance Group	Warhead	Airfoil Group	Weight
GBU-24/B	WGU-12B or -39/B	Mk 84	BSU-84/B	2,315 lb./ 1,052.3 kg.
GGBU-24A/B	WGU-12B or -39/B	BLU-109/B	BSU-84/B	2,350 lb./ 1,068.2 kg.
GBU-24B/B	WGU-12B or -39/B	BLU-109/B	BSU-84/B	2,350 lb./ 1,068.2 kg.
GBU-27/B	WGU-25/B or -39/B	BLU-109/B	BSU-88/B	2,170 lb./ 986.4 kg.
GBU-28/B	WGU-36A/B	BLU-113/B	BSG-92/B	4,700 lb./ 2,136.4 kg.

The first production versions of the Paveway III were the GBU-24 family, which entered service in the mid-1980s. Designed as the general purpose LGB, the GBU-24 quickly became the primary weapon of the F-111Fs of the 48th TFW at RAF Lakenheath. It is the airfoil group, with its large spring-deployed planar wings, that makes all the difference in expanding the launch and delivery envelope of the GBU-24. When the wings are fully extended some two seconds after the bomb is dropped, they have twice the lift area of the Paveway II-series airfoil group, and give the GBU-24 a glide ratio of 5:1, meaning that for every foot/meter of altitude lost in flight, the bomb can travel forward five feet/meters. This means that the launch envelope for the GBU-24 is vastly greater than the Paveway II-series bombs, and gives it the energy and maneuverability for a lot of tricks.

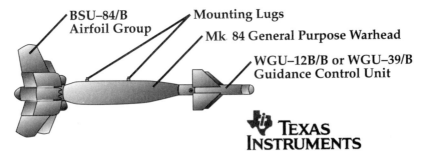

BSU–84/B Airfoil Group

Mounting Lugs

Mk 84 General Purpose Warhead

WGU–12B/B or WGU–39/B Guidance Control Unit

TEXAS INSTRUMENTS

A drawing of the GBU-24/B Paveway III Laser Guided Bomb. Jack Ryan Enterprises, Ltd., by Laura Alpher

The second version of the GBU-24 family, while a bit different, became one of the stars of Desert Storm. This variant has a BLU-109/B penetrating bomb warhead, designed to punch through heavy reinforced concrete and armor. Called a GBU-24/B, it was Saddam Hussein's greatest nightmare, and his worst tactical surprise when Desert Storm kicked off. With the exception of a handful of command bunkers outside of Baghdad, it was capable of destroying every hardened target in Iraq. This included the Yugoslav-built hardened aircraft shelters (HASs) that had been previously thought to be impervious, even to a near-miss by a tactical nuclear device! The GBU-24/B is composed of the same components as the basic GBU-24/B, with the difference of the BLU-109 being substituted for the Mk 84. In addition, there is a spacer attached to the bomb body called a ADG-769/B Hardback. This helps maintain the same tail clearances as the larger-diameter Mk 84. In addition, there is only one fuze, an FMU-143/B delayed action unit amounted in the rear of the BLU-109/B. Other than that, the two models are identical, with the necessary software to operate both models, already being built into the common guidance and control unit. A third variant, the GBU-24B/B is an improved GBU-24A/B.

The fourth variant of the Paveway III family is a unique version for the F-117A Nighthawk Stealth Fighter, the GBU-27/B. The reason for this is that the F-117A design was frozen before the new bomb was even in design, and the Lockheed designers had originally assumed that they would only have the older Paveway II-series weapons with their relatively small airfoil groups to fit into the weapons bays of the F-117s. With the coming of the Paveway III series weapons, though, the USAF wanted to get the new bombs, especially ones equipped with the BLU-109/B onto the new stealth birds. The problem was that the BSU-84/B airfoil group was too large to fit into the Nighthawk's weapons bays. This problem was overcome when the TI and Lockheed designers realized that the F-117A was almost never going to fly the kind of low-level delivery profiles that the F-111Fs and F-15Es were going to. In fact, the Nighthawk normally flies its weapons delivery profiles straight and level at various altitudes, dropping its precision weapons under the control of the pilot. Thus, the TI designers came up with a slightly different version of the fin group used on the Paveway II family, which fits nicely inside the limited volume of the F-117A weapons bay. The normal warhead of the GBU-27/B is the BLU-109/B, though the Hardback adapter is deleted because of the unique "trapeze" weapons handling gear of the Nighthawk.

The final version of the Paveway III family deserves special attention. It is the famous "Deep Throat" super penetrator bomb that was used on the last night of Desert Storm. Officially designated as the GBU-28/B. Its origins date back to August 1990, when the first planning for an offensive air campaign against Iraq began. As the planners in what was known as the Black Hole began to look at strategic targets around Baghdad, they noted a series of super-hard command and control (C^2) bunkers, so heavily built that there were doubts about the ability of the BLU-109/B warhead to penetrate and destroy them. With this in mind, a request was made to study the problem at the USAF Air Armament Division at Eglin AFB, Florida. Down at Eglin AFB, a quiet study was started to look over the problems associated with an improved penetrating bomb. In the study group, headed by Major Richard Wright, there was an engineer named Al Weimorts, who began to make some early sketches of a concept bomb that might just do the job. And that was where the idea stayed until the early BDA results from Desert Storm began to come in. By January 21st, 1991, it was clear that the BLU-109/B-equipped LGBs were just not getting the job done. All they had done to the big bunkers was scab the surface, and not much else. Worse, with more and more of the other Iraqi C^2 bunkers being destroyed, a greater percentage of the top Iraqi leadership was taking refuge in the big command bunkers and continuing operations. This made the destruction of those bunkers a top priority, and the word went out to the team down at Eglin to find a way to do so quickly.

Given their marching orders, TI, as well as the BLU-109/B team at Lockheed, got to work on a number of different problems at once. First there was the problem of the warhead. While the basic design of the BLU-109/B was sound, what was needed was something larger—longer and heavier, with a larger explosive payload. Also, because they had to bolt a modified Paveway III kit onto it, and because they had to maintain the necessary clearance to fly and drop it from either an F-111F or F-15E, it would *not* have a larger diameter than the BLU-109/B. This made for a long, skinny warhead section, with a long interior cavity, or "throat," for the explosive filler. Thus the bomb got the nickname "Deep Throat."

Next, to machine and finish a forged-steel blank would take months, and the Eglin team had days. Luckily, an engineer at the Lockheed plant where the BLU-109/Bs were made was a retired U.S. Army trooper who remembered a stock of old 8-inch/203mm howitzer gun barrels lying around (literally) at the Letterkenny Arsenal in Pennsylvania. Made of the same kind of hardened steel as the BLU-109/B, they had been happily rusting away for some time. By February 1st, 1991, a number of the old gun barrels were shipped to the Watervliet Army Arsenal in upstate New York and machined into the shape of what would become known as the BLU-113/B Super Penetrator. Eventually, around thirty-two of the BLU-113/Bs would be built for integration into what was going to be known as the GBU-28/B. Several inert (non-explosive) tests indicated that the new bomb was capable of doing the job. This included one test on a rocket sled at Holloman AFB, New Mexico, where it penetrated 22 feet/6.7 meters of reinforced structural concrete, and then continued on to career downrange for another mile or so without any damage whatsoever to the BLU-113/B. Each of the new warheads eventually weighed in at 4,700 lb./2,136.4 kg., and had to be hand-loaded with some 1,200 lb./545.45 kg. of explosive, and then integrated with the guidance kits from TI.

Those guidance kits were a whole story on their own. Meanwhile, the original Paveway III development team had long since moved onto other jobs within TI, and had to be reconstituted as quickly as possible. Murl Culp from Lockheed contacted TI and discussed the feasibility of guiding the new penetrator with a derivative Paveway III GCU. Luckily, Bob Peterson, an original Paveway III engineer, was still with the company, and was able to reassemble enough of the original team to get the ball rolling. And other members of the team were pulled off of other important TI programs to staff the effort. By February 12th, the TI/Lockheed team was down at Eglin AFB briefing guidance concepts to the Air Force.

Once the new guidance software was completed, the major testing normally associated with development of a new Paveway GCU would have to be accomplished in days rather than years. A key problem was access to the only wind tunnel in the Dallas/Fort Worth area capable of doing the testing required to develop and validate the new LGB's software. Owned then by LTV/Vought, it was heavily booked with projects, and the security around the GBU-28/B precluded doing anything special to "force" the owners to provide access for TI. Thus, TI would have to use the only open "window" on the tunnel's calendar, on the weekend of February 16/17, just four days away. Now, it should be remembered that at the time all of this was going on, TI, Lockheed, and the Air Force did not have any sort of contract for this project. What they did was done on a handshake and good faith, and TI decided to trust in that when they scheduled the tunnel time. They constructed a 1/4 subscale model to establish the ballistics of the new BLU-113/B/Paveway III combination, which was designated the GBU-28/B.

The tunnel testing was completed by the early hours of Monday, February 18th, and the effort now fell completely on the shoulders of the TI team. Over the next week or so, they worked around the clock to produce the software that would allow the bomb to guide successfully to a target. Almost as an afterthought, the Air Force called with an order for the first two guidance kits on the 19th, and the GBU-28/B was finally an official project, financially and contractually. Two days later, on the 21st, a TI-chartered aircraft loaded with four large airfoil groups took off from Love Field in Dallas, bound for Eglin AFB. These would be part of the actual kits that would be shipped to the Taif RSAFB, where the 48th TFW was based. The decision had been made that the F-111F would deliver the new bombs, mainly because the airframe was more mature than that of the F-15E.

On February 22nd, TI was asked to produce two more of the GBU-28/B guidance kits and ship them ASAP out to Nellis AFB, Nevada. The Air Force wanted to do a full-up test of the new bomb being dropped from an F-111F before it went to combat over Iraq. The ground war into Iraq and Kuwait was only hours from starting, and the Air Force wanted to be sure the system worked.

On the morning of February 24th, the final test of the new bomb took place. A fully integrated bomb (with an inert warhead; the explosive charge was not loaded) was dropped by an F-111F at a target on the Nellis AFB range. The results were stunning. Not only did the GBU-28/B hit the target as advertised, but it dug a hole over 100 feet/30.5 meters deep in desert caliche (hard clay soil with roughly the same consistency as concrete!). The BLU-113/B-equipped LGB was buried so deep, it could not be retrieved. It remains there to this day.

After the single "event" (as tests are sometimes called), TI programmed two GBU-28 GCUs (designated WSU-36A/B), and flew them out to Eglin AFB on Monday, February 25th. These were mated with two of the previously shipped airfoil groups, strapped to a pallet along with a pair of BLU-113/B warheads, loaded aboard a USAF C-141B StarLifter, and flown to Taif RSAFB on February 27th. Since the normal BSU-84/B planar wing section was too big to allow the proper ground clearance and separation from the F-111F, and a gliding bomb was not really required (the GBU-28/B was to be dropped from high altitude), a modified version of the GBU-27/B tail fin assembly was developed for attachment to the new bomb. Covered with signatures and messages from everyone who had handled them during the program, they were two of the oddest looking weapons ever built.

Within five hours of landing at Taif, the two bombs were loaded aboard a pair of 48th TFW F-111Fs, and their crews were briefed to hit a very special

The two GBU-28/B "Deep Throat" super penetrating bombs at the Royal Saudi Air Force Base at Taif just before being loaded onto F-111F fighter bombers of the 48th Tactical Fighter Wing (Provisional). The BLU-113/B warheads have already had their fin groups mounted, and the guidance sections will be mounted once loaded. *CAPTAIN ROB EVANS*

target that very night. For some time, a bunker known as Taji #2 had been monitored closely by elements of the U.S. intelligence community. Located at the al-Taji Airbase, approximately 15 nm./27.4 km. northwest of Baghdad, it had been hit no less that three times by F-117As with GBU-27/Bs early in the war. In the words of General Horner, they only "dug up the rose garden." Since that time, various estimates had suggested that the top national command authorities of Iraq, including possibly Saddam Hussein himself, were running the war from this bunker. With less than twelve hours left before the planned cease-fire, scheduled for 0800 Local Time (0500 Zulu) the next morning (February 28th), CENTAF was ordered to hit the bunker with the bombs. Each F-111F was loaded with a GBU-28/B under one wing and a single 2,000 lb./909.1 kg. GBU-24A/B under the other, for balance. Even so, while they taxied to takeoff position, the F-111s "leaned" to one side because of the weight imbalance.

On the night of February 27th/28th, 1991, the two F-111Fs took off and headed north towards the airfield northwest of Baghdad. The aircraft made their runs and dropped their bombs. They aimed for an air shaft on the top of the bunker, and at least one of the bombs hit its target. Penetrating the thick, reinforced concrete, it detonated in the heart of the bunker. The results were horrific. All six of the bunker's armored blast doors were blown off their hinges; then a huge glut of flame and debris swelled up. Anyone inside was clearly dead, though to this day we do not know who was there. Though they have never been confirmed, postwar rumors claim that a number of senior Iraqi civilian and military personnel perished in the destruction of Taji #2. But it's certain that the GBU-28/B did the job exactly as designed; it was an unqualified success.

With the war won, the quick-reaction program transitioned to a more normal type of USAF procurement. Approximately twenty-eight additional sets of BLU-113/Bs and GBU-28/B kits were produced so that a proper test program could be conducted. And some additional units were kept in reserve for combat use, should the need arise. In addition, the Air Force has contracted with TI for an additional one hundred GBU-28/B guidance kits; and a firm up in Pennsylvania is forging one hundred new production BLU-113/B warheads to go along. The idea is to provide U.S. national command authorities with a non-nuclear option to hit hardened targets like command bunkers and missile silos with precision munitions that do not generate a lot of collateral damage.

It's a staggering idea, and it is all due to the original vision of folks like Weldon Word, and his idea for a bomb with a beam of light for its guide. As for the future of the Paveway-series weapons, they may finally be coming to the end of the line. While new Paveway III kits are being manufactured by TI for U.S. and overseas customers, there are no new versions planned. The tactical limitations of LGBs, along with the rapid maturing of GPS technology, is making satellite navigation the guidance system of choice for the next generation of U.S. precision munitions. Nevertheless, Paveway LGBs will be the backbone of the USAF PGM capability well into the next century.

The Future: JSOW and JDAM

By now your head may be hurting slightly from the array of air-to-ground munitions in the previous pages. For what it is worth, USAF strike planners have similar problems when they consider the targets that need to be struck, the damage required to negate those targets, and the weapons required to do the job.

The folks down at Eglin AFB, Florida, who run the conventional munitions programs for the Air Force, are attacking the problem of what kinds of bombs to develop and buy. In particular, they're trying to buy fewer kinds of weapons that do more kinds of things. That was the basis for the TMD-series of CBUs like the CBU-87/B, as well as the Paveway III-series guidance kits; and it's at the core of the development of new weapons.

Several new and exciting kinds of air-to-ground weapons are being prepared for service with the Air Force. As might be expected in these days of limited budget dollars, weapons are usually joint-service ventures like the AIM-9X. In addition, they have been designed with many of the following criteria in mind:

- The use wherever possible of available, off-the-shelf components and technologies to lower risks and costs.
- Safe carriage and employment on the widest possible range of aircraft from all services, including fighters, bombers, and even attack helicopters.
- Improved accuracy over existing types of weapons, without the requirement of designation or data link guidance equipment.
- Enhanced weapons-delivery options, including greater standoff range and less exposure of the delivery aircraft to enemy air defenses.

A Texas Instruments AGM-154 Joint Standoff Weapon (JSOW) munitions dispenser. Guided by an onboard GPS satellite receiver, it will provide the ability to hit area-type targets from long standoff ranges.
ROCKWELL INTERNATIONAL

With these requirements in mind, let's explore two new programs that the Air Force is getting ready to put into service in the next few years.

The first of these is the ultimate answer to the problem of delivering cluster munitions into an impossibly heavy air defense environment, the AGM-154 Joint Standoff Weapon (JSOW). JSOW is the result of a joint Air Force/Navy/Marine effort to produce a new munitions dispenser which can be launched at long range toward the target, completely outside the range of enemy defenses. It started life as a Navy/Marine program called the Advanced Interdiction Weapons System (AIWS), which had a requirement for a full man-in-the-loop data link control system like the GBU-15. Texas Instruments won the AIWS competition in 1991, and in 1992, the AIWS requirement and program was merged with the Air Force's own standoff cluster munitions program to become JSOW. Like the TMD, it is designed to function as a submunition "truck," capable of carrying a wide variety of payloads; it can also be used from almost any tactical or bomber aircraft of any service. The key to JSOW is a technology I have often praised, the NAVSTAR Global Positioning System (GPS), which will be the primary baseline guidance system for every variant of the AGM-154. For the first time in history, a satellite navigation system will guide a weapon throughout its entire flight, from launch to weapons impact.

The AGM-154 is composed of a nose section containing the GPS-based guidance and flight control system, a weapons carriage bay topped by a folding planar wing system to provide lift during flight, and an aft guidance fin section. The 13.3 foot/4.1 meter-long JSOW, while not exactly stealthy, is definitely of a low-observable design. As designed, the JSOW is capable of gliding unpowered for up to 40 nm./73.1 km. before delivering its load of submunitions on target. Guidance accuracy for the GPS-based system is expected to be within 32.8 feet/10 meters in three dimensions, more than good enough for delivery of cluster weapons. The GPS-based guidance systems used on the new generation of precision munitions are actually hybrid systems, with a GPS receiver feeding positional updates to a small strapdown inertial guidance system which actually controls the flight-control system. In this way, the weapon can continue to the target with acceptable accuracy should the GPS system fail or be jammed.

Currently, two versions of the AGM-154 have been approved for production, one loaded with 145 BLU-97/B CEMs and the other with six of the BLU-108/B SFWs. These are expected to enter service late in the 1990s. There are also plans to produce versions with large (1,000 lb./454.5 kg.) unitary warhead and terminal guidance systems. Given the recent cancellation of the AGM-137 Tri-Service Standoff Attack Missile (TSSAM), this idea has to be considered a possibility. The new Northrop Brilliant Anti-Tank (BAT) weapon, which homes in on the sounds of enemy vehicles, and the Gator mine have also been considered for use on JSOW. And there are growth provisions for the addition of rocket and turbojet motors to extend range, as well as the possibility of enlarging the weapons carriage bay. There have even been proposals to produce "non-lethal" versions of JSOW, to provide logistical support for forward deployed troops such as special operations forces. Before you laugh too hard, consider how many Meals, Ready-to-Eat would fit into the 5.7 foot/1.7 meter-long bay of an AGM-154. It may be the ultimate expression of the statement that "every bomb is a political bomb."

The other munitions program the Air Force has pinned its hopes to is the Joint Direct Attack Munition System, or JDAM. Trust me when I say this, JDAM is *the* program that *must* work if the Air Force is to be a viable force into the 21st century. There is *that* much riding on it. The JDAM family of munitions is designed to replace the old Paveway II-series weapons, which are starting to show their age. Like JSOW, the JDAM program began as a pair of Navy/Marine and Air Force programs that were combined into a single joint requirement. Currently, the program is being competed for by two contractor teams consisting of McDonnell Douglas and Rockwell International on one side with Lockheed-Martin and Trimble Navigation on the other. Rockwell and Trimble are on the teams to supply GPS/inertial guidance system expertise, since that, as in JSOW, will be the primary guidance system for the JDAM family of munitions. Selection of a final winner is expected in 1996, with the weapons entering service in the late 1990s.

The idea is to produce a weapons family with the accuracy of the early LGBs, utilizing only a GPS/strapdown inertial-guidance system to find the target. This is the critical requirement. For the first time, aircraft without a laser-designator or data-link pod will be able to deliver precision weapons onto known targets. And it will do so without exposing the launching aircraft to direct fire by enemy defenses. Thus, stealth aircraft like the F-117A, F-22A, and B-2A will be able to use JDAM without generating telltale data link or laser designator emissions which might be detected by an enemy.

The basic features of the baseline JDAM family of weapons (called Phase I) includes the following:

- 32.8 foot/10 meter three-dimensional accuracy at the point of impact.
- A common guidance kit for every version of the weapon, independent of the warhead used.
- Interfaces with the most popular bomb warheads (Mk 83, Mk 84, and BLU-109/B).
- In-flight targeting and delivery, independent of weather and/or lighting conditions.
- Good standoff range (more than 8.5 nm./15.5 km. downrange and 2 nm./3.7 km. cross-range) and the ability to target more than one target/weapon at a time.

While this may sound like quite a lot to ask of a munition which has yet to even undergo its first engineering drop tests, the principals behind the JDAM system are both sound and mature. GPS/inertial guidance systems proved their worth during Desert Storm, and are more than capable of doing the job with

JDAM. And as we have mentioned earlier, JDAM may not even be the first GPS-aided bombs, if Northrop and Rockwell have their way.

As currently planned, there will be five separate versions of the Phase I JDAM family. They include:

Designation	Warhead	Weight	Planned Operator(s)
GBU-29(V)-1	Mk 84	2,250 lb./1,022.7 kg.	U.S. Air Force
GBU-29(V)-1	Mk 84	2,250 lb./1,022.7 kg.	U.S. Navy/ Marine Corps
GBU-29(V)-1	BLU-109/B	2,250 lb./1,022.7 kg.	U.S. Air Force
GBU-29(V)-1	BLU-109/B	2,250 lb./1,022.7 kg.	U.S. Navy/ Marine Corps
GBU-30(V)-1	Mk 83	1,145 lb./520.5 kg.	U.S. Air Force

Each JDAM kit will be composed of an aerodynamic nose cap which is bolted onto the nose fitting of the bomb warhead, and a guidance section/fin group which is bolted onto the rear. Contained in the fin group at the rear of the bomb will probably be a small GPS/receiver antenna system to pull in the signals from the satellites and feed navigational updates to the inertial guidance/steering system. Other than that, all mounting, fusing, and arming hardware will be identical to other PGMs.

As for their employment, all the pilot of an attacking aircraft will require is a known target location (preferably one with coordinates correlated with GPS accuracy), and a weapons delivery system capable of plotting a ballistic course to the target. While an onboard GPS receiver would be of great help, it

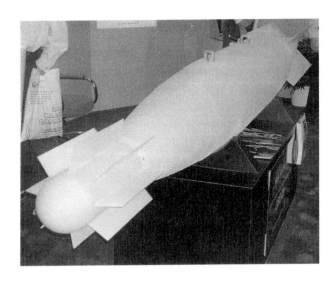

A mockup of the Lockheed Martin entry in the Joint Direct Attack Munition (JDAM) competition. Built around a conventional bomb warhead, it is guided by an onboard GPS satellite receiver to its target. McDonnell Douglas is the other JDAM competititor. *John D. Gresham*

is not necessary to the delivery of the JDAM munition. Once the bomb has been fed the target position and is launched, it will do its best, within the limits of the energy imparted by the launch aircraft, to head for the three-dimensional position of the target. Once there, it acts like any other bomb and explodes—in short, a very simple, yet very elegant solution to getting PGMs on target. Early tests of JDAM hardware on test benches are already showing accuracies in the 3.3-to-9.8 foot/1-to-3 meter range, without any other added guidance systems. This is the future of PGMs, where the attacking aircraft only has to know the position of a target to kill it.

Air-to-Ground Missiles

Ever since young David used a stone projected by a sling to slay the giant warrior Goliath from a safe distance, warriors have dreamed of weapons that allow them to attack from a distance that makes counterattack impossible. Standoff. This has been the idea behind almost every weapon innovation—from the catapult, to the cannon, to the Intercontinental Ballistic Missile (ICBM). During the 1940s and 1950s, a generation of designers and engineers worked to create long-range weapons. For Nazi Germany, there was the Fi-103 flying bomb, known better as *Vergeltungwaffe*-1, or V-1. Called the "Doodlebug" or "Buzz Bomb" by its victims, it was the first practical example of what we now call a cruise missile. Later, in the 1950s, standoff cruise missiles were produced to extend the reach of nuclear bombers and maritime strike aircraft.

None of these early standoff weapons had any real precision; the mission was simple delivery of a large warhead to the general target area. True standoff precision weapons had to wait for the development of electronic seeker technology in the 1960s. Earlier, we saw how the first precision seekers were developed for guided bombs like the Paveway-series LGBs, and the GBU-15, so that they could destroy point targets like bridges and bunkers. A precision guided missile combines seeker technology with a propulsion system to extend its range.

As we head towards the 21st century, the USAF has a growing array of standoff air-to-ground missiles (known by their AGM designator) for use against heavily defended targets. These weapons are highly specialized for the targets they are designed to destroy. They also tend to be expensive, with typical unit prices in the six-figure range. However, when compared to the cost of a lost aircraft ($20 million and up) and the human and political costs of lost or imprisoned aircrews, these weapons can be very cheap indeed.

AGM-65 Maverick

We'll start our look at what pilots like to call "gopher zappers" with the oldest air-to-ground missile in the USAF inventory, the AGM-65 Maverick. Maverick draws its roots from two different programs, the early electro-optical guided bomb projects and the Martin AGM-12 Bullpup (originally designated the ASM-N-7 Bullpup A by its first user, the U.S. Navy). Bullpup was an attempt to extend the range of the basic High Velocity Artillery Rocket (HVAR) used by U.S. aircraft since World War II. Bullpup provided a large warhead (250 lb./113.6 kg.), a rocket motor, and a guidance package to keep the whole thing on course. From a safe distance (8.8 nm./16.1 km.) one Bullpup could kill targets that previously required many aircraft with lots of bombs or unguided rockets. Guidance was provided by a command line-of-sight system, which sent the missile flying down a radio "pencil beam." All the operator had to do was keep the nose of his aircraft on the target, and the missile would fly down the beam and impact the target. When it came into service in 1959, it was a wonder to its operators, who saw it as something of a "silver bullet." The problem was that the AGM-12's guidance system compelled the combat aircrew to fly straight and level toward the target during the missile's entire time of flight.

In 1965, the Air Force began a program to develop a successor to the Bullpup. After a three-year competition between Hughes Missile Systems and Rockwell, Hughes won the contract in 1968. The development of the new missile proceeded smoothly, and it came into service in 1972 as the AGM-65A Maverick. Aircrews who saw the new weapon thought it looked like the big brother of the AIM-4/GAR-8 Falcon air-to-air missile, which was no surprise, since Hughes had also designed and built the Falcon. The Maverick shows its Hughes family roots, having the same general configuration as the Navy's much larger AIM-54 Phoenix air-to-air missile. Externally, the Maverick has changed very little in the last two decades that it has been in service. The airframe is 12 in./30.5 cm. in diameter and 98 in./248.9 cm. long. Wingspan of the cruciform guidance and stabilization fins is 28.3 in./71.9 cm. These dimensions make it the smallest, most compact AGM in the USAF inventory, one of the major reasons for its popularity.

It's what's inside that counts, and that is what differentiates the various versions of the AGM-65. The -A model Maverick, which first entered combat service during the Christmas bombing of North Vietnam in 1972, is an E/O guided weapon, much like the GBU-8 or GBU-15. Its main characteristics were a 5° field-of-view (FOV) DSU-27/B seeker, with a huge 125 lb./56.8 kg. shaped

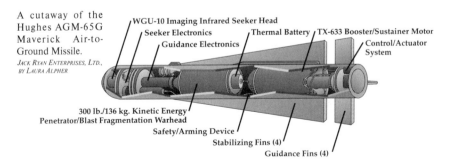

A cutaway of the Hughes AGM-65G Maverick Air-to-Ground Missile. *JACK RYAN ENTERPRISES, LTD., BY LAURA ALPHER*

WGU-10 Imaging Infrared Seeker Head
Seeker Electronics
Guidance Electronics
Thermal Battery
TX-633 Booster/Sustainer Motor
Control/Actuator System
300 lb./136 kg. Kinetic Energy Penetrator/Blast Fragmentation Warhead
Safety/Arming Device
Stabilizing Fins (4)
Guidance Fins (4)

charge warhead (that's really big for one of these!) that could cut through virtually any armor or bunker in existence. Weighing in at 463 lb./210 kg., it was powered by a Thiokol SR109-TC-1/TX-481 two-stage (boost and sustainer) solid propellant rocket motor, giving it a maximum range of roughly 13.2 nm./24.1 km. To fire it, the operator (the backseater of an F-4D Phantom II fighter) selected a missile and powered it up. Once the missile was "warm" with the onboard gyros running, the operator would view the picture from the missile's onboard black and white TV seeker and select a target with a set of crosshairs. Like other early E/O weapons, the -A model Maverick tracked its targets by looking for zones of contrast between light and dark areas. For example, a tank or bunker might appear as a dark shape on a lighter background, and this was what the TV seeker of the early Maverick was designed to track. Once the operator had the target in the crosshairs, he would press a switch to lock on the target, and the seeker would begin to track the target, regardless of the motion of the launching aircraft or the target. After confirming lock-on, all the operator had to do was to press the firing button to send the missile on its way, and the firing aircraft was free to maneuver or evade. All models of Maverick are very accurate. If the missile functions properly, it should place the warhead well within 5 feet/1.5 meters of the aimpoint, which makes it a deadly anti-tank weapon.

Early combat Maverick shots went extremely well, helped by favorable environmental conditions. About sixty were fired in North Vietnam in December 1972 (fairly cool, clear air), and hundreds more by the Israelis in the October 1973 Yom Kippur War (good contrast background, along with dry, clear air). Both situations favored the TV seeker of the -A model Maverick. But in the hazy, muggy summer weather of Central Europe, its effective range was often reduced; an E/O TV tracker had a hard time seeing the camouflaged tanks of the Warsaw Pact in Central Europe. Combined with the different lighting conditions and heavy air pollution, this limited the effectiveness of the AGM-65A. From a pilot's point of view, these conditions forced the user to get much closer to the target than is desirable. This problem was partially solved by reducing the FOV on the next version, the AGM-65B, to only 2.5°, which allowed for twice the magnification of the target scene by the missile optics. Also, for AGM-65s produced in FY-1981 and later, the rocket motor was replaced with an improved reduced smoke model. Nevertheless, the TV-series Mavericks remained difficult to use, especially in conditions of haze or ground cover, particularly by single-seat aircraft like the A-10 (the Warthog) and the F-16.

New versions of the Maverick were already on the way by the late 1970s. One idea was to make it into a laser-guided weapon like an LGB. A developmental version with a laser seeker, designated AGM-65C, was built by Rockwell. But the Air Force did not choose to put it into production (the USMC did, as the AGM-65E). This version also introduced a 300 lb./136.4 kg. blast fragmentation warhead with excellent penetration against everything from warships and bunkers to armored vehicles.

What everyone did want—including the Navy and a variety of foreign air forces—was a missile with a seeker that was immune to the problems of a visible-light TV tracking system. The answer was something entirely new—an Imaging Infrared (IIR) seeker. Like the Sidewinder missile, it would see the infrared (IR) energy given off by an engine or the body heat of a human being. However, instead of using a single detector element like the Sidewinder's seeker, the new Hughes seeker would use multiple elements clustered into a matrix called an imaging array. This array is similar to the photo-electronic pickups used in a home video camcorder. This made the seeker head, designated WGU-10/B, essentially a "poor man's" FLIR. Hughes designed the WGU-10/B to be a "common" seeker, which eventually was used on the IIR versions of the GBU-15, AGM-130, and the AGM-84E Standoff, Land Attack Missile (SLAM).

The IIR seeker integrated into a Maverick airframe proved to be a winner. The seeker was sensitive enough to see through smoke, haze, and fog to find its targets. Initially, the Air Force simply installed the new seeker onto the existing AGM-65B airframe with its 125 lb./56.8 kg. shaped charge warhead. Weighing in at 485 lb./220 kg., the AGM-65D, as it was designated, first arrived in service in 1983 and was very popular, especially in the A-10 community. They even found it could be used as a sensor during Desert Storm, when they would power up one missile on the rack and use its IIR seeker head video to help them navigate on night missions! The Navy and Marine Corps were also quick to see the advantages of the IIR seeker; and as soon as the production of the laser guided -E model was completed in 1985, Hughes began production of the Navy variant, the AGM-65F. This model utilized the large 300 lb./136 kg. blast fragmentation/penetrator warhead of the AGM-65E and was designed to provide U.S. Navy and Marine Corps aircraft with a serious punch against heavy land targets or ships like patrol craft and amphibious vessels. It too was a great success during Desert Storm. IIR Mavericks can be distinguished from their earlier TV E/O brethren by their drab green or gray paint (versus white for the TV Mavericks); and they have either a milky silver or translucent amber colored optical seeker window (the TV seeker uses a clear optical window).

The latest IIR Maverick variant, the AGM-65G, is still being produced for the U.S. Air Force. Weighing in at 670 lb./304.5 kg., this version takes advantage of everything that has been learned about building Mavericks to date. The AGM-65G's features include the WGU-10/B IIR seeker head, the 300 lb./136.4 kg. warhead, more reliable and accurate pneumatic control surface actuators, a digital autopilot, and the TX-633 reduced smoke rocket motor. Additionally, the -G model Maverick has a ship track "aimpoint biasing" mode, which allows the operator to pick an exact spot on a target where the missile will hit. This allows a pilot to designate the missile to hit at the waterline of a target vessel, greatly increasing the chance of critical flooding. When tied to a FLIR-based targeting system like LANTIRN, the AGM-65G is a weapon of deadly capability. (The unit price is $50,000 per missile in FY-1991 dollars.)

So, how do you fire a Maverick? Suppose that you are flying in the backseat of a F-15E Strike Eagle equipped with LANTIRN pods and carrying four AGM-65G IIR Mavericks. You are told to attack a column of enemy armor, stopping them for other aircraft following you to finish them off. You ingress (pilot talk for "approach") the target area and locate the armored column along a road. Using the LANTIRN hand controller, you target the lead vehicle in the column and automatically "hand-off" to the seeker the first missile. Then you repeat this set up for the last vehicle in the column (effectively trapping the vehicles in the middle of the column). Closing in for the attack run, you verify that both missiles are tracking their assigned targets, set the MASTER ARM switch to ON, wait for the missiles to come into range (up to 14 nm./25.6 km. at higher launch altitudes), and launch the missiles as fast as your finger can cycle on the firing button. The missiles should now be on their way to their targets. When each missile impacts, the AN/AAQ-14 will record the result (to provide BDA footage of the event). Before you say this sounds like an advertisement for Hughes and Raytheon (the primary and second source contractors respectively), be aware that over 90% of the Mavericks fired during the Gulf War successfully hit their targets, and most of these were TV E/O and early IIR versions of the missile.

Today, the Maverick missile program is going strong, with fairly bright prospects for the future, given the current defense budget climate worldwide. A number of other nations have continuing Maverick procurement programs of their own, with orders continuing to come in. As for new Maverick developments, there are several ideas being kicked around the engineering shops of Hughes's Tucson, Arizona, plant. Under evaluation is a variant with a new seeker that uses an active millimeter wave (MMW) radar to determine the exact shape of a target in virtually any weather conditions. Millimeter wave guidance uses radar waves small enough (less than a centimeter/0.4 inch) to resolve fine details on a target. The Maverick MMW seeker is only 9.45 in./24 cm. in diameter, so it fits neatly within the current dimensions of the AGM-65. Another option under consideration is to replace the rocket motor used on all previous versions of the Maverick with a turbojet power plant. Called the Longhorn project, it could triple the range of the AGM-65 without increasing the weight or significantly reducing the explosive payload. Neither modification is currently planned for production. Nevertheless, with over thirty thousand Mavericks built to date, the weapon has to be considered a success, with a long career still ahead of it.

AGM-88 HARM

On May 1st, 1960, over the farmlands of central Russia, a small air battle took place that forever changed the nature of air warfare. Almost 13 miles/21 kilometers in the sky, PVO-Strany, was desperately trying to shoot down one of their most hated enemies, a CIA Lockheed U-2 spy plane. It was a costly battle. Several of their own fighters were lost to "friendly fire," and the American intruder almost escaped. What won the day for them was the first success of a new tactical weapon, the surface-to-air missile (SAM). When Francis Gary Powers's U-2 was shot down by the proximity detonation of a S-75 Dvina/SA-2 SAM (NATO code-named Guideline), it set off a scramble to counter this new and lethal weapons technology.

"The best ECM in the world," said an Israeli general famously, "is a 500 lb./227.3 kg. bomb down the feedhorn of the missile tracking radar." He was right. But how many aircraft would he lose getting into position to hit a given SAM radar? Fixed SAM sites tend to be protected by layers of optically tracked AAA guns. Thus early USAF plans to hit such sites in Cuba (during the 1962 missile crisis) with tactical fighter bombers loaded with unguided rockets and canisters of napalm would have undoubtedly exacted a high price.

Meanwhile, the U.S. Navy, long a leader in SAM technology, began to think about the problem of suppressing SAM sites. In 1961, out at the same Naval Ordnance Test Station laboratory that had developed the Sidewinder and Sparrow AAMs, an idea was born that might provide a remedy. Known as an anti-radiation missile (ARM), it was quite simply a missile designed to home in on the emissions of the SAM tracking radar, guiding in to kill the radar. By killing the radar, and hopefully its skilled operators, the SAM site would effectively be "blinded" and unable to function. The first of these missiles was known as the ASM-N-10, later designated the AGM-45 Shrike, taking its name from a predatory bird that kills its prey by impaling them on the thorns or spikes of plants or fences. Simple in concept, the Shrike took some time to perfect; the first AGM-45 Shrike missiles entered fleet service in 1963.

Along with the development of the ARM came a vital piece of equipment which was required to make it functional, the radar homing and warning receiver (RHAW), or radar warning receiver (RWR) as it is known today. Amazing as it may sound, no U.S. tactical aircraft sent to Southeast Asia in 1965 went with any sort of warning system to tell the aircrew they were being tracked by enemy. Thus, when President Lyndon Johnson began the systematic bombing of North Vietnam, with Operations Flaming Dart and Rolling Thunder, USAF, USN, and USMC aircraft began to fall in numbers that were more than just disturbing.

Interestingly, the USAF took a different approach to suppressing SAMs than the Navy or the Marine Corps. The Navy/Marine policy on SAM suppression was just that: prosecute to suppress just long enough for the strike force of attack aircraft to hit their targets, and then run for the safety of the aircraft carrier or home base. In fact, the policy of avoiding duels with air defense sites is at the foundation of USN/USMC strike warfare doctrine even today. Thus, from early 1966, USN defense suppression efforts centered around A-4 Skyhawk attack aircraft equipped with an early RWR and a pair of the new ARMs.

The USAF doctrine is completely different. For the Air Force, it was not enough to scare the operators of the SAM and AAA radars. In the view of the Air Force leadership, those individuals, and their machines of war, were there to be killed. Thus, the Air Force formed a small force of specially configured aircraft and hand-picked, highly trained aircrews to do the critical job of radar hunting. These were the famous "Wild Weasels," initially flying two-seat versions of the famous F-100 Super Sabre, configured with RWR gear, rocket pods, and napalm canisters. Although they were successful in lowering losses from SAMs to the aircraft of the strike forces going "up north," their own losses were prohibitively high. Thus, integrating the new AGM-45 Shrike became a "crash" priority with the USAF. When this was done, losses among the Wild Weasel F-100Fs began to drop, and the crews began to have a future. Not much of one, though. Being on a Weasel crew was statistically suicidal in the early years of the Vietnam conflict.

However, the Shrike had significant tactical limitations and shortcomings. One big one was range. At high altitudes, the Shrike could hit radars some 21.7 nm./40.3 km. distant, while low altitude launches could be up to 15.6 nm./29 km. away. But in practice, launch ranges were usually less than half of the maximum, because certain functions necessary to targeting the missile had to be performed. Most dangerous of these was a maneuver known as a "Shrike pull-up." The launching aircraft had to go into a 15° climb just before launching the ARM; otherwise it would not successfully hit the target radar van. And if the enemy radar shut down while the Shrike was streaking down onto the target, the ARM was likely to miss, lacking as it did the necessary radar emissions for it to home in on. It was, as they say, a *very* tough business.

From the very beginning of its use, the Navy and Air Force were unhappy with the Shrike's performance. In 1969, the U.S. Navy conducted a Tactical Air Armament Study which looked into a shortcomings of Shrike and the whole range of USN/USMC air launched weaponry. From this study came a whole set of requirements which led to the beginning of a development program for a new ARM program. The new missile would be small, with the same general weight and shape as the Shrike, but with greater range, speed, accuracy, and lethality. Also, it would operate from the full range of USN/USMC tactical aircraft, both planned and in service, and would both outrun and outsmart the SAMs and radar operators for every Soviet and other potentially hostile SAM system, even those still under development. It was a tall order for the program engineers at NWC China Lake, California, when they began the new program in 1972. Called the High Speed Anti-Radiation Missile, or HARM, the new missile, designated AGM-88, would take over a decade to bring into service, and would undergo many of the same trials and problems suffered by other advanced missile systems, such as the AIM-120 AMRAAM.

HARM was the first really "smart" air-to-ground missile developed by the United States, using for the first time the new technology of microprocessors and computer software. In other words, HARM was a technical "stretch"—betting that a number of immature technologies ranging from high-impulse rocket motors to a new generation of RWRs would come together all at once, some years in the future, within some sort of cost ceiling. Not everything went as planned. Still, by 1974 Texas Instruments was selected as the prime HARM contractor, and advanced development was underway. And by 1978 the first test firings were underway at NWC China Lake. By FY-1981, the first eighty missiles were under contract, and they headed into fleet service in 1982.

The new missile was called the AGM-88A. And the AGM-88C1 (Texas Instruments) variant is the most common version produced today. The basic -C model missile weighs in at 798 lb./362.7 kg., is 164.2 in./417 cm. long, and is based on a 10.5 in./26.7 cm. diameter airframe with a forward (guidance) fin wingspan of 44 in./112 cm. At the front of the missile is the radome for the Texas Instruments Block IV seeker, which has vastly more capability than even the -B model birds of just a few years ago. Behind the bullet-shaped seeker dome are a series of broadband antennas, which are designed to provide all the functions of an aircraft RWR system, as well as providing passive targeting for the missile guidance system. When we use the term "broadband," we're talking about everything from .5 to 20 GHz; this covers everything from UHF radio transmissions to short-wavelength fire control and ground mapping radars. These antennas feed into a microprocessor controlled digital signal processor, which is capable of breaking down all the incoming signals and translating them into a prioritized target list. This is accomplished via the reprogrammable onboard threat library, which can be used "as is" by an aircrew or customized for a specific threat or situation. With the new seeker, even rotating air traffic control and phased array radars (like those used on the Aegis and Patriot SAM systems) can be effectively targeted and attacked.

Just aft of the seeker section is the warhead section. This is a 145 lb./65.9 kg. blast fragmentation-type unit, with a laser ranging proximity fuse, similar to that of the Sidewinder and the AMRAAM, which spews its twelve thousand tungsten cubes into the heart of the target radar. Behind the warhead section is the guidance/control section, which flies the missile during flight. This is accomplished by a digital autopilot equipped with a strapdown inertial guidance system, driving a series of electro-mechanical actuators which control the large guidance fins mounted along the mid-body of the AGM-88 airframe. Like the Paveway III, the autopilot allows the missile to fly the most energy efficient flight profile and make the most of the "smash" provided by the HARM's rocket motor. Located just aft of the guidance section is a TX-481 dual-grain (two stage), low smoke (to prevent observation), solid fuel motor supplied by

A cutaway drawing of the Texas Instruments AGM-88C1 High Speed Anti-Radiation Missile (HARM).
JACK RYAN ENTERPRISES, LTD., BY LAURA ALPHER

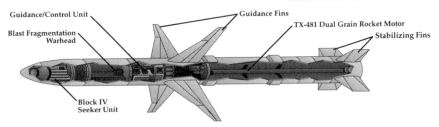

Guidance/Control Unit

Blast Fragmentation Warhead

Guidance Fins

TX-481 Dual Grain Rocket Motor

Stabilizing Fins

Block IV Seeker Unit

either Thiokol or Hercules. It is this motor that generates the incredible speed that gives the missile the first letter in its designation. The top speed, while classified, is probably greater than Mach 3, possibly as high as Mach 4 or 5. This allows it to outrun almost any SAM system in a "quick draw" contest, should that occur. It also provides for a vast increase in range over the Shrike, probably up to a maximum of perhaps 80 nm./146.3 km. from high altitudes (say 30,000 feet/9,144 meters), and 40 nm./73.2 km. when launched as low as 500 feet/152.4 meters. Normally, these ranges would probably be halved, to maintain a performance advantage over any SAMs that might be counterfired against the launching aircraft. The AGM-88 is normally carried on an LAU-118 standard launcher.

From the very beginnings of the HARM program, the Air Force maintained an interest in the new ARM. They too wanted the benefits of such a weapon, and joined in the program at their first opportunity. Initially, their participation included the development and integration of the APR-38 (later upgraded to the APR-47 standard) RWR suite on the F-4G Wild Weasel variant of the Phantom, which was the primary USAF aircraft assigned to the suppression of enemy air defenses (SEAD) mission at the time. The APR-38/47 is a group of RWR systems, tied together to allow the F-4G WSO (technically called an Electronic Warfare Officer or EWO, but known traditionally as the "bear") to accurately plot the positions and characteristics of hundreds of enemy threat emitters. By integrating HARM with this system, the F-4G became a radar hunter of amazing lethality, taking only one loss during Operation Desert Storm—and that happened because an Iraqi AAA round punched a hole in the aircraft's fuel tank; it wasn't able to land before running out of fuel. The crew survived the mishap without injury.

In addition to the dedicated Wild Weasel aircraft, the Air Force made several of their other new aircraft designs capable of carrying and firing the new ARM. Both new variants of the F-15 and F-16 can do so, given the right RWR systems, launch hardware, and software. And the F-16C has been extensively used to augment, and now replace, the aging F-4Gs that are on their last legs of service. As the last of the precious F-4Gs are going to the boneyard for a well-earned retirement, the F-16 is taking over all of the SEAD/HARM mission, thanks in part to the introduction of the ASQ-213 HARM Targeting System (HTS) pod. By combining the HTS pods with data exchanged from other F-16s via the Falcon's IDM, a rough approximation of the F-4G's SEAD capabilities can be reconstituted, without a gap in this badly needed resource.

So how would a pilot fire such a weapon? Well, let's imagine that we're flying a Block 50/52 F-16C, equipped with an ALR-56 RWR and an ASQ-213 HTS pod attached to the Station 5 (right) pod mount point. You and your wingman each have two HARMs on LAU-118 launchers at Stations 3 and 7. The two of you are flying a loose hunting formation ahead of a strike force, with a lateral separation of about 5 nm./9.1 km. You have been briefed about hitting a pair of Buk-1M/SA-11 Gadfly SAM sites on the ingress route of the strike force, and told to look out for possible mobile SAM launchers, which may have been moved into the area. The two of you have set up your IDMs to exchange HTS data and are flying subsonic at about 350 kt./640 kph into the target area. Down on the multi-function display at your right knee is the read-out for the HTS pod data, showing a rotating acquisition radar of the type used to pass targeting information to SAM transporter erector launcher and radar (TELAR) vehicles. At approximately 30 nm./54.9 km. to the target area, the two of you set up a pair of diagonal racetrack-shaped patterns and wait for the action to begin.

As the strike force begins to come up, you see a pair of symbols titled STA 11 come up on the MFD, with indefinite range indications. You call a warning to the strike force to go "heads up" for a possible SA-11 threat, and go to work. In a matter of seconds, your and your wingman's HTS pods have worked out approximate range and bearing to both sites. This done, the two of you each set up a HARM in RK MODE (RANGE KNOWN) and get ready to launch. Within a few seconds, the range to both SA-11 TELARs has settled down, and been fed automatically to the HARM, and you see the two vehicles going for a lock-on with their radars on your RWR. You select MASTER ARM ON and pull the trigger once to launch the missile from Station 3. As the missile flies off, you turn to keep on the edge of the TELAR's maximum range. Thirty seconds later, you see the symbology from both TELARs go off the air as they are destroyed by the two AGM-88s. The two of you now move out in front of the strike force to continue escorting them to the target area. About 10 nm./18.2 km. to the target, you get a sudden warning alarm from your RWR, indicating that a missile tracking radar has just locked up your Viper. A quick look at the RWR shows the STA 8 symbology indicative of an SA-8 Gecko TELAR somewhere off to the right front. You quickly select the SP Mode from the HARM options, the azimuth setting being automatically sent to the remaining HARM at Station 7. You squeeze the trigger one more time, call a warning to the force, and begin evasive maneuvers, punching out chaff as quickly as you can. Within a matter of seconds, the SA-8 TELAR goes off the air, another victim of the superior speed of the AGM-88. Meanwhile, the one missile it launched at you goes "stupid," flying off to self-destruct somewhere else. The force is safe for now, and you move to a covering position to make sure no wandering MiG tries to hassle your wingman or the rest of the force. Just another day's work.

Today the Texas Instruments AGM-88 production line is going strong, continuing to build the 2,018 replacement HARMs that were contracted to replenish the stock fired during Desert Storm, as well as the foreign orders that are being serviced. There are no known plans to replace the AGM-88 at this time; and there will probably be none in the near future, given the general stagnation in the worldwide SAM development market and the remaining growth potential in the HARM airframe. As for the AGM-88 HARM, it should remain the premier ARM in the world for at least the next ten years.

The Future: TSSAM and Beyond

The future of U.S. long range air launched standoff weapons is, to put it mildly, in disarray. This is the unhappy result of the cancellation of a weapon that the USAF and USN had bet the farm on—the Northrop Grumman AGM-137 Tri-Service Standoff Attack Missile. TSSAM was to have been a stealthy, super-accurate, long-range (180 nm./300 km.) guided missile with versions for the Navy and Air Force, and even a ground launched version for the Army. Unfortunately, development and program management problems drove up the cost of the program. And it took a severe hit when the Army dropped out several years ago.

Since the TSSAM program was canceled, the Air Force has been scrambling to figure out how to provide their combat aircraft with a viable precision standoff missile. The current plan has the USAF buying more of what they already have, ALCM-Cs. Several different options are under consideration to fill the gap left by the cancellation of TSSAM. Some of these include:

- Buying the clipped wing version of the AGM-142 Have Nap, and fitting it to the B-1B, the F-15E Strike Eagle, and the F-16C. This would provide a large part of the capability promised by the original TSSAM program.

- Retrofitting the IIR seeker developed for TSSAM to existing missile airframes like the AGM-86C/ALCM-C or the AGM-84E SLAM/SLAM-ER, which is a development of the Navy Harpoon anti-ship missile.

- Producing a reduced cost version of the AGM-137 TSSAM, with the stealth features installed only on the frontal surfaces of the airframe. This is probably the least likely option, given the current budget climate and the general lack of funding for new weapons systems.

Whatever the decisions reached in the halls of Congress, the Pentagon, and the USAF Material Command, there will have to be new gopher zappers, which will undoubtedly be joint programs with the Navy, and perhaps even foreign partners. That is perhaps the greatest impact of the New World Order on the worldwide weapons market—only through cooperation will the industry survive.

Air Combat Command: Not Your Father's Air Force

O nce upon a time in America, there was an Air Force. It was created in 1947 as a separate service (from the U.S. Army), with a simple set of goals: to deter our primary Cold War enemy, the Soviet Union, from expanding beyond its borders, and, if deterrence failed, to successfully fight the Soviets with the other armed services and achieve victory. For over forty-five years, the United States Air Force stood up to the challenge and outlasted its opponents. This is not to say it did so in the most efficient, economical, or even acceptable way. Its bitter turf battles with the U.S. Navy are legendary around Washington, D.C. Also, like all large organizations, the USAF was prone to internal conflicts. Throughout the Cold War, there were continuous squabbles between the primary commands of the USAF. The bomber pilots and ICBM missileers that made up the leadership of the Strategic Air Command (SAC) were always at odds with the fighter pilots who led the Tactical Air Command (TAC). If this was not divisive enough, the "combat" fliers at SAC and TAC scorned those who flew the transports for the Military Airlift Command (MAC), whom they considered "trash haulers."

And in 1991, the U.S. Air Force suffered the greatest disaster (save defeat in battle) that can befall a military force. Its primary enemy, the Soviet Union, collapsed as a result of the failure of the August Coup. Of course, only a truly sick and cynical observer of world events would have wished the Cold War to continue indefinitely. Yet scarcely anyone foresaw the end of the conflict between the U.S. and the USSR and the end of the bipolar world we'd known for half a century. Now, if you think *you* were surprised, you should have seen the shock of the armed services leadership!

Within the halls of the Pentagon, the leadership of the Air Force was quick to realize that with their primary threat nullified, and with severe budget cuts already planned by the Administration of President George Bush, they would have to remake themselves if they were to survive the coming lean years of the 1990s. Thus, in early 1992, USAF Chief of Staff General Merrill McPeak ordered a complete, USAF-wide reorganization. But don't call it a reorganization. Call it a revolution. It so stunned members of the service, they are still trying to fully understand it.

The three traditional flying commands, SAC, TAC, and MAC, were abolished, with combat aircraft (fighters, bombers, electronic warfare and theater transport aircraft) going to the newly formed Air Combat Command (ACC) headquartered at Langley Air Force Base. Virtually all heavy airlift (C-141, C-5, and C-17) and airborne tanker (KC-135 and KC-10) aircraft went to the newly formed Air Mobility Command (AMC), based at Scott AFB, Illinois. The strategic nuclear mission was handed off to a new unified (i.e. joint USAF/Navy) command called Strategic Command (STRATCOM). Incidently, STRATCOM does not own any of the bombers, submarines, or missiles that it operates.

On June 1st, 1992, when the reorganization took place, it was as if every major airline in America (and a few large service companies as well) had merged overnight and thrown their individual corporate cultures to the winds. As might be imagined, this has caused a great deal of stress and personal disorientation. It has also created one of the most powerful and diverse fighting forces in the world. Definitely a revolution! Let's take a look at it.

TAC to ACC: The Great Merger

When ACC was formed in June 1992, the man who was tasked as its first commander had the advantage of also being the last commander of TAC. Thus, General Michael Loh, USAF, had the unique distinction of commanding major USAF military commands on both sides of the great merger. A career fighter pilot, he suddenly found himself leading a force that would have been inconceivable just five years ago.

General Loh makes no secret of his tactical bias in the eternal struggle between the fighter pilots of TAC and the bomber pilots of SAC. It is even conceivable that on the night of May 31st, 1992, he may have hoisted a beer or two to celebrate the end of TAC's "true" enemy, the Armageddon-oriented bomber

General M. "Mike" Loh, USAF. General Loh was the first commander of the USAF Air Combat Command (ACC).
OFFICIAL U.S. AIR FORCE PHOTO

culture of SAC, which was to vanish at midnight that evening. But to listen to him now is to understand the transformation of the old Air Force he grew up in into the new one that he helped create. Gone is the cocky, triumphant fighter pilot. As he hands off command of ACC to General Joe Ralston there is an intense (you could define intensity by spending an hour with General Loh!), almost desperate drive to weld the formerly distinct elements of his new command into a single fighting force. Not in ten years, or even five. But now! Before they are needed again in some far-off, dangerous place. This is the reality that he faced as he finished his final year of command at ACC (he retired in the summer of 1995). His challenges have been simple but formidable. They included:

- Merging personnel, bases, and aircraft from all three of the former major flying commands (bombers from SAC, medium transports from MAC, and tactical aircraft from TAC) into a unified combat flying command.
- Continuing modernization of ACC aircraft, weapons, and equipment, despite the fiscal limitations of the 1990s.
- Maintaining operational and tactical proficiency when out-of-area (i.e., overseas) operations rates (Op Tempos, as they are known) for our forces have never been higher, and operations and maintenance budgets (per pilot and aircraft) have never been lower.
- Supporting Administration plans to be able to fight in two near-simultaneous major regional conflicts (MRCs) of the size that might be anticipated in Korea, or perhaps Iran.
- Doing all this in a time of planned drawdowns and budget shortfalls that are challenging even to those who survived the dark fiscal days of the 1970s.

ACC currently has units spread over the globe, conducting missions on a global scale. In Turkey, Saudi Arabia, and Italy, ACC aircraft are helping to enforce no-fly zones over Iraq and Bosnia. In Korea, ACC aircraft and personnel are providing muscle to diplomatic efforts to maintain peace and stability in that troubled region. And U.S.-based ACC aircraft were key to the recent efforts to build and enforce democracy in Haiti. All this while trying to maintain normal commitments in NATO, Latin America, and the Far East, as well as providing continental air defense for North America.

The ACC Mission

All this brings us to the question of just what are normal operations for ACC. To understand this requires a short history lesson. Back in the mid-1980s, during the Reagan buildup, questions were asked about the effectiveness of the military the buildup was buying. Less-than-perfect joint operations in Grenada (1983) and Libya (1986), along with the disaster of our intervention in Lebanon (1982 to 1984), were disturbing signs that more than just money was needed to get the most out of the American forces. The Congressional response was the Military Reform Act of 1986, known more popularly as Goldwater-Nichols, after its sponsors. Goldwater-Nichols reformed the various military chains of command, and concentrated actual power to command forces in the field in the hands of regional commanders in chief, or CinCs as they are called. These CinCs, of which there are currently eight, control all forces, regardless of service, that are assigned to their geographic area of responsibility (AOR) in the world. These joint commands range from the Middle East (U.S. Central Command, CENTCOM) to forces based in Europe (U.S. European Command, EUCOM). For example, anyone assigned to operate in Latin America would come under the command of General Barry McCaffrey, USA, who (at the time of this writing) is CinC of the U.S. Southern Command (SOUTHCOM) based in Panama. In addition, the Goldwater-Nichols bill strengthened the position of Chairman of the Joint Chiefs of Staff (JCS), so that the billet is now considered a cabinet-level position and the President's senior military advisor. The underlying idea was to clarify the chain of command between the civilian leadership of the national command authority in Washington, D.C., and the forward leadership of our armed forces in the field.

So far, Goldwater-Nichols seems to have worked, with joint operations from Panama to the Middle East running more smoothly than those of the post-Vietnam era. This is not to say that poor political objectives can't cause such operations to fail, as was proven in Somalia in 1992. On the contrary, Goldwater-Nichols places a much greater burden of responsibility for military operations on the civilian leadership of the United States, something future Presidential candidates might be wise to consider before seeking the office.

At this point, you might ask just what all this has to do with getting a wing of combat aircraft into action somewhere in the world? More than you might think, actually. Since the end of the Cold War, the military of the United States has increasingly become a home- or continental-based force. Just in the last five years, we have closed the bulk of our overseas bases in the Philippines, Germany, Spain, and many other countries. This means that interventions by U.S. armed forces are increasingly made at the request of a host nation or as part of a coalition of forces. Thus, the current U.S. military basing strategy has relatively few units forward based, with the CinCs frequently owning few or no forces of their own.

For example: When Iraq invaded Kuwait in August 1990, General H. Norman Schwarzkopf owned exactly *nothing* in the way of combat forces. All he had was a staff and a headquarters. So where did he get the nearly 500,000 soldiers, sailors, marines, and airmen who fought in Operation Desert Storm? Well, those forces were "packaged" and "chopped" to his command (CENTCOM) for the duration of the crisis in the Persian Gulf, and included units from virtually every other command in the U.S. armed forces. At the time, this action was regarded as something of an anomaly, but today it is a fundamental principle of our national defense strategy. By the year 2001, something like 90% of all U.S. forces will be based in the continental United States, meaning that if we want to intervene somewhere, we're going have to take our show on the road.

To support this shift in the U.S. defense paradigm, a new joint command has been created, called United States Atlantic Command (USACOM). In essence, this massive command "owns" virtually every military unit based in the continental United States. The role of USACOM is to be the "packager" of joint task forces for shipment to the various unified commands around the world. Delivery of the package is handled by the folks at U.S. Transportation Command (TRANSCOM) at Scott AFB, Illinois. TRANSCOM controls all the ships, heavy airlift, trucking, and rail assets needed to move the packaged forces to wherever they are needed.

This is where ACC comes in—as the one-stop supplier for USAF combat aircraft. If you need a wing of F-15s with AWACS support to keep a no-fly zone patrolled, ACC supplies the units that will make it happen. In addition, they can supply airbase construction teams (Red Horse battalions), Tactical Air Control Centers (TACCs), medical teams, and even field kitchens, for use at undeveloped airfield sites. They are also, as was demonstrated recently in Haiti, capable of deploying forces from their home bases in America directly into a crisis area.

ACC: The Force

So just what is ACC made up of? The slides of the "ACC Today" command briefing (September 1994) are full of numbers, some of them almost numbing in magnitude. Over 250,000 personnel, including 117,700 in the Air National Guard (ANG) and Air Force Reserves (AFRES). Twenty-five dedicated ACC bases, with ACC units "bedded down" at eleven other USAF installations. ACC boasts a force of some 3,230 aircraft (1,640 active, 1,590 ANG/AFRES) in some 160 different "battle management units," as they are called. These are distributed in four numbered air forces across the continental United States:

- **1st Air Force**—Provides fighters, radars, and other units as the primary air component of the North American Air Defense Command (NORAD).
- **8th Air Force**—Provides the bomber force for ACC, as well as being the primary air component for STRATCOM and USACOM.
- **9th Air Force**—Equipped mainly with fighter and transport aircraft, it is the primary air component for CENTCOM.
- **12th Air Force**—This is the primary air component for SOUTH-COM, as well as the airborne battle management component for STRATCOM.

In short, if it is a combat USAF aircraft, it belongs to ACC.

Headquartered at Langley AFB, Virginia, near Hampton Roads, ACC is commanded from the old TAC headquarters building. From here, General Joe Ralston (the current ACC commander) oversees one of the largest aerial combat units in the world today. But it's a shrinking unit, down from its 1980s high point of almost forty combat wings. In the fall of 1994, ACC was based around a force of some 22 1/2 combat wings. The calculus of counting military strength is an arcane science at best, but for our purposes, we will assume that a fighter wing equivalent (FWE) is composed of roughly seventy-two aircraft in three squadrons of twenty-four planes each. The bad news is that preplanned cuts will drop this number to 20 1/2 wings by 1996. Despite this, Generals Loh and Ralston have worked hard to make this force stretch to meet the requirements of the current Administration's two near-simultaneous MRCs strategy.

One way is to retrofit older airframes with the new series of precision munitions. Another is to make the limited number of new airframes (B-2As and F-22As) as capable as possible, so they might do individually more than the aircraft they will replace. In General Loh's view, any air force that buys new aircraft that are neither stealthy nor equipped with new generation precision and fire-and-forget weapons is committing a criminal act. This is not an extreme point of view; it is borne out by the results of the 1991 Persian Gulf War. The effectiveness of aircraft like the F-117A and the F-15E shows what can be done with modern systems and advanced aircraft engineering.

When you think of ACC today, the cutting edge of its capability is the fighter force. The word fighter is broadly defined. The USAF classifies any tactical combat aircraft as a fighter, regardless of whether it has an air-to-air capability or not. As shown in Table 1 below, the ACC fighter force is currently based around six different types of aircraft (F-15, F-16, F-15E, F-111, F-117, and A-10), which provide it with the bulk of its strike and interdiction capability. A further look shows that something like 25% of the ACC force is based overseas with United States Air Forces Europe (USAFE) and the Pacific Air Force (PACAF). These will almost certainly be pulled back to U.S. territory. In the Pacific, this has already begun, with units previously assigned to the Philippines being transferred to bases in Alaska, Okinawa, and Hawaii. Similar cuts and transfers are being made in Europe, with the bulk of the remaining USAFE units now based in the United Kingdom and Italy, with a continuing presence in Turkey.

Table 1 - ACC Fighter Aircraft Force

	ACC ACTIVE	USAFE/ PACAF	ANG/ AFRES	ANG AIR DEFENSE	TOTAL FORCE
F-15	186 (8 Sqd.)	168 (7 Sqd.)	54 (3 Sqd.)	36 (2 Sqd.)	444 (20 Sqd.)
F-16	234 (10 Sqd.)	240 (10 Sqd.)	504 (28 Sqd.)	144 (8 Sqd.)	1122 (56 Sqd.)
F-15E	90 (4 Sqd.)	72 (3 Sqd.)	N/A	N/A	162 (7 Sqd.)
F-111	58 (3 Sqd.)	N/A	N/A	N/A	58 (3 Sqd.)
F-117	36 (2 Sqd.)	N/A	N/A	N/A	36 (2 Sqd.)
A-10	72 (4 Sqd.)	54 (3 Sqd.)	126 (7 Sqd.)	N/A	252 (14 Sqd.)
Total	676 (31 Sqd.)	534 (23 Sqd.)	684 (38 Sqd.)	180 (10 Sqd.)	2074 (102 Sqd.)

An F-15E Strike Eagle of the 366th Wing's 391st Fighter Squadron taxis down the ramp at Mountain Home AFB to take off on a training mission. LANTIRN–pod equipped F-15Es and F-16Cs will provide the bulk of the USAF precision guided munitions capability until the introduction of JDAM and JSOW early in the 21st century. *JOHN D. GRESHAM*

Another point to notice is the small but significant force of air defense fighters which "chop" to the control of the North American Air Defense Command (NORAD) for purposes of continental air defense and airspace control. It is a sign of the times that these aircraft are no longer flown by active duty USAF personnel, but by units of the ANG. In fact, if you look closely, over 40% of the ACC fighter force is made up of AFRES/ANG units flown by dedicated weekend warriors who might fly you commercially from Washington to Boston on a normal weekday. This is the total force concept put forward after the Vietnam War, where reserve and national guard units are equipped with the same up-to-date equipment as the active components, and trained with them to be able to work together in time of crisis. For example, during Operations Desert Shield and Desert Storm, AFRES and ANG provided the bulk of the deterrent reserve for Korea, as well as virtually all of the air defense for the United States, while the bulk of the active force was fighting the war with Iraq. The process, called backfilling, is vital to the multiple MRC strategy, if it is to work.

As for the future, the good news is that there is a new airframe on the way to replace the F-15 Eagle, the backbone of the fighter and interceptor force for over two decades. When the F-22 arrives for service in the early part of the next decade, it will probably become the basic "heavy" fighter airframe for the USAF. The bad news is that the program will only see production of 442 fighter versions, about enough for four and a half wings of fighters in the current ACC structural scheme. In addition, there will be further cuts in the aircraft shown in Table 1 in some especially critical areas. The most likely place for cuts will be in the force of F-111Fs operated by the 27th Wing at Cannon AFB, New Mexico. While the Aardvarks of the 27th are some of the oldest and most expensive aircraft in the ACC force to operate and maintain (O&M), they also have the longest range and some of the best weapons systems in the whole of the USAF. Most importantly, to lose the entire force of F-111s, with their invaluable Pave Tack delivery systems, is to give up almost

A Rockwell B-1B Lancer bomber flies over the Egyptian pyramids during Operation Bright Star 93. Building upon their known and existing capabilities, ACC hopes to arm B-1s, B-2s, and B-52s with a variety of precision guided munitions to support their worldwide missions.

25% of the Air Force's PGM delivery capability. According to current ACC plans, the B-1B force will take over this role when the Joint Direct Attack Munition (JDAM) and Joint Standoff Weapon (JSOW) programs come on-line in the late 1990s. The problem is that none of the munitions these critical programs are designed to deliver is yet in service, meaning that if we prematurely retire aircraft capable of precision strikes, we will have a window of vulnerability that might prove critical in a time of crisis.

And then there is the shortage of F-15E Strike Eagle airframes. To sustain the current force of roughly two hundred F-15Es, ACC will need about forty additional airframes to make up for aircraft lost in accidents and projected combat attrition. Despite a hard fixed price offer by McDonnell Douglas ($50 million per copy), there is no money for such a sensible purchase. Lockheed has submitted a similar bid for its F-16 Block 50/52 Fighting Falcon, at $20 million per aircraft, and Northrop has submitted a bid of $595 million per aircraft for the B-2A Spirit. Money is just that tight right now.

"What the hell are we going to do with bombers?" When ACC was created in 1992, some of the former TAC-types were asking that question. And the answer they wanted to hear was: "We don't need them. Throw them the hell away." The TAC types were wrong. We need bombers; we need them bad.

Without bombers, General Loh would tell you today, there is absolutely no way ACC can hope to accomplish its assigned missions. Though they seem large and ponderous to fighter pilots, the big birds represent a known and ready capability to deliver massive amounts of firepower over great distances, with rapid responsiveness. Current ACC plans have the bombers armed with a variety of precision munitions (JDAMS and JSOW), conventional bombs (Mk 82/83/42, and CBU-87/89/97), and standoff missiles (ALCM-C/CALCM and

AGM-142 Have Nap), so they might provide the necessary firepower to prevail in a future conflict. And in time of international crisis, elements of the force of B-52Hs and the B-2 force may be chopped over to control of STRATCOM, to provide additional nuclear deterrence muscle. The Cold War may be over, but the need to present a credible nuclear deterrence force is still with us. Remember, settling our problems with Russia only leaves a couple of hundred potential enemies (countries, terrorist groups, etc.) to deal with out there in the world. Many of them are trying to acquire weapons of mass destruction, and the possibility of suffering nuclear annihilation from an overwhelming and undeniable U.S. deterrence force is one way to keep proliferation of such weapons under control.

Table 2 - ACC Bomber Aircraft Force

	ACTIVE FORCE	ANG/AFRES	TOTAL FORCE
B-52H	84 (6 Sqd.)	14 (1 Sqd.)	98 (7 Sqd.)
B-1B	75 (6 Sqd.)	16 (1 Sqd.)	91 (7 Sqd.)
B-2A	8 (1 Sqd.)	N/A	8 (1 Sqd.)
Total	167 (13 Sqd.)	30 (2 Sqd.)	197 (15 Sqd.)

As with the fighter force, the good news for the bomber community is that a new, highly capable airframe is on the way. With the B-2A, ACC has a penetrating bomber capable of flying a good payload into virtually any air-defense environment in the world. The bad news is that the USAF is only buying twenty of the production B-2s, with further production greatly in doubt. General Loh has stated his support for maintenance of the heavy bomber production capability, and obtained some $125 million in FY-1995 funding to keep the Northrop production line and its subcontractors alive while the question of further production is studied. ACC's long-term problem is to keep the bomber force viable in the face of pressure to cut ACC force levels.

This is where the long-standing disputes between the "fighter mafia" and "bomber barons" becomes most evident. The fighter supporters question both the ability of bombers to operate in a modern war and their relatively high O&M costs. The bomber supporters will tell you that fighters do not have the range or carrying capacity to haul the loads of precision munitions required in future conflicts. Who is right? In a manner of thinking, both of them. Generals Loh and Ralston, as well as the rest of the ACC leadership have tended to bet on the bird-in-the-hand theory, which is to say that the bombers are here, they are paid for, and as such should be made use of. Nevertheless, there will inevitably be cuts in the bomber force. Though General Loh would prefer to maintain a force of 180 bomber airframes on duty, this number will probably have to be cut, mostly though a mix of B-52H and B-1B mothballing.

To sustain a force of one hundred available bombers requires a total of about 180 airframes to cover those in test, training, refit, and maintenance. Note that I say mothballed, and not retired or scrapped. ACC wants the bomber airframes that are taken out of service to be protected, so they can be "bought back" should a crisis arise or attrition from combat casualties become critical. Moreover, the ACC leadership have done their best to buy back capabilities that were lost when the last of the B-52Gs were retired in 1993. During a recent visit to ACC headquarters at Langley AFB, General Loh was almost ecstatic when he heard that six B-52Hs of the 2nd Bombardment Wing at Barksdale AFB, Louisiana, had been made capable of launching the AGM-142 Have Nap standoff missile, and that their AGM-84 Harpoon anti-shipping missile and mining capabilities would also soon be restored. Such is the state of affairs in the U.S. military that a senior military leader is excited over a restored capability in just six airframes of a forty-year-old bomber design. It is something to keep in mind.

Of equal concern to the ACC leadership is the problem of their limited fleet of electronic warfare (EW) aircraft. EW aircraft are what is known as "force multipliers," and no aerial campaign in the last two decades has succeeded without them. Unfortunately, the linchpin of the USAF EW fleet, the SAM hunting Wild Weasel version of the venerable F-4G Phantom II, is—well—ancient. With the airframes hitting their twenty-fifth year of continuous service, it is essential to find a replacement airframe to do the mission of suppressing enemy air defenses. However, since there is absolutely no money to even consider producing a dedicated replacement Wild Weasel aircraft, the two remaining squadrons of F4-Gs will have to soldier on, supplemented by the hundred Block 50/52 F-16Cs equipped with the new Texas Instruments AN/ASQ-213 HARM Targeting System (HTS) pods and support from other ACC EW surveillance aircraft.

Table 3 – ACC Electronic Warfare Aircraft

	ACTIVE FORCE	ANG/AFRES	TOTAL FORCE
F-4G*	18 (1 Sqd.)	18 (1 Sqd.)	36 (2 Sqd.)
EF-111	24 (1 Sqd.)	N/A	24 (1 Sqd.)
EC-130H	10 (2 Sqd.)	N/A	10 (2 Sqd.)
Total	52 (4 Sqd.)	18 (1 Sqd.)	70 (5 Sqd.)

* Note: F-4G still retains its air-to-air capability

The other ACC EW airframes are in somewhat better shape, though their numbers are much lower than the ACC leadership would like. The EF-111A Raven (called the Spark 'Vark by their crews) fleet is in good shape. Unfortunately, they are scheduled to be retired in the next few years. The EC-130H Compass Call birds are also quite capable, though their lack of numbers is somewhat troubling.

Certainly the most diverse part of the ACC fleet is the aircraft that fall in the general category of support. At the top of the list is the fleet of E-3 Sentry airborne warning and control system (AWACS) aircraft. Few communities in

An EF-111A Raven of the 27th Fighter Wing standoff jamming aircraft on the ramp at Nellis AFB during Green Flag 94-3. These invaluable jammer aircraft are currently scheduled to be retired over the next few years because of budget cutbacks. *CRAIG E. KASTON*

the USAF have more temporary duty (TDY) assignment days than the 552nd Wing at Tinker AFB, Oklahoma. Like the other force multipliers, the E-3 community is limited by their relatively small number of airframes. In addition, they suffer because of their 1960s computer technology and less-than-efficient turbojet engines. The good news is that the AWACS Radar System Improvement Program (RSIP) should resolve the worst of the Sentry's problems, and the USAF is studying the retrofitting of new engines as well. In the long term, the next generation of surveillance aircraft will have to wait for some time, probably well into the 21st century.

Table 4 – ACC Support Aircraft Force

	ACC	USAFE/PACAF	ANG/AFRES	TOTAL FORCE
E-3	19 (4 Sqd.)	10 (2 Sqd.)	N/A	29 (6 Sqd.)
E-4	3 (1 Sqd.)	N/A	N/A	3 (1 Sqd.)
EC-135	6 (1 Sqd.)	N/A	N/A	6 (1 Sqd.)
EC-130E	6 (1 Sqd.)	N/A	N/A	6 (1 Sqd.)
OA-10	32 (4 Sqd.)	24 (3 Sqd.)	56 (7 Sqd.)	112 (14 Sqd.)
Total	66 (11 Sqd.)	34 (5 Sqd.)	56 (7 Sqd.)	156 (23 Sqd.)

The problem of numbers is also of concern to the EC-135 Looking Glass and EC-130 Airborne Control and Control Center (ABCCC) communities. These airborne command posts provide command and control for a variety of USAF operations. Both are invaluable national assets, and are beginning to get a bit long in the tooth. Watch for a replacement or supplement for these airframes in the next few years. Happier thoughts surround those in the OA-10 community, whose performance as forward air controllers during the recent Persian Gulf was nothing short of outstanding. Though short on all-weather/day-and-night systems, their crews and support personnel have taken their Warthog attitude of operations, and made lemonade from what some folks might consider lemons. Right now they are starting to consider using night vision goggles to get more out of their already busy birds. Finally, in one of the ironies of the 1992 mergers, ACC took over beddown and control of the fleet of E-4s. Once known as the "Doomsday Planes," these modified 747s still remain on alert to provide a secure, safe haven for the national command authorities in the event of a crisis or national emergency.

So what will be the next addition to the American fleet of support aircraft? Probably the new E-8 Joint Surveillance Tactical Reconnaissance Systems (JSTARS) aircraft, which will become available in the late-1990s. The E-8 (another modified 707 airframe) will provide information on ground forces the way the E-3 AWACS keeps an eye on airspace. While extremely expensive, the E-8 will undoubtedly become one of the crown jewels of the USAF fleet.

Nowhere in ACC is there a greater shortfall of capability, or more frustration, than in the airborne reconnaissance community. At the top of the problem list is the fleet of RF-4C Phantom II photo reconnaissance aircraft. These birds are antiquated and obsolete. They suffer from structural fatigue problems, short range (due to their thirsty J-79 turbojet engines), lack of modern radar warning receivers (RWRs), electronic countermeasures (ECM) gear, and outdated sensors. Only the loving care of their operators in units of the Nevada and Alabama ANG is keeping the RF-4C as a viable system. There had been plans to replace the RF-4C with a reconnaissance version of the F-16, carrying a podded version of the Advanced Tactical Reconnaissance System (ATARS). But when the system ran into technical problems, the USAF canceled the program. This caused much shock and displeasure for the other planned ATARS users, the U.S. Navy and the U.S. Marine Corps. Following this programmatic fiasco, as well as complaints with the overall direction of airborne reconnaissance, the Defense Airborne Reconnaissance Office (DARO) was created in 1993 to coordinate all airborne reconnaissance systems for all services. For now, though, the Air Force's contribution to the tactical photo reconnaissance mission is going to be limited to satellite assets from the National Reconnaissance Office (NRO), and the aging fleet of RF-4Cs.

Table 5 – ACC Reconnaissance Aircraft Force

	ACTIVE FORCE	ANG/AFRES	TOTAL FORCE
RC-135	6 (2 Sqd.)	N/A	6 (2 Sqd.)
U-2	24* (2 Sqd.)	N/A	24* (2 Sqd.)
RF-4C	N/A	36 (2 Sqd.)	36 (2 Sqd.)
Total	30 (4 Sqd.)	36 (2 Sqd.)	66 (6 Sqd.)

* Note: Estimated. Actual number is classified.

Operational-level reconnaissance assets are another thing entirely. The USAF fleet of U-2 reconnaissance aircraft is headed into its fifth decade of continuous service, and going strong. It is sometimes hard to believe that this Cold War icon has outlived even the aircraft that was designed to replace it, the SR-71 Blackbird. Presently, the U-2 is the best operational-level reconnaissance aircraft in the world, assuming a benign volume of airspace for it to operate in. The memory of what happened to Francis Gary Powers on May 1st, 1960 is still strong in the minds of the USAF, and they will not operate the U-2 anywhere where there is a significant surface-to-air missile (SAM) threat. How long will the U-2 continue to soldier on? Right now that is anyone's guess. It does the job, and nothing has yet come along which does the job better or cheaper.

Perhaps the most valuable airframe in the whole ACC finishes out our look at reconnaissance aircraft, the RC-135 Rivet Joint. These heavily modified airframes are packed from end to end with electronic surveillance equipment to locate enemy radars, communications centers, and command and control sites. The "RJs," as they are known, are literally electronic vacuum cleaners for electronic intelligence (ELINT)/signals intelligence (SIGINT), and thus are almost irreplaceable national assets. Again the problem is one of numbers. When we visited Nellis AFB in the spring of 1994, we saw two RJs working in the Green Flag exercises being held there. These aircraft were fully one third of the fleet. Meanwhile, Rivet Joint is becoming ever more important to the ACC mission, because their ability to locate and track SAM radars makes them vital in helping the F-16s assigned Wild Weasel duties find their targets and put their High Speed Radiation Missiles (HARMs) on target.

Of all the challenges borne by General Loh in the 1992 merger, certainly none was more alien to him than taking over beddown and command of the USAFs large fleet of C-130 Hercules transports. Tasked with the job of inter-theater transport, the C-130s are the backbone of combat logistics for deployed air units, and thus it makes perfect sense for them to be assigned to ACC. They also provide the bulk of combat airlift for the paratroopers of the 82nd Airborne Division within the XVIII Airborne Corps. The C-130 is yet another design with some four decades of service under its belt, with no end in sight. The C-130H model is still in production for the USAF and a number of other nations; and a new version, the C-130J, is being built and tested. It will likely come into service with the USAF in the early 21st century.

There are no plans to replace the basic C-130, and no perceived shortcomings in the design. The aircraft are structurally sound, and have no vices that anyone who flies them cares to complain about. In fact, if you look at Table 6, you will notice that the vast majority of the C-130 fleet is operated by the forces of the ANG and AFRES. The inter-theater transport mission is made-to-order for the Guard and Reserves, and will remain one of their most valuable contributions for decades to come. Thus, the C-130 will likely become the first combat aircraft to remain in production and service for five decades and in two different centuries.

Table 6 – ACC Transport/Tanker Aircraft Force

	ACTIVE FORCE	ANG/AFRES	TOTAL FORCE
C-130	102 (8 Sqd.)	280 (28 Sqd.)	382 (36 Sqd.)
C-21	13 (3 Sqd.)	N/A	13 (3 Sqd.)
C-27	9 (1 Sqd.)	N/A	9 (1 Sqd.)
KC-135	6 (1 Sqd.)	N/A	6 (1 Sqd.)
KC-10*	19 (2 Sqd.)	N/A	19 (2 Sqd.)
Total	149 (15 Sqd.)	280 (28 Sqd.)	429 (43 Sqd.)

* Note: May be returned to AMC.

In addition to the C-130s, ACC also took over the a small fleet of C-21 Learjets used for VIP travel, and twin-engine C-27 transports used for local logistical support in the Canal Zone down in Panama.

ACC has also been assigned a small, but significant force of KC-135 Stratotanker and KC-10 Extender aerial tanker aircraft. These have been assigned to various units, such as the 4th and 366th wings, to provide them with rapid-deployment capabilities.

Finally, there is the vital area of combat search and rescue (CSAR). Prior to the 1991 Gulf War, the CSAR mission was the property of the USAF Special Operations Command (USAFSOCOM). Their promise was that when the time came, their force of MH-53J Pave Low helicopters would be there to scoop up any fliers unfortunate enough to be shot down over enemy territory. There was just one little problem with this promise: It was a lie. It is not an exaggeration to say that the command leadership of the U.S. Central Command Special Operations Command (SOCCENT) was fixated on supporting the various teams of special operations ground forces operating in Iraq and Kuwait and not on picking up flyers unfortunate enough to get themselves shot down. Therefore, SOCCENT laid down an almost impossible set of criteria to be fulfilled before a rescue would be attempted. Thus, an F-15E Strike Eagle crew shot down in western Iraq spent days on the ground, waiting for a rescue mission that SOCCENT would not authorize, and which never came. Eventually they were captured, and they and their fellow aircrews were howling mad at the "snake eaters" of the special operations world for breaking what they considered to be a special covenant that dated back to the days of the Korean War. For forty years, U.S. combat aircrews took it as a matter of faith that if they were shot down, survived the ejection, and were free in enemy territory, their fellow warriors would stop the war, move heaven and earth, and risk their own lives to get to them before the enemy did. When that didn't happen; they felt betrayed. And they were right.

Table 7 – ACC Search and Rescue Aircraft Force

	ACTIVE FORCE	ANG/AFRES	TOTAL FORCE
UH-1	3 (1 Sqd.)	N/A	3 (1 Sqd.)
HH-60	20 (4 Sqd.)	28 (5 Sqd.)	48 (9 Sqd.)
HC-130	5 (1 Sqd.)	19 (4 Sqd.)	24 (5 Sqd.)
Total	28 (6 Sqd.)	47 (9 Sqd.)	75 (15 Sqd.)

Because ACC is committed to recreating that original covenant, CSAR has been the only real area of growth in the ACC inventory. Since the end of the Gulf War, the USAF has stood up a number of combat SAR squadrons dedicated to the CSAR mission. These are equipped with the latest version of the HH-60 Pave Hawk helicopter, together with HC-130 Hercules aircraft to provide both in-flight refueling as well as command and control for the rescue forces. In addition, ACC has built a CSAR weapons school at Nellis AFB, to make sure that the art of CSAR is never again lost.

The CSAR helicopter force is not limited to SAR operations. It is also used for exercise support, CSAR training, disaster relief, and even support during space shuttle launches. Nevertheless, the forces shown in Table 7 will always have one overriding imperative, to support the *combat* flyers of the USAF and their joint partners. First, last, and always!

Deployability: The ACC Style of War

So, you might ask, just how will ACC use their resources in future conflicts? Again, ACC's mission is to "package" USAF units for USACOM to be fed out to unified command JTFs. That is a fancy way of saying that ACC headquarters tells their folks where to go and how to get there. It also places the responsibility on ACC to train their people not only to use the array of weapons and equipment in the inventory, but to deploy and work with other JTF component units from other U.S. services (the Navy, Army, etc.), or those of other coalition/host nations. These basic weapons training skills are accommodated within the standard training system of USAF schools and squadrons. Local bombing, gunnery, and air-to-air training ranges are used to keep basic skills honed. Currently, the USAF has some thirty-eight live-fire bombing and gunnery ranges, six electronically scored bombing ranges, five electronic combat ranges, 775 air-to-air training range zones, and ten instrumented air-to-air (ACMI/TACTS) ranges. But to teach the more sophisticated skills of joint warfare, something more is required. These are the various Flag exercises that the USAF runs around the world. They teach USAF personnel, as well as the personnel of other services and countries, how to fight the kind of war we saw during 1991 in the Persian Gulf. These include:

- **Red Flag**—A series of five yearly composite force exercises run in the vast western training range complex north of Nellis AFB, Nevada. These are detailed war games run against simulated aggressor aircraft, ground threats, and target arrays, designed to teach units how to deploy and operate in a joint environment. Since its inception in 1975, air units from every U.S. military branch and twenty-one foreign air forces have participated in Red Flag.
- **Green Flag**—Essentially a Red Flag with real-world electronic warfare capabilities being exercised. Extremely expensive to run, these take place once a year at Nellis AFB, Nevada.
- **Blue Flag**—A large command post exercise designed to teach U.S. command staffs how to run theater-level deployment and combat operations.
- **Checkered Flag**—A large theater-level combat training exercise run several times a year. These exercises include direct participation of coalition/host nations. In 1994 alone, some twenty-one different nations from every continent in the world participated. These included such well-known allies as Australia and Saudi Arabia, as well as some less well-known participants such as Chile, Kenya, and Singapore.

And there are several other Flag exercises, with narrower goals. Other exercises are used to train specific types of units in particular scenarios. Some of the FY-1994 examples include:

- **Coronet Havoc**—F-117As from the 49th Fighter Wing at Holloman AFB, New Mexico, rapidly deployed from their home base to a base in the Netherlands.
- **Bright Star**—Aircraft from the 366th Wing at Mountain Home AFB, Idaho, ran a composite intervention wing deployment/combat exercise with the Egyptian Air Force, and other allies, in Egypt. This included deploying fighters and tankers to Cairo West Airfield in Egypt, as well as bombers and tankers to the Azores.
- **Global Power**—These demonstrations of bomber capability are usually run about eight times a year. For example, on the fourth anniversary of the Iraqi invasion of Kuwait, in 1994, two B-52Hs from the 2nd Bombardment Wing at Barksdale AFB, Louisiana, flew non-stop (with in-flight refueling) to Kuwait, where they delivered their conventional bomb load on a Kuwaiti training range, then continued around the world to their base. In another Global Power demonstration, B-1Bs from the 28th Bombardment Wing at Ellsworth AFB, South Dakota, also flew non-stop around the world (also with in-flight refueling support).

Another way of building skills and unit esprit is to hold weapons competitions. As might be imagined, these contests of skill appeal at a basic level to the ACC flyers, who by their very nature are competitive creatures. These include:

- **Gunsmoke**—This is ACCs biannual worldwide gunnery and bombing meet run every September of odd-numbered years at Nellis AFB, Nevada.

- **William Tell**—One of the longest-running exercises in USAF history, William Tell is ACC's worldwide air-to-air missile and gunnery meet held at Tyndall AFB, Florida. This is also a biannual event, run in even-numbered years.

- **Long Shot**—A new competition to ACC, Long Shot is a global power projection exercise which tests units' ability to both deploy and put combat power on target. Also a biannual, it is held during even-numbered years at Nellis AFB, Nevada.

- **Proud Shield**—A new event, this is the ACC long range bombing competition that is held at Barksdale AFB, Louisiana in odd-numbered years.

How does all of this training, exercising, competing, and expense pay off? Well, it gives us the best air force in the world for starters. No other air force trains as hard to go somewhere and fight as hard. Even such vaunted units as the air forces of Great Britain and Israel can't begin to match the mobility, capability, firepower, and professionalism of today's USAF.

So just how would ACC respond to an MRC? While the following comments reflect current ACC policy, as set down in their September 1994 command briefing, it should not be considered a one-size-fits-all kind of doctrine. The keystone of the responses is flexibility to the particular situation at hand.

The first part of any intervention is called the Contingency Response—how quickly different types of ACC units can be ready to move out to a crisis area. Consider the following types of ACC unit responses:

- **U.S.-Based Bombers**—Within three hours of any alert, every bomber unit in ACC is prepared to upload any ordnance in its required table of organization and equipment (TO&E), and launch the first cell of two or three aircraft on a mission. Following this, the units are required to maintain a continuous sortie rate (it varies with different types of bomber units) during the duration of the crisis. They also must be ready to deploy all of their equipment, aircraft, and personnel within seventy-two hours of an alert order for deployment to the crisis zone.

- **Active Fighters**—Active-duty ACC fighter units must be ready to deploy their first full squadron of aircraft within twenty-four hours, with all squadrons ready to move within seventy-two hours.

- **Reserve/Air National Guard Fighters**—These ACC units are given twenty-four hours to recall all personnel; they then must meet the same standard as active fighter units. First squadron wheels up in twenty-four hours, last bird in the air at seventy-two hours from the end of the mobilization period.

This is an impressive standard to meet, and one that the former bomber crews from SAC are proud to have brought with them to ACC. Now it should be said that not all ACC units would deploy to a crisis area all at once. Just the limitations of heavy airlift and available ramp space would restrict movement to those units absolutely required in the early stages of a crisis. Right now, the USAF is in the midst of the most serious airlift crisis in its history. With the C-141 fleet quickly coming to the end of its life, and the C-17 program only coming on-line slowly, the U.S. military's ability to rapidly deploy is greatly in question. This is one of the reasons for a new kind of ACC unit—the composite wing. It is designed to rapidly deploy airpower into a region with all the pieces necessary to start a successful air campaign. Three of these units have been formed to help get the ball rolling on any crisis response that might require USAF support. They include:

- **23rd Wing**—Based at Pope AFB, North Carolina, this unit is paired with the 82nd Airborne Division at Fort Bragg, North Carolina. Equipped with A/OA-10 Thunderbolt II attack fighters, F-16 Fighting Falcon fighters, and C-130 Hercules transports, it is designed to provide the first airborne units of the 82nd the kind of support that they would need early in a crisis.
- **347th Wing**—Located at Moody AFB, Georgia, the 347th is teamed with the 24th Mechanized Infantry Division at Fort Stewart, Georgia. Equipped with a similar TO&E to the 23rd, it will help support the only heavy armored unit in XVIII Airborne Corps.
- **366th Wing**—The crown jewel of ACCs quick-response strategy, the 366th, which is based at Mountain Home AFB, Idaho, is designed to provide a core air intervention capability on day one of a crisis. Composed of five different squadrons of F-15Cs Eagle fighters, F-15E Strike Eagle fighter bombers, F-16C Fighting Falcon strike fighters, B-1B Lancer heavy bombers, and KC-135R Stratotankers, the 366th is a miniature air force in a wing-sized package. It also contains a command and control element that can generate Air Tasking Orders (ATOs) for up to five hundred sorties a day.

Designed to deploy with less than half the normal number of heavy airlift sorties of normal combat wings, these composite wings are light on their feet and ready to move at a moment's notice. The price they pay is that they will only be able to operate for about a week on their own, before reinforcements will be required. Nevertheless, with the rapid response capability inherent in these composite wings, the commander of a JTF on the way to a trouble zone will have something waiting for him when he gets there. And that is more than General Horner had when he assumed the job of CENTCOM Forward in August 1990. It should also avoid the nightmare that met Lieutenant Colonel Howard Pope and his wingman when they arrived as the first elements of the 1st Fighter Wing in Dhahran, Saudi Arabia. Alighting on an almost empty airfield, expecting some kind of welcome from the Saudi authorities, what Pope got instead were directions to the arming and fueling pit, with instructions that he and his wingman would be on alert; and for the next twenty minutes (until the next pair of F-15s was due), they were the *only* American airpower in the region!

With all that behind us, let's consider the initial phase of a crisis. The President has decided to use force in response to the actions of a threat nation. The first units capable of responding to an emerging crisis would be bomber units and their associated tanker assets. The missions could cover a spectrum of possibilities. You might have B-52Hs hitting hardened enemy command and control facilities with penetrating AGM-142 Have Nap standoff guided bombs. Another possibility could have B-1Bs firing ALCM-C/CALCM cruise missiles into critical nodes of a threat nation's electrical power grid. Or B-2As might be penetrating enemy airspace to do precision drops of naval mines inside an enemy harbor or river estuary. Whatever the mission, the rapid application of airpower, and the demonstration of American will, probably have a significant effect on the actions of enemy leadership, as well as on the world scene. Thus, within twenty-four hours of the national command authority giving the order, the first bombers will have put ordnance on target. This done, they can return to the continental United States for another load, or continue on to a host nation base to raise their OpTempos even further by cutting the range to their targets.

Meanwhile, AMC will be positioning key command and control units, as well as airborne tanker assets, to support the massive flow of units and aircraft that will be headed towards the crisis. While this is happening, the first of the composite wings, the 366th, will deploy from its base at Mountain Home AFB, Idaho, to provide an initial JFACC capability in the forward area. In addition, if contingency ground forces are due to deploy, the 23rd (if the deploying unit is the 82nd Airborne Division) and/or the 347th (if the 24th Mechanized Infantry is used) will be getting ready to move and be in place when their associated ground units arrive in-theater. Unlike Operation Desert Shield, where this level of deployment took weeks, the whole sequence will take days. The idea is to respond so rapidly that a crisis can be contained, rather than become a drawn-out campaign.

With the initial phase completed, the deployment will transition to a more sustained pace. Additional fighter units will deploy, the bombers will continue their strike operations, and a sustained tanker air bridge will be established. During this transition phase, the 366th would be generating ATOs for all of the deployed forces, as well as for the bomber/tanker missions coming in from the United States. Should host or coalition aircraft wish to join in, they can supply their own command and control hookups into the 366th Air Operations Center (AOC). And if the crisis were to escalate, or the tempo of operations grow, you would probably see a full-sized theater-level JFACC Tactical Air Control Center (TACC) from one of the numbered air forces dispatched to relieve the 366th AOC. At this point, air operations would intensify, and you would see a sustained Op Tempo similar to that of Operation Desert Storm.

This is the current scheme for deploying airpower with ACC. Whether it survives the first hours of a crisis remains to be seen. But given the experience of some of the people who have worked on these plans, it represents the best use of the available ACC assets today. Of course, as new aircraft, weapons, and sensors come on-line, the plans will be altered to suit the new situation.

No military operations plan ever runs completely as designed. When General Horner laid out the deployment plan for Operation Desert Shield in August 1990, he did it in an office in CENTCOM headquarters at MacDill AFB near Tampa, by himself, on a pad of paper with a pencil. No other JTF commander will *ever* have to do that again. That is the promise that Mike Loh, Joe Ralston, and the ACC staff have made to unit commanders throughout this new air force that they have built.

ACC Tomorrow: Countdown to 2001

And what of the future? The next few years will be, if anything, more dangerous and uncertain than the last few. Given the wild rush of events since Mikhail Gorbachev took power in 1985, we can only imagine what the final years of the 20th century will bring.

So what will ACC look like as it moves towards the 21st century? Almost certainly it will be smaller. Older types of aircraft such as the B-52 and F-111 will disappear, and the small fleet of B-2A Spirit bombers will make itself felt. Also arriving will be the first of the new F-22A stealth air superiority fighters which will revolutionize air-to-air warfare. It would be nice to think that these new airframes will be bought in the kind of numbers that will make them decisive in future combat situations. But with B-2A production limited by Congress to a mere twenty airframes, and the F-22 production run planned at just 442 units, such hopes may be just that. Hopes. Nevertheless, it has been an Air Force tradition to equip their aircrews with the best that the American treasury can buy, despite the numbers involved. Also, there is a firm commitment by USAF leadership to keep critical design and manufacturing capabilities from wasting away. The USAF needs to maintain its share of the defense industrial base. Three areas that General Loh has identified as critical are:

- Design, development, testing, and production of bomber and fighter stealth airframes such as the F-22, F-117, and B-2.
- Design, development, testing, and production of heavy airlift aircraft such as the C-17, capable of carrying outsized cargo loads.

- High speed computer and electronics design to support improved avionics capabilities, as well as improving reliability and maintainability of new and existing aircraft.

In particular, he would like to see continued low-rate production (two to three a year) of the B-2, so that the bomber force might stabilize at around 120 airframes (say, 80 B-1Bs and 40 B-2s) at the turn of the century. In this way the force would remain both credible and survivable following the retirement of the last of the B-52s. As for the F-22, that is another problem. Recently, senior Administration officials proposed that the F-22 program should be "stretched out" so that the new fighter's service introduction would be delayed until around the year 2005. This would undoubtedly result in a rapid escalation of the program's cost and force ACC to push their already limited and aging fleet of F-15Cs to last another five years more than planned. It may well be that the program stretch will be required. But it will come at a high price in time and treasure. The old adage "Pay me now, or pay me later" was never truer than in the game of defense procurement.

As for the rest of the ACC combat force, there will be a modest series of upgrades. Addition of Global Positioning System (GPS) receivers and new Have Quick II radios will certainly be applied across the board. These are relatively low cost upgrades which will be felt across the whole of the USAF. A more subtle upgrade is being applied across the entire ACC fleet in the form of improved sensors to target improved weapons. Some of these are as simple as software upgrades to enable a greater percentage of the ACC fighter force to fire the AIM-120 AMRAAM missile. Others—such as adding the AN/ASQ-213 HTS pods to the Block 50/52 F-16C—cost a bit more, yet provide a cost-effective, interim replacement for an existing but dying capability. Still others, like the AIM-9X version of the classic Sidewinder air-to-air missile and the new series of air-to-ground munitions, are costly, but necessary to maintain the credibility of a shrinking force. It is important that Congress and the American people understand that the money spent on these programs is not just being spent to protect the stock values of defense contractor shareholders, but to maintain the very credibility of our military forces. A bit of money spent today may prevent an aggressor from deciding that tomorrow is a good day to test the will of America and her allies. A war never fought is always the cheapest war. We should always look for the *real* bargain.

Another financial problem for ACC, and the entire U.S. military, is that they must bear the burden of an unnecessary support infrastructure that is essentially a large public works program for members of Congress. Let me explain. Unless you have been on Venus the last few years, you probably have heard something about the Base Reduction and Closing (BRAC) Commission which has been recommending the closing or realignment (i.e. reorganization) of various surplus military facilities around the United States. The fights over which bases will remain and which will be closed have been among the most vicious and partisan in memory. Because of the loss of civilian jobs inherent in any base closing, individual members of the House of Representatives and U.S. Senate have taken the fight to keep pet facilities open to sometimes absurd lengths.

For the USAF and ACC, this has meant they have been forced to keep facilities open and paid for that they simply do not require or desire. For example, the USAF currently maintains five Air Logistics Centers (ALCs) around the United States. These are massive facilities, where the Air Force modifies or rebuilds aircraft of virtually every kind. However, the requirement for five ALCs was set for the USAF during the Cold War, not with the reduced force of today. Senior USAF officials have publicly stated to me that they only require two ALCs to service the current USAF fleet. The ALCs at Tinker AFB, Oklahoma (near Oklahoma City) and Hill AFB, Utah (near Ogden, Utah), have won awards for their facilities and personnel, and they can handle, with capacity and capability to spare, every aircraft in the USAF. Yet mainly due to the efforts of the congressional delegations of California, Texas, and Georgia where the endangered facilities are located, the Air Force has been unable to close any of the excess facilities. Between payroll and O&M costs, each ALC probably costs the USAF close to a billion dollars a year to keep open. Just the savings from closing these three facilities could support between ten and fifteen wings of combat aircraft every year!

Bases are, of course, not the only pork in the military budget. The USAF and other services are also forced to bear the financial strain of buying weapons and systems they do not need or desire, so that a contractor can be sustained in a home state or district. I wonder at times how the shame does not show on the faces of those elected and appointed to serve the people. So, will the Air Force and other services ever be allowed to cut the unnecessary overhead costs from their budgets? Doubtful to impossible. Closings cost votes, and the members of Congress much prefer to let our combat forces shrink than suffer a loss at the polls.

It should also be said that USAF leadership would love to restructure their support facilities to get more out of them. One of the more interesting ideas I have heard is the concept of merging all U.S. military flight test facilities and test pilot schools into a small group of consolidated facilities in the open areas of the western United States. This would allow the Department of Defense to close a number of facilities such as Naval Air Station (NAS) Patuxent River, Maryland, and Eglin AFB, Florida, while retaining a robust test capability at bases such as Edwards AFB and NAS Point Mugu, California. Again, hundreds of millions of dollars could be saved yearly, if only Congress and the Administration would allow it. So the next time you hear a member of Congress whining about the inefficiency and bloat in the U.S. military, send them a letter, fax, or e-mail, and ask them when they last closed a base in their home state or district! The burden of their pork is being borne by folks like General Ralston and his combat aircrews.

Despite these problems, ACC remains the single most powerful air force in the world today. In spite of the challenges and financial burdens that they bear, they will always do their best with what we the taxpayers care to give them. Let us hope that it is enough, and that they will not come back saying, "You could have done better."

The official badge of the 366th Wing, the "Gunfighters."   *U.S. AIR FORCE*

The 366th Wing: A Guided Tour

Audentes Fortuna Juvat–Fortune Favors the Bold.

— 366th Wing motto

You really have to want to get there, and it is not easy—some fifty miles outside Boise, Idaho, down Interstate 84 to a turnoff onto a road that seems to dead-end into nowhere. After about ten of the most desolate miles you will ever drive, you arrive at the gate. Your next impression is surprise, for what you have found is a state-of-the-art military facility in the middle of the Idaho desert, a place with the unlikely name of Mountain Home Air Force Base (AFB). The buildings are modern and trim, the flight line is vast and spacious. Then you notice the sign, "Home of the Gunfighters."

And so you get your first introduction to the most exciting combat unit in the U.S. Air Force today, the 366th Wing. Note that I say "Wing." Not "Fighter Wing" or "Bombardment Wing," but just "Wing." The 366th is made up of five flying squadrons, including a mix of fighters, bombers, and tankers, thus, its unofficial title of "Composite Wing." As such, it is controversial, since single-type aircraft wings have been the norm in the United States Air Force since World War II. Mixing up different kinds of aircraft in the same wing makes hardcore traditionalists very nervous. The traditionalists are wrong... in this case. If the Air Force is to meet all of its worldwide commitments, especially with the huge drawdown in Air Force strength since the end of the Cold War, they're going to need an edge. The 366th and the composite wing concept is just such an edge.

The Composite Wing Concept

The 366th is the product of Air Force experience in Operation Desert Storm... as well as what might have happened during Operation Desert Shield in August 1990 if Iraq had continued south into Saudi Arabia after the invasion of Kuwait. In that anxious time, because of its long reach and ability to react quickly, airpower was critical to the defense of the Saudi oil fields. And yet, except for a pair of United States Navy (USN) Carrier Air Wings (CVWs), American airpower was slow to reach the area; and the two CVWs would have had a hard time stopping any Iraqi advance south. It took weeks to deploy enough air units to block an Iraqi strike into Saudi Arabia or the Emirates. Worse yet was the condition of their units when they arrived. Munitions and supporting equipment they would need to sustain an air campaign were scarce.

When the forces were at last deployed, there were doubts about how effective they would be in this "come as you are" war—without time for the kind of detailed planning and meticulous preparation military organizations love. As it happened—fortunately—General Chuck Horner had six months (August '90 to January '91) to get his forces and supplies in place, plan his strikes, and train his forces before he initiated offensive air operations. But the next dictator with expansionist ambitions may not be so foolish as to give us six months to get ready.

Time. Time is the enemy if you are responding to a fast-breaking situation. Time always seems to be on the other guy's side. Given time, that dictator might gain recognition for his actions and (alleged) grievances in the halls of international organizations like the United Nations. He might also have time to dig in his forces and make their position too costly to recapture. Time can kill you. The British effort to retake the Falkland Islands from Argentina in 1982 ultimately hinged on their ability to rapidly move a handful of Harrier and Sea Harrier jump jets into the area to provide air cover for their forces. The planes had to travel eight thousand miles by ship. And the hard-fought air campaign barely resulted in victory.

Time. . . Quick response of integrated, combat ready airpower in a come-as-you-are war. . .

These thoughts buzzed around the collective brains of ACC. In Desert Shield we were lucky, they knew. But they also knew we needed something better than luck. One idea they tried came from the USAF's past—composite wings. These units have gone by many names. In World War II they were Air Commando Wings. During the Cold War they were Tactical Reconnaissance Wings. Whatever the name, they were created and used to solve an immediate problem.

In Saudi Arabia during the Gulf War at Al Kharj Air Base, the 4th Composite Wing (Provisional) was made up of an F-15C squadron from the 36th Tactical Fighter Wing (TFW) at Bitburg Airbase (AB), Germany, two squadrons of F-15Es from the 4th TFW at Seymour Johnson AFB, South Carolina, and a pair of Air National Guard (ANG) F-16 squadrons from New York and South Carolina. Another, even more unusual, composite unit was based at Incirlik AB in Turkey. Dubbed the 7440th Composite Wing, it was made up of no less than a dozen squadrons and detachments flying several different kinds of aircraft, a miniature air force unto itself. The 7440th was charged with running the air effort out of Turkey during Desert Storm (under the operational code name of Proven Force). And it represented the American effort in northern Iraq during and after the war, when it became the covering element for Operation Provide Comfort, the Kurdish relief effort in northern Iraq.

After the war, the lessons from Desert Storm were carefully analyzed to see what might have been done better, faster, and more efficiently. For the

USAF leadership back in the Pentagon, one obvious lesson was the need to rapidly move integrated, combat ready airpower into a crisis area, where it would either help defuse the developing crisis or actually begin combat operations, while follow-on forces arrived to take over the main effort.

As a result of these studies, the concept of special-purpose composite wings for specific missions was resurrected. Many different people within the Air Force had a hand in making this happen. General Mike Dugan, who was USAF Chief of Staff prior to Desert Shield and Desert Storm, proposed the idea to the USAF Air Staff. Following the war, the idea gained support from officers like Chuck Horner and Colonel John Warden who conducted a study of the concept. The final decision came from then-USAF Chief of Staff General Merrill "Tony" McPeak in the fall of 1991. As part of his general reorganization of the Air Force in 1992, McPeak authorized the creation of the 23rd Wing at Pope AFB, North Carolina, and the 366th Wing at Mountain Home AFB, Idaho. The 23rd was charged with supporting the rapid deployment units of the XVIII Airborne Corps (the primary ground component of CENTCOM), particularly the 82nd Airborne Division at nearby Fort Bragg, North Carolina, while the 366th Wing was formed to provide a rapidly deployable air interdiction force to deter or defeat enemy forces, and to provide a nucleus for other arriving air forces in an area. Both units were "stood up" in January 1992, being formed on the shells of two wings that were in the process of being shut down.

Getting the two wings up and running has created great challenges, the largest of which has been the cost of operating a unit with five different kinds of aircraft, ranging from fighters and bombers to tankers. Adverse publicity from a midair collision at Pope AFB didn't help either. In March 1994, a pair of 23rd Wing aircraft, an F-16 and a C-130, crashed into each other. The wreckage of the F-16 then struck a C-141 loaded with paratroopers from the 82nd Airborne, killing twenty-three and injuring dozens more.

After the crash, composite wings took a lot of flak from critics, who charged that the wide variety of aircraft flying in the pattern had something to do with the accident. The charge was absurd, and the critics knew it: Nellis AFB, Nevada is the largest and busiest air force base in the world. During exercises, Nellis often has over a dozen different aircraft types in the pattern at one time, and has not had a midair in *anyone's* memory. The reason the critics were upset had little to do with the tragic accident. They just hated the idea of composite wings.

Despite the difficulties, composite wings appear to be working—working so well that a third such unit, the 347th Wing at Moody AFB, Georgia, has been formed to work with the XVIII Airborne Corps. Meanwhile, the 23rd Wing completed a highly successful deployment to Kuwait during the crisis that erupted in the fall of 1994, when a pair of Iraqi Republican Guards Divisions moved into the Basra area. Two of the 23rd's squadrons, one each of F-16Cs and C-130s, rapidly deployed to the region as part of a much larger airpower deployment, with virtually every kind of USAF aircraft contributing (several hundred aircraft were involved). Though the 23rd did not fly combat sorties, this first real-world use of a composite wing has to be judged a success. The Iraqis backed off. This, in fact, is the ultimate goal of airpower: to be so formidable that a potential foe chooses not to fight.

The Gunfighters: A Unit History

The Air Force has always tended to form new units and disband existing ones with a reckless disregard for the niceties of military tradition. Thus, tracing the lineage of Air Force units can become a frustrating exercise, since the identifying unit numbers jump around so much. But following the story of the 366th is not at all frustrating; it is a unit with a long and proud service history.

As you walk into the wing headquarters building at 366 Gunfighter Boulevard (yes, that's really the address!), you are surrounded by evidence of that history. Photos, plaques, and citations cover the walls. The men who look out from those pictures seem almost to say to the new members of the wing, "This is what you must live up to."

The wing started life as the 366th Fighter Group at Richmond Army Air Base, Virginia. Flying P-47 Thunderbolt fighters, they moved to Thruxton, England, in January 1944, and began to fly missions over the continent in March of that year. During 1944, they flew cover for the Normandy invasion and subsequent breakout, right through the Battle of the Bulge in December. They flew their last mission on May 3rd, 1945, and became part of the postwar occupation force until their inactivation on August 20th, 1946.

The 366th Fighter Group was reactivated on January 1st, 1953, at Alexandria Air Force Base, Louisiana, as part of another unit, the 366th Fighter Bomber Wing, flying the P/F-51 Mustang and F-86 Sabrejet. After a series of European deployments, the Group converted in 1956 to the F-84F Thunderstreak, then in 1957 to the F-100 Super Sabre. At that time, the 366th Fighter Group was inactivated, with its flying squadrons being absorbed by the 366th Fighter Bomber Wing. The wing conducted an overseas deployment to Turkey and Italy during the Lebanon Crisis in 1958. Shortly afterwards, it was redesignated as the 366th Tactical Fighter Wing (TFW), but was inactivated again within a year. Cold War tensions in the early 1960s caused the 366th's reactivation, at Chaumont Airbase in France on April 30th, 1962. Flying F-84Fs again, they stayed at Chaumont for just fifteen months, then moved to Holloman AFB, New Mexico, in July 1963.

In February 1965, the 366th transitioned to the aircraft they are most closely identified with, the F-4C Phantom II. After spending a year getting accustomed to their new aircraft, they moved in March 1966 to Phan Rang Air Base in South Vietnam, and began their first combat operations since 1945. In October 1966, they moved to Danang Air Base and began to fly against targets in North Vietnam. On November 5th, two crews from the wing's 480th Tactical Fighter Squadron (TFS) scored their first kills against North

Vietnamese MiGs. The kills came hard, though, because of reliability problems with U.S. air-to-air missiles. In April 1967, the crews of the 366th began to fly with new 20mm Gatling gun pods slung under their Phantoms' bellies, and began to shoot MiGs out of the sky with regularity. When the slaughter of the MiGs was over in May 1967 (they scored a total of eleven kills during the period), the automatic cannons had earned the 366th the nickname they would carry from then on: "Gunfighters." In December 1967, the 366th converted to the -D model of the Phantom, continuing to fly out of Danang. For their air-to-air successes the previous year, they received a Presidential Unit Citation in December 1968. With the withdrawal of other USAF units in 1969 and 1970, they became the only wing stationed in South Vietnam. The wing was highly active during the 1972 Easter Invasion of the South, which forced a move to the Takhli Royal Thai Air Force Base in June of that year. During the period, they scored five more MiG kills over North Vietnam, earning another Presidential Unit Citation, awarded in 1974.

In October 1972, the wing abandoned its aircraft and equipment to other units at Takhli, and headed back to the United States to what has been their home ever since—Mountain Home AFB, Idaho. There they took over the F-111Fs and equipment of the inactivated 347th TFW, and in 1975, became the first Tactical Air Command (TAC) unit to win a Strategic Air Command (SAC) bombing competition, code-named High Noon. In August 1976, the wing deployed a squadron of F-111Fs to Korea to take part in a "show of force," following a border incident in which several U.S. soldiers were killed. Following the squadron's return in September of that year, the 366th sent its fleet of F-111Fs to the 48th TFW at RAF Lakenheath, England, in February 1977, under Operation Ready Switch. These were replaced by F-111As from the 474th TFW at Nellis AFB. Following the aircraft swap, the wing took over the training and replacement function for the F-111 community. They continued this mission throughout the 1980s, as well as taking on a new mission as the keeper of the Air Force's newest electronic warfare aircraft, the EF-111A Raven. Starting in 1981, the wing took delivery of these aircraft and trained to take them into combat. Eventually, the Ravens of the 366th went into action with the 390th Electronic Combat Squadron (ECS), providing jamming support for Operation Just Cause, the December 1989 invasion of Panama. But about this time, the planned post-Cold War drawdowns began to hit the 366th, with the 391st ECS being inactivated. Then, in August 1990, portions of the remaining Raven squadron, the 390th ECS, deployed to Taif Airbase in Saudi Arabia. There they served throughout Operation Desert Storm and the period just after. By March 1991, the bulk of the Squadron's aircraft and crews had returned to Mountain Home, where they awaited what seemed to be an inevitable inactivation under the planned Bush Administration force drawdown.

Then in April 1991, General McPeak's decision to remake the 366th into a composite wing was announced, and the people at Mountain Home began the process of turning an EW wing into the most powerful combat wing in the Air Force. In July 1991, Brigadier General William S. Hinton, Jr., took over the wing to supervise the transition. By the end of 1991, a small force of F-16s and F-15Es had arrived, and the squadrons began to form up. At the same time, the 366th continued to support the postwar no-fly zone over Iraq with the remaining EF-111As, deployed to Saudi Arabia for Operation Southern Watch.

As 1992 rolled along, the last of the wing's EF-111As were transferred to the 429th ECS of the 27th TFW at Cannon AFB, New Mexico; and in March 1992, the new composite wing squadrons were activated within the shells of the 366th's old squadrons. The 389th became the F-16 squadron, with the 390th and 391st being equipped with F-15Cs and F-15Es respectively. At the same time, new Operations and Logistics Groups were activated, joining the existing supporting units of the wing. In July, the 366th took control of the 34th Bombardment Squadron, equipped with B-52Gs and based at Castle AFB, California. While geographically separated from Mountain Home, the 34th is owned and operated by the 366th. The final squadron of the new organization came into being when the 22nd Air Refueling Squadron (ARS) brought their KC-135R tankers to Mountain Home in October of 1992. Now complete, the 366th began to train as a combined unit and to explore their new capabilities and equipment.

Over the next year, the wing continued to mature, though not without some changes and challenges. In July 1993, Brigadier General David J. McCloud arrived to take over from General Hinton, bringing with him the experience of two previous wing command tours. The highlight of the year was an overseas fall deployment to the Middle East as one of the core units of Operation Bright Star '94. Unfortunately, the 366th lost some ground at the end of 1993, when Secretary of Defense Les Aspin decreed the immediate retirement of the entire B-52G force. This included the 34th BS at Castle AFB, which was the last such unit to stand down (in November 1993). Despite the loss, Air Combat Command was solidly behind the composite wing concept, and provisions were made to replace the B-52s.

Aircraft from the 366th Wing fly over the Pyramids with fighters of the Egyptian Air Force during Operation Bright Star '93. With the wing deployed to Cairo West Airfield, Bright Star allowed it an early opportunity to test deployment plans in a "real world" environment.   OFFICIAL U.S. AIR FORCE PHOTO

As 1994 rolled around, there were big changes ahead for the 366th, starting with the arrival of a brand-new batch of Block 52 F-16Cs (with their powerful F-100-PW-229 engines), fresh off the Fort Worth assembly line. These were equipped with the new Texas Instruments AN/ASQ-213 HARM Targeting System (HTS) pods, as well as HARM missiles to conduct defense suppression missions. And in April, 1994 the 34th BS was reconstituted at Ellsworth AFB, South Dakota, equipped with the B-1B Lancer. Other additions included the Joint Tactical Information Data System (JTIDS) data link systems to the F-15Cs of the 390th FS, and AIM-120 AMRAAM missiles for every aircraft in the wing's three fighter squadrons.

The wing was still assimilating these changes in the winter of 1994 when a training deployment (Operation Northern Edge) took the 366th to Elmendorf AFB, Alaska, for Arctic operations with units from the Pacific Air Forces (PACAF). Then in April, the wing flew to Nellis AFB, Nevada, to become a core unit for the most important training exercise in ACC, Green Flag 94-3. Joined by units from all over ACC, the 366th spent two weeks testing out their planned concept of operations (CONOPS) in a real-world EW environment over the Nevada desert. This would be the last exercise for "Marshal" McCloud as commander; he turned over command of the Wing in August to Brigadier General Lansford "Lanny" Trapp, Jr.

Meanwhile, the 34th BS was standing up at Ellsworth AFB, watching nervously over their shoulders as their host unit, the 28th Bombardment Wing (BW), endured a Congressionally mandated readiness test known as Operation Dakota Challenge, to evaluate the continued viability of the B-1B within ACC. By late in 1994, the new squadron was ready for their own test, and it took part in a Global Power/Global Reach deployment to the Far East. Flying non-stop from Ellsworth, with the aid of midair refueling, two 34th BS Bones took part in the fiftieth anniversary of the retaking of the Philippines, dropping full loads of 500 lb./227.3 kg. bombs on a Leyte bomb range, then returning to Anderson AFB, Guam. After running training and "presence" missions to Korea, they returned to Ellsworth AFB on October 27th, 1994, less than six months after the 34th had stood up.

The 366th Wing is a unit on the move, headed into its sixth decade of service. From the aircrews who fly the missions to the enlisted airmen who turn the wrenches, pound the keyboards, and load the weapons, you can sense a feeling of pride in belonging to an elite team, the Gunfighters.

The 366th Wing Organization

The 366th Wing is a unique organization in the USAF, optimized for rapid deployment and immediate entry into combat. As such, it resembles the alert units of the former Strategic Air Command (SAC) more than the other components of Air Combat Command (ACC). This is not to say that the other combat wings of ACC are incapable of fast reaction. The performance of every

USAF unit rushed to Kuwait in the fall of 1994 is proof of that. But the 366th is designed for, and training for, deployment today. In the time it has taken you to read this book, the 366th could assemble a task force—or "package"—of aircraft that could be wheels up and on their way to a crisis spot almost anywhere in the world. The wing's claim is, "Integrated airpower, ready to go, on Day One!" As such, the 366th resembles a small independent air force, or one of the U.S. Navy Carrier Air Wings. Consider the following table:

366th Wing Squadron/Aircraft Capabilities

Squadron	Aircraft Type	PAA	Personnel	Capability
389th FS	F-16C Block 52	18	243	HTS/HARM
390th FS	F-15C MSIP	18	252	JTIDS
391st FS	F-15E	18	280	LANTIRN/PGM/Maverick
22nd ARS	KC-135R	6	176	C^3I/SATCOM
34th BS	B-1B	6	280	SATCOM/Jamming
Total		**66**	**1,231**	

The 366th has some capabilities that no other wing-sized unit in the Air Force provides. These include:

- It's the only combat wing combining fighters, fighter bombers, bombers, and tanker aircraft into a single integrated combat unit.
- It's the only combat wing with its own integrated command, control, and communications/intelligence (C^3I) element, capable of acting as a mini-JFACC and generating its own Air Tasking Orders (ATOs) for up to five hundred missions per day.
- It's the only combat wing which can plug detachments of other U.S. air units (USAF, USN, USMC, or U.S. Army), or even other countries' air units, into its C^3I capability.

The officer who commands this collection of units is a senior brigadier general with a minimum of one wing command tour before coming to the 366th. The officers and enlisted personnel have been hand-picked—chosen for their previous achievements in the USAF. And the aircrews in the flying squadrons have a high proportion of combat veterans from Desert Storm and Just Cause. Many are graduates from senior military schools like the Weapons School at Nellis AFB, Nevada, and the Air Command and Staff College. Even the young members of the line and maintenance crews are picked for their skill at making more out of less; for that philosophy is at the core of what the 366th is trying to do.

First a quick note about personnel. A normal tour of duty in a USAF unit is anywhere from two to three years. Military units are always in transition, and the 366th is no exception. When I first visited Mountain Home in April 1994, I arrived just as the cycle of rotations and replacements was beginning en masse for the founding members of the new wing structure. What follows is a "snapshot" of the 366th at that time, just as the wing was preparing for its trip to Nellis AFB for Green Flag 94-3. Where possible, I'll try to tell you what happened to people after that, and who might have replaced them. With that in mind, let's take a look at the 366th Wing.

366th Headquarters Squadron

The top of the 366th Wing organization is the Headquarters Squadron at the base/wing headquarters building on Gunfighter Boulevard. On the second floor is the commander's office, and in the top spot is Brigadier General David J. "Marshal" McCloud. The first time you meet him, you know why everyone calls him Marshal. Part of it is his build, well over six feet tall and lean as a rail. The other part is his reputation for leadership and action. Two previous wing command tours, quite unusual in the USAF, have given him ample experience to handle this job. He's flown just about every kind of tactical aircraft in the USAF inventory. He's flown everything from F-117A Night Hawks (from his time with the 37th TFW), to F-15Cs (from his command tour with the 1st TFW at Langley AFB, Virginia); and now he flies a new F-16C Block 52 (with the 389th FS) that bears his personal marking as the 366th's "Wing King." Flying skills are important for an air leader; they confer credibility in the eyes of the flight crews and establish a bond based on shared experience. And familiarity with a wide variety of aircraft is an asset not only because he may have to command the 366th Wing in combat, but also because he may have to act as a totally independent JFACC. In the early stages of a crisis, he could well find himself commanding attached units from the USAF or other U.S. armed services, or even from other coalition or host nations. And Dave McCloud would be flying combat missions, too. A commander, in his words, "should lead from the front."

The commander of the 366th Wing at Mountain Home AFB, Idaho, Brigadier General David "Marshal" McCloud, USAF.
OFFICIAL U.S. AIR FORCE PHOTO

The author with Brigadier General David "Marshal" McCloud, the commander of the 366th wing.

Other functions in the headquarters squadron include the Public Affairs Office (PAO). Usually this is an office that sends press releases about the Airman of the Month to hometown newspapers, and shepherds visiting VIPs on tours of the base. But the 366th PAO is additionally responsible for managing a major new program designed to supplement and replace the existing Mountain Home bombing range at Saylor Creek, near the Snake River Gorge to the east of the base. Saylor Creek is adequate for training in basic weapons delivery, but it lacks the necessary area and target arrays for conducting composite-strike-force training—the 366th's specialty. The new range complex needs to be close enough to Mountain Home AFB to allow strike-force training any time it is needed. So far, the proposal has encountered environmental and culturally oriented opposition from Federal and local bureaucrats. In fact, the proposal by the 366th and other USAF units would involve no dropping of live ordnance, and the land would actually be better protected than it is now, in the hands of the Department of the Interior.

Another major project run out of the headquarters squadron is the consolidation and building program which will bring the 34th BS from its present base at Ellsworth AFB to Mountain Home. This requires building additional ramp space and hangars capable of holding and servicing the big B-1Bs operated by the 34th.

The rest of the wing includes a series of functional groups, with specific roles in keeping the wing operable and combat ready. These include:

- **The 366th Operations Group**—Controls the flying squadrons and the range control squadron for the Wing.
- **366th Logistics Group**—Handles the various logistics, maintenance, supply, and transportation units in the 366th.
- **366th Combat Support Group**—Controls the combat engineering, communications, and services.
- **366th Medical Group**—Provides a range of medical and dental services for the wing and its dependents.

Each group must operate with great autonomy if the wing is to function properly. Let's look at each in detail.

366th Operations Group

The 366th Operations Group runs the flying squadrons of the wing. In April 1994, this unit was led by Colonel Robin E. Scott. A big man with a broad face and a marvelous sense of fun, he had his first job in the wing as commander of the 391st FS, the 366th's F-15E Strike Eagle squadron. Behind Scott's jolly smile is a mind that thinks all the time about getting the wing into combat faster. Every military unit has a mission briefing that is routinely delivered to visiting VIPs. When Scott gives the briefing on the 366th Wing concept of operations, he does it with passion and lots of direct answers to questions. The big question is how the wing would get to where it might have to fight in a crisis. The answer involves a lot of packaging and planning. Another question for the Operations Group is how the wing will fly and fight when it gets to the location of the crisis. The 366th may have to fight for up to a week without reinforcement or outside support. This is a tall order for only a handful of aircraft and aircrews, and it will require the wing leadership to make all the right decisions at the right time, and in the right order.

366th Operations Support Squadron. The 366th Operations Support Squadron (OSS) is the staff organization that runs the five flying squadrons of the Operations Group for Colonel Scott. Commanded by Lieutenant Colonel Gregg "Tank" Miller, it is the key to the whole 366th CONOPS plan. In addition to interfacing with the other groups of the wing, the 366th OSS provides the wing's ability to generate its own daily Air Tasking Orders (ATOs). ATOs furnish the script for everything that happens in the air, from the time and altitude for a tanker to establish a track to refuel other aircraft, down to whether the Army can fire artillery or guided missiles through a particular chunk of airspace at a particular time. One reason for the success of Operation Desert Storm was the quality of the ATOs built by General Horner's CENTAF staff. But the 366th has to do this job with a lot fewer people (forty-two vs. several hundred for the CENTAF staff), and less equipment. On deployment, the 366th OSS forms what is known as the 366th Air Operations Center (AOC), which brings its own tent city to operate from a "bare bones" base. Some good tools help make up for the lack of personnel.

The main tool is the Contingency Tactical Air Control System (TACS) Automated Planning System, or CTAPS. This is a network of computer work-stations that ties together a series of databases on intelligence, terrain, known targets, and aircraft capabilities, enabling the 366th AOC staff to rapidly build and distribute ATO plans to everyone in or attached to the wing. Each day's complete ATO (which can be several hundred pages of text) can be transmit-ted almost instantly via land line, printed hard copy, disk, or even a satellite communications link like the popular suitcase-sized Hammer Rick system. During Desert Storm hard copies had to be hand-carried out to CVWs in the Red Sea and Persian Gulf by airplane each day. Now almost every military air unit in the United States and allied nations has CTAPS-compatible equipment that allows them to receive and use an electronic ATO.

The process of building a day's ATO begins several days before it is exe-cuted. The Air Operations Center team is split into two twelve-hour shifts, with part of each shift working on the ATOs to be executed two and three days later, and the rest working on the ATO to be executed the next day. Once the ATO has been blessed by the AOC chief and the local JFACC (such as General McCloud), it can be distributed to the flying squadrons for execution of the next day's missions.

The 366th's ability to generate ATOs is limited by the number of person-nel that can be dedicated to the task. The estimate is that the 366th AOC staff could churn out ATOs for about five hundred daily sorties—comparable to a major exercise like Red/Green Flag (and about 10% to 20% of what the CENTAF staff generated during the 1991 Gulf War); and they could probably sustain this level of output for a week. After that the forty-two people on the team would doubtless be exhausted and require reinforcement. By that time, hopefully, a big, well-equipped CinC staff, like the 9th Air Force/CENTAF from Shaw AFB, South Carolina, would have arrived to relieve the 366th.

It is important to remember that the 366th Wing is designed as a "fire brigade," to deal with a crisis while more substantial forces are mustered and sent to assist. This tends to draw some grim humor from the members of the wing. They know exactly what the odds might be in a major crisis like Iraq or Iran, and that casualties might be the price of the job.

389th Fighter Squadron

The 389th FS, commanded by Lieutenant Colonel Stephen Wood, is the 366th Wing's F-16 squadron, and they are equipped with brand-new Block 52D F-16C Fighting Falcons. The 389th dates back to May 1943, when it was formed as part of the original 366th Fighter Group. Since that time, a 389th FS has usually been a part of the 366th's complement of units. Aircrews from the 389th were credited with twenty-nine air-to-air kills (twenty-three in World War II, six in Vietnam).

Currently, the 389th is equipped with eighteen Primary Authorized Aircraft (PAA), which refers to the combat strength of the unit. The actual

The official badge of the 389th Fighter Squadron.
U.S. AIR FORCE

total of aircraft controlled by the 389th FS (or any other USAF unit) is usually about one third greater than the PAA, and includes a small number of two-seat trainers (to maintain proficiency and certifications), as well as other F-16Cs that are either in the depot/maintenance pipeline or represent spares. In addition, the 366th is staffed at about 1.25 aircrew per flight position per aircraft, meaning that combat missions may have to be flown by wing support staff, who are rated as aircrews.

The F-16s of the 389th have been greatly "tricked out" with the addition of new systems designed to improve their capabilities over the original F-16s assigned to the 389th when it was formed. These include:

- The latest Block 50/52 software to allow the full use of the APG-68's radar modes.
- The capability to fire both the AIM-120 AMRAAM and AGM-88 HARM missiles.
- The addition of an ASQ-213 HTS pod for every aircraft in the squadron.

If you suspect, from this list of capabilities, that the 389th is working hard to get into the business of suppression of enemy air defenses (SEAD), you would be right on target. With the retirement of the F-4G force, there is no way that ACC can guarantee the commander of the 366th a detachment of Wild Weasels in the event of an emergency deployment. And with the APG-68/AIM-120 combination, the F-16s of the 389th can also take some of the air-to-air load off the F-15s of the 390th, when barrier combat air patrol (BARCAP) and strike escort missions are required. Of course, the 389th can also do traditional air-to-ground deliveries of iron AGM-65 Maverick missiles, as well as cluster bombs, if required. In short, the 389th FS

The official badge of the 390th Fighter
Squadron, the "Wild Boars." *U.S. Air Force*

provides exactly the kind of SEAD, air-to-air, and bombing capabilities
the 366th commander will require to react to a fast-changing crisis. It is the
wing's utility infielder.

390th Fighter Squadron (The Wild Boars)

Formed at the same time (May 1943) as the 389th, the 390th is the
366th's air superiority squadron. Equipped with F-15C Eagles, the 390th,
known as "the Wild Boars" (the 390th squadron ready room/bar has to be seen
to be believed!), has a long and colorful history. This includes 35.5 air-to-air
victories (33.5 in World War II, two in Vietnam) gained by 390th aircrews, as
well as the only service in Operations Desert Shield/Storm by a 366th unit.

The unit was "stood up" as an F-15C squadron in June 1992, commanded by Lieutenant Colonel Larry D. New, with twelve PAA aircraft. He
was succeeded by Lieutenant Colonel Peter J. Bunce, on March 28th, 1994, just
in time to take the squadron for Green Flag 94-3. Along with the new commander came the news that the 390th, together with its 366th sister F-15E Strike
Eagle squadron, the 391st FS, would be enlarged to eighteen PAA aircraft, the
same size as the 389th. This enlargement was a result of several exercises such
as Bright Star and Northern Edge which indicated that the twelve-aircraft
Eagle squadrons just did not have the critical mass to sustain a week of unreinforced operations. By late 1995, the first of the additional aircraft and crews
should arrive to join the Wild Boars.

The Boars are the shield of the 366th Wing. It is a classic air superiority
unit, with the range and firepower to clear the skies for the rest of the wing's aircraft. Their basic F-15Cs have been updated to provide improved capabilities,
including:

- The newest models of the AIM-9 Sidewinder and AIM-120 AMRAAM air-to-air missiles, as well as improved PGU-28 20mm cannon ammunition.
- The full F-15C MSIP improvement package, including the complete APG-70 radar package.
- The Joint Tactical Information Data System (JTIDS) data-link system.

The 390th is the only fighter squadron in the USAF that is fully equipped with the first-generation JTIDS terminals, and thus it can rightly claim to have the best "eyes" of any fighter squadron anywhere in the world. With JTIDS, it can work in tactical formations and situations previously unimaginable to fighter commanders. For example, the JTIDS data links allow each Eagle driver to pass along to any other JTIDS-equipped aircraft (E-3 Sentry, F-14D Tomcat, Tornado F.2, etc.) not only data about the targets detected by the F-15's onboard radar (position, altitude, course, heading, etc.), but also the aircraft's stores information (fuel, missiles, ammunition) and other critical tactical information. This means that a formation as small as two ships can cover a huge volume of airspace. This capability is especially critical for a fire brigade air unit like the 366th Wing, which can ill afford any kind of loss as it hangs on during what may be a week of unreinforced combat operations in a crisis.

391st Fighter Squadron (The Bold Tigers)

The "Bold Tigers" of the 391st FS are the heavy war hammer of the 366th Wing. No other strike aircraft in the world today provides an air commander with the power of the F-15E Strike Eagle, and the 391st gives General McCloud and the 366th Wing a weapon with the killing power of Excalibur.

The official Badge of the 391st Fighter Squadron, the "Bold Tigers." *U.S. Air Force*

Formed by Lieutenant Colonel Robin Scott (now a full colonel and the 366th Operations Group commander) in March 1992, the 391st is now led by Lieutenant Colonel Frank W. "Claw" Clawson, USAF, who took command in June 1993. The 391st is a big squadron from an aircrew standpoint (with two aircrew per aircraft). Like the 389th and 390th FSs, the 391st was formed in mid-1943, and has fought with the 366th through most of its history. Along the way, the aircrews of Bold Tigers have collected some seventeen kills (so far, all in World War II). In the Strike Eagle community, the 391st is the most coveted assignment in the Air Force.

"Claw" has a big job managing the most powerful unit in the 366th Wing. The squadron's capabilities include:

- The AAQ-13/14 LANTIRN FLIR/targeting system.
- Delivery of Paveway LGBs and GBU-15 E/O guided bombs.
- Delivery of the AGM-65 Maverick air-to-ground family of missiles.
- The same AIM-9 Sidewinder, AIM-120 AMRAAM, and M-61 Vulcan gun air-to-air armament as the F-15Cs of the 391st FS.

The Bold Tigers may soon gain additional weapons due to the cancellation of the AGM-137 TSSAM missile. These might include the AGM-130 version of the GBU-15, or the folding fin version of the AGM-142 Have Nap. The Strike Eagles of the 391st are also planned to acquire GPS receivers, JTIDS, and possibly satellite communications terminals, allowing commanders to order quick-reaction strikes on unbriefed targets while the planes are already in the air. When these improvements are completed in a few years, the fangs of the Tigers will be sharper still.

34th Bombardment Squadron (The Thunderbirds)

When the 366th Wing was put together in 1992, one of the more controversial decisions was inclusion of a small, but powerful, bomber squadron of B-52Gs. The big bombers have traditionally belonged to the Strategic Air Command and trained for global thermonuclear war. But as the nuclear deterrent bomber mission has gradually faded away, the B-52s have acquired more conventional capabilities. The "BUFFs" (the traditional nickname for the B-52; it stands, in polite company, for Big Ugly Fat Fella) of the 34th BS were equipped with "big beam" ordnance racks for carrying the AGM-142 Have Nap, and could launch the AGM-84 Harpoon and mines, as well as the AGM-86C cruise missile.

Originally formed as the 34th Aero Squadron in 1917, and later known as the "Thunderbirds," it brought a rich tradition to the 366th. It was one of the squadrons which supplied aircraft (B-25Bs) and crews for the famous Tokyo Raid by Jimmy Doolittle in 1942. Later, it saw service flying B-26s in the Korean War. It took delivery of its first B-52s and was renamed the 34th

The official badge of the 34th Bombardment Squadron, the "Thunderbirds." *U.S. AIR FORCE*

Bombardment Squadron (Heavy) in 1963 at Castle AFB, California, serving there until its inactivation in 1976. The squadron was reformed in July 1992 as the heavy bomber squadron for the 366th. After the retirement of the B-52G force, the squadron was reformed a few months later in April 1994 at Ellsworth AFB, South Dakota, as a B-1B Lancer squadron.

The 34th is commanded by Lieutenant Colonel Timothy Hopper, a highly professional, intense officer in his late thirties. A career bomber pilot, he has taken the challenge of rebuilding the 34th BS as a personal passion, and it shows. The challenges are many (especially in light of the B-1B's well-reported systems problems); and the 34th is fortunate to have the 28th Bombardment Wing (BW) as its host unit at Ellsworth AFB. Thanks to the leadership of Brigadier J.C. Wilson, Jr., the Bones of the 28th BW have exceeded the demanding performance standards mandated by the Congress in the Dakota Challenge Operational Readiness Inspection. As a unit making a transition to the B-1B, the 34th BS has benefited greatly from a close relationship with the highly experienced people of the 28th BW.

When they received their allotment of six PAA aircraft (the squadron carries a total of eleven B-1Bs on its balance sheet), they faced some severe challenges: The loss of the BUFFs in the Fall of 1993 eliminated the wing's long-range standoff weapons capability (the AGM-142 Have Nap, etc.). And the B-1B has always had a reputation as a "hangar queen" (an aircraft that spends most of its time indoors, waiting for repairs, spare parts, technical manual revisions, or software bug fixes). Nevertheless, they saw some opportunities in the Bone that the B-52 could not offer. These included:

- Vastly superior performance, especially in speed, maneuverability, and bomb capacity.
- Superior low-level penetration capability.

The commander of the 366th Wing's 34th Bombardment Squadron, Lieutenant Colonel Tim Hopper (right), on the ramp with one of his line officers. He has been the driving force behind getting the 34th combat ready in just six months from its reformation.

JOHN D. GRESHAM

- Greatly reduced radar and IR signature (about 1/100th as much as the B-52).
- Excellent avionics, including a Synthetic Aperture Radar, sensitive RWR, and a powerful radar jamming system.
- The best communications suite in the 366th Wing, including a UHF satellite communications terminal for in-flight target data reception.
- A precision weapons upgrade plan (CBU-87/89/97 with wind correction kits, GBU-29/30 JDAMS, AGM-145 JSOW, GPS receiver, etc.), which is part of ACC's "Bomber Roadmap."

With these capabilities, it is easy to see why Lieutenant Colonel Hopper and his squadron like to call their B-1Bs "Mo Bones" or "Mean Bones." In the short run, unfortunately, not all these capabilities will be available. In particular, JDAM and JSOW will slip some years in the future, despite the best efforts of the USAF Materiel Command and ACC. Nevertheless, Tim Hopper has his own ideas about how the wing might use the B-1B in combat. Some of them include:

- **Command and Control**—The wing might use the B-1B as a C^3I platform, using the synthetic aperture radar (SAR) capabilities of the Offensive Avionics Suite and the Bone's excellent communications capabilities much like a mini-JSTARS platform.
- **Standoff/Escort Jamming**—With the planned retirement of the EF-111A Raven force scheduled for FY-1997, the B-1B might

function as a jamming platform for the 366th Wing, using the Bone's ALQ-161 defensive countermeasures suite. With electronic warfare birds in short supply, the B-1B's RWR system might be able to supply radar targeting data to HARM-carrying F-16s from the 389th FS, if appropriate data links like JTIDS or an Improved Data Modem can be installed.

- **Composite Wing Strike**—With all the attention precision-guided weapons receive these days, it is sometimes forgotten that many potential targets for a unit like the 366th are of the "area" type, like troop concentrations, rail yards, truck parks, factories, etc. Area targets require large numbers of relatively small weapons to do significant damage, and the Bone is perfect for the job. With the B-1B capable of carrying up to eighty-four Mk 82 500 lb./227.3 kg. bombs or several dozen CBU-87/89/97 cluster bombs, the rest of the wing could use their SEAD and PGM capabilities to neutralize SAMs and AAA, after which the Bones could come in and lay waste to a target area.

Lieutenant Colonel Hopper and the 34th achieved a major step with the Global Power/Global Reach mission mentioned earlier. Now, they are looking forward to the planned system upgrades that will make them even more dangerous. When the massive construction project at Mountain Home AFB is completed in a few years, they can join the rest of the wing in Idaho.

Bridging the gulf between the fighter culture and the bomber culture can be a struggle for both communities. General McCloud told us a story about the first composite strike exercise that the 366th ran with the Bones. Several B-1B crews briefed with a strike force from the four other squadrons and headed down to the Nellis AFB ranges to run the mission. Afterwards, when the mission was debriefed, the pilot from one of the bomber crews confessed, "We did not understand a word you guys said on the radio." They have come a long way from that inauspicious beginning. When you consider what was achieved after just six months of operations, you can understand what Tim Hopper has accomplished.

22nd Air Refueling Squadron

The 22nd Air Refueling Squadron (ARS) is the only flying unit in the 366th Wing that does not shoot or drop things that explode. Yet, it is the key to the 366th's ability to instantly deploy and generate combat missions. Dave McCloud and the rest of the wing treasure the 22nd ARS more than diamonds . . . or even new -229 engines for all the fighters. Only two combat wings within ACC have their own tanker assets, and there is *nothing* more precious in air warfare than airborne fuel!

The 22nd ARS was one of the four original flying squadrons at Mountain Home AFB when the wing was reorganized back in 1992. Its first commander is Lieutenant Colonel John F. Gaughan II, whose boyish good looks conceal a

The official badge of the 22nd Aerial Refueling Squadron. *U.S. Air Force*

razor sharp mind. Originally formed in 1939 as a heavy bomber unit, the 22nd flew the B-17, B-25, and A-26 during World War II in the Pacific and China before being disestablished in 1945. Reborn in 1952 as an airborne tanker squadron flying KC-97s, it has served with SAC and ACC ever since. Along the way, the 22nd also flew the EC-135 before it was disestablished at the end of the Cold War in 1989. Like the rest of the 366th squadrons, it was reformed in 1992.

It was originally equipped with noisy, smoky, fuel-guzzling 1950s-era turbojets, but the 22nd's aircraft have now been refitted with modern CFM-56 turbofans to improve fuel economy and offload capacity. They are surprisingly young, at only about thirteen thousand hours of flight time average per airframe. Since the tankers have so little flight time, they avoided many of the stresses of repeated takeoff, pressurization and landing cycles that eventually wear out an airframe. The USAF is currently planning to fly the KC-135s until roughly the year 2020, a career of almost sixty years!

As for the 22nd ARS itself, because there is a lot of room in the KC-135, even when it is full of fuel, there is a lot more to their mission than just the complex aerial dance that allows fuel to pass to other aircraft. Still, the 22nd ARS is quite skilled at its primary job. For example, in fourteen days of operations at Green Flag 94-3 with just four aircraft, the 22nd flew ninety-seven sorties, refueling several hundred tactical sorties. Meanwhile, the big, open main compartment in the fuselage of the tanker can hold a lot of stuff. This includes:

- **Personnel Transport**—Each KC-135 can transport up to eighty passengers with their personal gear. This is enough to establish a small air-base cadre at their destination, as well as helping to relieve the burden on the limited resources of the Air Mobility Command (AMC).
- **Cargo Transport**—While they are currently limited to cargo which can be carried onboard by human muscle power, the

aircraft of the 22nd ARS can help out in the transport mission by taking on bulk cargo and lashing it carefully to the existing plywood floors.

- **Mission Planning/C³I**—During the hours the wing staff is in the air deploying to a crisis, these very people need to be getting ready to launch the first air strikes. In particular, the strike-planning staff needs to be close to its CTAPS terminals, taking in the latest intelligence and targeting data and generating the Air Tasking and Fragmentary Orders that must be finished before the first airplane can be loaded and fueled. Thus, Colonel Scott and the Operations Group staff came up with the "FAST CONOPS" plan. Four of the 22nd's tankers, loaded with personnel and equipment, fly ahead to make the host site ready to start operations as soon as the combat aircraft arrive. As quickly as possibly after an alert order, the first KC-135, known as FAST-1, would fly to the crisis area with a site survey team to evaluate exactly what the wing will need to deploy. Shortly after this, FAST-2 arrives with an Air Operations Center (AOC) team and the WICP (Wing Initial Communications Package) satellite communications equipment aboard. FAST-3 would carry the C³I element, with their CTAPS gear set up to work while in flight. Finally, FAST-4 would carry a staff of maintenance personnel and aircrews (in crew rest) to ready the aircraft and fly the first mission when they arrive in the crisis zone. In this way, the wing could fly its first mission within a few hours of arriving at the host airfield.

This capability is vitally important to the wing's planned CONOPS scheme, and could make all the difference in a crisis.

The 22nd ARS is working hard to improve its capabilities to support the wing. Although times are tough, and money for upgrades of support aircraft are short, there are continuing efforts to make the 22nd's aircraft more capable, which include:

- **Communications**—Provisions are being made to install a UHF satellite communications terminal aboard each of the tankers. This will allow transmission of high quality intelligence data, images, and teleconferencing to and from the FAST aircraft while in flight.

- **Cargo Handling**—One of the really *big* improvements is replacement of the KC-135s' original plywood floors with special fixtures, called Roll On/Roll Off (Ro/Ro) aluminum alloy floors, which will allow them to carry palletized cargo. This will greatly expand the variety of cargo the 22nd's tankers can carry, and help out a bit with the transportation crunch of getting the wing and all its stuff to the operating theater.

- **Navigational Systems**—A NAVSTAR GPS receiver is being installed to help with navigation and planning, as well as improving the accuracy of the autopilot. This should help in easing the aircrew workload, reducing fatigue on trans-oceanic flights when the 366th deploys.

These improvements will enhance the capabilities of the 22nd, though Lieutenant Colonel Gaughan and the rest of the wing's leadership still have a long wish list. At the top of the list is trading in the KC-135s for bigger, more modern KC-10 tankers, which can both pass and receive fuel in-flight and carry a large load of palletized cargo and personnel. This would allow the 22nd to both deploy *and* refuel while traveling overseas. Right now, it can only do one at a time. Unfortunately, these aircraft are closely held by the Air Mobility Command at Scott AFB, Illinois. Another item on the wish list is the installation of a refueling receptacle on the squadron's aircraft, a modification known as the "T-mod," which would make them into KC-135RTs. Again, though, money is the limiting factor in all of this, and the wing will probably have to make do with what it already has for the next few years, at least.

392nd Electronic Combat Range Squadron

The 392nd Electronic Combat Range Squadron was formed in 1985 to provide realistic electronic range training to the EF-111s of the 366th Wing when it had the standoff jamming mission within the USAF. Today, under its commander, Lieutenant Colonel Lynn B. Wheeless, USAF, it runs the facilities at Saylor Creek weapons training range.

366th Logistics Group

Combat units eat up a *lot* of supplies. Just one mission by the six B-1Bs of the 34th BS would use up 117 tons of bombs and over 148,250 gallons/551,886 liters of jet fuel. That is *one* mission by just *one* of the squadrons that might be controlled by the 366th Wing, and it in no way includes food, water, spare parts, black boxes, and all the other supplies that make a modern combat unit work. In high-intensity combat operations, the full 366th would consume several thousand tons of supplies a day, every day. Without a proper flow of supplies, the Gunfighters are just ground targets for some other air force to kill.

Commanded by Colonel Lee Hart, the 366th Logistics Support Group is composed of four squadrons responsible for supply, maintenance, and transportation. Without ground support personnel, there would not be anyone to load the bombs, fuel the planes, turn the wrenches, and move the cargo.

366th Logistics Support Squadron. Originally known as the 366th Sub Depot when it was formed in November 1942, the 366th Logistics Support Squadron is commanded by Major Louis M. Johnson, Jr. Redesignated in 1992, it has a mission to provide the wing with a steady supply of spare parts, tools, and equipment to help keep the 366th's aircraft in the air. As such, it handles ordering, storing, and distribution of thousands of items that go on or into the wing's airplanes.

366th Maintenance and Support Squadron. First activated in 1953, the 366th Maintenance and Supply Squadron is commanded by Lieutenant Colonel Ward E. Tyler III. Its mission, as you might guess, is to repair, test, and maintain all of the aircraft and other equipment that the wing carries on its books. This is a huge task, partly because the 366th has five different aircraft types, not to mention the variety of computers, generators, ramp service carts, test equipment, etc.

366th Supply Squadron. First stood up in 1953 with the other units of the Logistics Group, the 366th Supply Squadron is currently commanded by Major Jerry W. Pagett. Major Pagett and his team are tasked with maintaining the thousands of inventory items a combat unit like the 366th requires to keep moving. Like any other unit, this covers everything that would be needed by a small town, from food and fuel to soap and toilet paper. One of the big efforts of the folks in this unit is to combine, wherever possible, supply line items, so that the wing has fewer *different* things to take with it when it deploys.

366th Transportation Squadron. Commanded by Major William K. Bass, the 366th Transportation Squadron is a combination of a truck dispatch office, a passenger and cargo airline, and a warehousing and trucking company. Centered in a small cluster of offices and spaces in a hangar next to the flight line at Mountain Home, the Transportation Squadron is in charge of getting the wing and all its "stuff" from one place to another in a minimum of time, and with the least demand on AMC's limited airlift capacity. Heavy airlifters are scarce national assets, and they are spread very thin by the need to respond to multiple crises around the world.

Major Bass and his staff are constantly developing and refining contingency plans in their small hangar offices. Around the walls of their conference room are thirty small "white" boards, each representing a numbered load of equipment, cargo, and personnel to be loaded aboard a C-141B Starlifter, to support an "A" Package (the smallest force deployed by the Wing) of aircraft, equipment, and personnel. Now, this represents an ideal situation, with the wing deploying to an excellent host facility (like the Saudi bases used during Desert Shield and Desert Storm), with AMC standing by to send three dozen C-141s and some KC-10s to deploy the unit to the crisis area ASAP. In actuality, what will probably arrive, with only an hour or two of notice from AMC at Scott AFB, is a varied mix of heavy airlift aircraft. These may range from C-17s and C-5s, which carry a lot *more* than a C-141, to chartered civilian 747s and MD-11 freighters, which carry less and are limited to palletized cargo and perhaps small carts and vehicles. Since it is vital that certain loads and personnel arrive in a particular order, the unpredictability of airlift in a crisis sends the normally calm personnel under Major Bass into a frenzy, as they fire up laptop computers and check specifications to recalculate what and who will go onto a particular aircraft. Then they have to call homes and squadrons to order 366th wing personnel on standby to get themselves and their personal gear to the mobility office *now*! Although their job is to move the wing in a crisis, most of Major Bass's personnel will never leave Mountain Home AFB. Their lot in life is to push people, planes, and equipment forward to wherever the 366th is sent, but to stay home in the anxiety and emptiness that is a home base during a crisis.

366th Medical Group

The morale and quality of life on an Air Force base depend greatly on a well-managed, well-staffed medical group. This is not only to provide flight surgeons for the aircrews and combat medics for the ground personnel, but also general medical care for the families and dependents of the wing and base personnel. The geographic isolation of Mountain Home AFB makes this particularly important—the nearest major metropolitan hospital is more than fifty miles away.

Commanded by Colonel C. Bruce Green, MD, the 366th Medical Group provides medical services across the full range of missions. In addition, they are capable of deploying a field hospital with the wing, to provide medical services for the 366th and its attached units in the field.

366th Combat Support Group

The 366th Combat Support Group covers many specialized tasks and services such as engineering, communications, base security, and law enforcement, as well as food and sales services. Commanded by Colonel Robert G. Priest, the 366th Combat Support Group is the final slice in the 366th pie, and while its functions may seem secondary to the combat functions of the wing, rest assured that the quality-of-life issues faced by Colonel Priest's personnel are just as important to the success of the 366th's mission as the skills of the combat aviators in the flying squadrons.

366th Civil Engineering Squadron. Commanded by Lieutenant Colonel Cornelius Carmody, this unit allows the 366th to move into an unknown host airfield and make it fully operable. Doing this ranges from supplying and guaranteeing potable water and pure jet fuel to assuring the quality of the electrical power. On some deployments (such as to Saudi Arabia), this may be easy. But in other places, all the engineers can do is survey a bare bones base and transmit their construction requirements to an Air Force "Red Horse" airbase construction battalion. In a time that would amaze you, these units can take a patch of desert or jungle, add concrete and water, and build one of the world's busiest airports. The 366th engineers also oversee quality assurance on construction projects back at Mountain Home AFB.

366th Communications Squadron. Headed by Lieutenant Colonel Dennis J. Damiens, the 366th Communications Squadron is more than just a miniature phone company. It is a state-of-the-art organization that is absolutely vital if the Operations Squadron is to have anything to plug their CTAPS system terminals into. Colonel Damiens's crew can plug into virtually any kind of voice, data, or satellite system, ranging from commercial phone companies to the new MILSTAR system that is just coming on-line. In addition, they provide local communications support around Mountain Home AFB, and maintain all of the secure communications systems of the wing.

366th Security Police Squadron. Even the most law-abiding small town needs a police force. Mountain Home AFB is a small town with zero tolerance for drug and alcohol abuse, along with several billion dollars of irreplaceable assets that require extremely dependable protection. The Security Police Squadron, commanded by Lieutenant Colonel James E. Leist, serves the functions of that local police force. Additional duties include anti-terrorist intelligence while at home, and airbase defense when the wing is deployed overseas. If the wing were to deploy to an area with a serious local security threat, the Security Police Squadron would coordinate overall airbase defense, and any reinforcing units would plug in to them. This might include anything from an allied/host nation military police unit to Special Forces units specializing in anti-terrorist activities.

366th Services Squadron. The 366th Services Squadron, commanded by Major Timothy P. Fletcher, runs the mess halls, the officers's/enlisted clubs, the base commissary, and a host of other activities that make life bearable for military personnel. A good Services Squadron can make even the most desolate base into a duty station to remember. In the words of one young pilot, "They make Mountain Home a great place to come home to."

Outside Help: Other Attached Units

Despite the variety and capability of the units in the 366th Wing, there is no way they could go off to war all by themselves. While the Gunfighters can deal out death in several dozen interesting and creative ways, they are a bit short-handed when it comes to finding and identifying the targets to be terminated. This is not a flaw or weakness in the structure of the wing, because the Air Force generally guards reconnaisance and target intelligence assets quite closely, and parcels them out carefully. Since the 366th is solidly backed by the senior leadership at ACC, the wing is near the top of the priority list for reconnaisance and intelligence support of all kinds.

552nd Air Control Wing, Tinker AFB, Oklahoma

When ACC decided to set up the 366th as a composite wing, one idea they seriously considered was to give the wing its own small (three aircraft) squadron of E-3 Sentry Airborne Warning and Control Systems (AWACS) aircraft. Unfortunately, these aircraft are extremely scarce; only thirty-four were built for USAF service. Nevertheless, no significant force would normally deploy without AWACS support, and the 366th is high on the list of favored users. Thus, a standing arrangement has been made between the 366th Wing and ACC headquarters that in the event of a deployment, the parent unit for all USAF AWACS aircraft, the 552nd Air Control Wing (ACW), will supply a few of the precious eyes in the skies.

Based at Tinker AFB just east of Oklahoma City, Oklahoma, the 552nd is the sole operator of the big radar planes in U.S. service (in four Airborne Air Control Squadrons: the 463rd, 464th, 465th, and 466th). The 552nd maintains detachments all over the world, from Alaska to Turkey, and has become an important airborne tool of American diplomacy. But this has come at a high price for the overworked crews, who are routinely away from their homes and families for months at a time. The operational tempo has always been high for the crews of the 552nd Wing, probably too high. By the beginning of 1994, an average AWACS crew was spending over 180 days a year on temporary duty (TDY) assignments overseas. In mid-1994, Brigadier General Silas R. "Si" Johnson arrived at Tinker AFB to take over command of the wing. Si Johnson is a career multi-engine combat pilot, with thousands of hours in KC-135s and B-52s. Right now, the officers and enlisted personnel of the 552nd already feel the confidence of a strong hand on the reins of their wing and their community. They will need it too, because the demand for their unique capabilities continues unabated.

In order to keep a single AWACS aircraft airborne twenty-four hours a day, the 366th plans to deploy with a three aircraft AWACS detachment in the event of a crisis. The trick is to integrate the Sentry aircraft of the 552nd wing into the operations of the 366th wing, a task the two units have practiced extensively. This practice has included exercises to develop tactical procedures for the use of the 390th FS's F-15Cs with their new JTIDS data links, which makes them even more deadly, thanks to the "God's-eye view" of the E-3 radar and other sensors.

27th Fighter Wing, Cannon AFB, New Mexico

Another planned reinforcement for the 366th in a crisis deployment would be a detachment of four EF-111A Raven standoff jamming aircraft, currently based with the 27th Fighter Wing at Cannon AFB, Oklahoma. These powerful EW aircraft (using versions of the Hughes ALQ-99 jamming system) are the most capable tactical jamming aircraft in the USAF inventory. The USAF has used standoff jamming aircraft in raid packages since World War II, and no sane American strike force would care to enter hostile airspace without them. Unfortunately, the current Administration is planning to retire the Spark 'Varks (as they are called), along with the remaining force of F-111F fighter bombers, in FY-1997 and -98, with no planned replacement. This leaves ACC and the 366th in a world of hurt, and still requiring a standoff jammer of some kind. As an interim and very imperfect solution to this problem, Colonel Hopper and his creative folks at the 34th BS are working out tactics and techniques for using the B1-B as a standoff jammer. Meanwhile, the Ravens of the 27th FW are still available for deployments, and continue to support operations overseas in Iraq, Bosnia, and Haiti.

355th Electronic Combat Wing, Davis-Monthan AFB, Arizona

Buried in the depths of Colonel Scott's briefing charts on the 366th CONOPS plan is a note about a pair of aircraft known as EC-130H Compass Calls that will deploy with the Gunfighters. Festooned with an array of antennas, these odd-looking variants of the Lockheed Hercules are Signals Intelligence (SIGINT) and Electronic Intelligence (ELINT) platforms, with powerful jamming packages aboard. They act as virtual electronic vacuum cleaners, sucking up almost everything in the electromagnetic spectrum. After analyzing it to provide real-time targeting data on enemy command posts, SAM and AAA radar sites, and other electronic emitters, they pass them along via a JTIDS data link to other aircraft. They can also conduct standoff jamming of SAM and AAA radars, as well as communications jamming. Though there are only a handful of these valuable birds (residing in two squadrons, the 41st ECS and 43rd ECS of the 355th Wing at Davis-Monthan AFB near Tucson, Arizona) and their availability will always be limited, several of them with their highly skilled technicians would be assigned to the 366th in the event of an overseas deployment. Should the entire fleet be unavailable, ACC can also turn to a clip-on system known as Senior Scout, which can be installed as a package in any C-130 transport.

Joint Surveillance and Targeting System (Joint STARS)

While there is no active unit currently flying the E-8C Joint Surveillance and Targeting System (Joint STARS) radar aircraft, such a wing of these aircraft *will* be formed in the next few years with about two dozen planes assigned. It is likely that the new unit will be based at Tinker AFB, since so much work is done there on the old reliable 707-series airframes. Based around an SAR radar system with the ability to detect and identify moving and stationary ground targets, Joint STARS is probably the most important new aircraft being acquired by the USAF today. Given the fantastic performance of the two E-8A Joint STARS prototypes in locating and tracking Iraqi ground forces during Desert Storm, it is unlikely that the 366th would ever be sent into a crisis without this far-seeing eye in the sky. As soon as enough E-8Cs become operational in the late 1990s, ACC will probably provide a three aircraft detachment so that the 366th Wing will be able to monitor ground space as well as airspace.

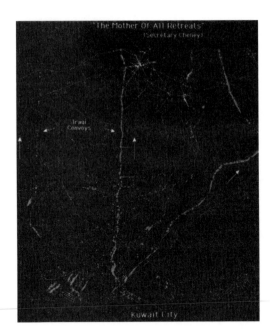

The famous "Mother of All Retreats" radar picture obtained by one of the prototype E-8A Joint -STARS aircraft during Operation Desert Storm.
NORTHROP GRUMMAN

Defense Airborne Reconnaissance Office (DARO)

When armies finally began to operate aircraft in the early 1900s, the first mission important to ground commanders was taking photos of enemy positions. Reconnaissance imagery is vital to a JFACC staff, because you have to be able to see a target before you can hit it. Then you need more pictures of the targets you have hit so that you can evaluate the damage. Unless a JFACC has photo-reconnaissance assets under his direct control, the whole process of planning, striking, and bomb damage assessment (BDA) starts breaking down. The bad news is that the USAF has just a few dozen aging RF-4C Phantom II tactical photo-reconnaissance aircraft in two Air National Guard squadrons. During Desert Storm, the lack of U.S. military tactical photo-reconnaissance forced the CENTAF staff to improvise, with a combination of aircraft and satellite systems controlled by different agencies, making effective BDA almost impossible. Following the war, Secretary of Defense William Perry, took the lesson to heart, and created the Defense Airborne Reconnaissance Office (DARO) to coordinate all reconnaissance within the earth's atmosphere. DARO shares space in the Pentagon with the National Reconnaissance Office (NRO—the agency that controls the earth orbiting reconnaissance satellites), and is run by Major General Kenneth Israel. DARO's charter is to take over all U.S. aerial recon programs and bring some order out of the chaos.

While many programs run by DARO remain highly classified, we do know that the staff in the Pentagon has initiated a series of UAV (Unmanned Aerial Vehicle, or pilotless drone) programs designed to replace or augment existing manned tactical systems. Since they are unencumbered by the weight

A General Atomics Predator Unmanned Aerial Vehicle (UAV) on a test flight. UAVs like the Predator will help form the backbone of the USAF's aerial reconnaissance capabilities in the 21st century.

GENERAL ATOMICS

and life-support requirements of a crew, or the need to return them safely in the event of a hostile response, UAVs will be more effective than manned aircraft in acquiring photo-reconnaissance data. UAVs can also loiter over an area of interest and study it, instead of just flying by at "the speed of heat" and snapping a single picture. At the same time, users of imagery products will need to develop some new attitudes and techniques. For example, rather than taking pictures of a particular target or Direct Mean Point of Impact (DMPI or "dimpy," as it is called), UAVs will monitor large areas, such as all of Kuwait or Bosnia, updating the situation map several times a day (and night). This means that while a JFACC staff may not see specific targets right before or right after a strike, they will be obtaining more and better information over time. In the long run, this big picture will provide better data for operational-level planning, especially when combined with high quality post-strike videotape from FLIR systems. During Desert Storm, these short video clips, when properly cross-referenced with other data, proved to be invaluable for BDA.

So far, none of the new UAV systems are operational, and only a few flying prototypes have seen any action. One of these, the Predator-series UAV manufactured by General Atomics Corporation of San Diego, California, is reported to have flown CIA-sponsored surveillance missions over Bosnia from a base in Albania and the Predators appear to have done well. These new systems, as well as the remnants of our older capabilities, should provide strike planners with adequate targeting data, as long as the satellite systems hold up. Nevertheless, airborne reconnaissance assets are going to be thin for at least a decade.

National Reconnaissance Office (NRO)

Though there are a number of intelligence gathering shortcomings at the tactical and theater levels of the American military, the United States has fortunately built an extremely robust capability for intelligence gathering from space.

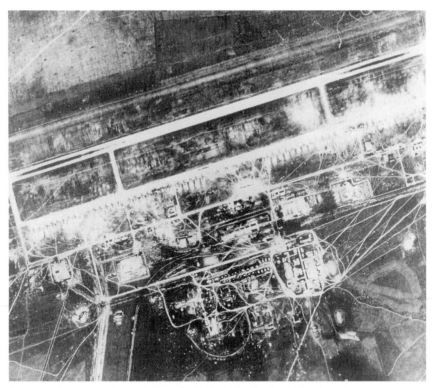

An early wide-area surveillance photograph of a Soviet bomber base, taken by a Corona photo, reconnaissance satellite in 1966. Much of the 366th's targeting information in a combat situation would come from such spaceraft in low Earth orbit.   *Official DOD Photo*

While it is no secret that America uses satellites for strategic-level intelligence gathering, the details of specific programs have until recently been closely held secrets. The first orbital photo reconnaissance satellites began operations in the 1960s under a covert CIA program called Corona, which had a NASA cover story as part of an orbital research program called Discoverer.

Luckily, the end of the Cold War has made available for wider use some space-based assets previously dedicated to watching the former Soviet Union. NRO has made an exceptional effort in the last few years to provide their "product" to a wider base of users within the U.S. military services. Today, the folks at the Central Imagery Office (CIO), the agency which handles and interprets imagery from both DARO and the NRO, are busy developing tactical systems to obtain and distribute satellite reconnaissance "products."

50th Space Wing/U.S. Space Command (USSPACECOM)

Coordinating America's military space activities is a major unified command, the U.S. Space Command based at Peterson AFB in Colorado Springs, Colorado, and commanded by General Joe Ashey. He also commands the

A Defense Support Program (DSP) -1 spacecraft is launched from the cargo bay of a space shuttle. DSP spacecraft like this would provide the 366th Wing with early warning of ballistic missile launches, as well as rough targeting of the launch sits.
OFFICIAL U.S. AIR FORCE PHOTO

USAF Space Command, and the North American Defense Command (NORAD), also based in the Colorado Springs, Colorado, area. Currently, those activities and their products include:

- **Ballistic Missile Warning**—Under a program known as the Project 647/Defense Support Program (DSP), several geosynchronous Earth-orbiting satellites with IR telescopes have the job of providing the National Command Authorities with warning of ballistic missile launches and prediction of their probable targets. Originally designed to provide warning against attacks by Soviet ICBM and SLBMs, the latest models of the DSP birds provided warning during Desert Storm of SCUD launches out of Iraq. Since then, they have been modified under a program called Talon Shield to provide warning and targeting for theater-level commanders to alert air defense warning and engagement systems (like the Patriot PAC-3/ERINT missile system).

- **Weather Data**—Pilots are very concerned with the weather they must fly through to reach their targets. For over three decades, the key element in military weather prediction has been a program called the Defense Meteorological Satellite Program (DMSP), which is designed to provide weather data of interest to military planners.
- **Communications**—Without question, the modern communications relay satellite, along with microelectronics and computers, is one of the wonders of the modern world. Currently, the military operates at least four types of communications satellites, with a fifth coming on-line. The first four are the Defense Satellite Communications System (DSCS) -II and -III-series relay vehicles, as well as the NATO-III and Fleet Satellite (FLTSAT) communication birds which have been in use for some time.

In 1995, the first of DoD's new secure communications relay systems named MILSTAR is coming on-line. One low data-rate satellite is currently being checked out in orbit and five more are on order, the last four greatly enhanced with medium-data-rate payloads. Hardened against anything an enemy might throw at it except a direct hit, it was designed for great resistance to enemy interception and jamming at the cost of limited (low) data rates and a limited number of channels. The program is therefore being restructured to provide much greater tactical utility to a wider community of users than just the National Command Authorities and strategic deterrent forces. One of the more interesting ideas being kicked around these days is that tactical aircraft like the F-15E Strike Eagle or F-16C Fighting Falcon might be fitted with MILSTAR-compatible communications terminals to receive targeting coordinates while in flight.

- **Navigational Support**—I have often sung the praises of the NAVISTAR GPS program every chance I can, for good reason. More than any other space-based system, this one that will soon touch the life of almost every person on Earth. The system is based around twenty-four satellites in six circular orbits. Aboard each bird is a series of highly accurate atomic clocks, which are calibrated daily from the control center on the ground. Each satellite transmits synchronized timing pulses from the clocks, and a highly accurate receiver measures the differences between the arrival times of signals from different satellites. The receiver does some fancy trigonometry and develops a highly accurate positional fix, as well as other data. The real beauty of the system is that it places the burden of "smarts" on the receiver system, which can be engineered into packages of amazing compactness and utility.

  GPS is set up to provide two different levels of precision: super-precise for military users with the appropriate code key, and less precise for everyone else, including the enemy. This means that civilian receivers are accurate to within about 100 meters/330 feet, and military receivers can generate 3-D positions to within 16 meters/52.8 feet, while also providing an anti-spoofing/ anti-jamming capability. In addition, the receivers can generate time readings accurate to within 100 Ns, and velocity readings accurate to within .1 meter per second/4 inches per second, which translates to errors of less than .2 knots/.37 kph! GPS receiver designers have found many uses for the system, from basic flight navigation to guiding weapons like cruise missiles and bombs. All this is possible in virtually any weather conditions, anywhere on Earth, or even in orbit around the Earth. Current DoD plans envision acquiring over eighty thousand GPS receivers, with over two thousand aircraft being built or modified to use the system.

While the systems mentioned above are owned by a variety of federal and military agencies, the operations of the birds are mostly controlled by a single organization, the 50th Space Wing (SW), based at Falcon AFB, Colorado, just down the street from NORAD and USSPACECOM headquarters. Currently commanded by Colonel Gregory L. Gilles, the 50th SW is something new in the space community, an operationally oriented unit designed to get the products of space into the hands of "real" users in the field. Broken into squadrons, it controls the operations and uses of literally tens of billions of dollars of orbital hardware. Yet when you look at the young men and women of the 50th SW, you see a lot of thick glasses and laptop computers, along with more than few science fiction novels. Don't be fooled, though, because these young space warriors are every bit as professional and dedicated to their tasks as are the aircrews in the ejection seats. In fact, their prideful motto, "In your face from outer space," says volumes about how they feel.

Each of the 50th SW's Space Operations Squadrons (SOSs) controls the satellites of a particular program or function. Some of the units of the 50th SW include:

- **1st SOS**—Provides support during launch and checkout of a variety of different satellite programs. For example, they are currently heavily tasked with checkout of the first MILSTAR orbital vehicles.
- **2nd SOS**—Is responsible for day-to-day operations, calibration, and maintenance of the GPS satellite constellation. Every day, they check and adjust, if required, the accuracy and timing of the onboard systems for every one of the GPS satellites.
- **3rd SOS**—Responsible for the operations and maintenance of the twenty-two operational DSCS-II and -III, NATO-III, and FLT-SAT communications satellites.

- **4th SOS**—Will, when it comes on-line, conduct the operations and maintenance of the constellation of MILSTAR communications satellites.
- **6th SOS**—Located at Offut AFB, Nebraska (adjacent to STRATCOM headquarters), this squadron controls the DMSP-series of meteorological satellites for USSPACECOM.

There are undoubtedly other SOS-type units assigned to control of "black" programs like the imaging and ELINT/SIGINT programs, but their story will have to wait for a future telling, after it has been declassified.

Space-based systems can be extremely valuable to a force going into combat. While many of these systems were directly tied to strategic missions during the Cold War, and thus closely held by the National Command Authorities, the end of that conflict has allowed almost every military commander to have some use for space. For many it will be the beautiful simplicity of things like the hand-held GPS receivers used during Desert Storm. For the 366th Wing, it will be the vital data flow delivered by the satellite dishes of the 366th Communications Squadron, which will distribute the products of the space infrastructure to the wing's users.

Cats and Dogs—Other Attached Units

In this chapter, you have seen how virtually anything can be plugged into the 366th Wing structure. Some of the specialized units that might be added to the wing on an "as required" basis by the National Command Authorities (NCAs) include:

- **Stealth Bombers/Fighters**—The B-2As and F-117As of the 509th BW and 49th FW respectively are irreplaceable national assets, closely controlled by the NCAs. Nevertheless, given the importance of the missions that the 366th would undertake, a detachment of F-117s might be assigned to the wing, or a strike by B-2s might be authorized, once they acquire a Precision Guided Munitions capability in the late 1990s.
- **Cruise Missiles**—The 366th does not currently have a capability to employ the AGM-86C aboard their B-1Bs, so any air-launched cruise missiles would have to come from one of the B-52 units equipped to do the job, such as the 2nd BW at Barksdale AFB in Louisiana. The B-52Hs of the 2nd BW can carry several types of standoff weapons, including the AGM-86C ALCM, and the AGM-142 Have Nap standoff missile. With their precision guidance systems, these formidable weapons could be launched from outside the range of enemy defenses. As an added bonus, the B-52s could be launched on their missions directly from the continental United States,

much as they were on the first night of Operation Desert Storm. In addition to the B-52s, the wing might also be able to task U.S. Navy ships and submarines to fire U/BGM-109 Tomahawk Land Attack Missiles (TLAMs). This would be possible now that the new GPS-equipped Block-III guidance systems have made it to the fleet. The use of GPS guidance systems greatly simplifies the process of mission planning for both the TLAMs and ALCM-Cs, requiring a minimum of support from the Defense Mapping Agency and other organizations.

- **Tankers**—One resource that Dave McCloud would tell you he *never* has enough of is airborne gas. It is almost certain that additional tankers would be assigned to the 366th Wing in the event of an emergency deployment. Most desired, of course, are the big KC-10A Extenders, because of their ability to take gas from other tankers, their truly huge giveaway capacity, and their ability to fuel either USAF aircraft with their boom receptacles, or USN/USMC/NATO aircraft with their drogue-and-probe units at the same time. Most likely, though, the reinforcing tankers would probably come from AMC's large pool of KC-135Rs, which have several decades of service ahead of them.

- **Inter-Theater Transport**—In any kind of deployment several squadrons of C-130 Hercules medium transports would be needed to move personnel and cargo from rear areas to the forward airfields. During Desert Shield and Desert Storm the press never noticed the vital job done by C-130 units (many were Air National Guard and Reserve squadrons) hauling bombs and missiles, spare parts, black boxes, food, and almost everything but fuel to the various wing airfields around the Persian Gulf. (The Saudis took care of the fuel.) Today, the logistical rules have not changed one bit, and this job would have to be done, or the wing's efforts would come to an immediate and grinding halt.

Of course, virtually any other kind of USAF flying unit could be plugged into the 366th Wing structure. This could range from the LANTIRN-equipped F-16Cs of the 388th FW at Hill AFB to beef up the wing's PGM delivery capability, to U-2s or RC-135 Rivet Joint reconnaissance aircraft from the 9th Reconnaissance Wing (RW) and 55th RW respectively. In fact, what goes overseas with the 366th Wing will probably be limited only by planners' imaginations, and what is available at the time.

CONOPS: The 366th Style of War

One of the viewgraphs you see during Colonel Scott's briefing on the Wing says, "The 366th Wing lives, works, plays, trains, deploys, and fights *TOGETHER*." It's easy enough to tell squadrons they will live at the same home base, but can you make them fight as one team? For the 366th, togetherness is more than just lip service. The togetherness shows in many ways, like on Friday nights when all the officers in the wing gather at the officers' club for happy hour. You don't see clusters of F-16 pilots, F-15 pilots, or tanker crews. Instead, you see mixed clusters, with waving arms describing formations (pilots can't really talk without their hands), new tactics, and ideas. These people really are interested in what is happening in the other units of the wing.

On a more practical level, a very impressive planning effort has gone into getting the Gunfighters ready to fight. These plans continue to be improved and refined, with a primary focus on getting the wing where it is going with less use of the Air Force's scarce heavy airlifters, and getting more out of the 366th's pool of aircraft and weapons. Let's look closer at the how the Gunfighters would get to a crisis.

Getting There: The 366th Wing Deployment Plan

The 366th library of deployment and operations plans is constantly growing on the disk drives and in the notebooks at the headquarters on Gunfighter Boulevard. We're going to look at just one of the deployment options—the movement of the wing to a well-developed base in a friendly host nation. By well-developed, we mean that the base has adequate facilities—aircraft shelters to house the wing, barracks or tent facilities for personnel, and stores of supplies such as fuel, water, and munitions compatible with USAF aircraft. Most friendly nations have supplies of jet fuel; and 80-series bomb warheads are quite common around the world. Also, the 366th might draw on prepositioned stores of such supplies, or access one of the maritime prepositioned ships stationed at places like Diego Garcia and Guam.

The 366th deployment scheme is designed around response forces packaged (i.e., sized and matched) to meet the particular crisis in question. It may be enough to send just a few fighters and tankers to a crisis zone to keep a lid on events until reinforcements can be assembled and sent. Other times, you may want to pile on into a given situation, to deter a particular rogue regime from making trouble. To keep things simple, the 366th Operations Group has designed a series of packages which allow the NCAs to quickly order a particular force into a crisis. The following chart shows the breakdown of the packages:

366th Wing Deployment Package Options

	A Package	A+ Package	B Package	B+ Package	C Package	C+ Package
F-15C	8	8	14	14	18	18
F-15E	8	8	14	14	18	18
F-16C	8	8	14	14	18	18
B-1B	0	4	0	6	0	6
KC-135R	4	4	5	5	6	6
E-3C*	3	3	3	3	3	3
EF-111A*	4	4	4	4	4	4
EC-130H*	2	2	2	2	2	2
Total	37	41	56	62	69	75

*Assets not controlled by 366th Wing.

As can be seen from the six options in the table, the smallest deployment unit, known as an A Package, includes twenty-four fighters and fighter bombers (eight F-15Cs, eight F-15Es, and eight F-16Cs), along with four KC-135Rs configured for FAST tanker deployment. The B and C Packages build upon the basic A Package by adding additional aircraft, until the entire Mountain Home force is committed. In addition, each package has a "plus" option, which adds a force of B-1B bombers from the 34th BS at Ellsworth AFB. You also may have noticed the force of support aircraft that is added to each package option. These are the E-3s, EF-111s, and EC-130s, which would accompany the wing on any deployment.

It would probably be impossible to deploy the entire Wing (a C+ Package) in one wave, due to the shortage of heavy airlift. Thus, for anything larger than an A Package, the wing is broken into separate waves, so that tanker and heavy transport aircraft can be utilized in shifts. For example, the deployment breakdown for a B Package would look like this:

B Package Deployment Schedule

	1st Wave	2nd Wave	Total
F-15C	8	6	14
F-15E	8	6	14
F-16C	8	6	14
B-1B*	4	2	6
KC-135R	4	1	5
E-3C	3	0	3
EF-111A	4	0	4
EC-130H	2	0	2
Total	41	21	62

* Indicates "plus" bomber option

The C+ Package, which is the largest option available, looks like this:

C+ Package Deployment Schedule

	1st Wave	2nd Wave	3rd Wave	Total
F-15C	8	6	4	18
F-15E	8	6	4	18
F-16C	8	6	4	18
B-1B*	4	2	0	6
KC-135R	4	1	1	6
E-3C	3	0	0	3
EF-111A	4	0	0	4
EC-130H	2	0	0	2
Total	41	21	13	75

* Indicates "plus" bomber package

Each wave would be separated by something like twenty-four to thirty-six hours, and would depend on tanker and airlift support to get certain key pieces of equipment and personnel onto the ground at the right time and in the right order. The matter of airlift cannot be overemphasized these days, since the force of AMC heavy airlift aircraft (C-141s, C-5s, and C-17s) is at the danger level when it comes to moving important stuff for top-priority units like the 366th. The AMC heavy airlift force in early 1995 consisted of the following aircraft:

USAF Heavy Lift Fleet

	Total	PAA
C-141	243	227
C-5	82	76
KC-10	59	57
C17	17	12
Total	401	372

Note: KC-10 limited to palletized cargo and passengers.

As you can see, the heavy airlift fleet is limited to less than 375 PAA aircraft assigned to units around the USAF. This situation is going to get worse as C-141s are retired faster than new C-17s are delivered. Whenever possible, AMC will try to use commercial freight aircraft from the Civil Air Reserve Fleet (CRAF), a pool of commercial freight aircraft subsidized by the U.S. Government and available to be drafted in a time of crisis. Another option for AMC is to charter freight aircraft from air carriers like UPS, Emery Air Freight, Federal Express, or even some of the huge Antonov 124 transports operated by the Russian flag carrier, Aeroflot.

As for the 366th Wing, they have worked hard to reduce their heavy airlift requirements to the bare minimum to get into operation at a host base in the minimum amount of time. The key is the number of C-141 loads it will take to get a particular package into action at the destination. Because the C-5 and C-17 can carry bigger loads of cargo (including outsized loads), and the KC-10 is limited to palletized cargo and personnel only, the load planners at the 366th Transport Squadron transportation office have to take this into account when they get the phone calls from AMC headquarters at Scott AFB. They plan for all kinds of possibilities. For example, consider the following notional table of airlift required to move various package combinations:

366th Package Deployment Transport Requirements

	A Package	A+ Package	B Package	B+ Package	C Package	C+ Package
Personnel (Deployed)	955	1,155	1,133	1,383	1,231	1,481
Weight (Short Tons)	549	732	824	1,190	1,098	1,464
C-141 Loads	30	40	45	65	60	80

Note: Above table is based upon fully equipped/stocked host base.

It should be noted that the above table is representative of only one particular planning scenario (the most optimistic actually), and should not be considered definitive. In fact, for bare-base operations, you should probably double the number of C-141 loads and throw in the services of one of the USAF Red Horse battalions.

Now, let's look back to our earlier example of an A Package going to a well-developed host base. As you can see, about thirty C-141s, along with appropriate tanker assets, would be needed to move the force overseas to the host operating base, and once the wing is in the air, the clock and the meter are running with regards to pushing cargo and supplies forward. What you see in the above table is just the down payment on a credible 366th deployment. A continuing logistics effort is vital to keeping the wing flying and operating up to its full potential, because on the ground the 366th is only a set of targets for another air force to destroy.

Hold Until Relieved: The 366th Style of Operations

Let's assume that General McCloud and the 366th Wing leadership has gotten the designated wing package to their host base. What happens next? Actually, well before the first combat aircraft has arrived, there will be a great deal of activity at the base, starting with the arrival of the FAST-1 tanker with its site survey team. Working quickly, they will size up the base, and using their own SATCOM link, will send back to Mountain Home the exact support requirements for the wing, so that the proper AMC airlift can be ordered and the right pallets and cargo can be loaded and sent on their way. Right after this comes FAST-2 with the AOC buildup team to establish the WICP satellite communications links back to Mountain Home and the Space Warfighting Center in Colorado Springs. Following this would be the C^3I element with their CTAPS equipment on FAST-3. This would be immediately moved to the AOC to keep the planning process going. Finally, FAST-4 would arrive, hopefully together with the first elements of the wing package with the aircrews and maintenance personnel necessary to fly the 366th's first missions.

So, just what might those missions be?

The Gunfighters are capable of almost any combat operation, except launching long range cruise missiles or doing a stealth penetration strike of an enemy air defense environment. Below is a chart of the different mission capabilities of the various aircraft of the 366th Wing (and attached units):

366th Mission Capabilities

	Day/Night Air-to-Air	Day Air-to-Ground	Night Air-to-Ground	Day/Night PGM	SEAD	Air-to-Air Refueling	C^3I	Standoff Jamming
F-15C	•							
F-15E	•	•	•	•				
F-16C	•	•		•	•			
B-1B		•	•	*			•	•
KC-135R						•	•	
E-3C							•	
EF-111A					•			•
EC-130H					•		•	•

* Indicates a future mission capability.

As can be seen, the Gunfighters provide a core capability to run rapid response air operations in a crisis initiated by a hostile government or force. The 366th is an aerial fire brigade, grudgingly willing to trade losses to buy time for the politicians back home to make up their minds, define a policy, and send forward reinforcement and/or replacement units. It is assumed that these would take over for the long-term campaign that would follow the commitment of a unit like the 366th. It is likely that the deployment of a package by the Gunfighters would be part of a joint operation with ground units from the Marine Corps or the Army's XVIII Airborne Corps. Just how they would fight in a crisis is therefore rather hard to specify, given the unpredictability of rogue states and other "bad guys" around the world. Thus, the 366th leadership will have to be both sneaky and imaginative in their use of their limited force of planes and aircrews.

The temptation to engage in an aerial form of guerrilla warfare must be balanced by the principles of mass and coordination that were proven during operations like Desert Storm and Just Cause. This means massing airpower assets, not just parceling them out wastefully and dangerously in penny packets. It also means looking for unconventional ways of hurting an opponent, so that that they can be caught looking somewhere else while the wing hits the "real" target. The Gunfighters Operations Staff must look for centers of gravity to hit, rather than punching away at an enemy's strength. The key to doing this is keeping their fighting edge sharp, and that means training and exercising. We'll take a look at the wing doing this in the next chapter, when we deploy with them to the biggest exercise they attend each year, Operation Green Flag at Nellis AFB, Nevada.

Getting Ready for War: Green Flag 94-3

An air force is more than an expensive collection of planes and personnel. A nation cannot just throw money and youth into building an aerial fighting force and expect to get anything more than a glorified flying club for military pageants. While an air force cannot win a war all by itself (despite what some zealots would like you to believe), since World War I *no* country has won a war without having a winning air force overhead. The history of the last six decades is filled with examples like France (1940), the Middle East Arabs (1967), and Iraq (1991), who spent a fortune on aircraft and had their heads handed to them when real combat came. Building a winning air force has relatively little to do with how much money a country spends.

Yes, air forces are hideously expensive. Figure on spending about $20 million for each modern single seat fighter, $2 million to select and train each pilot to a combat-ready level, and perhaps $100 million per wing per year, plus real estate costs for a no-frills air base. To maintain proficiency, your flight crews need to fly at least twenty hours a month, at a couple of thousands of dollars an hour. Don't forget to budget enough for administration, security, medical services, spare parts, practice ammunition, bombs, missiles, targets, and a thousand other details. Still, it isn't money alone that does the job. For starters, building an air force is a multi-generational task, which requires decades of investment in the cultivation of skills that are relatively rare and fragile. The best example of this is the Israeli Air Force, which uses a network of "talent scouts" with sophisticated psychological profiles to identify its future aircrews (and thus its future leaders) on the soccer fields and elementary schools while they are still pre-teen kids.

While such a system of selection may work for small countries with a few hundred aircraft and strong social cohesion, it would not be practical for a country of the size and diversity of the United States. America has an air force (actually several if you count the Navy, Marine, Army, and Coast Guard) with thousands of aircraft. Because of its worldwide responsibilities and interests, the U.S. has to reach deep to build its military forces, calling upon a wider range of skills and cultures than any other nation on earth. Backing up the selection of the right people is a massive industrial commitment, for only nations with a viable airframe industry can hope to avoid crippling dependence on one or two major powers for weapons, spare parts, and training.

There is a saying that goes, "If you think training is expensive, try ignorance!" Consider an example from the Vietnam War. Prior to the 1968 bombing halt over North Vietnam, both the Navy and Air Force suffered severely in air-to-air combat with the wily and agile MiG interceptors of the North Vietnamese Air Force. In fact, the critical kill/loss ratio was going decidedly against the Americans—only 3:1 (three MiGs shot down for every U.S. aircraft lost in air-to-air combat. Now, this doesn't sound bad until you consider that the MiGs and their pilots cost the North Vietnamese almost nothing to replace, and that fighting over friendly territory, a MiG pilot who ejected often lived to fight another day, while American aircrews who ejected stood a good chance of dying in a POW camp. In World War II, by way of contrast, the average kill/loss ratio was something like 8:1; and in Korea it was 13:1.

To improve the odds, the Navy launched a program of adversary flight training, flying practice missions against aircraft more agile than the F-4, including a few real MiG fighters that had found their way to the United States for evaluation and testing. The Navy opened the famous Top Gun school at NAS Miramar near San Diego, California, and a dozen or so classes of crews had cycled through by 1972. Every Navy pilot going to Southeast Asia received thorough intelligence briefings on the enemy aircraft and tactics that he would face.

The results were stunning. When the air war over North Vietnam started up again in 1972, the USAF still took a beating from the North Vietnamese, for a while losing more aircraft than they were shooting down. At one point the kill/loss ratio fell to only .89:1! Only the rapid introduction of electronic warning systems based on real-time intelligence saved the day for the Air Force, bringing the ratio back to a barely acceptable 2:1. But the Navy story was quite different. In a matter of weeks, the Navy fighters drove the North Vietnamese MiGs from the coastal zones; and at one time they had an incredible 31:0 kill/loss ratio. By the time of the cease-fire in early 1973, the ratio was a more realistic 13:1—a massive success compared to the Air Force's dismal performance during the same period. An unpopular war, fought under impossible political restrictions, was bad enough, but being outperformed in the air by the Navy was a burning humiliation for the USAF.

Today's U.S. Air Force is built on a foundation of education and training that only can be understood in terms of the bitter experience of USAF personnel in the skies over Southeast Asia in the 1960s and 1970s. The air force that America sent to the Persian Gulf in 1990 and 1991 was very much the product of the unacceptable cost of the Vietnam War and a twenty-year struggle by a generation of officers to exorcise the ghosts of dead comrades. Over the two decades since the end of that divisive conflict, the USAF has remade itself to ensure that its Vietnam experience will never happen again.

The Air Force Corporation

Like any large organization, the United States Air Force has a corporate culture. That culture is the product of its history and the collective experience of its people. Just like most big American corporations, it's had mergers and takeovers, reorganizations and purges. The Air Force Corporation started small, grew as a result of the vision of its founding members, and came into its own because it had a unique product at a time when it was needed. It has grown and shrunk as a result of competitive market forces in its own very specialized line of business, where the only customer is the U.S. Congress and ultimately the voters, taxpayers, lobbyists, and political interest groups that shape the lawmaking and budgeting process. Let's look at some of that history.

The Aeronautical Division of the U.S. Army Signal Corps was organized on August 1st, 1907, only four years after the Wright brothers' first powered flight. Commanded by a captain, the unit had one Wright biplane and a few mechanics. By 1914, it had become the Aviation Section of the Signal Corps, under a lieutenant colonel; and by 1918, after the United States entered World War I, it was upgraded to the Air Service, under a major general; and then in 1926, during a period of disarmament, it was downgraded to the Army Air Corps. On June 20th, 1941, with the threat of a new war on the horizon, it became the Army Air Forces, now led by a lieutenant general. By 1944, its strength had peaked at 2.3 million personnel, with tens of thousands of aircraft. Finally, on September 18th, 1947, after a forty-year struggle for identity, the U.S. Air Force was born, under the leadership of General Carl "Tooey" Spaatz.

Over the next five decades, its strength rose and fell, based on the perceived Soviet threat as well as its overseas commitments (Korea, Vietnam, the Persian Gulf, etc.). At the end of 1994, the Air Force consisted of 81,000 officers and 350,000 enlisted personnel; a ratio of one officer to every 4.3 enlisted, compared to an Army/Navy/Marine Corps ratio of about 1 to 10 or 12. More than half the officer corps consists of captains (O-3s) and majors (O-4s), ranks that have been especially hard hit by recent cutbacks. Under present downsizing plans, the active-duty Air Force will bottom out at around 400,000 people by 1996. There will also be about eighty thousand Reserve, 115,000 Air National Guard, and 195,000 civilian Air Force personnel working within the force. The Reserves consist of veterans who have completed their active duty and are available for recall in a national emergency on order of the President. The National Guard units evolved from the state militias of Colonial and Civil War times. Nominally under the command of their respective state governors (or commonwealth in the case of Puerto Rico), they can be called into federal service by a Presidential executive order. Many of the flight crews and maintenance personnel of U.S. commercial airlines serve in Reserve and National Guard units, and a major mobilization would wreak havoc on airline flight schedules, much as it did in 1990 during Operation Desert Shield.

The average age of USAF personnel is thirty-five for officers and twenty-nine for enlisted airmen. There are 66,000 women in the Air Force, some 15% of the officers and also 15% of the enlisted force, a proportion that has doubled since 1975. There are about three hundred female pilots and one hundred female navigators. In case you were wondering, an enlisted woman is addressed as "Airman." Only 17% of the officers were commissioned through the Air Force Academy, while 42% percent are Reserve Officer Training Corps

(ROTC) graduates. (The ROTC program is offered by a diminishing number of U.S. colleges and universities; in exchange for a commitment to take military science courses, attend summer training camps, and serve for a stated number of years, graduates receive a small stipend and a commission as a second lieutenant on graduation.) The rest are commissioned through Officer Candidate School (OCS) or other special programs such as the military medical recruiting program. Today's Air Force has approximately sixteen thousand pilots, seven thousand navigators, and 32,000 non-rated line officers in the grades of lieutenant colonel and below. There are almost three hundred generals (O-7s to O-10s) and about four thousand colonels (O-6s). Including National Guard and Reserve units, the Air Force operates about seven thousand aircraft, a number that is rapidly shrinking as entire types are taken out of service.

During World War II, when the U.S. Armed Forces were racially segregated, top Army Air Corps generals resisted the creation of "colored" flying units, arguing that "Negroes had no aptitude for flying." It took the personal intervention of Eleanor Roosevelt to force the creation of a black fighter squadron, which was trained at Tuskeegee, Alabama, and served with distinction in Italy. With major bases and senior officer hometowns heavily concentrated in the Southern states, the Air Force had a poor integration record, and for years the handful of black cadets admitted to the Air Force Academy and other training programs suffered extreme harassment and ostracism with quiet determination. Two of America's first black generals, Benjamin O. Davis and the famous "Chappie" James, came from the USAF—a tribute to the toughness of the men, and the system that created them. Things are a bit better today, though the Air Force remains the least ethnically diverse of the services. In 1994, Air Force officers were 89% Caucasian, 6% African-American, 2% Hispanic, and 3% other, mainly Asian-Americans. Enlisted ranks are a bit more diverse, with the breakdown being 76% Caucasian, 17% African-American, 4% Hispanic, and 3% Other. About 77% of officers and 67% of enlisted personnel are married, supporting a total of 570,000 dependent family members.

By law the Air Force is under the authority of a civilian Secretary of the Air Force, appointed by the President and confirmed by the Senate. Currently, this is the Honorable Sheila E. Widnall, the first woman to ever head a military service department. The highest ranking officer is the Chief of Staff of the Air Force, a four-star general appointed by the President to a three-year term and confirmed by the Senate. The present Chief of Staff is General Ronald R. Fogleman, who was previously the head of Air Mobility Command.

The Air Force is divided into eight Major Commands, each of which may include several numbered Air Forces. In 1995 the Major Commands were:

- **Air Combat Command (ACC)**—Formed by the 1992 merger of the Tactical Air Command, the Strategic Air Command, and elements of the Military Airlift Command, ACC, based at Langley AFB, Virginia, controls most of the fighter and bomber squadrons in service. Major components include the 1st Air

Force (Tyndall AFB, Florida), 8th Air Force (Barksdale AFB, Louisiana), 9th Air Force (Shaw AFB, South Carolina), and 12th Air Force (Davis-Monthan AFB, Arizona). It also controls the Weapons and Tactics Center at Nellis AFB, Nevada, and the Air Warfare Center at Eglin AFB, Florida.

- **Air Education and Training Command (AETC)**—Based at Randolph AFB, Texas, AETC was established in 1993 to provide unified management and direction to a vast infrastructure of schools, training squadrons, and advanced technical and professional programs, including the Air University at Maxwell AFB, Alabama. It has responsibility for the USAF Recruiting Service, but not for the Air Force Academy, at Colorado Springs, Colorado, whose superintendent reports directly to the Air Force Chief of Staff.

- **Air Force Material Command (AFMC)**—AFMC was established on July 1st, 1992, from what was previously the Air Force Systems Command, and is based at Wright-Patterson AFB, Ohio. AFMC is responsible for research, development, test, acquisition, and sustainment of weapons systems. It operates four major laboratories, the five air logistics depots, the School of Aerospace Medicine, the Test Pilot School, and many other centers and bases.

- **Air Force Space Command (AFSPC)**—Established on September 1st, 1982, AFSPC is based at Peterson AFB, Colorado. Major components include the Fourteenth Air Force at Vandenberg AFB, California (missile testing and some military satellite launches), the 20th Air Force at Francis E. Warren AFB, Wyoming (management of Minuteman and Peacekeeper ICBM squadrons, which come under the Operational Control of U.S. Strategic Command when they are on alert), and the Air Force Space Warfare Center at Falcon AFB, Colorado (management and tracking of defense-related satellites and space objects). AFSPC is a major part of U.S. Space Command, a unified command led by either an Air Force general or a Navy admiral.

- **Air Force Special Operations Command (AFSOC)**—Based at Hurlbut Field, Florida, AFSOC was established on May 22nd, 1990, as the Air Force component of the unified U.S. Special Operations Command (SOCOM). Primary missions include unconventional warfare, direct action, special reconnaissance, counter-terrorism, and foreign internal defense support. Secondary missions include humanitarian assistance, personnel recovery, and psychological and counter-narcotics operations. AFSOC's main operational units are the 16th Special Operations Wing, split-based at Hurlbut Field and Eglin AFB, the 352nd Special Operations Group at RAF Alconbury, Great Britain, and the 353rd Special Operations Group at Kadena AB, Japan. These units operate small numbers of AC-130 gunships, MC-130 transports, EC-130 electronic warfare birds, and night-capable helicopters like the MH-53 Pave Low and MH-60 Pave Hawk.

- **Air Mobility Command (AMC)**—AMC, which is based at Scott AFB, Illinois, was established on June 1st, 1992, replacing the Military Air Transport Command, while acquiring most of the tanker assets of the former Strategic Air Command. Major components are the 15th Air Force at March AFB, California (six wings), and the 21st Air Force at McGuire AFB, New Jersey (eight wings). The Commander of AMC also serves as Commander of U.S. Transportation Command (TRANSCOM), a unified command controlling America's military airlift, sealift, truck, and rail transportation assets.

- **Pacific Air Forces (PACAF)**—Based at Hickam AFB, Hawaii, near Pearl Harbor, PACAF is responsible for air operations in the vast Pacific and Asian theater. It includes the 5th Air Force at Yokota AFB, Japan; the 7th Air Force at Osan AB, South Korea; the 11th Air Force, at Elemendorf AFB, Alaska; and the tiny 13th Air Force at Andersen AFB, Guam. The loss of Clark AFB in the Philippines, which was damaged by the eruption of Mt. Pinatubo, and then abandoned after U.S. failure to negotiate an extension of the lease with the Filipino government, was a major setback to PACAF's forward presence in the Western Pacific. PACAF conducts most of its training exercises with Navy, Marine, and allied forces.

- **US Air Forces in Europe (USAFE)**—Headquartered at Ramstein AB, Germany, USAFE was a major element in the NATO defense structure that preserved the peace in Europe for over forty years. USAFE is coping with the effects of drastic force reductions resulting from the end of the Cold War, even as the operational demands of peacekeeping and humanitarian operations in Africa, Iraq, and the former Yugoslavia have increased. USAFE includes the 3rd Air Force at RAF Mildenhall, UK, 16th Air Force at Aviano AB, Italy, and 17th Air Force at Sembach, Germany.

In addition to the Major Commands, there are also many specialized agencies, services, and centers, such as the Air Weather Service, Air Force Safety Agency, Air Force Security Police, Air Intelligence, and medical services.

The basic operational unit of the Air Force is the wing, which typically occupies its own dedicated air base. Until recently most wings were commanded by colonels, but the more important wings are increasingly commanded by brigadier generals. A wing typically includes an operations group, which includes aircraft, aircrews, command and staff officers; a logistics group, which contains the maintenance and supply units; and a support group, which can include communications, security, engineering, finance, and other services. Most officers and airmen are assigned to smaller units called squadrons within each group. A wing can include any number of squadrons, from one to seven or more. A flying squadron typically includes eighteen to twenty-four fighters, eight to sixteen bombers, six to twelve tankers, or anything from two to twenty-four aircraft of other types. A large squadron may be divided, permanently or temporarily, into several flights or detachments. Several squadrons or detachments from several wings may be temporarily grouped into a provisional wing, as was often done during Operations Desert Shield and Desert Storm.

The Gunfighters Get Ready: The Road to Green Flag

How does a commander like Brigadier General Dave McCloud get his wing ready to go to war? You don't just slap together a bunch of people and aircraft, hand them a mission, and then expect them to do it without any training or experience. The USAF, insufficiently trained and lacking the experience that a previous war might have given, learned that lesson in the skies over North Vietnam. Never again would American pilots go into battle, only to have their ghosts taunt the survivors with the chant "You did not train me well enough."

When General McCloud took over the wing from General Hinton, he initiated an almost continuous, year-long schedule of training exercises, designed to prove the composite wing concept and to sharpen the skills of the personnel who had to make it work. Some difficulties had to be overcome to conduct effective training for the wing. These included:

- The limited range facilities at Mountain Home AFB for large composite-force training.
- Defining the 366th Wing's structure, particularly in the bomber, Eagle, and Strike Eagle squadrons.
- Reducing the wing's requirements for strategic airlift to deploy to a crisis area.
- The loss of the wing's standoff (AGM-142 Have Nap) and maritime (AGM-84 Harpoon and mining) capabilities when the B-52Gs of the 34th BS were retired in November 1993.
- Handling the transition of the F-16 squadron to the new Block 52 model Falcons, with the ASQ-213 HTS pods and AGM-88 HARM missiles for the SEAD (Suppression of Enemy Air Defense) mission.

"Marshal" McCloud and the wing staff plunged into their jobs with almost fanatical determination, and the results rapidly began to show.

In recent years, declining budgets and downsized forces have provided less and less money for flying hours. Most units of the USAF are desperately trying to hold the line at just twenty hours per month for proficiency and tactical training. When we visited the wing at Mountain Home, we heard a young fighter captain complaining that he had to fly over fifty hours the previous month, and he was tired! The 366th enjoys a high priority at ACC headquarters, and it shows up as extra money for flight hours, fuel, and spare parts. Another sign of the wing's high priority is the enlargement of the 390th (F-15C Eagle) and 391st (F-15E Strike Eagle) FSs to eighteen PAA aircraft each. Those birds are worth their weight in gold these days; to get more of them is unheard of. High priority also provides the wing with important little extras, like JTIDS terminals for the F-15Cs, and stressed steel Ro/Ro floors and satellite terminals for the KC-135R tankers of the 22nd ARS.

While General McCloud did wonders for the material side of the wing, it takes more than money and hardware to build a combat unit, especially when that unit is made up of five squadrons, all from different communities within the USAF, split between two separate bases. So General McCloud began a program of goodwill and coalition building among the five squadrons of the 366th. Where previously the personnel of a squadron spent their leisure time with members of their own little circle, now they were encouraged to mingle, to share ideas and experiences, and build the kind of comradeship that you need when you go to war. In the 366th command briefing (a presentation given to VIP visitors) you hear, "We live together. We train together. We play together. And we *fight* together!" This is more than just rhetoric. The very survival of the wing depends on working together.

The first real test of the new wing organization and its concept of operations (CONOPS) came in the fall of 1993, when the 366th Wing was chopped to CENTCOM to become the core air unit for Operation Bright Star-93, the yearly Middle East exercise. General McCloud deployed an A+ Package to North Africa, with the fighters, tankers, and command elements going to Cairo West Air Base in Egypt, and the bombers going to Lajes Air Base in the Azores. Over the next several weeks, the wing exercised with elements of several air forces, including Egypt's, and some U.S. Navy air units. Two important lessons learned were the need for more F-15 aircraft in the 390th and 391st FSs, and the urgency of reducing the amount of heavy airlift required to move the wing overseas.

In late 1993 came the announcement by Secretary of Defense Les Aspin that the entire fleet of B-52Gs would be retired within a matter of months. By November 1993, the last of the -G model BUFFs were history, and the 366th was without a long-range bomber component, or any maritime or standoff weapons capability. This hurt a lot, and ACC went to work to find a solution, not only for the Gunfighters, but for the whole Air Force. Soon after, the 389th FS began to take delivery from the Lockheed Fort Worth factory of their brand-new Block 52 F-16Cs, with the powerful new F100-PW-229 engines.

Good news arrived early in 1994, when ACC announced the formation of a new squadron of B-1B Lancers, the reborn 34th BS, to be co-resident with the 28th BW at Ellsworth AFB, South Dakota. While General McCloud still lacked the mining, maritime strike, or standoff weapons capabilities he had lost with the retirement of the B-52Gs, the B-1B squadron would bring some new capabilities to the wing. The work on reducing the number of C-141 loads required for deployment began to yield results, as sergeants at the squadron level found ways to leave more stuff behind and share resources among units. While the Air Force may look like an officers' club, without the work of the enlisted personnel, not one bomb would be loaded, not one plane fueled, not one engine changed.

During the winter, the Gunfighters went on a pair of deployments. One of these was a mobility exercise to Michigan, and the other to Alaska. This second one, dubbed Northern Edge, sent an A Package north to Elmendorf AFB, to play the role of an aggressor force in a large PACAF exercise. This let the 366th practice cold weather operations skills. Since they do not have any particular regional focus, just a fast response time, one week they may need to be ready to go to a desert environment, and the next week a jungle.

When they returned from Alaska, the Gunfighters threw themselves into the biggest challenge of 1994, getting ready for Operation Green Flag 94-3, the largest, most expensive, and most realistic annual training exercise in the Air Force. Run out of the huge range complex north of Nellis AFB in Nevada, Green Flag is the closest thing to war you're likely to run into, without actually having the other guys shoot back with live ammunition. The 366th Wing would make up the core force for this Green Flag exercise, with numerous other units plugging in under General McCloud's command. It was going to be a critical test of the Gunfighters and the composite wing concept. The entire wing began the move down to Nellis AFB in mid-April of 1994.

Nellis AFB: The Big Sky

Once upon a time, Las Vegas was just a dusty stop on the railroad across the desert from southern California. Later, after Bugsy Siegel started the gambling resort boom in the late '40s, it became a place where people went to escape. Today it is America's fastest-growing city, thanks to a construction boom brought on by an influx of retirees and tourism. Up on the north side of town, just off Interstate 15, is Nellis AFB, the USAF's biggest and busiest air base. Started during World War II as the Las Vegas Gunnery Range, Nellis was renamed to honor a local P-47 pilot who died during the war. After World War II, it remained a primary gunnery training center, with its complex of ranges to the north heavily used to teach pilots the art of shooting straight and true. It also has been home to combat units like the 474th TFW, which flew F-111s,

F-4s, and F-16s during the Cold War before it was disestablished. Nellis is a unique center for training, testing, and competition, with large, trackless desert ranges to the north, closed to civilian air traffic, and providing room for almost any kind of flying.

Nellis is home to the USAF Weapons and Tactics Center (W&TC, formerly the USAF Fighter Weapons Center), which expends over 45% of the USAF's practice munitions *worldwide*! Commanded by Lieutenant General Tom Griffith, the W&TC runs a range complex that covers much of southern Nevada. At any given time, there are almost 140 aircraft based at W&TC, flying some 37,000 sorties each year. The core of the W&TC is the 57th Wing (formerly the 57th Fighter Weapons Wing), whose personnel are distinguished by checkered yellow and black scarves worn with their flight suits. It is commanded by Colonel John Frisby, and its units include:

- **422nd Test and Evaluation Squadron (TES)**—Flying a combination of A-10A Thunderbolt IIs, F-15C/D/E Eagles and Strike Eagles, and F-16C/D Fighting Falcons, the 422nd TES is tasked with operation testing and tactics development for the USAF fighter force and their weapons.

- **USAF Weapons School (WS)**—This is a 5 1/2-month, graduate-level course in weapons, tactics, and strike planning. While only 7% of USAF aircrews are WS graduates, over 45% of wing commanders have attended the school. One measure of the effectiveness of WS training is aircrew performance during Desert Storm, where only 7% of the crews had successfully completed WS, but 66% of the air-to-air kills were accomplished by WS grads. The current curriculum includes a course for virtually every type of combat aircraft in the USAF inventory, as well as a special course for E-3 controllers. In 1994, the school was commanded by Colonel Bentley Rayburn.

- **561st FS**—Flying the F-4G Wild Weasel version of the Phantom, this is the last remaining active-duty squadron dedicated to the SEAD mission in the USAF. In recent years the squadron has been deployed to Turkey to support the air embargo over northern Iraq, and to Italy to fly similar operations over Bosnia. This highly respected and heavily tasked outfit is headed into its sunset years. The squadron has twenty-four PAA aircraft, with an additional eight F-4Gs as spares and pipeline aircraft.

- **414th Training Squadron (Adversary Tactics Division)**—With the deactivation of the 64th and 65th FSs, which were tasked with the adversary mission, this detachment of F-16C/D aircraft provides the W&TC with a small force of aggressor aircraft for realistic training.

- **Detachment 1, Ellsworth AFB**—This small detachment of B-1B and B-52H heavy bombers fulfills the same mission for the bomber force that the 422nd TES does for the fighter force. They are co-located with the 28th BW at Ellsworth AFB, but report back to the 57th Wing. Eventually, there will also be a B-2 detachment at Whiteman AFB, Missouri.

- **The Thunderbirds**—This renowned air demonstration squadron performs at air shows all around the world. Presently, they fly the Block 32 F-16C and -D Fighting Falcons. In 1994, Lieutenant Colonel Steve Anderson led the T-Birds through a demanding schedule of some seventy-two air shows, thrilling millions of viewers. The unit has eight aircraft, eleven officers, and between 130 and 140 enlisted personnel in any given year. An assignment to the Thunderbirds is a high honor, reserved for the best of the best, since this team, more than any other unit, represents the U.S. Air Force to the public.

- **549th Joint Tactics Squadron (JTS)**—Known as "Air Warrior," the 549th provides simulated close air support and debriefing services to the U.S. Army National Training Center (NTC) at Fort Irwin, California, about one hundred miles to the southwest. They fly the F-16C/D, and can now show visitors the results of their strikes in real time, thanks to a special data link to the NTC "Star Wars" building (a complex of high-tech three-dimensional real-time displays.) .

- **66th Air Rescue Squadron (RQS)**—This is one of four RQSs that were activated following the poor performance of the U.S. Special Operations Command in the Combat Search and Rescue (CSAR) mission during Desert Storm. Combat Search and Rescue gives aircrews confidence that if they are shot down behind enemy lines, well-trained and well-equipped professionals will be on the spot to find them and bring them home. When you read down the list of Medal of Honor recipients, you'll find quite a few CSAR aviators who sacrificed their lives trying to save others. When there are pilots around the bar, CSAR crews never have to buy their own drinks. Composed of 4 HH-60G Pave Hawk helicopters and a HC-130 Hercules tanker/C3I aircraft, the RQSs provide rapidly deployable CSAR forces, as well as supporting emergency rescue, safety, and security operations at Nellis AFB.

- **USAF Combat Rescue School**—Designed to provide a graduate-level Combat Search And Rescue training curriculum, the school flies the same HH-60G/HC-130 aircraft as the 66th RQS. In 1994, Lieutenant Colonel Ed LaFountaine commanded the school. The plan is to graduate two classes per year, as well as to provide testing and evaluation services for CSAR squadrons worldwide.

- **820th Red Horse Squadron**—This highly prized civil engineering unit can rapidly deploy anywhere in the world. Given a steady supply of water and concrete, the engineers can build a full air-base complex in a matter of days.
- **Federal Prison Camp (Area II)**—There is a medium security federal prison camp located on the Nellis base complex. One notable recent prisoner was former Undersecretary of the Navy Melvin Paisley, convicted on corruption charges in the late 1980s.
- **554th Range Squadron**—Commanded in 1994 by Colonel "Bud" Bennett, this organization monitors range safety and controls the flight activities for Nellis AFB and the various ranges to the north. In addition, the squadron provides local air traffic control for the FAA, feeding into the LAX control center in Los Angeles.

The twelve-thousand-square-mile/3 1/2-million-acre range complex fans out north of Las Vegas. There is enough range space to put the whole nation of Kuwait inside, with room to spare. Divided into a series of different ranges, or "areas" as they are called, the whole complex is instrumented with an electronic system known as the Red Flag Measurement and Debrief System (RFMDS). An aircraft flying over the complex can be constantly monitored, providing a continuous record of everything that happens overhead. Each area has a specific function. Some are live-fire gunnery and bombing ranges, while others have arrays of manned radar emitters designed to simulate enemy air defense systems. These include:

- **60-Series Ranges**—Test and evaluation, as well as WS training goes on here.
- **Ranges 71 and 76**—Deep strike-type targets that simulate a strategic weapons factory, SCUD launch sites, and an airfield.
- **Range 74**—This area simulates a Soviet-style mechanized battalion.
- **Range 75**—Simulates a follow-on supply convoy, typical of Iraqi columns attacked during Desert Storm.

These ranges are maintained by contractor personnel from Loral and Arcatia Associates, who spend their days servicing the target arrays and keeping the radar emitters working. There is also a Cubic Corp. Air Combat Maneuvering Instrumentation (ACMI) system, which can record and play back every movement and simulated weapon-firing in air-to-air combat engagements involving many aircraft. This instant-replay capability is heavily used by the Weapon School for after-action debriefings, in which pilots can review every mistake in slow motion from any three-dimensional viewpoint. Also located in the range complex is a legacy of the Cold War; the old nuclear testing range for the Department of Energy (DOE).

No account of Nellis AFB and its ranges would be complete without mention of the three (officially acknowledged) airfields inside the complex. The first of these is Indian Springs Airfield, where the Thunderbirds practice their routines. Indian Springs is also an emergency divert field during exercise and other activities. Farther north is the Tonopah Test Range (TTR) Air Base, which was constructed and used by the 37th TFW when they operated the F-117A Nighthawk stealth fighter. Following the Gulf War and its public exposure of the "black jets," the USAF transferred the 37th's aircraft and personnel to the 49th Fighter Wing at Holloman AFB, New Mexico. Today, Tonopah is frequently used by reserve and Marine aviation units to simulate operating out of a bare-bones base in the field. The last of the bases that we know about is the mysterious Groom Lake Test Facility, located in the heart of the Nellis AFB/DOE range complex. Based around a large dry lake, Groom Lake is similar in function to the USAF's main test facility at Edwards AFB, but the intense security would make you think the Russians were *still* coming. Known also as Area 51 and Dreamland, it was used during the testing of the Lockheed U-2 spy plane in the 1950s. It has been used ever since as a base for testing black (classified) aircraft, including the Lockheed SR-71 Blackbird, the D-21 reconnaissance drone, and the F-117A. It is also reportedly home to exploitation (i.e., technical evaluation) programs for foreign aircraft (MiGs, etc.), as well as black prototypes and technology demonstration aircraft. Whatever goes on there, the USAF is trying to expand the range boundaries to include several desert ridge lines that overlook the area, so civilian observers cannot see any part of the complex directly.

But our interest now at Nellis AFB has nothing to do with the black activities at Groom Lake; we've come to observe what goes on in the open light of day. In a word, Flags. The Flag-series exercises simulate real-world combat conditions in a relatively safe and secure environment. The best known of these is Red Flag, which started running in 1975. Conceived by the legendary Colonel "Moody" Suiter, Red Flag grew out of an alarming statistic of the war in Vietnam. If a pilot survived his first ten combat encounters, his chances of surviving a full combat tour would increase by over 300%. Such combat encounters help build "situational awareness," making an aircrew much more able to survive in the deadly air defense radar and missile thickets that the USAF has to penetrate. So Colonel Suiter got this bright idea: If you could provide those first ten combat missions in a safe stateside training environment, you might lose fewer aircraft and crews when a real war came along. Such training would also allow units to practice the complex art of strike warfare in large formations. Red Flag is designed to give every aircrew in a combat unit those first ten missions up on the Nellis AFB range complex, facing the most talented enemy force they will ever see. Every combat crew is supposed to go through at least one Red Flag during each two-year flying tour, to keep their flying and combat skills honed to a razor's edge. About six Red Flags are run annually, each consisting of a six-week training exercise, divided into three two-week segments.

The core unit is usually a combat wing. Each squadron from the core wing flies fifteen to twenty simulated combat missions during its two week training period. Supporting aircraft detachments (AWACS, tankers, jammers, etc.) make the training even more realistic. For twenty years, Red Flags have helped U.S. and allied combat aviators to prepare for war. The value of this training was proven in 1991, when aviators came back from missions over Iraq declaring, "It was just like Red Flag, except the Iraqis weren't as good."

Green Flag is a special exercise that runs each year at Nellis. Green Flag might be called a Red Flag with "'trons and teeth," Instead of practice bombs, Green Flag uses real bombs. Instead of simulated jamming and electronic countermeasures, Green Flag exposes aircrews to the full spectrum of electronic nastiness that can appear above the modern battlefield. Green Flag's only compromises with realism are that participants don't shoot live ammunition or real missiles at fellow aviators, and no planes are allowed to crash and burn.

Green Flags are very expensive, and difficult to set up. Vast amounts of weapons and decoys are expended during the simulated missions "up north." It isn't easy to assemble a force of scarce electronic warfare (EW) aircraft, such as the RC-135 Rivet Joints and the EC-130 Compass Calls, which are heavily committed to monitoring actual and potential crises around the world. Nevertheless, the USAF runs Green Flag each year to teach combat pilots how to operate in a full-scale electronic warfare environment. Green Flag is also an opportunity to test new tactics and equipment in a "near war" situation.

For 1994, ACC decided to dedicate the third rotation period (known as Green Flag 94-3) to testing the capabilities of the 366th Wing and the composite wing concept. The exercise would include a full overseas-style deployment, complete with the construction of a field-style Air Operations Center in a tent city next to the Red Flag headquarters on the south end of the base. Could a composite wing really function in a bare-bones field deployment? Could other units plug in to the 366th Wing's unique command and control structure? It would be a crucial test for the composite wing concept, and we were invited to observe the results. So in early April 1994, we headed west to join the 366th in their mock war, just outside the gambling capital of the country.

Green Flag 94-3 – Gunfighters Supreme

When we joined the 366th Wing at Mountain Home AFB, General McCloud was already getting ready to head down to Nellis AFB. With several days to get acquainted with the wing and its people, it was not too tough to sense the collective anxiety over the coming Green Flag test. We spent most of the next several weeks with the wing, and what follows is a "war diary" of the high points. It was an unprecedented inside look at how a unit like the Gunfighters would go to war.

Saturday, April 9th, 1994

We rose to a cold, rainy morning at Mountain Home AFB, and headed over to the 366th mobility office for processing. Instead of flying to Nellis AFB via commercial airliner (the standard procedure to save money as well as wear and tear on Air Force transports), the entire Wing would ride down on the FAST tankers of the 22nd ARS, just as if we were going to war; and we rode with them. The previous day, the first two FAST aircraft flew down to Nellis, taking with them an A package of eight F-15C Eagles, eight F-15E Strike Eagles, 8 F-16C Fighting Falcons, and four KC-135Rs. Since the new 34th BS with their B-1Bs were still getting organized, this trip would be fighters and tankers only. We were going to ride with about sixty members of the Gunfighters aboard FAST-3, the first aircraft to depart on this cold, wet morning.

At the Mobility Office we stacked our bags in a large, open wooden crate, sat down to have a cup of coffee, and listened to the safety and mobility briefing. In a little while, it came time to board the aircraft and head off. Once we and our gear were loaded, the four CFM-56 engines were started, and we took off. Heading south, we were shown around the aircraft by the crew chief/boomer. We got a look out of the boomer's position at the snow-capped Rocky Mountains, and a chance to "fly" the boom. Later, we went forward to learn about navigation from the attractive navigator, Captain Christine Brinkman. "Brink," as she is called, might look like a high school cheerleader, but she is one of two experienced female navigators in the 366th Wing. Nobody on our flight crew that day was as old as the airplane, which was manufactured by Boeing in FY-1960!

After learning from Brink how to navigate by "shooting the sun" through a sextant in the aircraft's ceiling, we sat back and enjoyed the relatively smooth, though noisy, ride of the venerable airplane. To help with the noise, the crew chief handed out little yellow foam earplugs. The cold inside the passenger compartment was another problem. We had been warned about the -135's poor heating system, so each of us wore a leather jacket to ward off the chill. Less than two hours after takeoff, we turned into the Nellis AFB traffic pattern to land. A few minutes later we taxied up to the transit ramp and cranked up the cargo hatch to disembark our gear. We had exchanged the rainy weather of Idaho for an unseasonably warm spring in southern Nevada.

Flocks of aircraft from units around the country were already arriving, and you could feel the excitement in the air. But the first job was to get the deployment team, ourselves included, bedded down for the duration of Green Flag. Though Nellis is a huge base, like so many others around the USAF, it is desperately short of temporary billeting quarters. Thus, most of the deployed personnel are billeted off base in a variety of hotel rooms and guest quarters in nearby Las Vegas. This housing arrangement is not considered a hardship by the aircrews, who eagerly headed off to collect rental cars from nearby McCarren Airport and claim their rooms. We stayed at a small hotel with the personnel of Lieutenant Colonel Clawson's 391st FS. By sundown, the Strike

The 366th Wing Air Operations Center (AOC), located adjacent to the Red Flag building at Nellis AFB. During Green Flag 94-3, the wing personnel in this tent city generated the Air Tasking Orders that were used by the Blue Forces. *John D Gresham*

Eagle crews had staked out the swimming pool and were discussing the best places to eat and gamble. Since Nellis is only a day's drive from Mountain Home, many of the aircrews' wives and girlfriends had driven down to share two weeks of fun and sun in Las Vegas. This deployment was a real favorite among family members, even though it was going to be a busy two weeks.

Sunday, April 10th , 1994

While most of us had a day to relax and rest, the personnel of Lieutenant Colonel "Tank" Miller's Operational Support Squadron were working hard setting up the wing's AOC in a small tent city in a side yard next to the Red Flag operations building, preparing the first of the Air Tasking Orders (ATOs). Even though the first missions of Green Flag 94-3 were not scheduled for two more days, the writing and cross-checking of ATOs needed to start at least seventy-two hours before they were actually executed. The Ops staff were working hard at their computer terminals to put together a Joint Integrated Prioritized Target List (JIPTL, the master list of bombing targets), as well as the Master Attack Plan for the entire exercise. Another vital document was the Air Coordination Order (ACO), which specified how the airspace around Nellis would be managed, or "deconflicted," to minimize the risk of a midair collision or other unpleasant incident. All this planning was supervised by Lieutenant Colonel Rich Tedesco, a combat F-15/WSO with a gift for assembling all the details that go into making an ATO.

An innovation that would be tried for the first time during Green Flag 94-3 was to pull all of the photo-intelligence data for the wing from the new U.S. SPACECOM Space Warfighting Center (SWC) at Falcon AFB,

Colorado. The SWC would process photographs taken by surveillance satellites, as well as information from other space-based assets, and immediately feed them to the 366th AOC over a satellite data link located adjacent to the communications tent. The wing would have no manned photo-reconnaissance aircraft for the exercise. Since only a handful of tactical reconnaissance aircraft remain in service, this reliance on satellite imagery for strike planning is quite realistic. The AOC crew would work late into the nights that were ahead, never really getting the rest they needed, but always reacting to the changes that are an inevitable part of the ATO building process.

Monday, April 11th, 1994

While the last of the attached air units were arriving, the wing's aircrews were either planning their first strike for the following day or taking guided tour flights over the Nellis ranges for familiarization with the terrain they would be flying over for the next two weeks.

The starting lineup of players for this Green Flag was impressive:

- **2-229th Attack Helicopter Regiment**—Twelve AH-64A Apache and six OH-58C Kiowa helicopters from the U.S. Army's 2-229th Attack Helicopter Regiment at Fort Rucker, Alabama.
- **27th FW**—Eight F-111F Aardvarks equipped with Pave Tack pods, and four EF-111A Ravens from the 27th FW at Cannon AFB, New Mexico.
- **55th Wing**—Two RC-135 Rivet Joint ELINT/SIGINT aircraft from the 55th Wing at Offut AFB near Omaha, Nebraska.
- **57th Wing**—Two Wild Weasel F-4G Phantoms from Nellis AFB's own 561st FS, as well as two F-16Cs from the 422nd TES.
- **187th FG, 160th FS**—To augment the aggressor aircraft from the Adversary Tactics Division, eight F-16C Fighting Falcons from the Alabama ANG were tasked to act as additional threat aircraft.
- **193rd Special Operations Group (SOG), 193rd Special Operations Squadron (SOS)**—The Pennsylvania ANG contributed an EC-130 with the Senior Scout "clip-on" EW system, from the 193rd SOG at Harrisburg IAP.
- **355th Wing**—Two EC-130H Compass Call jamming aircraft from the 355th Wing at Davis-Monthan AFB, Arizona.
- **388th FW**—Ten F-16C Fighting Falcons equipped with LANTIRN pods from the 388th FW at Hill AFB, Utah.
- **414th FS**—Four F-16C Fighting Falcons from the Nellis AFB Adversary Tactics Division, to provide aggressor support.
- **552nd ACW**—Two E-3B Sentrys from the 552nd ACW at Tinker AFB, Oklahoma.

By the time the last of the Green Flag participants had arrived, there were over two hundred aircraft on the ramp at Nellis AFB, quite an air force by itself.

After their familiarization flights, the crews attended a series of safety briefings, designed to minimize the chance of what the crews call "a sudden violation of the air/ground interface"—in other words, a crash. Not so long ago, accidents were unpleasantly common at Nellis, with more than thirty deaths from over two dozen crashes in the worst year, 1981. Those were the days when the USAF crews were just learning to fly low-level, and the high accident rate was the price paid to gain mastery of operations "at five hundred feet at the speed of heat!" Today the range controllers are fanatical about safety, with minimum above-ground-level altitudes and separations between aircraft rigorously enforced. A wing commander back in the 1980s was cashiered for telling his aircrews to ignore these minimums.

But the most fanatical care will not stop every bad thing from happening. Even before the exercise began, an Army AH-64A Apache attack helicopter went down in a snowstorm on a mountain while deploying from Fort Rucker, Alabama. The crew survived (thanks to the crash absorbing structure of the Apache) and was picked up by a HH-60G Pave Hawk from the 66th RQS (their first "save" as it turned out). Still, it was not a good omen.

The morning briefing was scheduled for 0630 (6:30 AM in civilian time), so everyone got to bed early.

Tuesday, April 12th, 1994—Day 1: Mission #1

The mass briefing room in the Red Flag building was crowded to capacity for the first mission of Green Flag 94-3. The 366th would be playing the role

A squadron planning room for one of the 366th's fighter units at Green Flag 94-3. The CTAPS mission-planning terminal is located in the pile of cases at the left.
JOHN D. GRESHAM

of the good guys, the Blue force. The adversary F-16s (bad guys) would be the Red Force. The object of the game was for Blue to crush the more numerous Reds by smashing their ground targets and shooting down their planes, while avoiding Blue losses. Even though General McCloud was in command, the Red Flag staff actually runs the show. After the weather and safety briefings, the 366th staff came in to give the Blue Force mission briefing. Following this, at 0645, the pilots and controllers of the aircraft and emitters from the Adversary Tactics Department (the Red Force) left for their own briefing. In a few hours war would break out on the northern ranges of the Nellis complex.

For the Red Force, the mission was simple: Stop the Blue Force. Today that would involve eight F-16Cs simulating the performance and tactics of the Russian MiG-29 Fulcrum. For the Blue Force, the first part of their plan was to strike at simulated enemy command facilities (bunkers) and strategic targets (SCUD launch sites). That would complete Phase I. In Phase II, Blue would gain air supremacy over Red by bombing airfields and SAM/AAA sites. Finally, in Phase III, Blue would bomb a variety of targets, mostly truck convoys and supply centers. The campaign was planned to last nine days, depending on the breaks of the referees and how well the bomb damage assessment (BDA) went.

The strike command would fall to the 366th Wing, though General McCloud would not personally lead the strike. A relative newcomer to his F-16, he swallowed his pride and flew as number six in a formation of six 389th FS F-16Cs assigned to hit a simulated SCUD site on the southern side of the event arena. Simultaneously, a quartet of 391st FS Strike Eagles were assigned to hit a nearby command bunker. On the northern side, the F-111Fs of the 27th FW and F-16Cs from the 388th FW would hit similar targets. The F-4Gs, EF-111As, an RC-135, and an EC-130 would provide EW and SEAD support, with two 22nd ARS KC-135Rs and an E-3C Sentry staying back to the eastern side of the range to support the Blue Force. In addition, a flight of U.S. Army AH-64A Apache attack helicopters would hit several Red Force radar sites, much as a joint Army/Air Force helicopter team (Task Force Normandy) did on the first night of Desert Storm. The big surprise of the Blue operation would be a new tactic devised by the Eagle drivers of the 366th. The Wild Boars of the 390th FS would form a virtual wall of Eagles to sweep enemy fighters from the path of the two strike forces. Netted together with their JTIDS data links and armed with simulated AIM-120 Slammers, they felt they could clear the skies ahead of the Blue Force with a minimum of losses.

Takeoff was at 0830, and the air below Sunrise Mountain rumbled as sixty aircraft clawed their way into the air. First off were the E-3 and the tankers, followed by the relatively slow EW birds. Then came the fighters. Each of the 389th FS F-16Cs were loaded with an AIM-9 Sidewinder training round, two 370 gallon/1,423 liter fuel tanks, two Mk 84 2,000 lb./909.1 kg. bombs, and an ALQ-131 jamming pod. Their decoy launchers were fully loaded with chaff and flare rounds; and like all the aircraft of the strike force, they would use their jam resistant Have Quick II radios to (hopefully) defeat the communications jammers of the adversary forces on the ground. Last off were the adversary F-16s of the 414th and the Alabama ANG, since they did not have any tanker support and fuel might be a bit tight for them. Up north at Indian Springs, the crews of the AH-64s launched from their forward operating base (FOB). Blue Force aircraft periodically refueled from the tankers to keep topped off. All they were waiting for now was the clearance from the range supervisor, and then they would listen for the "push" call from the air-to-air commander to start the run to the targets.

Up in front, the eight F-15Cs of the 390th FS began their push towards the gaggle of eight adversary F-16Cs defending the airspace in front of the Red Force target array. Making careful use of AWACS data and their APG-70 radars, the F-15Cs sorted out the targets, using the JTIDS links to assign a specific target F-16 to each Eagle. Then, on command, eight simulated AMRAAM shots were fired at the Red Force F-16s. Before they could react, the range controllers called seven of them "dead." The seven headed back to the "regeneration box," and the eighth fled west. The regeneration box is part penalty box and part safe haven located in the northwest corner of the range. If a dead adversary aircraft spends a few minutes in the box, the range controllers will resurrect or "regen" him, and allow the aircraft back into the fight. Since the U.S. Air Force trains to fight outnumbered against an enemy that can rapidly replace his losses, this is not so unrealistic.

Unfortunately for the Red Force, by the time they had all hit the regen box, the strikers were on their way in to their targets, and the adversary F-16s could only hit back in ones and twos. The Red Force faced a losing battle, since the Eagles of the 390th were still on the hunt, and the Strike Eagles and Fighting Falcons of the Blue Force were hitting the incoming aggressors with well-aimed Slammer shots. By the time the aggressor aircraft were headed back to the regeneration box for the fourth time, the strike forces were over their targets, hitting them precisely as planned.

For "Marshal" McCloud, this was the closest to war he had ever been, having just missed both Operations Just Cause and Desert Storm. Now he was "tail end Charlie" on day one of Green Flag 94-3, and things were going good. He stuck close to his element leader in the number-five F-16, and their ingress to the target area was textbook perfect. Six pilots set their weapons delivery computers for a "pop-up" attack, then pulled up, rolled, inverted, pulled through, and rolled wings level into a dive onto the simulated SCUD launch site. Lining up the "death dot" on the target, McCloud punched the release button, and when the computer was happy with the delivery parameters, the two Mk 84s were kicked off of the weapons racks. As he pulled out, he saw the explosions of two direct hits on the target, supremely satisfied at his first "combat" performance in the Viper. His element leader in number five had some sort of switchology problem, though, and his bombs did not drop. The pilot of the number-five Viper headed back to hit the target again, while General McCloud waited for him to return, orbiting nearby. Then suddenly, McCloud looked down and saw a Red Force F-16 chasing one of the Army AH-64As that was trying desperately to exit the target area after hitting a simulated radar site with AGM-114 Hellfire missiles and rockets. Switching to BORE mode, he dove down on the aggressor aircraft, rapidly setting up a shot with a simulated AIM-120 AMRAAM. In a matter of seconds, he had the radar lock and fired a simulated Slammer at a range of 1 nm./1.8 km., a perfect "in-his-lips missile shot." The range controllers immediately scored the Red F-16 dead, and as soon as McCloud's number five returned, he egressed the target area (pilot talk for "leave" or "go away") at high speed, hugging the contours of the mountains for cover to evade enemy SAMs and fighters.

By 1130 hours, all of the aircraft had recovered back to base, and the process of tallying up the results began. By 1330, range controllers and assessment teams had finished their jobs and were ready to present their findings at the mass debrief. The results were stunning. Every target had been hit, and only a few would require restrikes later in the campaign. The Red radars had either been successfully hit or suppressed, and the Blue EW aircraft were never in danger. Even better were the air-to-air results, thirty to four in favor of the Blue Force, a new Green Flag record. For General McCloud, it was a moment of personal triumph. Even though there were still eight days and seventeen more missions to go, the Gunfighters had won. Back in the 1970s and 1980s the aggressors and other Red Force players would regularly wreck the Blue Force plans; but Red would never get close during Green Flag 94-3. Even as we were watching the mass debrief, the second strike of the day was headed out, and the results were almost identical.

Wednesday, April 13th, 1994—Day 2: Mission 4

The following morning saw the transition to Phase II of the campaign plan, with Blue hitting airfields and SAM sites around the target ranges. This morning, we hung around the squadron ready rooms in the Red Flag building to watch the strike planning process. Each of the squadron rooms had a CTAPS terminal, networked into Rick Tedesco's Air Operations Center just a few yards away in the tent city outside. As we watched the staff officers work, my researcher, John Gresham, pointed to a photograph lying on one of the tables, his eyes wide with shock. As he opened his mouth to speak, one of the pilots said, "Don't worry. That stuff is unclassified these days." (The mild caution "Official Use Only" was stamped on the photo.) The photo showed the Mt. Helen Airfield; it clearly had been taken from a satellite; and it was stunningly detailed (with a resolution of about 3 feet/1 meter). Such imagery is quite ordinary, the pilot went on to explain. Just a few years ago this stuff was "Top Secret," but now it was the source of routine planning data for Green Flag exercises. The particular photo came from a series previously taken in preparation for Green Flag 94-3, but fresh bomb damage assessment (BDA) shots were being regularly downlinked from the Space Warfare Center in Colorado Springs. It truly is a new world order!

The crew of Ruben-40, a KC-135R of the 366th Wing's 22nd Aerial Refueling Squadron, flies a tanker mission during Green Flag 94-3. Brigadier General Dave "Marshal" McCloud, the 366th commander, sits between the pilot and copilot. Sitting at the navigation station to the right is Captain Ruben Villa.

That afternoon, General McCloud invited us to accompany him on a mission onboard one of the 22nd ARS KC-135R tankers. Since an opportunity to fly on an actual Green Flag mission is extremely rare for civilians, we gladly accepted, then headed off to have lunch and get ready to go flying. Normally, Green Flag 94-3 would have taken place in the most pleasant time of the year in Las Vegas, but the spring weather had turned into an unseasonable heat wave, with afternoon temperatures over 90°F/32°C. The cooling water spray nozzles over the flightline sunshades were running, and the Gatorade bottles were out for the ground crews. General Griffith had ordered heat precautions for all base personnel, and containers of bottled water were everywhere. We were sweating heavily on the ground, but we had our leather jackets ready for flying that afternoon.

A little after 1300, we drove out to the north end of the base flightline, where the large aircraft were parked. We were directed to the number-one 22nd ARS KC-135R (tail code 62-3572), and climbed aboard through the lower nose hatch into the hot interior. Inside we met our flight crew for today's mission: Captain Ken Rogers (the pilot), Second Lieutenant J.R. Twiford (copilot), Captain Ruben Villa (our navigator), and Staff Sergeant Shawn Hughes (the crew chief and boomer). Every mission is assigned a callsign, used for identification in radio communication. Our callsign today was Ruben-40. The tanker was loaded with over 80,000 lb./36,262 kg. of fuel, with a planned off-load of 42,000 lb./19,090 kg., and a maximum possible off-load of 62,000 lb./28,181 kg. Along with General McCloud was First Lieutenant Don Borchelt, one of the 366th Wing Public Affairs Officers. As soon as we were aboard, the hatches were sealed shut and the engines fired up. As we taxied out for takeoff,

Staff Sergeant Shawn Hughes, the crew chief and boomer of Ruben-40, working hard at his position in the rear of aircraft. Lying on his stomach, he is "flying" the refueling boom of the KC-135 into the refueling receptacle of a receiving aircraft. *JOHN D. GRESHAM*

Sergeant Hughes explained that our job was to top off six F-15E Strike Eagles from the 391st FS, so that the Bold Tigers would be full when they hit the start line at the push. The plan for the Bold Tigers' mission involved a lot of high speed flying down on the deck, which consumes fuel voraciously. We took off behind the E-3 AWACS, followed by another 22nd ARS tanker which would refuel other aircraft of the strike.

As we flew out to our refueling track, Captain Villa was kind enough to let us take turns sitting at the navigator's console, watching the radar screen to take navigation fixes of the surrounding mountain peaks. When we reached our tanking altitude of approximately 25,000 feet/7,620 meters, we began to cruise in a wide racetrack-shaped oval, waiting for Lieutenant Colonel Clawson and the rest of his Bold Tigers to come up and tank. Back at the boomer's position, Sergeant Hughes unstowed the boom and made ready to tank the incoming Strike Eagles.

Suddenly they were there, and Sergeant Hughes went to work, calmly and silently guiding the first of the big fighters into position to take its allotted 7,000 lb./3,181 kg. of fuel. Air-to-air refueling is about the most unnatural activity most of us are ever likely to see. A very big airliner flying about 350 knots/640 kph., full of flammable jet fuel, in direct physical contact with another airplane? The idea is totally demented. I will never be comfortable with it. Nevertheless, Sergeant Hughes and the F-15E crews made it look easy. And one after another, the Strike Eagles cycled into position to take their fuel. Then "Claw" Clawson, down in the lead Strike Eagle, looked up in the middle of tanking, recognized us taking pictures through the window, and calmly

An F-15E Strike Eagle of the 366th Wing's 391st Fighter Squadron (the "Bold Tigers") takes on fuel from a 22nd Aerial Refueling Squadron KC-135R tanker. Note the control fins of the refueling boom, which the boomer uses to guide it into the receiving aircraft's refueling receptacle. *CRAIG E. KASTON*

asked how things looked! Such is the skill from a lifetime of flying combat jets—you can carry on a normal conversation five miles above the earth, flying just ten yards away from an aircraft full of jet fuel, while your plane is locked onto a flying pipe taking on more fuel.

As each jet finished topping off, it would take station, flying in close formation on the tanker, until there were three F-15s on each side of Ruben-40. I was later told that this effectively merged all seven aircraft into one large radar contact, masking their true number from enemy surveillance. Then suddenly, the F-15s were headed down into the mountains, westward towards their targets. Once again, the Blue strike forces hit their targets with a minimum of losses, and the campaign plan moved on to its completion. Our mission done, we headed back to Nellis AFB, and the thought of dinner and some blackjack that night.

Friday, April 15th, 1994—Nellis AFB Officers' Club

By the end of the first week of Green Flag 94-3, the 366th and the other attached units of the Blue Force had racked up an impressive record of damage to targets and defending SAM/AAA sites, as well as killing a small air force of adversary F-16s. The first four days had been a clear victory for the Blue Force. The

A Soviet-built ZSU-23-4 mobile anti-aircraft gun system in the yard of the Nellis AFB threat training facility. This radar-controlled system is one of the significant threats to tactical aircraft, and can be studied by aircrews visiting the base during Red/Green Flag exercises and Weapons School.   *Craig E. Kaston*

366th and its attached units were breaking Red/Green Flag records like crazy, and the staff at the Adversary Tactics Division was starting to get a bit punchy.

So the Red Flag staff controlling the exercise decided something had to be done to keep things interesting: Starting the following Monday, the adversary F-16Cs would be allowed to use tactics simulating the very agile and capable Russian Su-27/35 Flanker (it resembles our F-15 Eagle). The rules of engagement would also be loosened for the Red Forces on the ground, making it easier for them to fire their simulated missiles at Blue aircraft.

We spent the afternoon touring the Threat Training Facility across the street from the Red Flag building, which maintains just about the finest collection of foreign military equipment anywhere in America (it's sometimes called the petting zoo). Everything from a French Roland SAM launcher to Russian MiGs can be viewed here. Just ten years ago, the whole facility was highly classified; but now, the Air Force lets Boy Scouts and civic leaders tour the facility. What a change the end of the Cold War has made!

As the week wore down, and the last mission of the day came in, the thoughts of the aviators and staff officers turned to the observance of a Red/Green Flag tradition: Friday night at the Nellis O-Club. Now it should be said that given the pressures for moral, physical, and mental perfection, such celebrations are kept to a bare minimum. But to remove the camaraderie of Friday night at the club would be to remove one of the most important social institutions in the pilots' lives. Thus, after appropriate assigning of designated drivers and agreement about the time we would all return to the hotel, we headed down to the Nellis AFB Officers' Club for a long evening of "Happy Hour."

Colonel Robin Scott, the 366th Wing Operations Group commander (handling billiard balls at left), referees a game of Crud for members of wing at the Nellis AFB Officers' Club on a Friday night.

JOHN D. GRESHAM

The original O-Club that stood during the glory days of the 1970s and 1980s had been torn down a few years back and replaced by a building now used as the open officers' mess and club. The present building, though splendid in its own way, lacks some of the historic character of the old club. To make up for this, the builders of the new facility kept the old club's tabletops (where generations of fighter pilots had burned in their names and messages with woodburning irons) and recycled them as wall panels. As you walk by, you see the names of aces and wild weasels, POWs and MIAs, Medal of Honor winners, and MiG killers; and it is hard not to stare at names of people you know, people you will never know, and those you wish you had known.

As the bar area fills up, the evening begins to get more lively. The music is a mix of rock and country, and it is *loud*! Every generation of USAF fliers has gone to war with their own brand of music. Where World War II vets took Glenn Miller and Tommy Dorsey records with them, and the Vietnam-era fliers had Jimi Hendrix and Janis Joplin, today's aircrews seem to enjoy country/rock music as the tunes for their times. Back in the '80s, the old days of Red Flag, Friday night was the time for macho contests or even fights in the parking lot, but such behavior does not fly in today's Air Force. Luckily, there is a game called Crud to absorb the competitive energy of the aircrews. Crud is an odd little contest, with elements of soccer, racquetball, and billiards all mixed together. Played on a pool table with a pair of billiard balls, it is a full-contact sport for teams of two or more. The idea is to use a cue ball to hit the other ball (you use your bare hands to throw the cue ball), while it bounces around the table. You play in ordered relays, and either a break in the order or a missed ball results in a score. The game requires a referee, and this is inevitably the senior officer present. Normally this would have been General McCloud, but he was attending General Loh's annual wing commanders' conference, so Colonel Robin Scott took over. The Nellis O-Club bar has the finest playing area, called a Crud Pit, in the country. The walls are lined with sandbags, and there is plenty of space to set down long-necked bottles of beer (the favorite of the pilots) while you are playing.

As the evening wore on, and the music got slower so the couples could dance, some of us, including Lieutenant Colonels Clawson and "Boom-Boom" Turcott, moved to a corner to talk. Toasts were drunk to departed friends, and everyone went their way for the weekend. By midnight, only the AOC staff was still working, the lights in their tent city still glowing as they planned the Phase III strikes for the second week of Green Flag 94-3.

Monday, April 18th, 1994

Every April 18th the USAF commemorates Jimmy Doolittle's bombing raid on Japan (Doolittle had recently passed away). This day, however, safety was uppermost in the minds of the Green Flag controllers: Most fatal Red/Green Flag accidents take place on Monday after the weekend break. Throughout the day, especially at the briefings, the safety rules were hammered into the aircrews as they were admonishied to "take it easy" while they got back into the "groove" of flying. A special safety video was played for the crews just before they headed to their aircraft. With a deafening musical backup from ZZ-Top playing "Viva Las Vegas" (appropriate, don't you think?), it was five minutes of near misses and accidents that will *never* be shown to the public. The idea was to shock the fliers a bit and make them think.

We sat in on the afternoon briefing in anticipation of watching the live action on the big screen RFMDS (Red Flag Measurement and Debrief System), while the afternoon strikes hit their targets. There were new wrinkles in the balance of forces this day, as the Red Force got their new simulated Flanker fighters, and the Red ground units got their new rules of engagement. There was a shift away from using live ordnance and decoys, since they were in short supply. That morning, we had watched LANTIRN videotapes showing LGB and IIR Maverick missile deliveries, and it was easy to see why the uprange target arrays had taken such a beating the previous week. There is a general shortage of targets at Nellis AFB, and the range crews have to be creative to keep the ranges stocked with fresh ones.

Mother Nature had also decided to spice up the exercise with some variety. The weather had changed, and layers of heavy cloud hung over the northern range areas. Extra precautions would be needed to guarantee deconfliction between aircraft, along with special weather reconnaissance flights to determine if conditions were good enough to run the missions safely. The morning flight had gone all right, but eight hours of the desert sun had stirred up the air considerably, making the weather a bit dicey.

By 1400, we were comfortably seated in the viewing theater in the Red Flag building, staring at a projected screen display of the situation up on the northern ranges. We had a "God's-eye view" of the action on both sides, and we could identify various aircraft by color codes. The radio chatter on the squadron nets was piped in, giving us the feeling that we were watching some sort of bizarre video game with an audio track. Today's Blue Force targets were restrikes on SCUD and supply convoy targets that needed to be hit again. From the Red Force, with their "new" airplanes and enhanced ROE, came new tactics. They would attempt to disrupt the strike by attacking Blue's High Value Heavy Airframe Aircraft (HVHAA) such as the E-3, the Rivet Joint, or the tankers. Using a decoy force of aggressor F-16s down low, they would bait the 390th's "wall of Eagles"; then they would send two other F-16s into a ballistic "zoom" climb over the top of the F-15s to get at the HVHAAs. This would draw off the escorting Eagles from the strike forces, allowing regenerated aggressor aircraft more freedom of action against the strike aircraft. Red had tried this tactic unsuccessfully several times before, but the combination of the weather and the new rules made them think it might work this time.

The weather recon birds almost canceled the mission, but at the last minute, they allowed the exercise to continue with flight restrictions between 15,000 and 25,000 feet/4,572 and 6,720 meters. The wall of Eagles moved forward, and the "push" call launched the Blue strike force toward the targets. It was a mess. The cloud deck divided the sky into high and low zones, creating two separate fights for the Eagles. The two aggressor F-16s made their move over the top, but they did not go unnoticed. The AWACS aircraft saw what was happening and called for support from the F-15s. The two Red Falcons got close, but not close enough for a shot at the HVHAAs before the Eagles drove them off. Still, the Eagle drivers were agitated that night over dinner. They would have to find ways to adjust their "wall" tactics for bad weather.

And then it happened. Everyone was already on the way out when an emergency call came in that one of the U.S. Army OH-58C helicopters was down. . . and it was bad. Everyone went silent. The 66th RQS rushed a HH-60G Pave Hawk up to the crash site to look for survivors. But there were no survivors. Both crewmen, officers from the 2-229 Attack Helicopter Regiment at Fort Rucker, Alabama, had perished in the crash. It was the first fatal accident to take place during a Flag exercise in over three years, and it cast a pall over the rest of the day.

In early 1995, the causes of the crash are still being assessed, though it appears that the chopper hit a rock wall of a mountain while returning to Indian Springs. The old Monday-after-the-weekend jinx had struck again, and the Green Flag staff was not happy. They immediately went on a tear with the aircrews to review safety and ROE instructions. Dinner that night did not taste very good.

Three Block 52 F-16Cs of the 366th Wing's 389th Fighter Squadron peel away from a 22nd Aerial Refueling Squadron KC-135R tanker, on their way to targets on the Nellis AFB ranges during Green Flag 94-3. *JOHN D. GRESHAM*

Tuesday, April 19th, 1994 —
Adversary Tactics Operations Center

Today we would view the morning mission from the Adversary Tactics Control Center, then fly an afternoon tanker mission with the 22nd ARS. Our host, Major Steve Cutshell, gave us the Red side of the Green Flag story. He confessed that the 366th had given the Red Force challenges they had never experienced before, and that subsequent exercises might require more Air National Guard F-16s to reinforce the Red air forces. On the other hand, the ground-based Red forces had done well, considering the age of the equipment. The wily contractor personnel who live uprange and operate the emitters have years of experience. Indeed, they could probably teach the Russians a thing or two about how to use their systems! Red communications jamming against the Have Quick II radios had been fairly effective, though it tended to wipe out their own communications. And Red's radar jamming usually worked, though the newest U.S. airborne radars with advanced signal processing can out-fox most ground-based jammers, or just burn through them with raw power.

That afternoon, we headed back out to the HVHAA ramp, and were pleasantly surprised to find we were assigned to the same aircraft (62-3572) and crew we rode with the previous week. This time we were the second tanker in the flight, called "Refit," and our callsign was Ruben-50. We would refuel six F-16s from the 389th FS that were going to strike targets on the southern side of the range, as well as a pair of F-4G Wild Weasel aircraft from the 561st FS at Nellis AFB. The Vipers would each get 5,000 lb./2,272 kg. of fuel, with 8,000 lb./3,636 kg. going to each of the Weasels. Since the F-4s had the shortest "legs" of any aircraft in the strike force, they would tank last, to be as full as possible when the push to the targets came. Takeoff went smoothly, though

An F-4G Wild Weasel aircraft from the 57th Wing's 561st Fighter Squadron pulls away from a 22nd Aerial Refueling Squadron KC-135R tanker during Green Flag 94-3. These defense-suppression aircraft are rapidly being replaced by F-16Cs equipped with the AQS-213 HARM Targeting System pod.

JOHN D. GRESHAM

there was a lot more cloud cover this afternoon, a residue of the previous day's thunderstorms. This made for a rough ride, and Sergeant Hughes's skills were taxed to keep the tanking on schedule. He had particular difficulty with the old refueling receptacles of the Phantoms; their tricky (and now worn-out) refueling probe latching mechanism had trouble establishing and maintaining a solid connection. Nevertheless, he managed to fill everyone up, and they all made the mission push on time.

Then, just as we were scheduled to head home, there was an urgent radio call from the Blue Force air-to-air mission commander. Several aggressor F-16s had finally made it over the top, and were chasing several of the HVHAAs, including us! Luckily, a couple of Eagles hunted them down, but it was now clearly too risky to leave the big birds unescorted during missions. For the rest of the week, until it was certain that all the airborne Red aircraft had been killed, there would be fighter cover for the HVHAAs.

Friday, April 22nd, 1994

As the last missions finished up, the 366th and the other units prepared to pack up and head back to their home bases. While the Gunfighters had "won," that really was not the intention of the exercise or the true measure of what was achieved. Much more important: The composite wing concept was validated, at least as far as the resources of Nellis were capable of testing it.

For the 366th Wing itself, there was a mass of data to be analyzed, assessed, and acted upon when they got back to Mountain Home AFB. As the last missions were flown and the ground crews started packing up their gear onto the FAST tankers, everyone could take pride in his or her own contribution. The raw steel that General Hinton had passed on to General McCloud the previous year was now a sharp sword, though it might still require some polishing. That could wait for tomorrow. Today the Gunfighters were going home to their families. As we joined them, it gave us much to reflect on, for we had seen more than any civilian had seen before about how the USAF gets ready for war.

Afterwards

Later in 1994, we returned to Mountain Home AFB to see how the wing was implementing the changes that emerged from Green Flag 94-3. In the few months since the deployment, many jobs in the wing had changed hands. When we arrived, Dave McCloud had less than a week left in command of the 366th; his next assignment was a staff job for General Joe Ralston (now the ACC commander) in the Operations Directorate of the Air Staff. This was a good omen for his future promotability to lieutenant general (he made the list "under the zone" in early 1995). McCloud's replacement, Brigadier General "Lanny" Trapp, came from the A-10 wing at Davis-Monthan AFB in Arizona, and chose an F-15E Strike Eagle as the new "Wing King" aircraft. Colonel Robin Scott had left to attend the U.S. Army War College at Carlisle Barracks, Pennsylvania. Lieutenant Colonel Clawson, now promoted to full Colonel, moved over to the wing staff. Roger "Boom-Boom" Turcott, who had given John Gresham his ride, moved up to command the "Bold Tigers." And the 34th BS became fully operational with its B-1Bs. It conducted its first Global Power/Global Reach mission just six months after "standing up." The steady flow of new personnel is a positive sign that the wing is alive and healthy.

Finally, there was one more big exercise for the 366th Wing in the fall of 1994—Joint Task Force (JTF)-95. JTF-95 was planned to team elements of the new Atlantic Command (a carrier battle group and a Marine expeditionary unit) in a combined exercise. But just as the exercise was kicking off, the U.S. intervention in Haiti and an emergency deployment to Kuwait took away the Atlantic Command assets, wiping out the entire JTF-95 exercise package. In our "new world order," global events seem to be keeping military units too busy to train for the future. In a time when we are contemplating further force structure cutbacks, that is something to think about.

Operation Golden Gate
Southeast Asia

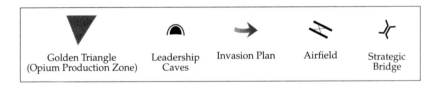

| Golden Triangle (Opium Production Zone) | Leadership Caves | Invasion Plan | Airfield | Strategic Bridge |

Operation Golden Gate. *Jack Ryan Enterprises, Ltd., by Laura Alpher*

Roles and Missions: The 366th Wing in the Real World

As we have seen, the power a composite wing like the 366th can bring to bear in a time of war is impressive, possibly even decisive. But how might this power actually be used in a crisis? The question is often on the minds of a number of folks, from the JCS Tank in the Pentagon to the flightline at Mountain Home AFB, Idaho. (Currently, only one of the three USAF composite wings assigned to ACC, the 23rd at Pope AFB, South Carolina, has ever been deployed during a crisis.) The decision when and where to use the 366th, with its unique capabilities, will be a tough judgment call for the national command authorities who will order it deployed and the regional CinCs who will command it during a crisis.

The following scenario is designed to show you some of the possibilities. I hope it will help you understand the capabilities of the 366th Wing and of modern airpower in general. The composite wings of ACC, along with the carrier air wings (CVWs) on our aircraft carriers, are going to be our aerial fire brigades for the next generation or so. If the last few years have been any indication, the coming decades will be violent enough to make the Cold War look no more frightening than an election in Chicago.

Operation Golden Gate–Vietnam, May 2000

The inevitability of the event seemed so clear in retrospect, yet this did not mitigate the surprise. South Vietnam, once deluged by American and other Western influences, simply never bought into the Marxist-Leninist orthodoxy of the North. And while Hanoi was able to make it stick for a generation, the demise of their governing philosophy everywhere else in the world only encouraged the South to go its own way. The leader was a former chieftan with the Central Office for South Vietnam (COSVN–the former Viet Cong headquarters) with his own reasons for rebellion. Only 5 feet/1.5 meters tall and thin, even by Vietnamese standards, Duc Oanh had been an earnest and effective foe of the RVN and its American protectors. Wounded twice in combat actions and nearly buried alive by a B-52 Arc Light mission in 1970, he'd carried the banner for his beliefs, only to be shunted to a minor post office job when the North finally overran Saigon in 1975. What began as personal resentment in Duc's mind grew into a dream as he watched the North stagnate while the South fought the ideological reins well enough to begin something akin to genuine national development. He saw the perversion of his people's revolution by the ruling council of the North as final proof of the folly of the old men who ruled this corner of the world. One day, the dream formed into action.

Many former revolutionary soldiers shared Duc's feelings.

The coup that followed was anything but bloodless. In eight violent hours of darkness, combat veterans of the Vietnamese Army systematically assassinated their own senior officers during parties following the twenty-fifth anniversary Liberation Day ceremonies on April 30th. By dawn most of the military formations in the southern half of Vietnam had either been decapitated or had new leadership. And from Radio Saigon (nobody but foreigners had ever called it Ho Chih Minh City) went out a cry of renewed Southern independence that caught every news and intelligence agency in the world by total surprise.

Hanoi's first reaction was predictably intemperate.

The People's Republic of China was the only nation with any inkling of what was happening—Duc had established covert links to that government, whose hatred of Hanoi was every bit as deep as his own—and by noon the first international recognition of the revolutionary government had been announced. As for the Americans, the timing was too close to an American election. The President—himself a veteran of the aerial campaign against Hanoi in the 1970s and one of a generation of former warriors with a personal promise to make that lost war right—had to act.

Communist Party Headquarters, Saigon, May 1st, 2000, 0930 Hours

The Party headquarters in Saigon had originally been built by the French as Saigon's city hall. The wide corridors, arched windows, and high ceilings with slowly rotating fans gave the building an air of faded colonial elegance. But the wiring was almost as bad as the plumbing. The emergency diesel generator in the basement had been delivered from East Germany in the 1970s, and was inoperable for lack of parts. Brownouts and complete power outages in the city had grown more frequent lately, as the arthritic Vietnamese economy and crumbling infrastructure were increasingly unable to meet payments on oil shipments, even at the subsidized "friendship price" the Chinese comrades offered to help prop up one of the world's three remaining Communist states.

Vu Xuan Linh, Chairman of the city's Party Committee and effective ruler of a metropolitan region of over five million people, was not surprised when the lights went out. That happened often enough. He *was* surprised, though, when he heard bursts of automatic fire in the corridor outside, and a ragged crowd of men armed with sticks, hand tools, and a few AKMs taken from the still-warm bodies of the dead guards outside burst into the office, grabbed his speechless body, and hurled it from the third-floor window. As the pavement rushed up to smash him, he only had time to wonder why the crowd in the plaza outside was waving those tattered, forbidden yellow flags with three horizontal red stripes.

Tho Xuan Airfield, Vietnam,
May 1st, 2000, 1445 Hours

The phone lines to the South were down, and the few military posts that had not thrown down their weapons or joined the rebels were getting out only fragmentary reports. The rebels seemed to have some sort of electronic jammers (ham radio gear actually) and knew how to use them. But the CNN news feed on TV in the ready room of the 923rd Fighter Regiment was clear and chilling. Saigon, Danang, Hue, even small provincial towns like Dalat and Ban Me Thuot, all seemed to have broken out in a mad carnival of mutiny, vandalism, looting, and murder of government and party officials. Colonel Nguyen Tri Loc, chief political officer of the Vietnam People's Air Force (VNPAF) Fighter Command, could see that he was facing the greatest challenge of his career. He would have to send his pilots into action against their own people.

"Airmen," he said quietly to the two dozen pilots in the ready room, "this is the most serious crisis Vietnam has faced in a generation. Your grandfathers shed their blood to drive out the French imperialists. Your fathers shed their blood to drive out the Americans. If this criminal counterrevolutionary uprising is not crushed swiftly, all their sacrifices will have been for nothing, and your children will become slaves of international monopoly capitalism. Remember your training, and your aim will be true. The Party and the Nation are depending on you."

The pilots looked straight ahead, stood to attention, and filed out to the flight line. There were no sidelong glances or murmurs of conversation. The colonel had no idea what they were thinking, and that made him uneasy. The 923rd was trained for the ground attack role, operating some 24 Su-22M-3 Fitters. Twenty were flyable today, an excellent maintenance performance considering the difficulty of keeping the temperamental Tumansky engines running without regular factory overhauls. The range of over 600 miles/983 km. for this mission would limit the ordnance each could deliver on downtown Saigon to either two pods of 57mm rockets, or two napalm canisters. The most urgent target was the secret police headquarters. If the rebels could secure the building and its voluminous records, it would be a disaster. (The Party leaders had learned well the lessons of the overthrow of the German Democratic Republic.) After striking the city hall, the broadcasting stations, the Caravelle Hotel, and other likely centers of the revolt, the planes would recover at Danang, if that airfield was still secure, or alternatively at Cam Ranh Bay, then refuel and return to Tho Xuan to re-arm. There were no target folders, but every pilot was given a large-scale city map. The latest weather satellite pictures indicated that after some morning showers, it would be clear over most of the South. There was no up-to-date reconnaissance beyond what every pilot could see on CNN. The air defense missile sites around Bien Hoa and Tan Son Nhut airport had been thoroughly sabotaged by their loyal crews before they were evacuated, but there was no way of knowing how many hand-held SAMs and anti-aircraft guns had fallen into the hands of the rebels. The regiment took off in five four-ship waves, spaced a few minutes apart.

HQ PACAF (U.S. Pacific Command Air Forces), Hickam AFB, Hawaii

"Looks as if the VNPAF is making a full court press," General Russ Dewey, commander of the U.S. Pacific Air Forces, observed as the situation display flickered with the latest updates. "We haven't seen this much activity out of them since, oh, hell, back in '72."

"There's still no word from the Pentagon," Admiral Roy Shapiro, the Commander in Chief, Pacific (CINCPAC), replied. "Not that we could do much right now, even if we got a green light." You didn't have to see the gold wings above the admiral's chestful of ribbons to tell that he was an aviator. He had flown off carrier decks in the Gulf of Tonkin, out of Subic Bay and Clark Field in the Philippines, out of Andersen AFB on Guam, the Marine base at Kadena on Okinawa, and a dozen other places that were now mostly memories. It was the kind of situation that was every CinC's worst nightmare. Another Major Regional Contingency (MRC) was shaping up, and the nearest airpower that U.S. Pacific Command controlled was exactly two squadrons of 8th TFW F-16s in Korea, two thousand long, long air miles away.

Downtown Saigon, May 3rd, 2000, 2035 Hours

There was still some daylight fading in the western sky as the planes came in from the north low and fast. Because the mission had been laid on in a hurry and the ground crews had humped whatever ordnance was immediately available in the closest bunkers at Gia Lam and Hue, they had been loaded with 250 kg. incendiary and fragmentation bombs.

The slaughter in the streets, thronged with celebrating crowds, was appalling. Months later the International Committee of the Red Cross estimated that over five thousand people had been killed outright and about fifteen thousand seriously burned or injured. No one would ever know for sure—the provisional city government committee reluctantly had to order the dead buried in mass graves for reasons of public health. Some of the fires burned for days, but not as hotly as the wave of rage and revulsion that swept through the normally docile and apolitical Saigonese population. Even worse from the point of view of the world press was what happened to the visitors that made up Vietnam's major cash industry—tourism. Better than two hundred foreigners, mostly businessmen from Europe or Japan, were checked in at the Caravelle

Hotel in Saigon. Most of them were eating an early dinner or drinking in the world-famous bar. There were also about a hundred elderly American Vietnam War veterans in the country, invited by the Hanoi government to visit old battlefields and exorcise ancient demons. The original idea behind their visit, in fact, had been to speed along the normalization of U.S.-Vietnamese relations. Unfortunately for them, and for Hanoi, the pilots of four MiG-27 attack fighters had been told that the Caravelle was under rebel control.

It is one of the realities of our time that satellite news networks are the finest intelligence-gathering agencies in the world. Though Hanoi denied conducting the strike, a Sky News TV crew from Britain had it on tape, with the yellow stars clearly visible on the MiGs. The tape was uplinked immediately to the global satellite network.

The United Nations Security Council, New York City, May 4th, 2000

The first Security Council resolution came up for a vote within hours of the airing of the tape; the pictures from Saigon had shocked even the hardened diplomats of this cynical group.

RESOLUTION 1397

The Security Council,

Recognizing the belligerent status of the Provisional Government of the Republic of Vietnam,

Alarmed by the bombing of Saigon by aircraft of the Democratic Republic of Vietnam, and continuing attacks on civilian targets in southern Vietnam by land, naval, and air forces of the DRV,

Determining that there exists a breach of international peace and security by the DRV,

Acting under Articles 39 and 40 of the Charter of the United Nations:

1. *Condemns* the DRV attack on the Republic of Vietnam;

2. *Demands* the immediate and unconditional withdrawal of DRV forces to positions North of the 17th parallel;

3. *Calls upon* the Provisional Government of the Republic of Vietnam and the Government of the Democratic Republic of Vietnam to begin immediately intensive negotiations for the resolution of their differences and supports all efforts in this

regard, and especially those of the Association of Southeast Asian Nations;

4. *Orders* that the DRV shall be the object of a UN-sanctioned air, ground, and naval quarantine of all products considered supportive to military efforts against RVN;

5. *Authorizes* that member nations providing forces for the quarantine may use military force consistent with their own security, and the enforcement of the previously mentioned action;

6. *Decides* to meet again as necessary to consider further steps to ensure compliance with the present resolution.

The motion had been proposed by the ambassador from France, the one-time colonial ruler of the region. It called for a UN-enforced isolation of the South until such time as UN-supervised elections could be conducted. Some speculated that the French proposal was offered in order to soothe old feelings of guilt going back three generations. The other Security Council members barely had time to call in to their various departments and ministries of State to obtain instructions. The surprise came when the vote by the permanent members was taken.

"The United States of America?"

"Yes."

"The United Kingdom?"

"Affirmative."

"The Republic of France?"

"Oui."

"The Russian Federation?"

"Da."

"Japan?"

"Hai!"

"The People's Republic of China?"

There was a long, tense pause while everyone waited for the simultaneous translation. "Madame Chairman, China abstains." In capitals around the world, the great and powerful sucked in their breath.

The White House, Washington D.C., May 5th, 2000, 0015 Hours

"How the hell does the UN Security Council expect us to back them up when they won't even tell us what they want ahead of time?" the National Security Advisor raged to the President, the Cabinet, and the Joint Chiefs of Staff.

"Mitch," the President said in his best soothing fighter jock voice, "we have a unique opportunity here with regards to Southeast Asia, and I intend to take full advantage of it."

"I agree, Mr. President, but what do we use for bases and deployment support? We've gutted our forces in the region and have almost zero influence within the governments that run those places," the National Security Advisor pointed out correctly. "And on top of that, we're down to zero carrier battle groups in the Western Pacific, after that little problem with the *Eisenhower* battle group last week."

A Cypriot supertanker outbound from the Persian Gulf had plowed into the side of the USS *Dwight D. Eisenhower* (CVN-68), killing over fifty U.S. sailors and causing a massive hole in the supercarrier amidships. The tanker sank. With the big ship under tow to Newport News, Virginia, for repairs at the builder's yard, it would be at least three weeks until another battle group could be assembled and dispatched to the Western Pacific.

"This is going nowhere," thought the Chairman of the Joint Chiefs, and he noisily cleared his throat to gain the attention of the assembled group. When he spoke, it was with the controlled authority that had made him the first Marine to ever hold the post. "I should point out that nations do not have allies, but common interests. Things are getting a bit crazy over there. Which means a lot of people over there are eager for the craziness to go away. Which means I think we can count on the leadership of that region offering us some options, if we're just ready to make use of them. Let me make several suggestions." As he spoke, and wrote ideas on a white board at the end of the conference room, a few thin smiles began to crack on the faces of the attendees. The National Security Advisor was among those smiling.

Communist Party Headquarters, Hanoi, May 6th, 0345 Hours

It had been a long night for the Leadership Council of the Communist Party of Vietnam, and the meeting was still not over. A bunch of elderly, has-been revolutionaries, thought General Truong Le, the Vietnamese Defense Minister, trying to hold on to the memory of a war long since gone, with ideals long since dead. The Premier himself may have been a veteran of Dien Bien Phu and Hue, but even those in this room did not have the personal courage to point out that his service had been as a staff headquarters political officer. Now these old men were going to decide the fate of two nations, and they were not viewing the situation with any sense of reality.

"We will not stand for this interference in our internal politics by the capitalist powers," stated the Premier flatly.

"What would you have us do against the power of nations like America and Russia?" asked the Defense Minister. "We are a third-rate power facing the most technologically advanced societies in the world."

"Precisely the kind of negativism that our Great Leader Ho had to overcome during the Liberation decades ago. Where would we be now if they had listened then to defeatist drones like you?" barked the Premier. "I'll tell you what we are going to do to the weak-willed dogs that call themselves the leaders of countries," he continued. "We're going to declare a blockade around the whole of the so-called-RVN, just like the one the UN thinks they can slap around us. Then we'll see who chokes first!" He finished the statement by slapping the meaty palm of his hand on the polished conference table, stunning the assembled members of the council.

"But that means that we are granting de facto recognition of the RVN in the process," protested the Foreign Minister.

"I should also point out that this action carries with it certain international responsibilities, and is almost certain to place our forces directly into conflict with the UN forces that will be deployed to this area," said General Truong Le calmly, "and that their so-called rules of engagement will never be as insane as the ones they imposed on themselves during the Wars of Liberation."

"I speak for the Council," said the Premier coldly. "The action will go forward as I have ordered it!" Nobody on the Council tried to protest.

Mountain Home AFB, Idaho,
May 6th, 2000, 2300 Hours

No Vietnam veterans flew tactical aircraft for the U.S. Air Force . . . they hadn't in years. A few senior officers remembered going "downtown," but these were generals; and if they were allowed in fighters at all, they had to satisfy themselves with two-seaters. But the colonels and the majors were veterans of another air war. They knew what it was like to fight where their targets were *not* picked by a politician in the Oval Office.

Now the 366th logistics officer took her place in front of the map. "Okay, ladies and gentlemen, we're going to run another no-fly-zone operation with a possible air offensive somewhere in the rub," she said. "Now, where the hell are we going?"

"The F-16s and tankers will bed down initially at Takhli, about one hundred miles north of Bangkok. Seems that the Thais got real cooperative when the bombing in Saigon started a few days ago. In fact, everyone has been that way." The officer grinned. "Good facilities. The Royal Thai AF has operated F-16s there for years. Excellent runway—it was built long enough to handle 'hot day' takeoffs of F-105s. The rest of the wing, for now, will go to U-Tapao, right on the coast about seventy miles southeast of Bangkok. The facilities are great.

We can bring seagoing tankers of jet fuel and munition ships right into the port. We're going to forward-base the Combat SAR guys up-country at a Thai Army airfield called Sakon Nakhon and a little opium-smuggling airstrip called Chiang Rai in the middle of the Golden Triangle. It's hairy up there; we'll need some heavy security on the ground. The guys down at Fort Benning at the JFK School are sending some instructors and volunteers to take care of that problem. Meanwhile we'll be working to reactivate old air bases at Udon and Korat about two hundred miles northeast of Bangkok for any other coalition nations that send in forces later. Great locations, but the Royal Thai Air Force abandoned them a few years ago, and it'll take a lot of engineer work to make the jungle and cobras give 'em back."

Brigadier General Jack "the Knife" Perry, the 366th commander, looked at the map, and memories flooded back. For the first time in years, he desperately wanted a cigarette. "Thank you, Colonel," he told his logistics officer, who seemed much too young for the silver eagles on her shoulder boards. "Now how do we get there, Kurt?" He turned to his operations officer.

"The State Department guys are still twisting arms over some of the overflight rights, but it looks like we can do a Great Circle." That was the shortest and hence most economical route between any two points on the globe. "First stage: Mountain Home to Elmendorf, Alaska. If the weather permits, we can put some tankers at Shemya for refueling, but the ramp space there is tight. Second stage: Elmendorf to Yokota and Misawa, Japan. The Russians will let us base a squadron of ANG tankers at Petropavlovsk, as long as we buy the fuel from them and pay in hard currency. In emergencies they say we can divert to any of their fields in Kamchatka or Sakhalin. No diplomatic problem with Yokota and Misawa so far, but the Japs want us in and out fast, with *no* publicity. Third stage is Misawa to Taiwan. The ROC Air Force is rolling out the red carpet. We can use the civil airports at Taipei International, Tai Chung, Kao Hsiung, and all their military fields. No way to maintain OPSEC"—Operations Security—"on such short notice, but the ROCs will try to keep the media camera crews out of the landing patterns. The last stage gets complicated. We had planned on staging tankers out of Kai Tak Airport at Hong Kong; but the Chicoms said, not just no, but *Hell, NO!* Seems they don't ever want to be accused of a stab in the back, like Poles accused the Russians back in '39. So, we have to pre-position tankers at Manila, Kota Kinbalu in Malaysia, and Brunei. The Filipinos are gouging us for landing rights, so we can't count on Manila. We can get some Australian tanker support out of Singapore, but we're still working on how much."

The general nodded. Good staff work on short notice. His scarred index finger traced a line on the map, skirting the Chinese mainland air-defense buffer zone. "How about a shortcut across Vietnam?" he said, with a wicked grin.

"No way, sir. That's not the way we've trained to deploy," the ops officer said with an answering smile. "By that point our crews will be tired, and we don't want to risk tangling with their air defenses before we've had a chance to knock them down a little. It would be a bad start for the mission if we lost a few planes just to save a couple of hours' flight time."

The general reluctantly nodded. There was no point in staging another "Doolittle Raid" as a stunt. The way to win an air campaign was by the book.

Over the South China Sea, May 7th, 2000, 1500 Hours

It had been a long trip, and double issues of "piddle packs" had been the order of the day. For the aircrews of the 366th's A+ Package on their way to Thailand, it had been a day of contrasts. From the desert of Idaho, to the cold mountains of Alaska, now down to the equatorial jungles. They had one more refueling to go in about an hour, and were looking forward to seeing the tankers. The eight F-15Es of the 391st TFS, in two four-ship formations spaced a few miles apart, were cruising southwest at their most economical speed and altitude, about 470 knots/859.5 kph. at 20,000 feet. The Strike Eagles were combat loaded with a mix of GBU-24 LGBs, AGM-65 Mavericks, GBU-15s, and three 630 gallon/2,377 liter fuel tanks, as well as the usual load of two AIM-120 and two AIM-9 air-to-air missiles. They were accompanied by eight F-16Cs of the 389th, each armed with a pair of AGM-88 HARM missiles, an AN/ASQ-213 HARM Targeting System (HTS) pod, an external ALQ-131 jamming pod, two AIM-9s, two AIM-120s, and a pair of 370 gallon/1,396 liter fuel tanks. These two groups were being escorted by eight F-15Cs of the 390th FS, armed with a full load of four AIM-120 AMRAAM and four AIM-9 Sidewinder AAMs. These last were headed "downhill" to 18,000 feet/5,486 meters, where they would meet up with a pair of KC-10A tankers to top off for the final run into Thailand.

At the moment, each group was doing different things to prepare the aircraft for the planned embargo of the North, as well as staying ready for any trouble from the Vietnamese off to the west. The ROE were *Warning Yellow— Weapons Hold,* which allowed the fighters to defend themselves if they were threatened in any way. The UN resolution clearly allowed them to do so, though everyone in the formation was quietly hoping that this contingency would not involve any expenditure of ordnance or loss of life. The F-15Es were testing their LANTIRN targeting pods, and were using their APG-70 radars to shoot a series of radar maps to help with the target planning that was already going on in Fast-3, the command-and-control KC-135R of the 22nd ARS, which was already coming in to land at U-Tapao. The F-15Cs were testing their JTIDS data links to make sure that they functioned as advertised. And the F-16Cs of the 389th were calibrating their HTS pods and Improved Data Modems (IDMs) on known SAM sites along the Vietnamese shore to their right. The F-16s were all "netted" together, and the leader of the second flight had just turned on his gun camera video recorder when the radar warning receiver began to bleep. "What the ****," Captain Julio "Frito" Salazar, lead pilot of the second flight of F-16s, said. "Somebody down there is tracking us!"

The frigates *Dau Tranh* ("Struggle") and *Giai Phong* ("Liberation") were the pride of the Vietnamese Navy. Originally built for the Soviet KGB as heavily armed Krivak-III maritime patrol vessels, they had been acquired by Hanoi for little more than their scrap value and carefully refitted with French weapons systems and Japanese electronics, though they retained the twin ZIF-122/ SA-N-4 Gecko missile launcher forward. The cost of maintaining the ships was high, but the Party leaders judged that the political cost of conceding control of the Gulf of Tonkin and the South China Sea was even higher. Following standing orders, the ships fired up their gas turbine engines and raced out to sea at the first sign of trouble, lest they be trapped in Haiphong harbor by mines. Rear Admiral Vu Hung Van, flying his flag in *Dau Tranh,* had mission orders to blockade the southern Vietnamese coast, isolating the rebels while the People's Army crushed them.

"Admiral, aircraft bearing thirty degrees, at least ten, maybe more, in tactical formation. Definitely not friendly. If they maintain course and speed they will be within missile range in about five minutes."

"That will be our old friends the Americans," said the admiral, as an enigmatic smile crossed his weather-beaten face. "Let us prepare to welcome them." CNN had provided live coverage of the first movements of the American aircraft, and he knew what was coming. He also knew his duty and orders, and punched the button on the console for General Quarters.

Things began to happen at electronic speeds, beyond the range of human reflexes. As the fire control computers on the Vietnamese frigates began to develop target solutions, they commanded the tracking radars to switch to a higher pulse rate. At the same moment, HTS pods on the F-16s immediately detected this ominous development and alerted the pilots flashing the code STA 8 in two spots in the corner of the digital display of their ALR-56M radar-warning receivers (RWRs). It also told them that the Pop Group fire control radars of the two ships were in a firing mode, ready to launch. Captain Salazar reacted quickly. He immediately called a warning to the other aircraft of the package, and began to rapidly move his fingers over the HOTAS controls on his control stick and throttle. As he did, he called to his wingman, 1st Lieutenant Jack "the Bear" Savage, to hit the northernmost target with his HARMS, while he took the southern one. The IDMs linked the data from the HTS pods, and in a matter of seconds both aircraft had range and bearing solutions to their targets. It took only a few seconds more for the two pilots to set up the HARM missiles and launch them. Then the pilots turned on their jamming pods, set up their countermeasures dispensers, and made ready to evade the SAMs of the two frigates.

Ten seconds after the General Quarters alarm sounded, four SA-N-4 Gecko/4K33 missiles rose from the ships, while the four HARM missiles descended from the planes. The range was down to 5 miles/8.2 km. as the 100mm gun turrets of the frigates began slewing toward the black specks in the clear tropical sky. Diving in at over 4,500 feet per second/1,372 meters per second, the HARMs won the race. The proximity fuzes detonated above the ships, showering them with thousands of tungsten fragments and chunks of still-burning rocket motor fuel. Admiral Vu and his bridge crew were dead before they knew what had happened. The fragments from the HARMs' warheads virtually shredded the two frigates, starting fires in the forward weapons magazines of both ships, as well as rupturing the fuel tanks. The SA-N-4s, deprived of terminal guidance, followed a graceful ballistic arc until the fuzes timed out and they self-destructed.

The lead Strike Eagle had captured the whole engagement on the videotape recorder of his LANTIRN targeting pod. Two hours later, just a few minutes after he touched down in Thailand, the imagery of the first shots fired in what was now being called Operation Golden Gate was being relayed by satellite datalink to Washington. The good parts were rushed through declassification by a rather sharp Pentagon PAO, just in time to make the evening news. The Vietnamese would regret firing the first shots at the 366th. *Giai Phong* limped into Cam Ranh Bay, where the surviving crew mutinied and joined the rebellion. *Dau Tranh* blew up and sank when the fires reached the forward missile magazine. A Chinese freighter picked up the survivors a few days later. They were neither grateful for the rescue nor well treated by their rescuers.

Hanoi, Vietnam,
May 7th, 2000, 1500 Hours

The Military Committee of the Party had ordered all senior cadres to study diligently the lessons of the 1991 Gulf War. If the Americans, or even worse, the damned Chinese came again (they had attempted an invasion of Vietnam in 1979), the command-and-control centers of *this* nation would not be caught sitting around the capital waiting to be decapitated. The top-secret dispersal and evacuation plan was worked out in detail, but the details were changed at random intervals, and there were never any practice exercises, to reduce the risk that a high-level defection could fatally compromise the plan.

The first lesson of the 1991 Persian Gulf War for the leadership of bandit nations was that underground bunkers were a trap. They would be pinpointed by satellite reconnaissance, targeted, and smashed by precision-guided penetrating bombs. So the Party would take refuge in the vast network of natural caverns that abounded in the mountains north and west of the city. Centuries of bat droppings were cleared out, and carefully camouflaged remote antennas for French-built spread-spectrum cellular phone systems were installed; but otherwise, preparations were kept to a minimum, and no road construction was permitted in the vicinity of the cave entrances.

Following the incident between the frigates and the 366th's A+ Package, the UN Security Council voted another resolution, this one designating the Hanoi regime as an outlaw government and authorizing the use of force. When word of this was received from the Vietnamese delegation in New York, the leadership evacuation plan was activated. The plan was executed so smoothly that the foreign diplomatic and journalistic community in Hanoi never got a hint that anything was amiss until virtually the entire Party and Government structure had vanished from the city. Thus it came about that elderly members of the Central Committee found themselves being winched down in darkness from rickety old Mi-8 HIP helicopters through the forest canopy and into tiny clearings, where National Security Force guards led them to underground hideouts connected by comm links that were difficult to intercept and almost impossible to jam.

The White House, Washington, D.C., May 7th, 2000, 1800 Hours

"Mitch, I'm going to have to fulfill a few legal obligations to make this enforcement business happen the way you and the UN Security Council want it done," the JCS Chairman said to the National Security Advisor in his office.

"What might those be, Jack?" the National Security Advisor asked coyly.

"I'm talking about assassination, Mitch. Not that it's illegal; but we do have to do some paperwork to make it all nice and okay. Especially the part about a signed Presidential National Security Finding showing that the continued existence of the Hanoi regime is a clear threat to the security and safety of the region," replied the annoyed JCS Chairman.

"Will this do?" said the NSC Advisor, handing the big Marine a leather binder with the seal of the President on it. The JCS Chairman looked it over carefully, taking his time as he flipped through the pages. He stopped abruptly when he reached the last page with the signature blocks.

"Nice touch having the Speaker of the House and the President Pro Tem of the Senate endorse it . . . makes it all nice and bipartisan," the general observed.

"We thought it would add a certain moral conviction to the effort, especially since most of the veterans killed at the Caravelle were from the senator's home state," replied the National Security Advisor. "It just took some time to staff it through the Justice Department and the UN Security Council. Everyone wants to keep this most nasty of actions as tidy as possible. If, of course, your folks at the 366th can make it happen."

The 366th Wing Tactical Operations Center, RTAFB U-Tapao, Thailand, May 8th, 2000, 2200 Hours

"All right, Bob," Brigadier General Jack Perry, the 366th's commander and the resident JFACC of the UN-sponsored action, said, "give us a rundown on operations to date."

"Yes sir," the colonel commanding the Operations Center said. "We've been running no-fly operations in the southern part of Vietnam for two days now, and we seem to have things under control so far. The light grays"—

F-15Cs—"from the 390th have gotten an even dozen MiG kills so far, and VNPAF air activity outside their borders has virtually ceased. Also, the movement of Vietnamese units and supplies from the north has slowed greatly, and they have a backup of trains going from Hue back through Thanh Hoa to Hanoi."

"How about troop movements headed south?" the commander asked.

"Well sir, that's not so good," the colonel observed. "Satellite photos show large formations of light troops moving south on foot, with most of them headed for Mu Gia Pass and the old Ho Chi Minh Trail routes. National estimates make their numbers at approximately fifty thousand, in four identifiable divisions. They appear to have nothing heavier than personal weapons, and there are very few vehicles supporting them. Looks like a modern-day version of the Long March. They'll be through the pass and on the trail in less than a week. After that, you're going to have one nasty civil war down south."

"Just wonderful!" observed General Perry. He then asked the logistics chief, "And what happy news do you have for me, Harry?"

Lieutenant Colonel Harry Carpenter looked down at the notes on his laptop computer and began to speak. "Sir, the last elements of the C-Package arrived this afternoon. The Bones from the 34th will start mining operations of all northern harbors, rivers, and estuaries tonight. It will take about two nights to get them closed off. The UN posted the warning to navigators right after the embargo resolution was passed, and Lloyds threatened to pull the coverage from any ship still in harbor after 0000 local time tonight. The B-1Bs will start laying the eggs around 0400 local tomorrow, with activation in forty-eight hours."

"How about escorts and ROE?" the general inquired.

"Per your orders, sir," the lieutenant colonel replied, "no bomber shall drop any mine without logging it with a PY-code GPS receiver supplying the position. Also, each B-1B will be escorted by an F-15C loaded for air superiority and an F-16C with HARMs and HTS for defense suppression, if required. For tonight at least, the dark grays over at the 391st will do the no-fly job for us until that's done." He took a long breath and continued. "As for supplies and reinforcements, there's good news coming. Our old friends, the 8th FS from the 49th Wing at Holloman AFB, have just arrived this evening with twelve F-117s to help out with our leadership hunting, should that work out. In addition, we've been getting little bits and pieces of other things, like two RC-135 Rivet Joints to help out with the SIGINT problem. We also got two more E-3Cs from Tinker, to help out the three we already have. The first of the French and British fighters will arrive in about six days, as soon as they can get their tanker support settled. As for logistics, the first of the prepositioned ships will arrive tomorrow, so we can stop sweating ordnance and fuel supplies. The Alert Brigade of the 82nd Airborne and 7th Marine Expeditionary Brigade are standing by to help with the peacekeeping duties, if there ever are any. They'll bring elements of MAW-3"—Marine Air Wing Three—"and the 23rd Wing at Pope AFB if they ever arrive." He gave a rueful smile at that, knowing that things were not going well in the area they were about to discuss.

"Okay, ladies and gentlemen," General Perry announced, "lets get down to cases. What the hell happened to the enemy leadership, our designated center of gravity? Where are our damned targets? I want some dammed DMPIs, and I want them *now!* I'm listening. I'm waiting for an answer." The young brigadier had been under heavy stress already, and was now seriously irritated by a stupid tropical rash he had picked up in this hellhole, by the disappearance of the North Vietnamese national leadership, and by the dumb stares of his bright young intelligence officers. Had he been more of a screamer, he might have enjoyed a late night snack of lieutenant's butt on rye. But now, all he wanted was a target set for his Strike Eagles to hit.

Five hours later, the general was awakened in his hooch by the Operations Chief and Major Goldberg, a particularly disheveled-looking officer, even for an intelligence weenie. After rising and turning the overworked air conditioner to its maximum setting, the general sat down across a small table from the two officers and said, "This had better be good."

Goldberg pushed a book across the table. The paper binding was yellowed and stained, and the edges of the pages were ragged. It was in French:

LES CAVES DE TONKIN, INVESTIGATIONS PRELIMINAIRES GEOLOGIQUES, ARCHAEOLOGIQUES ET ZOOLOGIQUES, 1936

"What the hell is this, Major. I don't speak Frog," the General snarled, realizing he would have to stop saying that when their French coalition partners arrived.

"The Caves of Tonkin, sir. Back in the thirties, a French geographer named DuBois did a thorough exploration of the karst caverns near Hanoi. I figured that's where they might be hiding their command and control infrastructure, so I called. . .an. . .old friend in Paris. She tracked this down for me. Please be careful with the fold-out maps in the back, sir. The paper is kind of brittle, but they're better than anything that NRO, DMA, or USGS could come up with."

The general picked up the book, leafed through it, and unfolded the first map as carefully as he would have treated the original manuscript of the Constitution. After two hours of study with Goldberg translating—as the first rays of sunlight began to light the eastern sky—he handed it back, almost reverently. "Get this all translated, and get the maps digitized and correlated to our datum references. Also, get access to someone who's an expert on the geology of limestone karsts. Now. That means right now, Major!"

A sigh of relief passed around the room. "We got 'em," the three officers muttered simultaneously. As the trio broke up, another thought about the French came to Major Goldberg, and he decided to make another phone call.

U-Tapao Royal Thai AFB, May 9th, 2000, 2300 Hours

The twelve F-117s lifted off from U-Tapao, topped off their tanks from a pair of 22nd ARS KC-135Rs well out of radar coverage, and headed northeast. Through their FLIR imaging equipment, not a few pilots looked down on Thud Ridge, the karst finger pointed southeast towards Hanoi, which had guided their fathers and grandfathers in daylight on their own missions "downtown." But this was a different time, and the new USAF preferred to fight at night, when the optically aimed AAA batteries were largely useless. One of their targets was the Paul Doumer Bridge, proof that at least one colonel who had experienced the Vietnam War on the *CBS Evening News* had a sense of humor. The mission was to turn Hanoi into a darkened, isolated city, and do it in a single night. The whole purpose of the mission was deception, albeit deception with highly desirable effects. The missiles were still there, the SA-2s and -3s from the 1970s, and a few newer systems were in place, bought from Russia or cash-strapped clients of the now-defunct Soviet Union. Hanoi thought it still had a formidable air-defense system, remembering how many American aircraft had fallen in its rice paddies. Indeed, there was a large museum of such trophies. It is often said that countries prepare to fight the last war. But in the case of Hanoi, the war they planned to fight was *two* wars back.

Two hours later, the lieutenant colonel flying the lead Nighthawk looked with satisfaction on the image of the Paul Doumer Bridge as he began his attack run. A generation earlier, at the dawn of the age of precision guided weapons, his father had led a flight of four F-4Ds with Paveway I LGBs against this same bridge. Now he was flying serenely over Hanoi, with not a shot flying up at him, lining up on the same structure his dad had nearly died for exactly twenty-seven years ago this day. His target was a bridge piling, which provided structural support for the center of the bridge, in the deepest part of the Red River channel. The two GBU-27/Bs with their BLU-109/B warheads dropped accurately and hit the target with a pair of huge explosions. When the FLIR screen cleared, he smiled at the result. On either side of the piling, the bridge was down, like a giant V into the river. The piling itself looked as if it had been chopped off by a meat cleaver, the support tower having been completely destroyed. It would be a while until this link in the Hanoi-Hue railroad would be fixed.

Ten seconds after his bombs hit, he saw the flash off to his right of two more LGBs taking out the air defense command center at Gia Lam Airfield. Seconds later, the Party headquarters went up. Other targets went up as well. The thermal power plant took two GBU-27/Bs into the foundation of the turbine room, throwing the delicate mechanisms out of alignment, tearing them apart like lunatic pinwheels from hell. In all, ten targets in the Hanoi area went up in a matter of just three minutes. Meanwhile, two additional F-117s took out the "Dragon's Jaw" Bridge at Thanh Hoa and the hardened Vietnamese II Corps command post at Hue. As the city went dark and panic erupted among the junior officers and bureaucrats left behind to supervise the functions of the government, the real targets of tonight's strike began to pay the price for their arrogance.

The Caves of Tonkin, Northwest of Hanoi, May 10th, 2000, 0055 Hours

The rule was that nothing would go into the caves that could not be hand-carried to the entrance on a narrow footpath. Six champion athletes of the People's Army had the honor of carrying the 300-kg./660-lb. steel blast door almost 10 miles/16.3 km. from the nearest road. The engineers calculated that it would withstand the overpressure from any conceivable near-miss by a conventional weapon, and it was located far enough down a twisting passage that any guided weapon would have to be as agile as a Habù to negotiate the two right-angle turns. The Sergeant of the Guards at the entrance to the blast door was startled when he turned and saw the Defense Minister, General Truong Le, standing before him. "Comrade General, you cannot go outside."

"Comrade Sergeant, they won't let me smoke down there. I appeal to your fraternal revolutionary spirit. Take pity on an old man who is dying for a cigarette."

The general had been a recruit in Giap's army at Dien Bien Phu. He had led a battalion in the bitter street fighting in Hue during Tet. He had commanded a division during the final liberation of the South in 1975, then a corps on the Chinese border during the 1979 war with their hated Chinese neighbors. He might be Chief of Staff for the People's Army of Vietnam, but he was still close to his peasant roots. A big man by Vietnamese standards, he lived simply, and had refused to use political influence to get his sons cushy jobs in the Party. The soldiers loved him. His request was a breach of discipline, but the general and the sergeant stepped outside the cave entrance together into the cool night air for a smoke, carefully closing the blast door behind them. This ensured that they would be the only survivors of what was about to happen.

The two RC-135 Rivet Joint aircraft were working with a C-130 Hercules equipped with a Senior Scout clip-on SIGINT system to isolate the final locations of what were now being called "the leadership caves" from the minute emissions of the French-supplied cellular phone equipment used for their communications. The idea had come to Major Goldberg when he remembered a small notice he had seen on an Internet newsgroup several months before about a French firm in Toulon selling several million francs' worth of satellite cellular equipment to the Vietnamese government. He talked the situation over with the newly arrived French liaison officer, sent ahead to scout for the squadron of Rafale fighters that was due to arrive in three days. A phone call was made to the electronics firm and the company controlling the satellite cellular service contract for the Vietnamese. After finding out that the service had been almost unused until a few days earlier, and exactly what frequencies the phones transmitted on, it was a simple matter to have one of the NSA SIGINT satellites identify a rough location for the cellular activity.

The three aircraft refined their positions, then handed them off, via their own MILSTAR satellite links, to an inbound strike force of 366th Wing aircraft. The Vietnamese leadership was in the 366th's sight, and the gun was cocked.

General Perry was flying this one himself in his own F-15E Strike Eagle, known as Wing King. Tonight's mission had it flying at 16,000 feet/4,876.8 meters, loaded with four GBU-24/B penetrating 2,000-lb./909.1-kg. bombs. He had ordered a maximum effort for this evening's mission, and the maintenance chiefs had done themselves proud, getting sixteen of the complex birds into the air. The real kudos, though, had to go to the enlisted ordies from the bomb shops, who had switched plans for the evening and managed to build up the necessary LGBs to arm the dark grays, as well as getting the necessary mines into the B-1Bs for their last night of mining.

"Final update coming in over the MILSTAR link, sir," said Captain Asi "Ahab" Ontra, the general's personal WSO, over the intercom. The general smiled in his oxygen mask at the report. Ontra was one of the growing number of Moslems making a career for themselves in the U.S. military. Born in the Detroit area, with its large population of Lebanese immigrants, he may have been a bit too "dry" on Friday nights at the officers' club, but a better operator of the LANTIRN system was not to be found in the 366th. Now they were on their way to kill a government.

"How many of the caves have they identified?" asked the wing commander.

"Nineteen so far, sir. Major Goldberg seems to feel that may be all of them, sir," replied the young WSO.

"Have they told us what our target for tonight is?" the general inquired.

"They're not sure, sir . . . maybe some kind of military command center," the young man speculated.

"Okay. How long to target?" the general asked.

"Two minutes, sir. Your steering cue is up!" came the curt reply. It was all business now.

The Defense Minister shared a Camel with the young sergeant and sucked in the smoke and night air. Any other time, it would have been a beautiful night. Now his country was at war again, fighting for its pride . . . its self-respect . . . its identity . . . though he himself was beginning to question all of that. He looked over at the young soldier sharing a smoke with him and wondered what kind of nation he and the rest of the Party Leadership Council were going to hand over to this brave man.

"Target in sight, sir. Ten seconds to drop," Ahab called to General Perry, the green glow from the FLIR image on the Multi-Function Display lighting his face as he worked the two hand controllers to set up the LGB delivery.

"Roger, Master Arm on. Your pickle is hot. Stand by!" called General Perry over the intercom. As he did, the AAQ-14 LANTIRN targeting pod fired a short laser burst at the top of the karst to establish the range to target. This done, the time-to-drop clock counted down to zero. Then the four GBU-24/Bs dropped in rapid succession. They fell quickly, speeding up to over 900 fps./274.3 mps. When they were fifteen seconds from impact, Captain Ontra fired the laser again at the top of the limestone mountain, painting it with laser light. Again, a countdown clock in his FLIR MFD counted down to zero.

It was the memory of a younger man that saved him at that moment. There was only time for General Truong Le to yell, "*Get Down!*" to the sergeant, before the four bombs impacted the top of the karst. For a moment, the old man thought that the weapons has been duds, though that illusion was rapidly dispelled when the delayed-action fuzes fired the charges in the BLU-109/B warheads. There was no way the weapons could fully penetrate the limestone strata to reach the caves below. They did not have to. The tail-mounted fuzes had been set to detonate at the same moment, setting up the equivalent of a small earthquake within the soft rock. At once, a vertical shear wave was formed, heading down into the karst. It collapsed the cave tunnels below, like eggs under an elephant. Everyone inside was killed instantly. Meanwhile, the sudden collapse of the caves caused a huge overpressure of air in the tunnel entrance, blowing the blast door off its hinges with a "bang" and a "whoosh." The rogue door was flung out of the twisting cave tunnel like a sheet of paper. It missed the Defense Minister and his young comrade by inches as it careened off into the jungle. As the silence returned to the night, the old general heard other dull explosions, as twelve more targets were hit in exactly the same way. Instinctively knowing what was happening, he stood transfixed as the distant flashes announced the end of the Vietnamese Communist Party.

He was still standing when the young sergeant asked, "Shouldn't we report this to someone, Comrade General?"

The old man thanked the darkness for not showing his embarrassment to the young soldier. Then he replied as the last of the rolling thunder of the bombs died away, "Yes. And Sergeant, thank you for reminding me of my duty. Would you care to accompany me, please?" With that, they headed down the trail, back to the road, and hopefully, to Yen Bai Airfield some 20 km./12 miles away.

Yen Bai Airfield, Northwest of Hanoi, May 10th, 2000, 1412 Hours

The Party Military Committee's study of the 1991 Gulf War had derived one important lesson about air power: *Use it or lose it.* The VNPAF would not cower in shelters waiting to be destroyed. It would go down fighting from dispersed airstrips like this one. So it was that Colonel Nguyen Tri Loc, formerly the chief political officer of the VNPAF, found himself commanding the remains of the 931st Fighter Regiment, following the death of its commander from a Yankee AMRAAM missile three days previously. The 931st now consisted of just nine flyable MiG-29Cs and a rugged antique AN-2 biplane. These had narrowly escaped from the burning and exploding rubble of the air defense command center at Gia Lam Airport northwest of Hanoi only hours ago. The colonel had realized that the Americans were not making his planes a target unless they were actually flying. The unit's first attempt to break the aerial blockade had resulted in the loss of five of his precious MiG-29s to long-range AMRAAM shots. Since that time, they had been whittled down to the survivors that resided in the earth and concrete shelters surrounding the airfield's perimeter.

The colonel had almost lost his own life two nights before, while trying to intercept one of the big B-1B bombers on a mining mission. He had flown alone that night, trying to hide in the clutter with his IFF transponder off, just in case they were trying to use that against him also. He had just sighted the black monster in the mouth of the Red River near Nam Dien when he saw the flash of a Sidewinder missile coming at him from an escorting F-16. Only a quick snapshot with one of his own R-73/AA-11 Archer missiles and a rapid run behind a nearby karst saved his life.

At the time, the incident severely shook him, though now he was just furious, angered by his regiment's impotence against the aerial invaders. He and the surviving planes and pilots lived at the discretion of a hostile opponent, only as long as they did not threaten them. That was the reason why the Yankees wiped out the surface-to-air rocket batteries that protected his base here in the Vietnamese highlands valley from which it drew its name. When the survivors of the four rocket batteries returned, they were cursing the HARM missiles that destroyed their engagement radars like thunderbolts from the blue. Despite this loss, the People's Army was still providing base defense, in the form of a few well-hidden S-60 57mm AAA guns, and some shoulder-fired missile teams equipped with the Chinese version of the SA-16, dug in on hilltops to the south and west.

Just finding the American intruders was almost impossible. Every intercept radar site in North Vietnam had been taken out in the first few days of the American intervention. So for early warning the colonel had only an Inmarsat-P satellite phone that connected him to agents on the ground in Thailand. He knew when a strike or patrol left Takhli or U-Tapao, but he could only guess where it was headed; and more than once he had scrambled his handful of fighters, wasting precious fuel and alerting the ever-vigilant AWACS planes, only to discover that aircraft had doglegged somewhere too far for him to have a chance at interception.

But today would be different. Several flights of F-15Es had just struck one of the last of the leadership cavern complexes, and an urgent coded message on the satellite phone told him that their return route would pass almost directly over his position. The odds for once were more than two to one in his favor. He would have the advantage of surprise, and this might be the last chance for the 931st Regiment to strike a blow before it was targeted and wiped out for good. He headed to his MiG, strapped in, and gave the order for the rest of the regiment to start engines. As the last of the howling Klimov RD-33 engines came to life, Colonel Nguyen Tri Loc taxied his MiG out for what would be the last air battle of the Vietnam People's Air Force.

General Perry brought the Wing King away from its target run and pulled into the standard Strike Eagle trailing formation. This had two pairs of F-15Es, with the trailing pair up to four miles behind the first two. Because he and his wingman had hit a large leadership cave complex that was close to the old PRC/Vietnamese northwest rail line, they had wound up as the trailing pair in the formation for the return leg of the mission, which would take them within five miles/8.2 km. of the Yen Bai Airbase. The Gunfighters' commander was elated. The last of the leadership caves had been destroyed by a total of eight GBU-24/Bs. Amazingly, the last of the Leadership Council had insisted on staying in their own private grave complex, even when warned about the imminent danger posed by the 366th's penetration bombs. It was as if they'd realized their time was up . . . like old elephants going off to die. General Perry smiled. For once, those responsible for making war on innocent people had themselves paid with their lives. Justice. His eyes were scanning the cockpit, looking for signs of mechanical and systems problems, when they fixed on the moving map display, and froze.

"Ahab," the general snapped, "get me an SAR picture of the runway at Yen Bai. Do it now!"

The young captain immediately slewed the big dish of the APG-70 radar around to the left and painted the airfield, just coming into sight now about 20 miles/32.8 km. distant. The Synthetic Aperture Radar (SAR) mode gave them photographic-quality images of ground targets from many miles away; targets as small as 8 feet/2.4 meters in size could be imaged. Both men stared tensely at the image in their MFDs. What they saw chilled them both, for on the screen were eight or nine small targets, clearly identifiable as aircraft. General Perry saw that most of them were clustered at what he remembered from satellite photos of the base as an arming and fueling pit. Two others were clearly getting ready for a takeoff roll. Immediately, he yelled over the intercom for Captain Ontra to take another sweep with the APG-70 in SAR mode, and saw that two more of the aircraft were missing from the arming pit. From the back seat, he heard his WSO mumble, "Oh, Allah!" They were in trouble.

Colonel Nguyen and his wingman stayed low in the valley, not turning on their radars or any other electronic gear which might reveal their positions or intentions. As they rocketed on full afterburner through the saddle at the western end of the valley, they pulled up and sighted a pair of the Yankee Eagle strike aircraft directly in front of them. Nguyen exulted as he set this up, and called to his wingman, "Captain Tran, you attack the right-hand target, I'll take the left one." With that, he checked his sensors. His Infrared Search And Track

(IRST) system, contained in a small transparent ball in the nose, was giving him a good lock for his two R-73/AA-11 Archer short-range IR missiles. But the range was still too long, so he activated the RLPK-29/Slot Back radar, and set up a shot with his two R-27/AA-10 Alamo long-range radar-homing missiles. When the HUD showed the lead Eagle locked up, he depressed the trigger twice, and the two missiles were on their way. At the same time, he saw Tran's missiles leap off their launch rails and head for the second American fighter.

"Oh, Christ!" thought General Perry as he saw the smoke trails from the missiles angle up towards the leading pair of Strike Eagle Flight. He jammed a finger on the guard frequency transmit button and yelled, "Harry! Tony! Alamos coming up. Get the hell out of there *now!*" Both Strike Eagle crews reacted with trained precision, doing everything right. In the back seats, the WSOs immediately activated their defensive electronic countermeasures (ECM) systems, then began to hit the buttons for the ALE-47 chaff/decoy launchers to dispense metalized plastic strips and flares to try and decoy the incoming missiles. In the front cockpits, each of the pilots jammed the throttles of their twin F-100-PW-229 engines to Zone 5, afterburner, and racked their fighters in a sweeping left hand turn towards the oncoming danger. They almost got away with it.

One of Captain Tran's missiles failed in mid-flight, and the other was decoyed by the Strike Eagle's internal ECM system, flying off into the western sky. The lead Eagle had no such luck. While the first missile went after a chaff decoy, the second was dead on target. It struck the F-15E at the base of the port wing, detonating there and taking it off completely. As the big fighter began to cartwheel into a spin, both crewmen activated their ACES II ejection seats and headed for a "nylon letdown" and God-knows-what on the ground. General Perry shook off the shock from the suddenness of the strike and realized that three or four more flights of MiG-29s just like this one were about to do the same thing to the remaining three planes of his strike force. He had to act fast, and time was burning.

But then things slowed down, as the adrenaline rush compressed time and events into a dizzying swirl. He slammed the twin throttles of the -229 engines to afterburner and punched the button for the radio channel again, thinking of the two men in their chutes as he spoke. "Tony, extend and get back into the fight when you can. Get us some CSAR"—combat search and rescue— "support up here to look for the guys." He then turned his attention to his wingman, a young First Lieutenant named Billy "Jack" Bowles, a full-blooded Cherokee from Oklahoma. He called over, "Billy, get the flight taking off *now* with Slammers. *Now!* Then try and extend and reassemble to the west."

Next he called to Captain Ontra in the backseat and ordered, "Lock up the second airborne pair with Slammers. Get the ECM going. And get me a raid count with the FLIR."

He needn't have said anything. Already, Ahab had the APG-70 in TWS mode, searching for and finding the second pair of Fulcrums. He quickly set up an AIM-120 Slammer for each of the approaching MiGs and fired them in **Fire-and-Update mode.** The two missiles quickly ate up the 5 miles/8.2 km. to the two Vietnamese fighters, obliterating them in a pair of dirty orange explosions. There were no survivors.

He heard Ontra in the backseat yell, "Splash two," over the guard channel, and heard a similar call from Lieutenant Bowles.

In his headset he heard the duty AWACS calling, "This is Disco-1 on guard. Bandits . . . I repeat . . . multiple bandits at Bullseye"—Hanoi —"295 degrees for 85" (85 miles/139.3 km). "King flight is engaged. King-3 is down. CSAR support is on the way. Oilcan flight, engage. Your code is BUSTER" (full afterburner). "I repeat. Your code is Buster!" The young female captain at the controller console of the AWACS was excited, but doing her duty. Now all General Perry had to do was stay alive for five minutes, and four F-15Cs from the 390th would be here to save their collective asses.

Colonel Nguyen, elated with his ambush of the first Strike Eagle, led Captain Tran towards the ground to avoid being ambushed himself. But as the two MiGs popped up over a ridge, his elation died. In addition to the two white American parachutes, there were four dirty balls of smoke, with trails heading down.

His men had paid the price for his victory. Now he had to avenge them. He again activated his radar and began to search for targets. He noticed he had lost Captain Tran from his wing and decided to keep going on his own.

The Trail to Yen Bai Airfield,
May 10th, 2000, 1422 Hours

General Truong Le stared in wonder at the air battle going on above his head, cheering like a boy at a soccer match when he saw the Strike Eagle go down. But then he watched in horror as four of the Fulcrums died in a matter of seconds with their pilots. "Four more young Vietnamese lost. For what?" he thought. Then he noticed the two Americans in their parachutes descending towards the ground. He and the sergeant rushed to the landing site and caught both men while they were struggling out of their parachute harnesses. The sergeant suggested that he should shoot them as retribution for the deaths of the MiG pilots, but the general decided that he had seen enough men die for one day, and motioned the two men down the trail to Yen Bai Airfield.

The "Furball" West of Yen Bai Airfield,
May 10th, 2000, 1423 Hours

Colonel Nguyen saw a lone Strike Eagle chasing a MiG-29 in the distance, crossing his nose from left to right. He was racking his fighter in a tight turn to the right in an effort to save his comrade in the MiG when he saw an

AIM-9 Sidewinder missile leap out and shred the Eagle's quarry into a streaming fireball. Luckily, the pilot ejected, a rare Vietnamese survivor of this battle. Meanwhile, Nguyen was trying to catch up to the enemy strike fighter to get a shot when he saw a flash in his rearview mirror.

General Perry saw a lone MiG chasing Lieutenant Bowles in King-2 and made a conversion turn to the enemy fighter's rear. He had to kill this guy fast. Selecting SIDE mode from the HOTAS controls, he waited for the tone in his headset to settle down to a continuous scream. At a range of 2,500 feet/762 meters, he triggered the missile, which rapidly ate up the distance to the Fulcrum's port engine. It impacted the engine's afterburner can, contact detonating and blowing the back of the engine to pieces, taking with it the port rudder and horizontal stabilizer. Amazingly, the MiG continued to fly, the starboard engine, rudder, and stabilizer continuing to function. Cursing the tiny warhead of the AIM-9M, he switched the armament controls to GUN.

Colonel Nguyen heard and felt a huge bang in the rear of his MiG; then all the port engine annunciators flashed red in warning. He chopped the port throttle and popped the port side fire bottle to contain the fire that had broken out in the shattered engine. The bird was still flying, and perhaps he might get it home to Yen Bai. But seconds later, he felt a thumping in the control stick and throttle console, and the cockpit exploded with a flash and a sudden darkness. It was the last sight he would see.

General Perry placed the MiG in the firing cone of the gunsight, let the range close to under 1,000 feet/304.8 meters, and fired a three-second burst from the M61 Vulcan cannon in the Eagle's starboard wing root. The stream of PGU-28 armor-piercing/incendiary shells walked up the spine of the aircraft and eventually filled the enemy fighter's cockpit with explosions and smoke. The Fulcrum fell off and began to spin down to the ground. Eventually it impacted in a fireball, a funeral pyre to Colonel Nguyen and the Vietnamese People's Air Force. A quick check of the radar and radio showed only the two surviving Strike Eagles of King flight and the incoming flight of F-15Cs. He turned the nose of the big fighter to the southwest and began to think about fueling from the duty tanker and heading home. It had been a long ten minutes.

Captain Tran landed his MiG-29, the only surviving aircraft of the 931st Regiment's last air battle. As he taxied into a shelter, he cut the engines and allowed his head to fall forward against the control panel as he mumbled an old saying from an American Western film he had once seen, "From every massacre there is always one survivor. . . . " He did not notice the old general and the sergeant when they walked by with their prisoners. His only thought was that he was very tired and never wanted to fly again.

Meanwhile, the Defense Minister was curious about the AN-2 biplane at the end of the field, and asked one of the ground personnel if a pilot was available to fly him and his guests back to Hanoi. The annoyed crew chief was about to curse at the old man in the grimy uniform when he saw the gold braid and stars. He ran off to ask Captain Tran to get ready to fly one more time.

Royal Palace, Hue,
May 11th, 2000

Amid the chaos of the Coalition airstrikes on the leadership caves, it took several hours to establish that the Defense Minister General Truong Le was the senior surviving official of the DRV. From Bach Mai, the general had called Beijing, and the Chinese comrades had patched him through to Duc Oanh's temporary headquarters at Bien Hoa Air Base outside Saigon. Their conversation was brief, frank, and cordial. Both parties were well aware that every intelligence agency with two SIGINT analysts to rub together was recording, translating, and analyzing every word. At times like these in the life of nations, symbolism was important. So they agreed to meet face-to-face in the most politically symbolic location in their country, the walled and moated Royal Palace complex in Hue.

"I regret that I never had the opportunity to serve under your leadership," said Duc.

"I regret that I did not have a hundred thousand soldiers like you," said the general. "We have to end this conflict before our people suffer irreparable harm. What will it take to keep our country together?"

"We would like to propose a return to the provisions of the 1954 Geneva agreements. We both know that our people have little experience with elections. It will take generations for democracy to take root in this land we both love. We had better start soon, by working out a constitution. I would be honored if you would stand for election as President. I would be honored to serve as your Vice President."

The signing of the agreement was a formality. The photo of the old general and the middle-aged former guerrilla and postal clerk embracing in tears was a Pulitzer Prize winner.

366th Tactical Operations Center,
RTNAS U-Tapo, May 11, 2000

General Perry sat in his command cell and looked out the window upon the scene of his force of B-1Bs and F-15Es, uploading maximum loads of CBU-87 cluster bombs. The sight sickened him, because of where the deadly "eggs" were scheduled to be dropped. After the completion of the last mission against the leadership caves the previous day, he had received an order from the National Security Council, with an endorsement from the UN Security Council, to begin mass cluster bomb strikes against the four DRV infantry divisions moving up the eastern slope of Mu Gia Pass. It would be a slaughter when the canisters of CEMs opened over the exposed troops, filling the air with hot metal, fire, and screams. The vision filled him with remorse. Unfortunately, if the fifty thousand men of those units did not return to their barracks in the DRV, the action was going to be necessary. The great nations of the world had allowed the people of this region of the world to draw them into conflicts too many times to allow it to happen again. Thus, the fifty thousand young men marching to Mu Gia were doomed, unless the guys running things in Hanoi came to their senses. The knock at his door broke the spell of his thought, and he turned to see Major Goldberg standing in his door with a message flimsy in his hand and a broad grin on his face. "Good news, sir," said the younger man. "Messages from both security councils."

The general took the fragile paper and read the short message. It was a cease-fire. The DRV had sued for terms under the old 1954 accord, and there was going to be peace. The ground units of the peacekeeping force were being assembled and would be on their way within hours. He went limp from relief, and it was a long minute before he could look at Major Goldberg.

"Major, tell the ordies that they are to download those munitions dispensers immediately. Then pass the word that we're to plan for peacekeeping and enforcement operations. We may be here a while doing that. Lastly, please try and get a line on the two crewmen from King-3 through the UN. I want to know about them ASAP."

The major said "Yes, sir," saluted, and left the room.

Security Council, United Nations, New York

RESOLUTION 1398

The Security Council,

Recognizing the collapse of civil government and lawful authority in the DRV,

Concerned over the loss of life, destruction of property, and environmental damage resulting from the continuation of hostilities in Southeast Asia,

Determined to restore conditions of peace, justice, and democracy throughout the territory of the Republic of Vietnam and the former DRV:

1. *Declares* that the provisions of the 1954 Geneva Accords regarding free elections throughout the northern and southern regions of Vietnam are to be implemented within six months of the date of this resolution,

2. *Authorizes* the Secretary General to nominate a Vietnam Electoral Commission, representing all segments of the Vietnamese people, including those presently residing outside Vietnam, to publish and disseminate throughout the territory under control of the Provisional Government of the Republic of Vietnam and the territory of the former DRV regulations for the conduct of political parties, candidates, and electoral campaigns, in accordance with international standards of fairness and equal access,

3. *Authorizes* the Secretary General to take all necessary action to ensure that voter registration and balloting are conducted without fraud, coercion, or violation of human rights,

4. *Encourages* all member nations to provide technical assistance, electoral observers, and material contributions to support the implementation of this resolution,

5 *Requests* the Secretary General to provide a progress report on the implementation of this resolution no later than thirty days from this date.

The "Yes" vote was unanimous.

Mountain Home AFB, Idaho, July 4th, 2000

The entire wing had staged out of Elmendorf AFB in Alaska in order to make the final leg home as one formation. The UN peacekeeping force had relieved the wing of its duties the day before, and the no-fly operation had been concluded with the implementation of the final UN resolution. Now, as the formation broke into the base pattern, General Perry saw thousands of people waiting on the flight line for what he know was going to be an incredible homecoming. Somewhere down there was the President of the United States, ready to pin on medals and make the campaign speech of a lifetime. Also down there were representatives of the UN Security Council, to award the wing its special streamer for peacekeeping. Best of all, though, was that his family was down there—and the family of every deployed member of the wing, including the two downed Strike Eagle crewmen. The new Vietnamese Vice President had taken personal responsibility for getting them home, and Perry made a mental note to write a letter of thanks to the man. As he broke his Strike Eagle into the pattern, he smiled in the knowledge that this time there was going to be a parade for the Gunfighters coming home from Vietnam.

Conclusion

A irpower is a tool with many limitations, but in its short history it has profoundly transformed the nature of war. As a navy can move across oceans to strike without warning at a hostile shore, so too aircraft can appear over the very heart of a country on the first day—or in the first minutes—of hostilities, bringing the war instantly to people and places which in the past could only be reached after years of campaigning and the loss of countless lives. At the same time defenses against air attack—interceptors, ground-based anti-aircraft guns, and surface-to-air missiles—have also improved rapidly, in testimony to the threat of this new military capability. But the race in military history between offensive and defensive technologies generally works in favor of the offense.

America has recently developed two revolutionary offensive capabilities. The first, stealth, denies an enemy the ability to detect, and therefore protect against, a deep and damaging strike. Stealth is not black magic; it is a technical fact. When used properly in the design of an aircraft, missile, ship, or even submarine, stealth gives the attacker a decisive advantage over almost any kind of sensor from radars to sonars. The second capability, precision-guided munitions (PGMs), gives the attacker the means not so much to do explosive "surgery" as to use his weapons with a far higher degree of efficiency. No longer is laying down a carpet of bombs on a target a viable political or military option. Given the worldwide abhorrence of collateral damage from air strikes, use of PGMs is not only desirable, but may become required in the future. The combination of these two technological capabilities offers our national leadership opportunities unknown since the demise of a small and vicious sovereignty in the Middle East whose name has come into the English lexicon as a curse—Assassin. During the Middle Ages, from their mountain fortress in Lebanon, the military-religious Order of the Hashishin preserved their independence by killing any caliph, khan, sultan, emperor, or shah who dared to threaten them.

War is, after all, nothing more than organized murder, sanctioned by a government. And while war might sometimes be necessary, the more quickly and efficiently it can be concluded, the less harm is done to innocent people in the process. The very horror of war has, in recent times, sometimes deterred its necessity. This is a source of hope for the future survival of our species. The first sign of that hope was the inability of "civilized" nations to bring themselves to use their most potent weapons—thermonuclear arms—during the Cold War.

Despite deep and fundamental differences in philosophy that throughout history were the basis for major conflict, the balance of terror that thermonuclear weapons imposed (known euphemistically as Mutually Assured Destruction or MAD) kept the peace, such as it was. The weapons and the military units designed to use them, we ought to remember, were in place for two generations, always ready for a push of the button. Yet the button wasn't pushed, because rationality somehow took precedence over ideology. Thank God.

Part of that rationality was motivated by the advance of airpower (if we may include strategic missiles and orbital satellites in the definition), and the immediate future could well see a further application of the same principle. Thus, the mating of stealth technology and PGMs today means that the decision-makers who send young men off to die can now be targeted directly. No one is truly safe from such a precision attack, and personal vulnerability might well make a dictator think twice and then again before committing his country to war—if, that is, America develops the doctrine and installs the capability to target those who instigate war. Clausewitz liked to talk about an enemy's "center of gravity," meaning those things which a nation had to protect in order to survive. But the real center of gravity of any nation is its decision-makers, be they presidents, prime ministers, dictators, or juntas. No person becomes a chief of state, or group a leadership team, in order to suffer. The exercise of power, especially for despots, is heady wine indeed. Hiding in deep bunkers (which may no longer be safe in any case) cannot be fun. Nor is traveling about with the constant knowledge that a single enemy intelligence officer, or a domestic traitor, needs to finger the target only one time. What has emerged, then, is the ability to apply the well-named MAD principle of nuclear arms to conventional weapons, to fight a war with ultimate efficiency.

This idea is still what some might call "blue-sky"; but it is a fact that the capability now exists (even though we never quite managed to turn off Saddam Hussein's personal radio transceiver). The ability to strike deep and strike accurately could well become the best excuse for people to find something other than war as an instrument of international policy.

To use airpower effectively one must understand its limits, as well as it capabilities:

- **Airpower Is Costly.** It is easy to be appalled by the notion of a twenty million dollar fighter, a fifty million dollar fighter bomber, or a five hundred million dollar stealth bomber. But the dollar cost of an aircraft does not even begin to measure the true cost of airpower. It costs thousands of dollars an hour to keep even the simplest jet trainer in the air. An effective air force requires a vast infrastructure of training, maintenance, and administrative support. It requires a whole range of specialized industries that draw talent and productive resources away from other sectors of the economy.

- **Airpower Is Fragile.** On June 22nd, 1941, most of the Soviet "Frontal Aviation" tactical aircraft were caught on the ground and destroyed by the German Luftwaffe. Six months later, on December 8th, virtually the entire U.S. Army air force in the Philippines was caught on the ground and destroyed by Japanese air attacks on Clark Field. On June 5th, 1967, most of the offensive power of the Egyptian Air Force was caught on the ground and destroyed in a single morning's work by Israeli Air Force attacks. Even more fragile than the airplanes themselves is the network of radars, command centers, communications facilities, fuel systems, and munitions depots that make airpower possible. An entire air force can be wiped out in a few hours. As the Iraqis learned in the Gulf War, even the most strongly built shelters cannot protect an air force that has lost control of the air space above them.

- **Airpower Is Not a Substitute for Clear Military Objectives.** Especially when it is used piecemeal, for limited political purposes. This was the clear lesson of Vietnam, where hundreds of American and South Vietnamese aircraft were shot down between 1964 and 1972 without inflicting strategically significant damage on the elusive enemy. Years earlier, political limitations on the use of airpower helped to turn the Korean War from a decisive Allied military victory into a protracted stalemate. Even the Israelis, so skillful in the political employment of airpower, have conducted hundreds of air strikes on "terrorist bases" without significant impact on the political base of the terrorist threat to the Israeli people. The "limited punitive air strike" may play well on the evening news to a domestic audience, but it generally only serves to solidify the enemy's will to resist. All too often, it also serves as a "hostage delivery system," leaving hapless downed aircrews as bargaining chips in the hands of the enemy. A good example was the 1983 raid by U.S. Navy aircraft on Syrian antiaircraft positions in Lebanon. The result was two aircraft lost, another damaged, one pilot killed, and another captured by the Syrians, requiring the intervention of the Reverend Jesse Jackson to obtain his release. A lousy trade for a few AAA guns!

Ironically, naval and land power *can* serve as limited political tools where airpower cannot, because an airplane does not establish *presence*. For decades, the presence of the U.S. Army in Europe and Korea deterred Communist attack, even when that Army turned into a hollow shell in the post-Vietnam period. The presence of the U.S. Navy in the Western Pacific and the Indian Ocean has a similar stabilizing geopolitical influence.

Consider the current attempts of the Western powers to influence events in the former Yugoslavia. NATO combat air patrols (Operation Deny Flight), airstrikes on Bosnian Serb military positions, and a multinational naval blockade in the Adriatic have failed to change the behavior of the Bosnian Serbs in any significant way, because they do not reach the Serbian center of gravity in Belgrade. But the token presence of a few hundred U.S. paratroops as a UN peacekeeping force in Macedonia has preserved the existence of that fragile republic. Even Serbs are not crazy enough to directly challenge United States ground forces. Symbolically speaking, when you shoot down my airplane, that is an unfortunate incident, but when you kill my soldiers or sink my ship, that is an act of war.

Perhaps airpower will never conquer ground. Perhaps airpower cannot linger in place as long as ships. But airpower can take the fight to the enemy's heart and brain in a way and with a speed impossible for the more traditional fighting arms. It is, moreover, almost entirely an American invention which, like democracy, has changed the face of the world.

Glossary

A-12	Lockheed high-altitude, high-speed low-observable interceptor developed in the 1960s. Never went into service, but served as the basis for the development of the SR-71 Blackbird. Not to be confused with McDonnell Douglas A-12 Avenger, a 1990s Navy program for a stealthy carrier strike aircraft, canceled due to cost overruns and program mismanagement.
AAA	Anti-Aircraft Artillery (AAA), also called "triple-A" or "flak."
Aardvark	Nickname for the F-111 fighter bomber, derived from its large nose and ungainly appearance. The F-111 never received an official name.
ABCCC	Airborne Battlefield Command and Control Center. An EC-130E aircraft equipped with communications equipment and staff.
ACC	Air Combat Command. Major command of the USAF formed in 1992 by the merger of the Strategic Air Command (bombers and tankers) and the Tactical Air Command (fighters).
ACES II	Standard USAF ejection seat built by McDonnell Douglas based on an original design by the Weber Corporation. ACES II is a "zero-zero" seat, which means that it can save the crew person's life (at the risk of some injury) down to zero airspeed and zero altitude, as long as the aircraft is not inverted.
ACM	Air Combat Maneuvering. The art of getting into position to shoot the other guy, preferably from behind, before he can shoot you.
AFB	Air Force Base. NATO or Allied bases are usually identified simply as AB (air base). The Royal Air Force designates its bases by place name, i.e. RAF Lakenheath.
Afterburner	Device that injects fuel into the exhaust nozzle of a jet engine, boosting thrust at the cost of greater fuel consumption. Called "Reheat" by the British.
AGL	Above Ground Level. A practical way of measuring altitude for pilots, even though engineers prefer the more absolute measure ASL, "Above Sea Level."
AI	Airborne Intercept; usually used to describe a type of radar or missile.
AIM-9 Sidewinder	Heat-seeking missile family, used by the Air Force, Navy, Marines, Army, and many export customers. Variants are designated by a letter, such as AIM-9L or AIM-9X.
AMC	Air Mobility Command. Major USAF command that controls most transports and tankers. Based at Scott AFB, Illinois.

AMRAAM	AIM-120 Advanced Medium Range Air-to-Air Missile. First modern air-to-air missile to use programmable microprocessors with active radar homing (missile has its own radar transmitter, allowing "fire and forget" tactics).
ANG	Air National Guard. Air Force reserve units nominally under the control of and partially funded by state governments. Many ANG flight crews and ground crews work in the airline or aviation industries.
Angels	Altitude in thousands of feet. "Angels fifteen" means 15,000 feet.
AOC	Air Operations Center.
API	Armor Piercing Incendiary. A type of ammunition favored for use against armored ground vehicles.
Aspect	The angle from which a target is seen. From the front an aircraft presents a relatively small target; from above or below it presents a comparatively large target.
ATF	Advanced Tactical Fighter. Original program name for the F-22.
ATO	Air Tasking Order. A planning document that lists every aircraft sortie and target for a given day's operations. Preparation of the ATO requires careful "deconfliction" to ensure the safety of friendly aircraft. During Desert Storm the ATOs ran to thousands of pages each day.
Avionics	General term for all the electronic systems on an aircraft, including radar, communications, flight control, navigation, identification, and fire control computers. Components of an avionics system are increasingly interconnected by a "data bus" or high-speed digital network.
AWACS	Airborne Warning and Control System. Specifically used to describe the Boeing E-3 Sentry family, but also used generically to describe similar types used by other Air Forces.
Bandit	Fighter pilot jargon for a confirmed enemy aircraft. An older term, still used by some English-speaking air forces, is "Bogey."
Bar	One sweep of a radar beam, typically a few degrees in altitude and 60 to 120 degrees in width.
BARCAP	Barrier Combat Air Patrol. A fighter operation intended to prevent enemy aircraft from passing through a defined airspace. A BARCAP is typically established along the most likely enemy area of approach, involving relays of fighters that are continuously relieved in place.
BDA	Bomb Damage Assessment. The controversial art of determining from fuzzy imagery and contradictory intelligence whether or not a particular target has been destroyed or rendered inoperative.
Bingo	The point when an aircraft has just enough fuel remaining to return safely to a friendly base. At this point, a rational pilot will attempt to disengage, unless there is an extremely compelling reason to put the aircraft at risk.
BLU	Air Force nomenclature for a "bomb" or "munition."
Boresight Mode	When a radar beam or electro-optical device is pointed straight ahead (12 o'clock).

BVR	Beyond Visual Range; usually used in reference to radar-guided air-to-air missiles. "Visual range" depends on the weather, how recently the windscreen was cleaned and polished, and the pilot's visual acuity, but against a fighter-sized target rarely exceeds 10 miles (16 km.).
BW	Bomber Wing (traditionally Bombardment Wing).
C-130 Hercules	Lockheed tactical transport. Four Allison T56 turboprops. Over two thousand of these classic aircraft have been built since 1955 and it is still in production. Hero of 1976 Israeli hostage rescue mission to Entebbe, Uganda. Many models and variants, including AC-130U gunship and EC-130H communications jammer. New C-130J under development has advanced avionics and new Allison T406 engine with six-bladed propellers. Standard transport has maximum takeoff weight of 175,000 lb./80,000 kg.
C-141 Starlifter	Long-range heavy lift transport, built by Lockheed, entered service in 1964. Four TF33 turbofan engines. About 227 remain in service, subject to weight restrictions due to airframe fatigue. Equipped for in-flight refueling. Maximum takeoff weight 325,000 pounds.
C-17 Globemaster III	Heavy-lift McDonnell Douglas transport designed for operation into short, unimproved runways. Four P&W F117 turbofan engines. Maximum takeoff weight 585,000 lb./266,000 kg. Advanced cockpit with flight crew of two plus enlisted loadmaster in cargo bay. Only forty aircraft currently funded.
C-5B Galaxy	Long-range Lockheed Martin heavy lift transport. Four TF39 turbofan engines. Maximum takeoff weight is 837,000 pounds. Nose structure swings up and tail ramp drops down for rapid loading and unloading. About eighty-two in service.
C³I	Command, Control, Communications, and Intelligence; the components and targets of information warfare. Pronounced "see-three-eye."
Call Sign	(1) An identifying name and number assigned to an aircraft for a particular mission. Aircraft in the same flight will usually have consecutive numbers. (2) A nickname given to an aviator by his/her squadron mates and retained throughout his/her flying career, often humorous.
Canard	Small fixed or movable wing located forward of an aircraft's main wing. This is the French word for "duck," from an early French aircraft (c. 1910) that first used this feature and was nicknamed "the Duck." Canard-type designs are generally very resistant to stalling.
Canopy	The transparent bubble that covers the cockpit of an aircraft. Usually made of Plexiglas, or polycarbonate, sometimes with a microscopically thin layer of radar-absorbing material. Easily scratched or abraded by sand or hail. Ejection seats have a means of explosively jettisoning or fracturing the canopy to reduce the chance of injury during ejection.
CAP	Combat Air Patrol, a basic fighter tactic that involves cruising economically at high or medium altitude over a designated area searching for enemy aircraft.

CBU	Cluster Bomb Unit. A munition that is fuzed to explode at low altitude, scattering large numbers of "submunitions" over an area target. Submunitions can be explosive grenades, delayed-action mines, antitank warheads, or other specialized devices.
CENTAF	The Air Force component of U.S. Central Command, including units deployed to bases in Kuwait, Saudi Arabia, and other states in the Gulf region. The Commander of CENTAF is an Air Force lieutenant general, who typically also commands 9th Air Force based at Shaw AFB, South Carolina.
CENTCOM	United States Central Command, a unified (joint service) command with an area of responsibility in the Middle East and Southwest Asia. Headquartered at McDill AFB, Florida, and generally commanded by an Army four-star general. CENTCOM normally commands no major combat units, but in a crisis situation it would rapidly be reinforced by units of the Army's XVIIIth Airborne Corps, the U.S. Marine Corps, and Allied forces.
Chaff	Bundles of thin strips of aluminum foil or metallized plastic film that are ejected from an aircraft to confuse hostile radar. A chaff cloud creates a temporary "smokescreen" that makes it difficult for radar to pick out real targets. The effectiveness of chaff depends on matching the length of the chaff strips to the wavelength of the radar.
Chop	To assign a unit to the command of a different headquarters. For example, in a Middle Eastern crisis the 366th Wing might be chopped to CENTCOM (U.S. Central Command). Term is probably derived from Cantonese pronunciation of the Chinese word for a seal used to sign official documents. "In-chop" and "out-chop" designate the official dates that a unit arrives in or departs a particular theater of operations.
CinC	Commander in Chief. Used to designate the senior officer, typically a four-star general or admiral in charge of a major command, such as CINCPAC (Commander in Chief of the U.S. Pacific Command).
CMUP	Conventional Munitions Upgrade Program. U.S. Air Force initiative to develop new families of low-cost improved conventional bombs.
CONOPS	Concept of Operations. The commander's guidance to subordinate units on the conduct of a campaign.
CTAPS	Contingency Tactical Air Control System Automated Planning System. A transportable network of computer workstations, linking various databases required for the generation of an Air Tasking Order.
CVW	Carrier Air Wing. A force of Navy aircraft organized for operation from an aircraft carrier. Typically includes one fighter squadron, two attack squadrons, and small units of helicopters and anti-submarine, electronic warfare and early warning radar planes. U.S. Marine Corps air units may be assigned to a carrier air wing.
CW	Continuous Wave. A type of radar that emits energy continuously, rather than in pulses.
DARO	Defense Airborne Reconnaisance Office. A Pentagon agency created in 1992, charged with fixing the mess in U.S. airborne recon.

DMPI	Direct Mean Point of Impact. The exact geographical coordinates of a target, used for mission planning. Pronounced "dimpy."
Drag	The force that resists the motion of a vehicle through a gaseous or liquid medium. The opposite force is lift. Also the practice of cross-dressing in clothing of the opposite sex for informal squadron entertainment events.
DSCS	Defense Satellite Communication System. A family of geosynchronous satellites and ground terminals ranging from 33-inch airborne antennas to 60-foot ground dishes. The current generation, DSCS III includes five satellites, providing global coverage. Some earlier DSCS II satellites are still operational.
E-2C Hawkeye	U.S. Navy carrier-based twin-turboprop airborne early warning aircraft built by Grumman. Large radar in saucer-shaped rotating antenna housing. Entered service in 1964. Also operated by France, Israel, and Japan.
E/O	Electro-optical. A general term for sensors that use video, infrared, or laser technology for assisting navigation or locating, tracking or designating targets.
ECM	Electronic Countermeasures. Any use of the electromagnetic spectrum to confuse, degrade, or defeat hostile radars, sensors, or radio communications. The term ECCM (electronic counter-countermeasures) is used to describe active or passive defensive measures against enemy ECM, such as frequency-hopping or spread-spectrum waveforms.
EF-111 Raven	Electronic warfare version of the F-111 fighter bomber. Nicknamed "Spark 'Vark."
ELINT	Electronic Intelligence. Interception and analysis of radar, radio, and other electromagnetic emissions in order to determine enemy location, numbers, and capabilities.
Energy	In pilot jargon, the sum total of kinetic energy (speed) and potential energy (altitude) that an aircraft or missile has at a given instant. The concept of "energy maneuverability" developed by Colonel John Boyd is a fundamental idea in air-to-air tactics. Turning and other forms of maneuvering quickly use up energy, making an aircraft vulnerable to an enemy with more energy. The faster an aircraft can accelerate, the more quickly it can regain lost energy.
FAC	Forward Air Controller. Designates both the aircraft and the pilot with the dangerous mission of circling over a battlefield to locate targets and direct strike aircraft.
FADEC	Full Authority Digital Engine Control. A computer that monitors jet engine performance and pilot throttle inputs and regulates fuel supply for maximum efficiency.
Flameout	The unintended loss of combustion inside a jet engine, due to a disruption of air flow. This can be extremely serious if the flight crew is unable to restart the affected engine.
Flap	A hinged control surface, usually on the trailing edge of a wing, commonly used to increase lift during takeoff and drag during landing.

Flare	(1) A pyrotechnic device ejected by an aircraft as a countermeasure to heat-seeking missiles. (2) A pitch-up maneuver to bleed off energy, performed during landing, just before touching down.
FLIR	Forward Looking Infrared. An electro-optical device similar to a television camera that "sees" in the infrared spectrum rather than visible light. A FLIR displays an image based on minute temperature variations in its field of view, so that hot engine exhaust ducts, for example, appear as bright spots.
Fur Ball	A confused dogfight involving a large number of aircraft on each side. Derived from the cartoonist's typical representation of fights between cats and dogs.
G force	One G is the force exerted by Earth's gravity on stationary objects at sea level. High-energy maneuvers can subject the aircraft and pilot to as much as 9 Gs. Some advanced missiles can pull as much as 60 Gs in a turn.
G-suit	Aircrew garment with inflatable bladders connected to a pressure-regulating system. During high-G maneuvers the suit compresses the legs and abdomen to prevent pooling of blood in the lower body that might deprive the brain of oxygen, causing "gray-out" or, in extreme cases, GLOC (G-induced loss of consciousness).
GBU	Guided Bomb Unit. General term for a class of precision-guided munitions.
GHz	Gigahertz. A measure of frequency, 1,000,000,000 cycles per second.
"Glass Cockpit"	Design that replaces indivdual flight gauges and instruments with multi-function electronic display screens. A few mechanical gauges are usually retained for emergency backup.
Goldwater-Nichols	Common name for the Military Reform Act of 1986, which created a series of unified commands cutting across traditional service boundaries and strengthened the power of the Chairman of the Joint Chiefs of Staff.
GPS	Global Positioning System. A constellation of twenty-two Navstar satellites in inclined Earth orbits, which continously broadcast navigational signals synchronized by ultra-precise atomic clocks. At least four satellites are usually in transit across the sky visible from any point on Earth outside the polar regions. A specialized computer built into a portable receiver can derive highly accurate position and velocity information by correlating data from three or more satellites. An encoded part of the signal is reserved for military use. A similar, incomplete Russian system is called GLONASS.
Green Flag	A series of realistic Air Force training exercises conducted at Nellis AFB to evaluate doctrine, training, tactics, readiness, and leadership at the squadron and wing level.
HARM	AGM-88 High Speed Anti-Radiation Missile, produced by Texas Instruments. Mach 2+ with 146 lb. blast-fragmentation warhead. Typically fired 35 to 55 miles from target, but maximum range is greater.
Have Blue	Original Lockheed "Skunk Works" prototype for the F-117 Stealth fighter. Considerably smaller than the production aircraft, and still highly classified.

Have Nap	AGM-142 heavy medium range (50 mi./80 km.) standoff air-to-ground missile. Developed by Israeli Rafael Company, and co-produced by Lockheed Martin.
Have Quick	A family of jam-resistant secure airborne radios operating in the UHF band utilizing frequency hopping.
HEI	High Explosive Incendiary. A type of ammunition commonly used with air-to-air guns.
HOTAS	Hands on Throttle and Stick. A cockpit flight control unit that allows the pilot to regulate engine power settings and steering commands with one hand.
HUD	Heads-Up Display. A transparent screen above the cockpit instruments on which critical flight, target and weapons information is projected so that the pilot need not look down to read gauges and displays during an engagement. Current HUD technology provides wide-angle display of radar and sensor data.
HVHAA	High Value Heavy Airframe Aircraft. Air Force term for a big, slow, vulnerable, and extremely valuable aircraft such as an AWACS or tanker that must be protected at all costs.
IFF	Identification Friend or Foe. A radio frequency system designed to reduce the risk of shooting down friendly aircraft. An IFF "interrogator" on one aircraft transmits a coded message intended for the IFF "transponder" on an unknown target. If the proper coded reply is received, the target is reported as friendly. If no reply is received, the target is reported as unknown. IFF codes are changed frequently in wartime, but lack of an IFF response is not enough to classify a target as hostile, since the transponder may be inoperative or turned off.
IIR	Imaging Infrared. An electro-optical device similar to a video camera that "sees" small differences in temperature and displays them as levels of contrast or false colors on an operator's display screen.
IL-76 Candid	Russian four-turbofan heavy transport. Maximum takeoff weight of 375,000 lb./170,000 kg. Designed to operate from relatively short, unpaved runways. Exported to many Soviet client states.
ILS	Instrument Landing System. A radio-frequency device installed at some airfields that assists the pilot of a suitably equipped aircraft in landing during conditions of poor visibility.
INS	Inertial Navigation System. A device that determines location and velocity by sensing the acceleration and direction of every movement after the system is initialized or updated at a known point. Conventional INS systems using mechanical gyroscopes are subject to "drift" after hours of continuous operation. Ring-laser gyros sense motion by measuring the frequency shift of laser pulses in two counter-rotating rings, and are much more accurate. The advantage of an INS is that it requires no external transmission to determine location.
Interdiction	Use of airpower to disrupt or prevent the movement of enemy military units and supplies by attacking transportation routes, vehicles, and bridges deep in the enemy's rear.

IOC	Initial Operational Capability. The point in the life cycle of a weapon system when it officially enters service and is considered ready for combat, with all training, spare parts, technical manuals, and software complete. The more complex the system, the greater the chance that the originally scheduled IOC will slip.
IRBM	Intermediate Range Ballistic Missile. A rocket (typically two-stage) designed to deliver a warhead over regional rather than intercontinental distances. This class of weapons was eliminated by treaty and obsolescence from U.S. and Russian strategic forces, but is rapidly proliferating in various world trouble spots, despite international efforts to limit the export of ballistic missile technologies.
J-3	Operations officer on a joint staff, responsible for assisting the commander in the planning and execution of military operations.
JCS	Joint Chiefs of Staff. The senior U.S. military command level, responsible for advising the President on matters of national defense. The JCS consists of a Chairman, who may be drawn from any service, the Chief of Naval Operations, the Chief of Staff of the Army, the Commandant of the Marine Corps, and the Chief of Staff of the Air Force.
JDAM	Joint Direct Attack Munition. A general-purpose Mk 83 or Mk 84 bomb or BLU-109 cluster bomb with an inertial guidance package and miniature GPS receiver in a modified tail cone. Initial operational capability originally planned for 1997. Intended for use on Air Force and Navy strike aircraft.
JFACC	Joint Forces Air Component Commander. The officer who has operational control over all air units and air assets assigned to a theater of operations. The JFACC is typically drawn from the service that has the greatest amount of airpower in the area of operations, and reports directly to the theater commander in chief.
Jink	A violent zigzag maneuver intended to confuse enemy tracking or fire-control systems.
Joy Stick	The control stick of a fixed-wing aircraft. Moving the stick forward or back makes the nose pitch up or down. Moving the stick left or right makes the aircraft bank in the corresponding direction. The rudder is separately controlled by foot pedals.
JP-5	Standard U.S. Air Force jet fuel. A petroleum distillate similar to kerosene.
JSOW	AGM-154 Joint Standoff Weapon. A 1000-pound glide bomb with 25 mile range, using INS/GPS guidance, intended to become operational in the late 1990s. The Air Force verson will carry six BLU-108s.
Joint Stars	Joint Surveillance and Targeting Attack Radar System. An Army/Air Force program to deploy about 20 Boeing E-8C aircraft equipped with powerful side-looking synthetic aperture radar to detect moving ground targets at long range. Two E-8A prototypes rushed to Saudi Arabia were very successful in Desert Storm night operations.
JTF	Joint Task Force. A military unit composed of elements of two or more services, commanded by a relatively senior officer. JTFs may be organized

for a specific mission, or maintained as semi-permanent organizations, such as the anti-drug JTF-4 based in Florida.

JTIDS Joint Tactical Information Distribution System. Planned replacement for obsolete existing U.S. and some NATO air, land, and sea high-capacity radio data links. JTIDS operates in the L-band (960–1215 MHz) using frequency-hopping and encryption. Maximum range is 300 to 500 miles. JTIDS allows units with dissimilar computer systems to share sensor, position, weapon, and other data to construct a unified tactical situation display.

KARI The Iraqi Integrated Air Defense System, combining French and Soviet radars, missiles, fighter aircraft, and command, control, and communications systems. Largely neutralized during the Desert Storm air campaign, it may have been partially rebuilt after the war. Name said to be derived from Irak (french for Iraq) spelled backwards.

KC-10 Extender Heavy tanker/transport based on Douglas DC-10 wide-body commercial airliner. There are fifty-nine aircraft in service, some modified with drogue refueling hose reel as well as tail boom. Three CF6 turbofan engines. Maximum takeoff weight 590,000 lbs.

Knot Nautical miles per hour. Often used by U.S. Air Force and Navy to measure aircraft speeds, particularly in the subsonic range. One knot equals one nautical mile per hour.

LANTIRN Low Altitude Navigation Targeting Infrared for Night. A pair of pods mounted on the F-15E and certain F-16C/D aircraft. The AAQ-13 Navigation Pod combines a forward-looking infrared sensor and a terrain following radar. The AAQ-14 Targeting Pod combines a forward looking infrared and laser target designator. Entire System is built by Lockheed Martin and tightly integrated with the aircraft's flight control and weapons delivery software.

LGB Laser-guided bomb.

"Loose Deuce" A two-aircraft formation consisting of a lead and a wingman, separated by a relatively large horizontal and vertical distance, but capable of mutual support and communication.

M-61 Vulcan Six barreled rotary ("Gatling") 20mm cannon used as standard weapon on U.S. aircraft. Very high rate of fire. Also mounted on Army vehicles and Navy ships for short-range anti aircraft defense.

Mach The speed of sound at sea level (760 feet per second). An aircraft's Mach number is dependent on altitude, since sound travels faster in a denser medium. Named for Ernst Mach (1838–1916), Austrian physicist.

Maverick AGM-65 family of air-to-surface missiles, produced since 1971 by Hughes and Raytheon with a variety of guidance and warhead configurations.

MFD Multi-Function Display. A small video monitor or flat panel display on an aircraft control panel that allows the operator to display and manipulate different kinds of sensor information, status indications, warnings, and system diagnostic data.

MiG	Russian acronym for the Mikoyan-Gurevich Design Bureau, developers of some of the greatest fighter aircraft in history, including the MiG-17 and MiG-29. Survived the breakup of the Soviet Union, and is actively competing in the global arms market.
MiG-23	Soviet single-turbojet, single seat variable geometry fighter. Widely exported in large numbers with many variants. A 23mm cannon and up to six missile rails. First flight in 1967. MiG-27 strike fighter is similar, but radar is replaced with laser rangefinder/designator. NATO reporting name is Flogger. No longer in production.
MIL-STD-1553	U.S. Military Standard that defines cable specifications, connectors, and data formats for a digital data-bus, or high-speed network for aircraft, naval, or ground-based electronic systems. One of the most successful standards in aviation history.
MRC	Major Regional Contingency. Current Pentagon euphemism for small war or crisis requiring intervention of U.S. military forces as directed by the President.
MRE	Meals, Ready to Eat. Military field rations in individual serving packs. Eaten by Air Force personnel on deployment until regular dining facilities can be constructed. Humorously known as "Meals Rejected by Ethiopians."
Nautical mile	6076 feet. Not to be confused with Statute Mile, which is 5280 feet. The historical reasons for the difference would be tedious to explain.
NBC	Nuclear, Biological, Chemical. General term for weapons of mass destruction, including nuclear bombs or weapons designed to disperse radioactive material, toxic gases, liquids, or powders, and infectious microorganisms or biological toxins. Forbidden by many international treaties that have been widely ignored.
NORAD	North American Air Defense Command. Joint U.S.–Canadian headquarters located inside Cheyenne Mountain, Colorado, responsible for air defense of North America. CINCNORAD is also the Commander of U.S. Space Command.
NRO	National Reconnaissance Office. Formerly super-secret intelligence agency established in late 1950s within the Department of Defense, not officially acknowledged to exist until 1990s. Responsible for procurement, operation and management of various types of reconnaissance satellites. A separate organization, the Central Imagery Office (CIO), is responsible for processing, interpretation, and dissemination of satellite imagery.
O&M	Operations and Maintenance. A major budget category for most military units.
Optempo	Operational Tempo. Subjective measure of the intensity of military operations. In combat high optempo can overwhelm the enemy's ability to respond, at the risk of burning out your own forces. In peacetime a high optempo can adversely affect morale and exhaust budgeted funds.
Ordnance	Weapons, ammunition, or other consumable armament. Frequently misspelled.

PAA	Primary Aircraft Authorized. The number of planes allocated to a unit for the performance of its operational mission. PAA is the basis for budgeting manpower, support equipment, and flying hours. In some cases, a unit may have fewer aircraft because of delivery schedule slippage or accidents. Units may also have more aircraft than their PAA, such as trainers, spare "maintenance floats," or inoperable "hangar queens."
PAO	Public Affairs Officer. Military staff officer responsible for media relations, coordination with civil authorities, VIP escort duties, and similar chores.
Pave Penny	A laser spot tracker pod originally used on Air Force A-10 and A-7 aircraft for delivery of laser-guided bombs. This simple device has no laser target designator, so targets must be designated by another aircraft. Pods from retired A-7s are currently being rebuilt for installation on F-16s.
Pave Pillar	Air Force program for the development of a new generation of modular electronic components for new generation combat aircraft.
Pave Tack	An early laser-target designator pod developed by Ford Aeronutronic (now Loral) used on the F-111 and other aircraft.
Paveway	Generic term for laser-guided Mk. 80-series bombs.
PGM	Precision-Guided Munition. Commonly called a "smart bomb."
Pitch	Change of an aircraft's attitude relative to its lateral axis (a line drawn from left to right through the center of gravity). Pitch up and the nose rises; pitch down and the nose drops.
"Pucker Factor"	Flight crew anxiety level. Typically related to highly stressful combat situations such as major aircraft system malfunctions while under fire from enemy missiles.
PVO	Protivo-vozdushnoye Ogranicheniye Strany, Russian for anti-air defense. The independent branch of the former Soviet, now Russian, armed forces charged with homeland defense against enemy bombers and ballistic missiles.
Pylon	A structure attached to the wing or fuselage of an aircraft that supports an engine, fuel tank, weapon, or external pod. The pylon itself may be removable, in which case it is attached to a "hard point" that provides a mechanical and electrical interface.
RAM	Radar Absorbing Material. Metal or metal-oxide particles or fibers embedded in synthetic resin applied as a coating or surface treatment on radar-reflective areas of a vehicle in order to reduce its radar cross section. A particular RAM formulation may be specific to a narrow band of the radar frequency spectrum.
RC-135V Rivet Joint	Program name for electronic reconnaissance aircraft, operated by 55th Wing based at Offutt AFB, Nebraska. Used in Saudi Arabia during Desert Shield/Desert Storm.
Red Flag	Regularly scheduled (about five per year) combat squadron training exercises held at Nellis AFB, Nevada. Every crew flies ten different missions on a highly instrumented range.

Red Horse U.S. Air Force engineering units (of squadron/battalion size) equipped and trained for rapid construction or repair or runways and airbase facilities.

Revetment An area adjacent to a runway or taxiway, surrounded by a protective wall or mound or earth, where aircraft may be dispersed for temporary shelter, refueling or rearming.

RFMDS Red Flag Measurement and Debrief System. Electronic monitoring and recording system at Nellis AFB used to evaluate performance and tactics of aircraft participating in training exercises.

ROE Rules of Engagement. Guidance, often determined at the highest levels of government, regarding how and when flight crews may employ their weapons. In air to air combat, ROE usually specify specific criteria for identifying a non-friendly aircraft as hostile. In air-to-ground combat, ROE usually forbids attacking targets likely to involve significant collateral damage to civilian populations or religious sites. Regardless of the ROE, the right of self-defense against direct armed attack is never denied.

Roll Change of an aircraft's attitude relative to its longitudinal axis (a line drawn from nose to tail through the center of gravity). Roll to port and the aircraft tilts to the left; roll to starboard and it tilts to the right. Roll also describes a class of aerobatic maneuvers, such as the barrel roll.

RWR Radar Warning Receiver. An electronic detector tuned to one or more hostile radar frequencies and linked to an alarm that alerts the pilot to the approximate direction, and possibly the type, of threat. Similar in concept to automotive police radar detectors. Also known as a RHAW (Radar Homing and Warning Receiver).

S-60 Soviet 57-mm antiaircraft gun. Highly mobile. Very lethal at low altitudes, it may be radar or optically aimed.

SA-2 Soviet surface-to-air missile. Introduced in the 1950s and frequently updated. Excellent performance at high altitude. Western reporting name is Guideline.

SA-3 Soviet surface-to-air missile. Soviet designation is S-125 Neva. Western reporting name is Goa. Improved low-altitude performance. Operation since early 1960s.

SA-6 Soviet surface-to-air missile. Western reporting name is Gainful. Semiactive radar homing. Proved highly effective in Egyptian service during 1973 Mideast War.

SA-8 Soviet short-range surface-to-air missile. Western reporting name is Gecko.

SALT Strategic Arms Limitation Treaty. One of a series of agreements beginning in 1972, between the United States and the former Soviet Union, designed to limit the number and type of nuclear delivery systems and warheads.

SAM Surface-to-air missile. A guided missile with the primary mission of engaging enemy aircraft. Most SAMs use rocket propulsion and some type of radar or infrared guidance.

SAR	Search and Rescue (sometimes written as CSAR, Combat Search and Rescue). An urgent and dangerous mission to recover shot-down flight crew or survivors from enemy-controlled territory or waters. Typically involves very low-altitude covert helicopter flights with or without fighter escort.
SAR	Synthetic-Aperture Radar. An aircraft radar (or operating mode of a multi-function radar) that can produce highly accurate ground maps.
SCUD	Western reporting name for the Soviet R-11 (SCUD-A) and R-17 (SCUD-B) short-range ballistic missile. Based largely on World War II German technology. Range of 110–180 miles with 1000 kg./ 2200 lb. warhead. Inaccurate inertial guidance. Can be transported and erected for launch by large truck. Widely exported to Iraq, North Korea, and other Soviet client states. Iraq modified basic SCUD design to produce longer-ranged Al Abbas and Al Hussein missiles with much smaller warheads.
SEAD	Suppression of Enemy Air Defenses. This requires enticing the enemy to light up search and track radars, launch SAMs, or fire anti-aircraft guns, which can then be target for destruction or neutralization by jamming and other countermeasures. SEAD was a primary mission of Wild Weasel aircraft. With the retirement of the remaining F-4G Wild Weasels, the SEAD mission will be taken over by specially trained and equipped F-16s.
SIGINT	Signal Intelligence. Interception, decoding, and analysis of enemy communications traffic.
Skunk Works®	Lockheed's Burbank, California, Advanced Development group, created during World War II by engineer Clarence "Kelly" Johnson. Developed the U-2, SR-71, F-117, and other secret aircraft. The name and skunk cartoon logo are copyrighted by Lockheed.
Slat	A long, narrow movable control surface, usually along the leading edge of the wing, to provide additional lift during takeoff.
Slave Mode	Any system mode that causes the sensor of a weapon to lock onto a target being tracked by the sensor onboard the aircraft. For example, the infrared seeker on a Sidewinder missile can be "slaved" to a target tracked by the aircraft's radar.
SNECMA	Societe Nationale d'Etude et de Construction de Moteurs d'Avions (National Aircraft Engine Research and Construction Company). French state-owned jet engine builder; financially troubled but technically proficient.
Sortie	The basic unit of airpower: one complete combat mission by one aircraft. "Sortie generation" is the ability of an air unit to re-arm, re-fuel, and service aircraft for repeated missions in a given period.
SOS	Space Operations Squadron.
Spar	A long load-carrying beam in the structure of a wing.
Sparrow	AIM-7 family of long-range radar guided air-to-air missiles produced by Raytheon. Variants include the ship-launched Sea Sparrow.

Stall	Sudden lost of lift when the airflow separates from the wing surface. May be caused by a variety of maneuvers, such as climbing too steeply with insufficient thrust. "Compressor stall" is a different phenomenon that occurs inside a turbine engine.
START	Strategic Arms Reduction Treaty. One of a series of agreements between the United States and the former Soviet Union to reduce the number of deployed nuclear delivery systems and warheads.
Stealth	A combination of design features, technologies, and materials, some highly classified, designed to reduce the radar, visual, infrared, and acoustic signature of an aircraft, ship, or other vehicle to the point where effective enemy detection and countermeasures are extremely unlikely before the vehicle has completed its mission and escaped. The F-117A is the best known modern example.
STOVL	Short Takeoff, Vertical Landing. Capability of certain vectored-thrust aircraft, notably the Harrier. Short takeoff is assisted by a fixed "ski-jump" ramp.
T-38 Talon	Twin-turbojet advanced trainer; over 1100 built by Northrop. Entered service in 1961. First supersonic aircraft specifically designed as a trainer.
T-3A Firefly	Lightweight two-seat propeller driven trainer based on British Slingsby T67. Used by U.S. Air Force for screening of prospective pilots. Top speed 178 mph., ceiling 19,000 ft.
TAC	Tactical Air Command. Former major command of the U.S. Air Force responsible for most fighter aircraft wings. Merged into Air Combat Command in 1992.
TACC	Tactical Air Control Center. A staff organization responsible for planning and coordinating air force combat and support operations in a given area.
TDY	Temporary Duty. A military assignment to a location away from one's normal duty station. TDY generally involves separation from family and entitles personnel to supplementary pay and allowances.
TELAR	Transporter Erector Launcher and Radar. A tracked or wheeled vehicle, typically of Soviet design, equipped to carry and launch one or more surface-to-air missiles. Often equipped with optical tracking systems and command, control, and communications electronics.
TERCOM	Terrain Contour Matching. A cruise missile guidance concept that relies on a radar altimeter and a stored digital map of elevations along the line of flight. Flight plans require detailed and lengthy preparation, and cannot be generated for relatively flat, featureless terrain.
TFR	Terrain-Following Radar. A low-powered radar that scans the terrain ahead during low-level flight and either automatically commands the flight-control system to avoid hitting the ground, or sounds a warning to the pilot to pull up when necessary.
TFW	Tactical Fighter Wing. A unit of three fighter squadrons and supporting units.

TO&E	Table of Organization and Equipment. The official document that prescribes in detail the structure and authorized assets of a military unit.
Top Gun	The U.S. Navy Fighter Weapon School, scheduled to relocate from NAS Miramar, California, to NAS LeMoore, California. Responsible for training fleet pilots in air-combat maneuvering.
TSSAM	Tri-service Standoff Attack Missile (AGM-137). A stealthy, long-range precision-guided munition for Air Force, Navy, and Army (ground-launched) use; cancelled in 1994 when the projected unit cost exceeded $2 million. Air-launched version intended for B-1B, B2, B-52, F-16, and F-22 weighed about 2300 lb./ 1045 kg. with a range of less than 375 miles/600 km.
U-2	High-altitude (over 90,000 ft./27,430 m.) reconnaissance aircraft originally developed in the 1950s for the Central Intelligence Agency by Lockheed. Single J57, later J75, turbojet. Many variants with diverse sensors operated by the USAF and NASA (civilian research).
UAV	Unmanned Aerial Vehicle. Also known as a drone or RPV (remotely piloted vehicle). A recoverable pilotless aircraft, either remotely controlled over a radio-data link, or pre-programmed with an advanced autopilot. The U.S. Air Force has tended to resist any use of UAVs, except as targets, because they take jobs away from pilots. There are also real safety concerns about operating UAVs and manned aircraft in the same airspace, since UAVs are usually small and hard to see.
UPT	Undergraduate Pilot Training.
Variable Geometry	Ability of an aircraft to change the sweep of its wings in flight, to optimize performance for a given speed and altitude.
Viewgraph	An overhead-projector transparency or slide used in briefings or presentations. Sometimes used as a term of derision for a project that is incompletely developed, as: "His plan was nothing but a set of viewgraphs."
Warthog	Nickname for the A-10 Thunderbolt.
Waypoint	Pre-set navigational reference point on an aircraft's flight plan. May include geographical coordinates, plus altitude, speed, and time-of-arrival data.
WCMD	Wind-Corrected Munitions Dispenser. A cluster bomb with an inertial-guidance system and GPS receiver, allowing accurate delivery from high altitudes. Intended for use on the B-1B, beginning around 2002.
WICP	Wing Initial Communications Package. A set of radios, satellite communications antennas, portable electric power generators, and related equipment maintained by selected Air Force wings for rapid emergency deployment to remote locations.
Wild Weasel	An aircraft configured with Radar Homing and Warning (RHAW) gear and Anti-Radiation Missiles (ARMs) operated to suppress enemy surface-to-air missile sites. Originally performed by F-100F, F-105F, and F-4G Phantom II aircraft, this mission will increasingly be borne by specially trained and equipped F-16Cs.

William Tell	An air-superiority competition held every other year at Tyndall AFB, Florida. Live-fire missions are conducted over the Gulf of Mexico.
WSO	Weapons System Officer. The backseater in an F-15E or F-111. Pronounced "wizzo." Although not specifically trained as a pilot, the WSO usually acquires basic flying skills.
XO	Executive Officer. Second in command of a squadron or equivalent unit.
Yaw	Change of an aircraft's attitude relative to its vertical axis (a line drawn from top to bottom through the center of gravity). Yaw to port and the nose points further to the left; yaw to starboard and the nose points further to the right.
ZSU-23-4	Soviet four-barreled 23mm antiaircraft gun on light tank chassis with radar and optical fire control. Deadly against unarmored low-altitude aircraft. Usually employed together with mobile SAM launchers. Russian nickname is Shilka.

Bibliography

BOOKS:

Adams, James. *Bull's Eye: The Assassination and Life of Supergun Inventor Gerald Bull.* Times Books, 1992.

Adan, Avraham (Bren). *On the Banks of the Suez.* Presidio Press, 1980.

Allen, Charles. *Thunder and Lightning: The RAF in the Gulf.* HMSO, 1991.

Allen Thomas B. *War Games: The Secret World of Creators, Players and Policy Makers Rehearsing World War III Today.* McGraw-Hill, 1987.

—— and Polmar, Norman. *Merchants of Treason.* Dell Publishing, 1988.

Allison, Graham T. *Essence of Decision.* Little Brown, 1971.

Arnett, Peter. *Live from the Battlefield: From Vietnam to Baghdad.* Simon & Schuster, 1994.

Asher, Jerry, with Hammel, Eric. *Duel for the Golan: The 100-Hour Battle that Saved Israel.* Morrow Publishers, 1987.

Atkinson, Rick. *Crusade: The Untold Story of the Persian Gulf War.* Houghton Mifflin, 1993.

Baker, A.D. *Combat Fleets of the World 1993.* The Naval Institute Press, 1993.

Ballard, Jack S. *The United States Air Force in Southeast Asia.* U.S. Government Printing Office.

Barker, AJ. *The Yom Kippur War.* Ballantine Books, 1974.

Barron, John. *MiG Pilot: The Final Escape of Lt. Belenko.* Avon Books, 1980.

Basel, G.I. *Pak Six.* Associated Creative Writers, 1982.

Bathurst, Robert B. *Understanding the Soviet Navy: A Handbook.* U.S. Government Printing Office, 1979.

Baxter, William P. *Soviet AirLand: Battle Tactics.* Presidio Press, 1986.

Berry, F. Clifton, Jr. *Strike Aircraft: The Vietnam War.* Bantam Books, 1987.

—— *Gadget Warfare: The Vietnam War.* Bantam Books, 1988.

Beschloss, Michael R. *May Day.* Harper & Row, 1986.

—— and Talbott, Strobe. *At the Highest Levels.* Little Brown, 1993.

Bishop, Chris, and Donald, David. *The Encyclopedia of World Military Power.* The Military Press, 1986.

Bishop, Edward. *Wellington Bomber.* Ballantine Books, 1974.

Blackwell, James. *Thunder in the Desert: The Strategy and Tactics of the Persian Gulf War.* Bantam Books, 1991.

Blair, Colonel Arthur H., USA (Ret.). *At War in the Gulf.* A&M University Press, 1992.

Bodansky, Yossef. *Crisis in Korea: The Emergence of a New and Dangerous Nuclear Power.* SPI Books, 1994.

Bonnanni, Pete. *Art of the Kill: A Comprehensive Guide to Modern Air Combat.* Spectrum Holobyte, 1993.

Boyne, Walter J. *Clash of Wings: World War II in the Air.* Simon & Schuster, 1994.

Bradin, James W. *From Hot Air to Hellfire: The History of Army Attack Aviation.* Presidio Press, 1994.

Braybrook, Roy. *British Aerospace Harrier and Sea Harrier.* Osprey/Motorbooks International, 1984.

—— *Soviet Combat Aircraft.* Osprey/Motorbooks International, 1991.

Broughton, Colonel Jack, USAF (Ret.). *Thud Ridge.* Bantam Books, 1969.

—— *Going Downtown: The War against Hanoi and Washington.* Orion Books, 1988.

Brown, Captain Eric M., RN. *Duels in the Sky: World War II Naval Aircraft in Combat.* Naval Institute Press, 1988.

Brown, David F. *Birds of Prey: Aircraft, Nose Art and Mission Markings of Desert Storm/Shield.* U.S. Government Printing Office, 1993.

Brugioni, Dino A. *Eyeball to Eyeball: The Cuban Missile Crisis.* Random House, 1991.

Burrows, William E. *Exploring Space: Voyages in the Solar System and Beyond.* Random House, 1990.

—— and Windrem, Robert. *Critical Mass.* Simon & Schuster, 1994.

Burton, James G. *The Pentagon Wars: Reformers Challenge the Old Guard.* Naval Institute Press, 1993.

Butowski, Piotr, with Miller, Jay. *OKB MiG: A History of the Design Bureau and Its Aircraft.* Specialty Press, 1991.

Caidin, Martin. *The Night Hamburg Died.* Bantam Books, 1960.

—— *Flying Forts: The B-17 in World War II.* Ballantine Books, 1968.

Caldwell, Donald L. *The Epic Saga of Germany's Greatest Fighter Wing: JG 26, Top Guns of the Luftwaffe.* Orion Books, 1991.

Campbell, Glenn. *Area 51, Viewer's Guide.* Glenn Campbell-HCR, 1994.

Carter, Kit C., and Mueller, Robert. *The Army Air Forces in World War II: Combat Chronology 1941-1945.* U.S. Government Printing Office, 1973.

Chadwick, Frank. *Gulf War Fact Book.* GDW, 1992.

Chant, Christopher. *Encyclopedia of Modern Aircraft Armament.* IMP Publishing Services Ltd., 1988.

Chinnery, Philip D. *Life on the Line.* St. Martins Press, 1988.

Clancy, Tom. *The Hunt for Red October.* The Berkley Publishing Group, 1985.

—— *Red Storm Rising.* G.P. Putnam's Sons, 1986.

—— *The Cardinal of the Kremlin.* G.P. Putnam's Sons, 1988.

—— *The Sum of All Fears.* G.P. Putnam's Sons, 1991.

—— *Submarine: A Guided Tour Inside a Nuclear Warship.* Berkley, 1993.

—— *Armored Cav: A Guided Tour of an Armored Cavalry Regiment.* Berkley, 1994.

—— *Debt of Honor.* G.P. Putnam's Sons, 1994.

Cline, Ray S. *Secrets, Spies and Scholars.* Acropolis, 1976.

Clodfelter, Mark. *The Limits of Airpower: The American Bombing of North Vietnam.* Free Press, 1989.

Cochran, Thomas; Arkin, William; Norris, Robert; and Sands, Jeffrey. *Soviet Nuclear Weapons*. Harper & Row, 1989.

Cohen, Colonel Eliezer "Cheetah." *Israel's Best Defense: The First Full Story of Israeli Air Force.* Orion Books, 1993.

Cohen, Dr. Elliot A. *Gulf War Air Power Survey Summary Report.* U.S. Government Printing Office, 1993.

—— *Gulf War Air Power Survey Volume I.* U.S. Government Printing Office, 1993.

—— *Gulf War Air Power Survey Volume II.* U.S. Government Printing Office, 1993.

—— *Gulf War Air Power Survey Volume III.* U.S. Government Printing Office, 1993.

—— *Gulf War Air Power Survey Volume IV.* U.S. Government Printing Office, 1993.

—— *Gulf War Air Power Survey Volume V.* U.S. Government Printing Office, 1993.

Cohen, Elliot A., and Gooch, John. *Military Misfortunes: The Anatomy of Failure in War.* Free Press, 1990.

Copeland, Peter. *She Went to War: The Rhonda Cornum Story.* Presidio Press, 1992.

Coyne, James P. *Airpower in the Gulf.* Air Force Association, 1992.

Creech, Bill. *The Five Pillars of TQM: How to Make Total Quality Management Work for You.* Dutton, 1994.

Crickmore, Paul F. *Lockheed SR-71: The Secret Missions Exposed.* Osprey Aerospace, 1993.

Crow, Admiral William J., Jr. *The Line of Fire: From Washington to the Gulf, the Politics and Battles of the New Military.* Simon & Schuster, 1993.

Cunningham, Randy, with Ethell, Jeff. *Fox Two: The Story of America's First Ace in Vietnam.* Chaplin Fighter Museum, 1984.

Darwish, Adel, and Alexander, Gregory. *Unholy Babylon: The Secret History of Saddam's War.* St Martin's Press, 1991.

David, Peter. *Triumph in the Desert.* Random House, 1991.

Davis, Larry. *MIG Alley: Air-to-Air Combat over Korea.* Squadron/Signal Publications, 1978.

Dawood, N.J. (editor). *The Koran.* Penguin Books, 1956.

Dean, David J. *The Air Force Role in Low Intensity Conflict.* Air University Press, 1986.

Divine, Robert A. *The Sputnik Challenge.* Oxford, 1993.

Doleman, Edgar C., Jr. *The Vietnam Experience: Tools of War.* Boston Publishing Company, 1985.

Doolittle, Jimmy, with Glines, Carol V. *An Autobiography by General James H. "Jimmy" Doolittle: I Could Never Be So Lucky Again.* Bantam Books, 1991.

Dorr, Robert F. *Air War Hanoi.* Blanford Press, 1988.

—— *Vietnam MiG Killers.* Motorbooks, 1988.

—— *Desert Shield – The Build Up: The Complete Story.* Motorbooks, 1991.

—— *Desert Storm Air War.* Motorbooks, 1991.

—— *F-86 Sabre: History of the Sabre and FJ Fury.* Motorbooks, 1993.

—— and Taylor, Norman E. *U.S. Air Force Nose Art: Into the 90s.* Specialty Press, 1993.

Dunnigan, James F., and Bay, Austin. *From Shield to Storm.* Morrow Books, 1992.

—— and Martel, Williams. *How to Stop a War: Lessons on Two Hundred Years of War and Peace.* Doubleday Books, 1987.

Dupuy, Colonel T.N., USA (Ret.). *The Evolution of Weapons and Warfare.* Bobbs-Merrill, 1980.

—— *Options of Command.* Hippocrene Books, Inc., 1984.

—— *Numbers, Predictions & War: The Use of History to Evaluate and Predict the Outcome of Armed Conflict.* Hero Books, 1985.

—— *Understanding War: History and Theory of Combat.* Paragon House, 1987.

—— *Attrition: Forecasting Battle Casualties and Equipment Losses in Modern War.* Hero Books, 1990.

—— *Understanding Defeat: How to Recover From Loss in Battle to Gain Victory in War.* Paragon House, 1990.

—— *Saddam Hussein: Scenarios and Strategies for the Gulf War.* Warner Books, 1991.

—— *Future Wars: The World's Most Dangerous Flashpoints.* Warner Books, 1993.

Dzhus, Alexander M. *Soviet Wings: Modern Soviet Military Aircraft.* Greenhill Books, 1991.

Edwards, Major John E., USA (Ret.). *Combat Service Support Guide.* 2nd Edition. Stackpole Books, 1993.

Eighth Military History Symposium USAF Academy. *Air Power and Warfare.* U.S. Government Printing Office, 1978.

Eshel, David. *The U.S. Rapid Development Forces.* Arco Publishing, Inc., 1985.

Ethell, Jeffrey L., and Price, Alfred. *One Day in a Long War: May 10, 1972, Air War, North Vietnam.* Random House, 1989.

—— and Sand, Robert T. *Fighter Command: American Fighters in Original WWII Color.* Motorbooks, 1991.

—— and Simonsen, Clarence. *The History of Aircraft.* Ethell and Simonsen, 1991.

Finney, Robert T. *History of the Air Corps Tactical School, 1920-1940.* U.S. Government Printing Office, 1992.

Fisher, David E. *A Race on the Edge of Time.* McGraw Hill, 1988.

Flaherty, Thomas J. *Carrier Warfare.* Time Life Books, 1991.

—— *Air Combat.* Time Life Books, 1990.

Fletcher, Harry R. *U.S. Air Force Reference Series: Air Force Bases.* U.S. Government Printing Office, 1993.

Flintham, Victor. *Air Wars and Aircraft: A Detailed Record of Air Combat, 1945 to Present.* Facts on File, 1990.

Ford, Brian. *German Secret Weapons: Blueprint for Mars.* Ballantine Books, 1969.

Francillon, Rene J. *Tonkin Gulf Yacht Club: U.S. Carrier Operations off Vietnam.* Naval Institute Press, 1988.

Freeman, Roger A. *The Mighty Eighth: In Color.* Specialty Press, 1993.

—— *The Mighty Eighth: The History of the Units, Men, and Machines of the U.S. 8th Air Force.* Motorbooks International, 1993.

—— *The Mighty Eighth: War Diary.* Motorbooks International, 1993.

—— *The Mighty Eighth: War Manual.* Motorbooks International, 1993.

Fricker, John. *Battle for Pakistan.* Ian Allen, 1979.

Friedman, Norman. *Desert Victory: The War For Kuwait.* Naval Institute Press, 1991.

—— *The Naval Institute Guide to World Naval Weapons Systems 1991/92.* Naval Institute Press, 1994.

—— *The Naval Institute Guide to World Naval Weapons Systems.* Naval Institute Press, 1994.

Furtrell, Robert F. *The United States Air Force in Southeast Asia: The Advisory Years to 1965.* U.S. Government Printing Office, 1981.

—— *The United States Air Force in Korea.* U.S. Government Printing Office, 1983.

Galland, Adolf. *The First and the Last.* Chaplin Museum Press, 1986.

Gann, Ernest K. *The Black Watch: The Men Who Fly America's Secret Spy Planes.* Random House, 1989.

Garnett, Graham Christian. *Against All Odds: The Battle of Britain.* The Rococo Group, 1990.

Garrett, Dan. *Wings of Freedom.* Lockheed-Ft. Worth, 1988.

Gibson, James Williams. *The Perfect War: Technowar in Vietnam.* Atlantic Monthly Press, 1986.

Gordon, Yefim, and Rigmant, Vladimir. *MiG-15.* Motorbooks, 1993.

Gribkov, General Anatoli I., and Smith, General William Y. *Operation Anadyr: U.S. and Soviet Generals Recount the Cuban Missile Crisis.* Edition, Inc., 1994.

Gropman, Lt. Colonel Alan L. *Airpower and the Airlift Evacuation of Kham Duc.* Airpower Research Institute, 1979.

Gumble, Bruce L. *The International Countermeasures Handbook.* EW Communications Inc., 1987.

Gunston, Bill. *Mikoyan MiG-21.* Osprey Publishing Limited, 1986.

—— with Gilchrist, Peter. *Jet Bombers: From the Messerschmitt Me 262 to the Stealth B-2.* Osprey Aerospace, 1993.

Halberstadt, Hans. *Desert Storm: Ground War.* Motorbooks, 1991.

—— *F-15E Strike Eagle.* Windrow & Greene, 1992.

Hall, George. *Air Guard: America's Flying Militia.* Presidio Press, 1990.

Hallion, Dr. Richard P. *On the Frontier: Flight Research at Dryden, 1946-1981.* National and Aeronautics and Space Administration, 1984.

—— *The Literature of Aeronautics, Astronautics and Air Power.* U.S. Government Printing Office, 1984.

—— *Rise of the Fighter Aircraft, 1914-1918.* The Nautical & Aviation Publishing Co., 1988.

—— *Storm over Iraq: Air Power and the Gulf War.* Smithsonian Books, 1992.

—— *Strike from the Sky: The History of Battlefield Air Attack, 1911-1945.* Smithsonian Books, 1989.

Hanak, Walter. *Aces and Aerial Victories.* U.S. Government Printing Office, 1979.

Hansen, Chuck. *U.S. Nuclear Weapons.* Orion Books, 1988.

Hanson, Victor Davis. *The Western Way of War: Infantry Battle in Classical Greece,* Alfred Knopf Publishers, 1989.

Hartcup, Guy. *The Silent Revolution.* Brassey's, 1993.

Hastings, Max. *Bomber Command: Churchill's Epic Campaign.* Simon & Schuster, 1989.

Heiferman, Ron. *Flying Tigers: Chennault in China,* Ballantine Books, 1971.

Heinlein, Robert A. *Starship Troopers.* Ace Books, 1959.

Heinmann, Edward, Rausa, Rosario, and Van Every, K.E. *Aircraft Design.* Nautical & Aviation Publishing Co., 1985.

Hersh, Seymour M. *The Samson Option.* Random House, 1991.

Hess, William. *B-17 Flying Fortress.* Ballantine Books, 1974.

Hilsman, Roger. *George Bush vs. Saddam Hussein: Military Success! Political Failure?* Lyford Books, 1992.

Holley, I.B., Jr. *The U.S. Special Studies: Ideas and Weapons.* U.S. Government Printing Office, 1983.

Hudson, Heather E. *Communication Satellites: Their Development and Impact.* Free Press, 1990.

Hurley, Colonel Alfred, USAF, and Erhart, Major Robert C., USAF. *Air Power and Warfare.* U.S. Government Printing Office, 1978.

Jessup, John E., Jr., and Coakley, Robert W. *A Guide to the Study and Use of Military History.* U.S. Government Printing Office, 1991.

Jomini, Baron Antoine Henri de. *The Art of War.* Green Hill Books, 1992.

Joss, John. *Strike: U.S. Naval Strike Warfare Center.* Presidio Press, 1989.

Kahn, David. *Seizing the Enigma: The Race to Break the German U-Boat Codes, 1939-1943.* Houghton Mifflin Company, 1991.

Kaplan, Philip. *Little Friends: The Fighter Pilot Experience in World War II England.* Random House, 1991.

—— *Round the Clock.* Random House, 1993.

—— and Collier, Richard. *Their Finest Hour: The Battle of Britain Remembered.* Abbeville Press, 1989.

—— and Smith, Rex Alan. *One Last Look.* Cross River Press, 1983.

Keegan, John. *A History of Warfare.* Alfred A. Knopf, 1993.

Kelly, Orr. *Hornet: The Inside Story of the F/A-18.* Presidio Press, 1990.

Kenney, George C. *General Kenney Reports.* Office of Air Force History, 1987.

Kerr, E. Batlett. *Flames over Tokyo.* Donald I. Fine, Inc., 1991.

Kinzey, Bert. *The Fury of Desert Storm: The Air Campaign.* McGraw-Hill, 1991.

—— *U.S. Aircraft and Armament of Operation Desert Storm.* Kalmbach Books, 1993.

Kissinger, Henry. *Henry Kissinger: Diplomacy.* Simon & Schuster, 1994.

Knott, Captain Richard C., USN. *The Naval Aviation Guide.* Naval Institute Press, 1985.

Kohn, Richard H., and Harahan, Joseph P. *USAF Warrior Studies.* Coward McCann, Inc., 1942.

—— *Air Superiority in World War II and Korea.* U.S. Government Printing Office, 1983.

—— *Air Interdiction in World War II, Korea, and Vietnam.* U.S. Government Printing Office, 1990.

Korb, Edward L. *The World's Missile Systems.* General Dynamics, Pamona Division, 1988.

Kyle, Colonel James H., USAF (Ret.). *The Guts to Try.* Orion Books, 1990.

Lake, Jon. *MiG-29: Soviet Superfighter.* Osprey Publishing, 1989.

—— *McDonnell F-4 Phantom-Spirit in the Skies.* Aerospace Publishing Ltd., 1992.

Lambert, Mark. *Jane's All the World's Aircraft 1991-92.* Jane's Publishing Group, 1992.

Lavalle, Major A.J.C. *Last Flight from Saigon.* Office of Air Force History, 1978.

—— *The Tale of Two Bridges and the Battle for the Skies over North Vietnam.* Office of Air Force History, 1978.

—— *The Vietnamese Air Force, 1951-1975, and Analysis of Its Role in Combat and Fourteen Hours at Koh Tang.* Office of Air Force History, 1978.

—— *Airpower and the 1972 Spring Invasion.* Airpower Research Institute, 1979.

Lehman, John. *Making War.* Scribners, 1992.

Levinson, Jeffrey L. *Alpha Strike Vietnam: The Navy's Air War, 1964-1973.* Presidio Press, 1989.

Liddell-Hart, B. H., *Strategy.* Frederick A. Praeger, Inc., 1967.

Lindsey, Robert. *The Flight of the Falcon.* Simon & Schuster, 1983.

Luttwak, Edward, and Koehl, Stuart L. *The Dictionary of Modern War: A Guide to the Ideas, Institutions and Weapons of Modern Military Power.* Harper Collins, 1991.

Macedonia, Raymond M. *Getting it Right.* Morrow Publishing, 1993.

Makower, Joel. *The Air and Space Catalog: The Complete Sourcebook to Everything in the Universe.* Vintage Tilden Press, 1989.

Manning, Robert. *The Vietnam Experience: The North.* Boston Publishing Company, 1986.

Marolds, Edward J. *Carrier Operations: The Vietnam War.* Bantam Books, 1987.

Mason, Francis K. *Battle over Britain.* Aston Publications, 1990.

Mason, Tony. *To Inherit the Skies: From Spitfire to Tornado.* Brassey's, 1990.

McCarthy, Brigadier General James R., USAF, and Rayfield, Colonel Robert, E., USAF. *Linebacker II: A View from the Rock.* Office of Air Force History, 1978.

McConnell, Malcolm. *Just Cause: The Real Story of America's High-Tech Invasion of Panama.* St. Martin's Press, 1991.

McFarland, Stephen L., and Newton, Wesley Phillips. *The Command of the Sky.* Smithsonian, 1991.

McKinnon, Dan. *Bullseye – Iraq.* Berkley, 1987.

Meisner, Arnold. *Desert Storm: Sea War.* Motorbooks, 1991.

Mersky, Peter B., and Polmar, Norman. *The Naval War in Vietnam.* Kennsington Books, 1981.

Micheletti, Eric. *Operation Daguet: The French Air Force in the Gulf War.* Concord Publications Company, 1991.

Middlebrook, Martin. *Task Force: The Falklands War, 1982.* Penguin Books, 1987.

Miller, Samuel Duncan. *U.S. Air Force Reference Series: An Aero Space Bibliography.* U.S. Government Printing Office, 1986.

Morrison, Bob. *Operation Desert Sabre: The Desert Rat's Liberation of Kuwait.* Concord, 1991.

Morroco, John. *The Vietnam Experience: Thunder from Above.* Boston Publishing Company, 1984.

—— *The Vietnam Experience: Rain of Fire.* Boston Publishing Company, 1985.

Morse, Stan. *Gulf Air War Debrief.* Aerospace Publishing Limited, 1991.

Musciano, Walter A. *Messerschmitt Aces.* TAB/Aero Books, 1990.

Nakdimon, Shlomo. *First Strike: The Exclusive Story of How Israel Foiled Iraq's Attempt to Get the Bomb.* Summit Books, 1987.

Nalty, Bernard C. *The United States Air Force Special Studies: Air Power and the Fight for the Khe Sanh.* U.S. Government Printing Office, 1986.

Neafeld, Jacob. *Ballistic Missiles in the United States Air Force.* U.S. Government Printing Office, 1992.

Nelson, Derek, and Parsons, Dave. *Hell-Bent for Leather.* Motorbooks, 1990.

Neustadt, Richard E., and May, Ernest R. *Thinking in Time: The Uses of History for Decision Makers.* Free Press, 1986.

Newhouse, John. *War and Peace in the Nuclear Age.* Alfred Knopf Publications, 1989.

Nichols, Commander John B., USN (Ret.), and Tillman, Barrett. *On Yankee Station: The Naval Air War over Vietnam.* Naval Institute Press, 1987.

Nissen, Jack. *Winning the Radar War.* St. Martin's Press, 1987.

Norby, M.O. *Soviet Aerospace Handbook.* U.S. Government Printing Office, 1978.

Nordeen, Lon. *Fighters over Israel: The Story of the Israeli Air Force from the War of Independence to the Beakaa Valley.* Orion Books, 1990.

O'Ballance, Edgar. *No Victor, No Vanquished.* Presidio Press, 1978.

Office of the Secretary of Defense. *Conduct of the Persian Gulf War.* U.S. Government Printing Office, 1992.

Ogley, Bob. *Doodlebugs and Rockets.* Froglets Publications, 1992.

O'Neill, Richard. *Suicide Squads of World War II.* Salamander Books, 1981.

Orange, Vincent. *Coningham: A Biography of Air Marshall Sir Arthur Coningham.* U.S. Government Printing Office, 1992.

Pagonis, Lt. General William G., with Cruikshank, Jeffrey L. *Moving Mountains: Lesson in Leadership and Logistics from the Gulf War.* HBS Press, 1992.

Parrish, Thomas. *The American Codebreakers: The U.S. Role in Ultra.* Scarborough Publishers, 1986.

Parsons, Dave, and Nelson, Derek. *Bandits!* Motorbooks, 1993.

Paszek, Lawrence J. *U.S. Air Force Reference Series: A Guide to Documentary Sources.* U.S. Government Printing Office, 1986.

Peebles, Curtis. *Guardians: Strategic Reconnaissance Satellites.* Presidio Press, 1987.

—— *The Moby Dick Project.* Smithsonian Institute, 1991.

Penkovskiy, Oleg. T*he Penkovskiy Papers.* Avon Books, 1965.

Perla, Peter P. *The Art of Wargaming.* Naval Institute Press, 1990.

Perret, Geoffrey. *Winged Victory: The Army Air Forces in World War II.* Random House, 1993.

Petersen, Philip A. *Soviet Air Power and the Pursuit of New Military Options.* United States Air Force, 1979.

Pocock, Chris. *Dragon Lady: The History of the U-2 Spyplane.* Motorbooks International, 1989.

Polmar, Norman, and Laur, Timothy. *Strategic Air Command.* Nautical & Aviation, 1990.

Pretty, Ronald T. *Jane's Weapon Systems 1981-82.* Jane's Publishing Company Limited, 1981.

Price, Dr. Alfred. *Battle of Britain: 18 August 1940, The Hardest Day.* Granada Books, 1980.

—— *Air Battle Central Europe.* Warner Books, 1986.

—— *Instrument of Darkness: The History of Electronic Warfare.* Peninsula Publishing, 1987.

—— *The History of U.S. Electronic Warfare.* Association of Old Crows, 1989.

Rapoport, Anatol (editor). *Carl von Clausewitz on War.* Penguin Books, 1968.

Ravenstein, Charles A. *The U.S. Air Force Reference Series: Air Force Combat Wings 1947-1977.* U.S. Government Printing Office, 1984.

Rentoul, Ian, and Wakeford, Tom. *Gulf War: British Air Arms.* Concord, 1991.

Richelson, Jeffrey T. *The U.S. Intelligence Community.* Ballinger Publishing Company, 1985.

—— *Sword and Shield: Soviet Intelligence and Security Apparatus.* Ballinger Publishing Company, 1986.

—— *American Espionage and the Soviet Target.* William Morrow and Company, 1987.

—— *America's Secret Eyes in Space.* Harper & Row Publishers, 1990.

Robbins, Christopher. *The Ravens.* Simon & Schuster, 1987.

Rogers, Will and Sharon, with Gregston, Gene. *Storm Center: The USS Vincennes and Iran Air Flight 655.* Naval Institute Press, 1992.

Santoli, Al. *Leading the Way: How Vietnam Veterans Rebuilt the U.S. Military.* Ballantine Books, 1993.

Schlight, John. *The War in South Vietnam: The Years of the Offensive, 1965-1968.* U.S. Government Printing Office, 1988.

Schmitt, Gary. *Silent Warfare: Understanding the World of Intelligence.* Brassey's (U.S.), 1993.

Schwarzkopf, H. Norman, with Petre, Peter. *General H. Norman Schwarzkopf, the Autobiography: It Doesn't Take a Hero.* Bantam Books, 1992.

Scutts, Jerry. *Wrecking Crew: The 388th Tactical Fighter Wing in Vietnam.* Warner Books, 1990.

Sharp, Admiral U.S.G., USN (Ret.). *Strategy for Defeat.* Presidio Press, 1978.

Sharpe, Captain Richard, RN. *Jane's Fighting Ships 1989-90.* Jane's Publishing Company, 1990.

Shaw, Robert L. *Fighter Combat: Tactics and Maneuvering.* Naval Institute Press, 1985.

Shawcross, William. *Sideshow: Kissinger, Nixon and the Destruction of Cambodia.* Simon & Schuster, 1977.

Sheehan, John W., Jr. *Gunsmoke: USAF Worldwide Gunnery Meet.* Motorbooks, 1990.

Sheehan, Neil. *The Pentagon Papers.* Bantam Books, 1971.

Simonsen, Erik. *This Is Stealth: The F-117 and B-2 in Color.* Greenhill Books, 1992.

Sims, Edward H. *Fighter Tactics and Strategy 1914-1970.* Harper & Row Publishers, 1972.

Smallwood, William L. *Warthog: Flying the A-10 in the Gulf War.* Brassey's (U.S.), 1993.

—— *Strike Eagle: Flying the F15E in the Gulf War.* Brassey's, 1994.

Smith, Peter C. *Close Air Support: An Illustrated History, 1914 to the Present.* Orion Books, 1990.

Spick, Mike. *The Ace Factory.* Avon War, 1988.

—— and Wheeler, Barry. *Modern Aircraft Markings.* Salamander Books Ltd., 1992.

Stevenson, William. *90 Minutes at Entebbe.* Bantam Books, 1976.

Stockdale, Jim and Sybil. *In Love and War.* Naval Institute Press, 1990.

Straubel, James H. *Crusade for Airpower.* Aerospace Education Foundation, 1982.

Sturu, Colonel William D., Jr. *F-16 Falcon.* General Dynamics, 1976.

Summers, Colonel Henry G., Jr., USA (Ret.). *On Strategy II: A Critical Analysis of the Gulf War.* Dell Publishing, 1992.

Sweetman, John. *Schweinfurt: Disaster in the Skies.* Ballantine Books, 1971.

—— *The Dambusters Raid.* Motorbooks, 1990.

Talbott, Strobe. *Deadly Gambits.* Alfred Knopf, Inc., 1984.

—— *The Master of the Game.* Alfred Knopf, Inc., 1988.

Terraine, John. *A Time for Company: The Royal Air Force in the European War, 1939-1945.* Macmillan Publishing Company, 1985.

Thornborough, Anthony. *Sky Spies: The Decades of Airborne Reconnaissance, Arms and Armour.* 1993.

Tilford, Earl H., Jr. *Search and Rescue.* U.S. Government Printing Office, 1992.

Toffler, Alvin and Heidi. *War and Anti-War: Survival at the Dawn of the 21st Century.* Little Brown, 1993.

Toliver, Colonel Raymond F., and Constable, Trevor J. *Fighter General: The Life of Adolf Galland.* AmPress, 1990.

Townsend, Peter. *Duel of Eagles.* Simon & Schuster, 1959.

Tubbs, D.B. *Lancaster Bomber.* Ballantine Books, 1972.

U.S. Military Air Force Academy. *The Intelligence Revolution.* U.S. Government Printing Office, 1988.

Ulanoff, Brigadier General Stanley M., USAF, and Eshel, Lt. Colonel David, IDF (Ret.). *The Fighting Israeli Air Force.* Arco Publishing, 1985.

U.S. News and World Report Staff. *Triumph without Victory: The Unreported History of the Persian Gulf War.* Random House, 1992.

Valenzi, Kathleen D. *Forged in Steel: U.S. Marine Corps Aviation.* Howell Press, 1987.

Venkus, Colonel Robert E. *Raid on Qaddafi.* St Martin's Press, 1992.

Volkman, Ernest, and Baggett, Blaine. *Secret Intelligence: The Inside Story of America's Espionage Empire.* Doubleday, 1989.

Wagner, William. *Lightning Bugs and Other Reconnaissance Drones.* Aero Publishers, 1982.
—— *Fireflies and Other UAV's.* Midland Publishing Limited, 1992.

Waller, Douglas C. *The Commandos: The Inside Story of America's Secret Soldiers.* Simon & Schuster, 1994.

Ward, Sharkey, DSC, AFC, RN. *Sea Harrier over the Falklands: A Maverick at War.* Naval Institute Press, 1992.

Warden, Colonel John A., III, USAF. *The Air Campaign: Planning for Combat.* Brassey's, 1989.

Ware, Lewis B. *Low Intensity Conflict in the Third World.* U.S. Government Printing Office, 1988.

Warnock, A. Timothy. *The Battle against the U-Boat in the American Theater: The U.S. Army Air Forces in World War II.* U.S. Government Printing Office, 1992.

Watson, Bruce; George, Bruce; Tsouras, Peter; Cyr, B.L. *Military Lessons of the Gulf War.* Greenhill Books, 1991.

Wedertz, Bill. *Dictionary of Naval Abbreviations.* Naval Institute Press, 1977.

Weinberger, Caspar. *Fighting for Peace.* Warner Books, 1990.

Wesgall, Johnathan M. *Operation Crossroads: The Atomic Tests at Bikini Atoll.* Naval Institute Press, 1994.

Wilcox, Robert K. *Scream of Eagles.* John F. Wiley & Sons, 1990.

Winnefeld, James A., and Johnson, Dana J. *Joint Air Operation.* Naval Institute Press, 1993.

Winnefeld, James; Niblack, David; and Johnson, David. *A League of Airmen: U.S. Air Power in the Gulf War.* Rand Project Air Force, 1994.

Winter, Frank H. *The First Golden Age of Rocketry.* Smithsonian Institution, 1990.

Wood, Derek. *Project Cancelled: The Disaster of Britain's Abandoned Aircraft Projects.* Jane's Publishing Inc., 1986.

Woodward, Sandy. *One Hundred Days: The Memoirs of the Falklands Battle Group Commander.* Naval Institute Press, 1992.

Yergin, Daniel. *The Prize: The Epic Quest for Oil, Money & Power.* Simon & Schuster, 1991.

Yonay, Ehud. *No Margin for Error.* Pantheon, 1993.

Zaloga, Steven J. *Red Thrust: Attack on the Central Front, Soviet Tactics and Capabilities in the 1990's.* Presidio Press, 1989.

—— *Target America: The Soviet Union and the Strategic Arms Race, 1945-1964.* Presidio Press, 1993.

Zuyev, Alexander, with McConnell, Malcom. *Fulcrum: A Top Gun Pilot's Escape from the Soviet Empire.* Warner Books, 1992.

Pamphlets:

Department of the Air Force Reaching Globally, Reaching Powerfully: The United States Air Force in the Gulf War. Department of the Air Force, 1991.

GPS-A Guide to the Next Utility. Trimble Navigation, 1989.

Measuring Effects of Payload and Radius Differences of Fighter Aircraft. Rand, 1993.

Space Log – 1993. TRW, 1994.

TRW Space Data. 4th Edition. TRW, 1992.

Wings at War Series, No. 2: Airborne Assault on Holland. Headquarters, Army Air Forces, 1992.

Wings at War Series, No. 2: Air Ground Teamwork on the Western Front. Headquarters, Army Air Forces, 1992.

Wings at War Series, No. 2: Pacific Counterblow. Headquarters, Army Air Forces, 1992.

Wings at War Series, No. 2: Sunday Punch in Normandy. Headquarters, Army Air Forces, 1992.

Wings at War Series, No. 2: The AAF in Northwest Africa. Headquarters, Army Air Forces, 1992.

Wings at War Series, No. 2: The AAF of Southern France. Headquarters, Army Air Forces, 1992.

Magazines:

Air and Space Smithsonian

Air Force

Air Force Monthly

Airman

Airpower Journal

Aviation Week and Space Technology

Code One

Command: Military History, Strategy & Analysis

Naval History

Proceedings

Royal Air Force Yearbook 1992

Royal Air Force Yearbook 1993

The Economist

The Hook

Thunderbirds

USAF Weapons Review

U.S. News and World Report

World Airpower Journal

Videotapes:

AGM-137 (TTSSAM). U.S. Air Force, 9/6/94.

Army TACMS. Loral Vought Systems.

Astrovision Music Video (B-2). Northrop Television Communications, 1994.

BLU-109B: Penetrate and Destroy. Lockheed Missiles and Space Company.

Bold Tigers. McDonnell Douglas.

B-1B: Top Performer for the U.S. Air Force. Time, 1991.

The B-2 Legacy, Northrop Grumman, 1994.

The Canadian Forces in the Persian Gulf. DGPA-Director General Public Affairs, 1991.

CIA: The Secret Files Parts 1-4. A&E Home Video, 1992.

CNN ISAR Demo. Defense Systems & Electronics Group, 4/21/93.

C-17: The 2nd Year. McDonnell Douglas Teleproductions.

F/A-18 Hornet 94. McDonnell Douglas, Northrop Grumman, General Electric, Hughes, 1994.

Fighter Air Combat Trainer. Spectrum HoloByte, 1993.

Fire and Steel. McDonnell Douglas.

Flight-F-15 Eagle. Network Project Ltd., 1989.

F-16's in Iraq and New Glory. Multimedia Group.

F-22 Plane, F-117 Fighter. United Technologies, 1994.

Harrier II Plus Remanufacture Program. McDonnell Douglas, 1994.

Hercules and Beyond. Lockheed Aeronautical Systems Company.

Hercules Multi-Mission Aircraft. Lockheed Aeronautical Systems Company.

Heroes of the Storm. Media Center.

It's about Performance. Sight & Sound Media.

Joint Stars. Grumman.

Joint Stars One System Multiple Missions. Grumman.

JSOW Update 1994. Texas Instruments, 1994.

Loral Aeronutronic-Pave Tack Exec. Version. Loral.

MAG-13 Music Video — Long Version. McDonnell Douglas.

Manufacturing the B-2: A New Approach. Television Communications, 7/29/94.

Navy League 1992. Hornet Team, 1992.

Navy League 1992. McDonnell Douglas & Northrop.

Navy League 1993. Hornet Team, 1993.

Navy League 1993. McDonnell Douglas, Northrop, General Electric, Hughes, 1993.

New Developments in the Harpoon and Slam, Media Center.

New Legacy, A. Northrop Television Communications, 1994.

Night Strike Fighter FA-18. McDonnell Douglas, Northrop, General Electric, Hughes.

90 Days: The Chairman Quarterly Report. McDonnell Douglas. 1989.

Nite Hawk F/A-18 Targeting FLIR Video. Loral Aeronutronic.

Nobody Does it Better. McDonnell Douglas.

OM94008 Lantim Turning Night into Day: OM94154 Lantim/Pathfinder Cockpit Display. Martin Marietta, 9/29/94.

On the Road Again. McDonnell Douglas, Northrop, General Elec., Hughes.

Operation Desert Storm Nite Hawk and Pave Tack FLIR Video for IRIS. Loral Aeronutronic.

Paveway Stock Footage. Defense Systems & Electronics Group.

Predator Presentation & 2 MPV Shots. Loral Aeronutronic.

Slam/Slam ER Product Video. Media Center.

Slam Video Composite. Media Center.

Stealth and Survivability Revision 5. Television Communications.

Storm from the Sea. Naval Institute, 1991.

Three Hits in a Row. Loral Vought Systems, 1994.

United States Air Force ATF-23. Northrop McDonnell Douglas Team.

War in the Gulf Video Series Volumes 1-4. Video Ordance Inc., 1991.

Wings of the Red Star, Volumes 1, 2 and 3. The Discovery Channel, 1993.

Wings over the Gulf, Star Volumes 1, 2 and 3. The Discovery Channel, 1991.

Games:

Ace of Aces of Jet Eagles. NOVA Game Designs, Inc.

Ace of Aces Wingleader. NOVA Game Designs, Inc.

Ace of Aces WWI Air Combat Game. NOVA Game Designs, Inc.

Air Strike: Modern Air-to-Ground Combat. Game Designers Workshop.

Air Superiority: Modern Jet Air Combat. Game Designers Workshop.

Captain's Edition Harpoon. GDW Games.

Dawn Patrol: Role-Playing Game of WWI Air Combat. TSR Hobbies.

Flight Leader: The Game of Air-to-Air Jet Combat Tactics, 1950-Present. The Avalon Hill Game Company, 1985.

Harpoon. Game Designers Workshop.

Over the Reich: WWII Air Combat over Europe. Clash of Arms Games.

Phase Line Smash. GDW.

The Speed of Heat: Air Combat over Korea and Vietnam. Clash of Arms Games.

12 O'Clock High: The WWII Aerial Action Card Game. Wild West Productions.